Britain

1945–2007

Collins

Published by Collins
An imprint of
HarperCollinsPublishers
77–85 Fulham Palace Road
Hammersmith
London
W6 8JB

Browse the complete Collins catalogue
at www.collinseducation.com

© HarperCollinsPublishers Limited
2008

10 9 8 7 6 5 4 3 2 1

ISBN 978-0-00-726873-3

British Library Cataloguing in
Publication Data
A Catalogue record for this
publication is available from the
British Library

Original series commissioned by
Graham Bradbury
This edition commissioned by
Michael Upchurch
Edited by Graham Bradbury
Design and typesetting by Derek Lee
Cover design by Joerg
Hartmannsgruber, White-card
Map Artwork by Tony Richardson
Picture research by Celia Dearing
and Michael Upchurch
Production by Simon Moore
Indexed by Malcolm Henley, Henley
Indexing
Printed and bound by Printing
Express Ltd, Hong Kong

ACKNOWLEDGEMENTS
Every effort had been made to
contact the holders of copyright
material, but if any have been
inadvertently overlooked the
publishers will be pleased to make
the necessary arrangements at the
first opportunity.

HarperCollins for the extracts from
*The Conservatives: A History from
Their Origins to 1965* by Lord Butler
(editor) (1977) and *Statecraft* by
Margaret Thatcher (2002).
Macmillan for the extracts from
British Political Facts by David and
Gareth Butler (1994). Pearson for
the extracts from *The Attlee
Governments* by Kevin Jeffreys
(Longman, 1992) and *The
Conservative Party and British
Politics, 1902–51* by Stuart Bell
(Longman, 1995). Penguin Books
for the extract from *Divided Ulster*
by Liam de Paor (1971). Routledge
for the extracts from *Britain since
1945: A Political History* by D. Childs
(1992).

The publishers would like to thank
the following for permission to
reproduce pictures on these pages.
T=Top, B=Bottom, L=Left, R=Right,
C=Centre

Getty images 22, 25, 34, 37, 44, 55,
73, 74, 103, 111, 120, 136, 151, 167
(C), 198, 210, 249; AFP/Getty
Images 78, 119, 167 (T), 197 (B),
201, 202, 230, 262;
Popperfoto/Getty Images 143, 234;
Chaloner Woods/ Getty Images 218;
Douglas Miller/ Getty Images 222;
Martin Rowson/ Guardian News &
Media Ltd 2006 48; NI
Syndication/The Sun 80, 197 (T);
© 2002 Credit:Topham / AP 160;
© Steve Bell 2005 167 (B);
Unknown 62, 88, 90, 176, 188, 191,
240, 247, 253, 257;
www.cartoonstock.com / Robert
Thompson 81.

Contents

Study and examination skills

This section of the book is designed to aid Sixth Form students in their preparation for public examinations in History.

- Differences between GCSE and Sixth Form History
- Extended writing: the structured question and the essay
- How to handle sources in Sixth Form History
- Historical interpretation
- Progression in Sixth Form History
- Examination technique

Differences between GCSE and Sixth Form History

- The amount of factual knowledge required for answers to Sixth Form History questions is more detailed than at GCSE. Factual knowledge in the Sixth Form is used as supporting evidence to help answer historical questions. Knowing the facts is important, but not as important as knowing that factual knowledge supports historical analysis.

- Extended writing is more important in Sixth Form History. Students will be expected to answer either structured questions or essays.

Structured questions require students to answer more than one question on a given topic. For example:

(a) What problems faced Clement Attlee when he became prime minister in 1945?

(b) How successful was Attlee, and his government, in dealing with these problems by 1951?

Each part of the structured question demands a different approach.

Essay questions require students to produce one answer to a given question. For example:

To what extent was Mrs Thatcher successful in foreign affairs in the period 1979 to 1990?

Similarities with GCSE

● **Source analysis and evaluation**
The skills in handling historical sources, which were acquired at GCSE, are developed in Sixth Form History. In the Sixth Form, sources have to be analysed in their historical context, so a good factual knowledge of the subject is important.

● **Historical interpretations**
Skills in historical interpretation at GCSE are also developed in Sixth Form

History. The ability to put forward different historical interpretations is important. Students will also be expected to explain why different historical interpretations have occurred.

Extended writing: the structured question and the essay

When faced with extended writing in Sixth Form History students can improve their performance by following a simple routine that attempts to ensure they achieve their best performance.

Answering the question

What are the command instructions?
Different questions require different types of response. For instance, 'In what ways' requires students to point out the various ways something took place in History; 'Why' questions expect students to deal with the causes or consequences of an historical event.

'How far' or 'To what extent' questions require students to produce a balanced, analytical answer. Usually, this will take the form of the case for and the case against an historical question.

Are there key words or phrases that require definition or explanation?
It is important for students to show that they understand the meaning of the question. To do this, certain historical terms or words require explanation. For instance, if a question asked 'how far' a politician was an 'innovator', an explanation of the word 'innovator' would be required.

Does the question have specific dates or issues that require coverage?
If the question mentions specific dates, these must be adhered to. For instance, if you are asked to answer a question on British foreign policy, it might state 'in the period 1945 to 1951'.

Planning your answer

Once you have decided on what the question requires, write a brief plan. For structured questions this may be brief. This is a useful procedure to make sure that you have ordered the information you require for your answer in the most effective way. For instance, in a balanced, analytical answer this may take the form of jotting down the main points for and against an historical issue raised in the question.

Writing the answer

Communication skills
The quality of written English is important in Sixth Form History. The way you present your ideas on paper can affect the quality of your answer. Therefore, punctuation, spelling and grammar, which were awarded marks at GCSE, require close attention. Use a dictionary if you are unsure of a word's meaning or spelling. Use the glossary of terms you will find in this book to help you.

The quality of your written English will not determine the Level of Response you receive for your answer. It may well determine what mark you receive within a level.

To help you understand this point ask your teacher to see a mark scheme published by your examination board. For instance, you may be awarded Level 2 (10–15 marks) by an examiner. The quality of written English may be a factor in deciding which mark you receive within that level. Will it be 10 or 15 or a mark in between?

The introduction

For structured questions you may wish to dispense with an introduction altogether and begin writing reasons to support an answer straight away. However, essay answers should begin with an introduction. These should be both concise and precise. Introductions help 'concentrate the mind' on the question you are about to answer. Remember, do not try to write a conclusion as your opening sentence. Instead, outline briefly the areas you intend to discuss in your answer.

Balancing analysis with factual evidence

It is important to remember that factual knowledge should be used to support analysis. Merely 'telling the story' of an historical event is not enough. A structured question or essay should contain separate paragraphs, each addressing an analytical point that helps to answer the question. If, for example, the question asks for reasons why Harold Wilson won the 1964 general election, each paragraph should provide a reason which explains why this occurred. In order to support and sustain the analysis evidence is required. Therefore, your factual knowledge should be used to substantiate analysis. Good structured question and essay answers integrate analysis and factual knowledge.

Seeing connections between reasons

In dealing with 'why'-type questions it is important to remember that the reasons for an historical event might be interconnected. Therefore, it is important to mention the connections between reasons. Also, it might be important to identify a hierarchy of reasons – that is, are some reasons more important than others in explaining an historical event?

Using quotations and statistical data

One aspect of supporting evidence that sustains analysis is the use of quotations. These can be from either a historian or a contemporary. However, unless these quotations are linked with analysis and supporting evidence, they tend to be of little value.

It can also be useful to support analysis with statistical data. In questions that deal with social and economic change, precise statistics that support your argument can be very persuasive.

The conclusion

All structured questions and essays require conclusions. If, for example, a question requires a discussion of 'how far' you agree with a question, you should offer a judgement in your conclusion. Don't be afraid of this – say what you think. If you write an analytical answer, ably supported by factual evidence, you may under-perform because you have not provided a conclusion that deals directly with the question.

Source analysis

Source analysis forms an integral part of the study of History.

In dealing with sources you should be aware that historical sources must be used 'in historical context' in Sixth Form History. This means you must understand the historical topic to which the source refers. Therefore, in this book sources are used with the factual information in each chapter. Also, specific source analysis questions are included at the end of most chapters.

How to handle sources in Sixth Form History

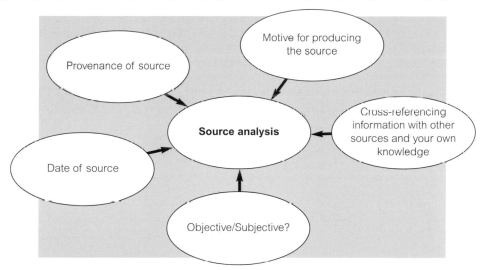

In dealing with sources, a number of basic hints will allow you to deal effectively with source-based questions and to build on your knowledge and skill in using sources at GCSE.

Written sources

Attribution or provenance and date
It is important to identify who has written the source and when it was written. This information can be very important. If, for instance, a source was written by Mrs Thatcher in 1983, this information will be of considerable importance if you are asked about the usefulness (utility) or reliability of the source as evidence of British policy in that year.

It is important to note that just because a source is a primary source does not mean it is more useful or less reliable than a secondary source. Both primary and secondary sources need to be analysed to decide how useful and reliable they are. This can be determined by studying other issues.

Is the content factual or opinionated?
Once you have identified the author and date of the source, it is important to study its content. The content may be factual, stating what has happened or what may happen. On the other hand, it may contain opinions that should be handled with caution. These may contain bias. Even if a source is mainly factual, there might be important and deliberate gaps in factual evidence that can make a source biased and unreliable. Usually, written sources contain elements of both opinion and factual evidence. It is important to judge the balance between these two parts.

Has the source been written for a particular audience?
To determine the reliability of a source it is important to know to whom it is directed. For instance, a public speech may be made to achieve a particular purpose and may not contain the author's true beliefs or feelings. In contrast, a private diary entry may be much more reliable in this respect.

Corroborative evidence
To test whether or not a source is reliable, the use of other evidence to support or corroborate the information it contains is important. Cross-referencing with other sources is a way of achieving this, so is cross-referencing with historical information contained within a chapter.

Visual sources

Cartoons

Cartoons are a popular form of source used at both GCSE and in Sixth Form History. However, analysing cartoons can be a demanding exercise. Not only will you be expected to understand the content of the cartoon, you may also have to explain a written caption – which appears usually at the bottom of the cartoon. In addition, cartoons will need placing in historical context. Therefore, a good knowledge of the subject matter of the topic of the cartoon will be important.

Photographs

'The camera never lies'! This phrase is not always true. When analysing photographs, study the attribution/provenance and date. Photographs can be changed so they are not always an accurate visual representation of events. Also, to test whether or not a photograph is a good representation of events you will need corroborative evidence.

Maps

Maps which appear in Sixth Form History are predominantly secondary sources. These are used to support factual coverage in the text by providing information in a different medium. Therefore, to assess whether or not information contained in maps is accurate or useful, reference should be made to other information. It is also important with written sources to check the attribution and date. These could be significant.

Statistical data and graphs

It is important when dealing with this type of source to check carefully the nature of the information contained in data or in a graph. It might state that the information is in tons (tonnes) or another measurement. Be careful to check if the information is in index numbers. These are a statistical device where a base year is chosen and given the figure 100. All other figures are based on a percentage difference from that base year. For instance, if 1945 is taken as a base year for motor car production, it is given the figure of 100. If the index number for motor car production in 1979 is 217 it means that motor car production has increased by 117 per cent above the 1945 figure.

An important point to remember when dealing with data and graphs over a period of time is to identify trends and patterns in the information. Merely describing the information in written form is not enough.

Historical interpretation

An important feature of both GCSE and Sixth Form History is the issue of historical interpretation. In Sixth Form History it is important for students to be able to explain why historians differ, or have differed, in their interpretation of the past.

Availability of evidence

An important reason is the availability of evidence on which to base historical judgements. As new evidence comes to light, a historian today may have more information on which to base judgements than historians in the past.

'A philosophy of history?'

Many historians have a specific view of history that will affect the way they make their historical judgements. For instance, Marxist historians – who take the view from the writings of Karl Marx the founder of modern socialism – believe that society has been made up of competing economic and social classes. They also place considerable importance on economic reasons in human decision making. Therefore, a Marxist historian of fascism may take a completely different viewpoint to a non-Marxist historian.

The role of the individual

Some historians have seen past history as being moulded by the acts of specific individuals who have changed history. Attlee, Wilson and Thatcher are seen as individuals whose personality and beliefs changed the course of British history. Other historians have tended to 'downplay' the role of individuals; instead, they highlight the importance of more general social, economic and political change.

Placing different emphasis on the same historical evidence

Even if historians do not possess different philosophies of history or place different emphasis on the role of the individual, it is still possible for them to disagree because they place different emphases on aspects of the same factual evidence. As a result, Sixth Form History should be seen as a subject that encourages debate about the past based on historical evidence.

Progression in Sixth Form History

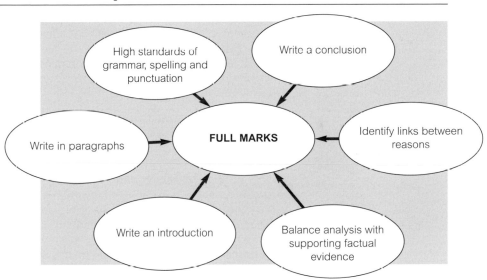

The ability to achieve high standards in Sixth Form History involves the acquisition of a number of skills:

- Good written communication skills
- Acquiring a sound factual knowledge
- Evaluating factual evidence and making historical conclusions based on that evidence
- Source analysis
- Understanding the nature of historical interpretation
- Understanding the causes and consequences of historical events

- Understanding themes in history which will involve a study of a specific topic over a long period of time

- Understanding the ideas of change and continuity associated with themes.

Students should be aware that the acquisition of these skills will take place gradually over the time spent in the Sixth Form. At the beginning of the course, the main emphasis may be on the acquisition of factual knowledge, particularly when the body of knowledge studied at GCSE was different.

When dealing with causation, students will have to build on their skills from GCSE. They will not only be expected to identify reasons for an historical event but also to provide a hierarchy of causes. They should identify the main causes and less important causes. They may also identify that causes may be interconnected and linked. Progression in Sixth Form History will come with answering the questions at the end of each sub-section in this book and practising the skills outlined through the use of the factual knowledge contained in the book.

Examination technique

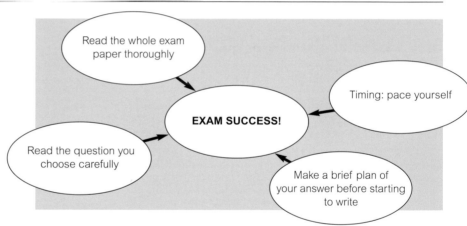

The ultimate challenge for any Sixth Form historian is the ability to produce quality work under examination conditions. Examinations will take the form of either modular examinations taken in January and June or an 'end of course' set of examinations.

Here is some advice on how to improve your performance in an examination.

- Read the whole examination paper thoroughly
  Make sure that the questions you choose are those for which you can produce a good answer. Don't rush – allow time to decide which questions to choose. It is probably too late to change your mind half way through answering a question.

- Read the question very carefully
  Once you have made the decision to answer a specific question, read it very carefully. Make sure you understand the precise demands of the question. Think about what is required in your answer. It is much better to think about this before you start writing, rather than trying to steer your essay in a different direction half way through.

Revision tips

Even before the examination begins make sure that you have revised thoroughly. Revision tips on the main topics in this book appear on the Collins website:

www.collinseducation.com

- Make a brief plan
Sketch out what you intend to include in your answer. Order the points you want to make. Examiners are not impressed with additional information included at the end of the essay, with indicators such as arrows or asterisks.

- Pace yourself as you write
Success in examinations has a lot to do with successful time management. If, for instance, you have to answer an essay question in approximately 45 minutes, then you should be one-third of the way through after 15 minutes. With 30 minutes gone, you should start writing the last third of your answer.

Where a question is divided into sub-questions, make sure you look at the mark tariff for each question. If in a 20-mark question a sub-question is worth a maximum of 5 marks, then you should spend approximately one-quarter of the time allocated for the whole question on this sub-question.

1 Britain 1945–2007: A synoptic overview

Key Issues

- How did Britain's position change from imperial power to member of the European Union?

- To what extent was British society and the economy transformed in the period 1945–2007

- How far did the British political system change between 1945 and 2007?

The decline of imperial power

In 1945 Britain was one of the world's greatest imperial powers. The British Empire traversed the globe, containing one third of the world's population. 1945 was the British Commonwealth and Empire's finest hour. It had fought Germany, Italy and Japan in a global conflict, and won. The war had cost the Empire over 350,000 dead, and large parts of urban Britain had been devastated by aerial attack. Yet Britain was one of the 'Big Three' powers, along with the USA and USSR, that decided the fate of the post-war world at Yalta and Potsdam in 1945.

By 2007 Britain's position had been transformed. From 1945, Britain withdrew from virtually its entire Empire, and only Gibraltar, Bermuda, the Falkland Islands and a scattering of other islands around the world remained. One of the great successes of the period 1945 to 2007 was the transformation of the British Empire into the Commonwealth, a multiracial association of states.

The biggest peaceful transfer of political power in world history occurred in 1947 when Britain gave independence to India and Pakistan. However, this peaceful process was not possible in every case. In Malaya and Kenya Britain fought guerrilla wars before these states received independence. In 1982 one of Britain's last 'colonial' wars was the defence of the Falkland Islands against Argentine invasion and occupation.

By 2007 Britain had replaced the role of imperial power with another role. Britain no longer had the financial and military power to act independently on the world stage – as was made clear as early as the Suez Crisis in 1956. From 1949, during the Cold War and after, Britain became an important – but junior – partner of NATO. Britain's move from global imperial power reached a turning-point in 1973 when it made the momentous decision to join the European Economic Community, which by 2007 had become the European Union.

The transformation of British society and the economy

In 1945, Britain was recovering from six years of world war. Large areas of British cities had been severely damaged by aerial attack. The economy was virtually bankrupt, and post-war rationing and this 'age of austerity' continued into the 1950s. Yet Britain was still one of the largest economies in the world, after the USA and USSR. In 2007 Britain was still a major economy, ranking fifth in the world. However, the source of Britain's economic wealth had changed – almost out of all recognition. In 1945 Britain was a major manufacturing nation and a producer of coal as an energy source. From the 1950s Britain's share of world manufacturing began to decline, and by the early 1980s its manufacturing sector entered a crisis, shedding millions of jobs. To replace manufacturing, Britain developed a strong service sector, offering international banking, insurance, electronics and computer-based technology to the world. In addition, from the late 1970s Britain became a major producer of oil, with the development of the North Sea oilfields. So why did Britain lose its strong world economic position? First, two world wars had a major effect on world trade, and with it, Britain's economic prosperity. During both world wars Britain lost markets, mainly to the USA. In addition, the development of textiles, shipbuilding and steel industries in countries such as Japan, Korea and Taiwan reduced the demands for British goods. By 2007, China and India provided further international competition in manufacturing.

According to the historian Geoffrey Owen, Britain's decline was due to a lack of competition within industries. However, it can also be attributed to poor industrial relations – weak management and militant trade unions have both been to blame for Britain's economic decline in the 1960s to 1980s. The decision to join the European Economic Community, in 1973, gave Britain the opportunity to participate in a large European market. In addition, structural reforms during the Thatcher years (1979–1990) increased productivity, reduced government debt and increased flexibility in the labour market. In 1987, deregulation of the City of London financial institutions ensured that London would remain one of the world's great financial centres.

As the economy changed, so did society. The post-war period was associated with a housing boom and the transformation of urban life, with the creation of new towns, such as Harlow, and new suburbs. In the mid-1950s Britain was building 300,000 homes per year, and the post-war economic growth was being translated into a rise in real incomes. In the 1950s, for the first time, teenagers had real economic power, helping to fuel the popular music and fashion industries. The 'Swinging Sixties' saw major changes in social values. The popular heroes of the 1960s were pop groups, such as the Beatles and the Rolling Stones. Homosexuality and abortion were legalised, the contraceptive pill became widely available, and a greater social equality developed in what had long been a class-ridden society. In 1964, for example, Harold Wilson became the first prime minister not to have gone to an independent school..

However, changes in society were not always for the better. The 1970s was a decade of major industrial unrest. Major strikes in 1971–72 and 1973–74 by the miners, and in 1978–79 by many public sector workers, brought Britain to a standstill. The UK economy also suffered a serious decline caused by the combination of rising inflation and rising unemployment. The arrival of Mrs Thatcher as Prime Minister, in 1979, brought a period of radical readjustment. Trade union powers were limited, the economy changed rapidly from a manufacturing-based to service sector-based economy and in the process, from 1979–83 suffered a serious economic recession, with unemployment rising above 3 million. The mid- and late 1980s, however, brought rapid economic growth, and saw the rise of a new social phenomenon: the Yuppy (young, urban professional).

After another brief recession in 1989–92, Britain entered a period of sustained economic growth, the longest for 150 years. And by 2007 Britain had experienced a decade of low, stable inflation, low unemployment and constant economic growth.

Multicultural Britain

British society also changed dramatically in other ways. In 1948 the ship *Empire Windrush* brought the first of a number of immigrants from the West Indies to work in the UK economy. By the late 1970s, Britain had large numbers of immigrants from the West Indies and South Asia. Like immigrants before them, most notably the Irish and Jews, these new immigrants lived in ethnic neighbourhoods in the towns and cities. But the arrival of new immigrants caused social tension. Race riots occurred in Notting Hill in London in 1958 and, later, riots involving ethnic minorities occurred across several of Britain's major cities, most notably in the early 1980s. Much of the rioting was caused by discrimination and the alienation felt by new immigrants. As a result, the government passed anti-discrimination legislation and encouraged multiculturalism. By 2007, Britain had become a multi-ethnic community. However, concerns were raised about the division and alienation that multiculturalism had delivered. This was mostly aimed at the Muslim community, especially after 2005's 7/7 bombing in London by Muslim extremists.

A disunited kingdom?

Britain as a political community has also changed dramatically. By 2007 a 'disunited kingdom' had been created, with Scotland and Wales receiving their own governments and legislatures in 1999. But the worst problem within the UK since 1945 was the 'Troubles' in Northern Ireland. Here – within a part of the UK – a guerrilla war, involving Republican and Loyalist paramilitary groups and the British armed forces, lasted from 1969 to 1998. From 1998 peace had been restored to Northern Ireland. But this meant that the unity of the United Kingdom had been undermined because a foreign state (the Republic of Ireland) now had an official role in the affairs of Northern Ireland.

The changing fortunes of the Conservative and Labour Parties

The period 1945 to 2007 was dominated by two national parties, the Conservatives and Labour. No other party held government in the period. This did not mean minor parties did not have influence. The Liberal Party recovered from a low point in the 1951 general election, when it won only six seats to 2005 when, as the Liberal Democrats, it won sixty-two seats. And between 1977 and 1978 Labour governed with the support of the Liberals. Also, regional parties fared well. The Ulster Unionists, for example, supported the Conservatives in 1994 to 1997, in return for their support on Northern Ireland issues.

In 1945 Labour won its first outright victory in a general election. From 1945 to 1951 it introduced extensive social and economic reforms which established the Welfare State. Labour subsequently won elections in 1964, 1966 and 1974, when the party was under the leadership of Harold

Wilson. However, for much of the second half of the twentieth century the Conservatives were the dominant party. They held power from 1951 to 1964, from 1970 to 1974, and from 1979 to 1997. For much of the period the Conservatives portrayed themselves as the national party, gaining votes across all social classes. Labour was portrayed as a class party under the financial influence of the trade union movement. The low point in Labour Party fortunes came in 1983 when they suffered a landslide defeat under the leadership of Michael Foot.

In the period 1983 to 1997 the Labour Party reorganised, rebranding itself as 'New Labour' under Tony Blair, the leader from 1994. In 1997 Labour won its greatest ever electoral victory. This was followed by two further victories in 2001 and 2005. As a result, it had replaced the Conservatives as the major political party in Britain.

The media

In 1945 the media in Britain comprised newspapers, the radio and the cinema. Although television existed, it was still in its infancy and very few Britons possessed a TV set. By 2007 the media had been transformed. Virtually every house possessed television. In addition, the choice of TV channel had gone from one (the BBC) in 1945, to over 600 terrestial, cable and satellite channels in 2007.

In addition, the late twentieth century saw a technological revolution in the media. The videocassette recorder became available in the 1970s, followed by the development of the CD and DVD. In the 1990s the availability of personal computers allowed households to access the internet and the worldwide web, and by 2007 mobile phones had developed into a social necessity.

This does not mean that newspapers lost their influence. The acquisition of the *Sun* newspaper by Rupert Murdoch, in the early 1970s, started a revolution in the production and content of popular newspapers. By the 1990s the *Sun* had 4 million daily readers, and was regarded as having a major influence on the outcome of the 1992, 1997 and 2001 general elections.

By 2007 the average Briton possessed a wide variety of technological means to access various forms of media. As a result, political parties adopted the new technology to get over their political message. In 2006, for example, David Cameron, the Conservative leader, started his own 'blog' on the internet.

1. Construct a timeline from 1945 to 2007, using the information contained above. On the timeline, locate what you think were the major events in the development of Britain between 1945 and 2007.

2. Using a table like the one below, identify areas where Britain changed in the period between 1945 and 2007. Also identify any areas where you think Britain experienced minimal change.

Having completed your table, write down in what areas you think Britain has experienced the greatest change, and where you think the least change has occurred. Give reasons for your answer.

	1945	2007	Change or continuity?
International position			
Society			
Economy			
Political parties			
Scotland, Wales, Northern Ireland			
Media			
Multicultural Britain			

2 The Labour Party, 1945–2007

Key Issues

■ How successful were the Labour governments in the period 1945 to 2007?

■ What problems did the Labour Party experience while in opposition?

■ What has been the influence of the left of the Labour Party on its policy-making?

Framework of Events

1940	Labour enters wartime coalition with Clement Attlee as Deputy Leader
1945	Labour wins general election: Clement Attlee becomes Prime Minister
	Economic loan negotiated with the Americans
1947	Nationalisation of coal mines
	Grant of independence to India and Pakistan
1948	Nationalisation of railways
	Foundation of National Health Service
1949	Devaluation of the pound
1950	General election: Labour returned with a small majority
1951	Festival of Britain
	General election: Conservatives win under Winston Churchill
1955	General election: Conservatives increase majority under Anthony Eden
	Hugh Gaitskell becomes leader of the Labour Party following Attlee
1956	Publication of Anthony Crosland's *The Future of Socialism* arguing for a revision of policy and attitudes within the Labour Party
	Suez Crisis
1959	General election: Conservatives increase majority under Macmillan
1960	Labour Party adopts a policy opposing British possession of nuclear weapons
1961	Hugh Gaitskell fails in his attempt to revise Clause IV of the party's constitution defining aims and objectives
1963	Hugh Gaitskell dies, replaced by Harold Wilson as leader
	Wilson's speech to party conference on 'the white heat of technology'
1964	General election: Labour win with small majority
1965	Rhodesia unilaterally declares independence
1966	General election: Labour returned with large majority
	Emergency budget: government spending cut to preserve pound
1967	Pound devalued. Abortion legalised
1968	Commonwealth Immigration Act restricts immigration to Britain
	Attempt to reform House of Lords abandoned in view of opposition within House of Commons
1969	White Paper 'In Place of Strife' tries to modernise industrial relations practices. Opposed by trade unions and backbench MPs

1970	Equal Pay Act establishes the right of equal pay for women workers
	General election: Conservatives win under Edward Heath
1972	Minority of Labour MPs support Heath to get bill allowing Britain to join the European Economic Community through Parliament
1973	Publication of 'Labour's Programme 1973' disowned by party leadership
	Miners' strike. Oil crisis
1974	February: Labour forms minority government after general election
	October: Labour wins general election with small minority
1975	Referendum on Britain's membership of European Economic Community overwhelmingly endorses membership
1976	Harold Wilson resigns as leader, replaced by James Callaghan
	Government applies for loan from International Monetary Fund (IMF) to help solve economic crisis
	Government spending cut in order to meet IMF loan conditions
1978–9	'Winter of discontent' as public sector workers strike for more money
1979	General election: Conservatives under Margaret Thatcher win
1980	James Callaghan resigns as leader, replaced by Michael Foot
1981	Denis Healey narrowly beats Tony Benn in contest for deputy leadership
	Departure of 25 MPs under Roy Jenkins and David Owen to form Social Democratic Party
1983	General election: Conservatives increase majority under Margaret Thatcher – worst result for Labour since 1935
	Michael Foot resigns as leader, replaced by Neil Kinnock
1985	Neil Kinnock attacks influence of Militant Tendency within party in speech at Labour Party Conference
1986	Peter Mandelson appointed as Director of Communications
1987	General election: Conservatives returned with slightly reduced majority under Margaret Thatcher
1988–9	Policy review fundamentally modernises Party policies
1992	General election: Conservatives win under John Major, but with a much reduced majority
	Neil Kinnock resigns as leader, replaced by John Smith
1994	John Smith dies suddenly, replaced as leader by Tony Blair
1995	Party membership overwhelmingly approve a new set of Party values and objectives to replace the old Clause IV of the Party Constitution.
1997	General election: Labour wins with large majority
1998	Good Friday Agreement on Northern Ireland
	Devolution given to Wales and Scotland (operational from 1999)
2001	Tony Blair wins a second landslide victory over the Conservative Party, led by William Hague
2005	Tony Blair becomes the first Labour leader to win three general elections
2007	Tony Blair retires as Labour's most successful leader and is replaced as prime minister by chancellor of the exchequer, Gordon Brown.

Overview

FEW observers looking at the result of the 1945 general election, in which Labour had a massive parliamentary majority, would have guessed that in the following 55 years, Labour would be in power for only 20 of them. Indeed the post-war record of the Party has been exceptionally patchy.

Nobody would deny the achievements of Attlee's administration between 1945 and 1951 that radically changed society, with nationalised industries and the National Health Service, and a start made in repairing the neglect of centuries in housing and education. Abroad Labour began the disengagement from Empire and established Britain very firmly as a key member of the Atlantic alliance during the Cold War.

Perhaps the greatest achievement was the creation of a **post-war consensus** that lasted 30 years, in which Labour and Conservative parties alike were committed to Keynesian economic policies of high public spending in order to keep unemployment under control. This led to a period of prosperity the like of which had never been experienced before – even if neither party were able to reverse Britain's decline as an economic, political or military world power.

Post-war consensus: Many contemporary commentators have argued that between the late 1940s and mid 1970s the main political parties shared common beliefs and policies in the field of economic, social and foreign policies. Historians are now beginning to question whether this was so. (See the case study in historical interpretation, chapter 3, section 8.)

Yet the achievements of the Wilson and Callaghan administrations of the 1960s and 1970s are much less certain. Improvements were certainly made to the lives of the poorest in society, but for all that there is a feeling that they could have done much more. The 1964–70 government particularly promised much and delivered little. A decade later the Wilson and Callaghan administrations between 1974 and 1979 were constrained by a precarious parliamentary majority. The decisions made at the time of the International Monetary Fund (IMF) Loan crisis in 1976 were a precursor to the policies of Margaret Thatcher and her successors, including Tony Blair.

The internal history of the Labour Party has not been a happy one. For much of the period under discussion the Party was split to varying degrees between left and right. In the 1950s the split was mainly (but not exclusively) between MPs in the **Parliamentary Labour Party**. Even though the election in 1963 of Harold Wilson, perceived as being on the left of the Party, brought about a truce between the two factions, their rivalry continued throughout the 1964–70 government and to a lesser extent between 1974–79. A much greater threat, indeed one which nearly destroyed the Labour Party, came with the rise of unrest among ordinary members in the 1960s and 1970s. MPs were less involved, although the leader of the movement, Tony Benn, was a prominent and important cabinet minister. The Party nearly tore itself apart during a period of self-inflicted infighting between 1980 and 1983. It took the 1983 election result, the worst for 50 years, to persuade people at all levels within Labour that things had to change. Even so it took nearly a decade and a half, and an almost total revision of everything the Party ever stood for, for Labour to become re-electable.

Parliamentary Labour Party (PLP): Organisation of Labour MPs and representatives of Labour peers. Until 1982 alone elected leader and deputy leader of the Party. Elects members of shadow cabinet, but not cabinet ministers who are appointed by the Prime Minister.

The fate of Labour governments has also depended on co-operation with all parts of the labour movement, particularly trade unions. The embarrassing climb down by Harold Wilson and Barbara Castle over mild plans to reform trade unions damaged the standing of the government with the electorate. In 1979 the government's inability to control union militancy during the 'Winter of Discontent' directly led to the election of the Conservatives.

During the Thatcher years (1979–90) the Labour Party went through major changes. Under Michael Foot (1979–83) the party veered to the left and suffered a humiliating defeat in the 1983 general election. However, under Foot's successors as leader, Neill Kinnock (1983–92) and John Smith (1992–94), the party went through a major reform of its organisation and policy. By 1994 the party had shed its left-wing image and competed with the Conservatives for the centre ground of British politics. The beneficiary of these change was Tony Blair, Labour leader from 1994 to 2007. He 'rebranded' the party as 'New Labour' and exploited divisions within the Conservative Party to win three resounding electoral victories in 1997, 2001 and 2005. Under Blair, Britain experienced an almost unprecedented period of stable economic growth, with both low inflation and low unemployment. And by 2007, Labour had replaced the Conservatives as the 'natural' party in government for the United Kingdom.

From the points above, what do you regard as successes for the Labour Party and what do you regard as failures? Explain your answer.

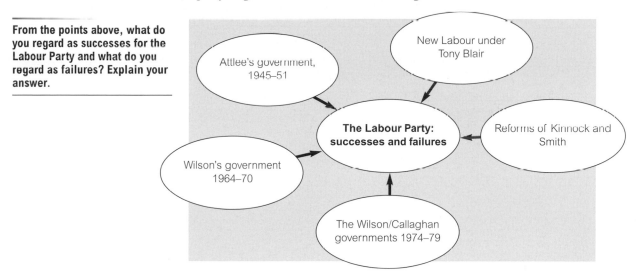

2.1 'Quite a day' – Labour and the election of 1945

The election of the Labour Government in 1945 was probably the greatest British political upset of the 20th century. Politicians of all parties and the press were united in their belief that the British people would reward Winston Churchill for his leadership during the recent war with a renewed mandate to prepare the country for the post-war world. Opinion polls, however, which politicians had yet to learn to rely on, had long told a different story.

Labour's victory was convincing. It had a majority of 146 seats over all other parties. For the first time it broke out of its industrial heartlands of the north to win seats in southern England; such as High Wycombe and Winchester, as well as suburban areas such as respectable Wimbledon. The party even won a few rural seats, mainly in Norfolk.

For party members the victory was an event they would always remember. Fifty years on, in 1995, Donald Matheson in Liverpool recalled: 'We went **on the knocker** and we leafleted and whatnot. We didn't expect to win. Everybody quoted Wordsworth "Bliss was it in that dawn to be alive". It was like that. It really was. We really thought "Everything is going to be all right now".' (*Generating Socialism*, 1995) Even the normally cautious Attlee, the new Prime Minister, noted in his diary that election day 'had been quite an exciting day'.

The Labour victory was even more impressive considering the Party's dismal electoral performance since its foundation as the Labour Representation Committee in February 1900. The number of Labour MPs had risen to 154 in the 1935 general election – the last before the outbreak of war – but even so they were considerably outnumbered by the Conservatives and their allies in the National Government.

The 1930s saw a revision of Labour's aims culminating in *Labour's Immediate Programme* published in 1937. Many of the points in the

On the knocker: Going house to house finding out how residents would be voting at the election

Programme would find their way into the manifesto put to the country in 1945, such as the nationalisation of the Bank of England and the coal mines. Labour's leaders were also able to capitalise on the growing interest in left-wing politics, as well as concern over the appeasement policies of the Conservatives under Neville Chamberlain. In the years before the outbreak of war in 1939 the party campaigned hard against the appeasement of Nazi Germany. As a result the party attracted an increasing number of intellectuals and academics. Hugh Gaitskell, Anthony Crosland and Douglas Jay became members in the 1930s. Barbara Castle and Harold Wilson, among many others, joined during the War. They helped to ensure that for the first time the party had carefully thought-out proposals.

In the difficult days of May 1940, Labour entered the new Coalition government led by Winston Churchill. The price for their entry was full partnership in running the war. Many of the Labour's leaders became ministers: Clement Attlee became Deputy Prime Minister, Ernest Bevin Minister of Labour, and Herbert Morrison Home Secretary. Labour ministers tended to be responsible for domestic matters, as Churchill was uninterested in the **Home Front**. The effective way in which the ministers handled their responsibilities encouraged confidence in the belief that a Labour government would be run sensibly. Of the senior ministers in the first Labour Cabinet only Aneurin Bevan had not held government office before.

For many, their experiences during the war transformed their political outlook. It quickly became accepted that Britain was fighting for a better post-war world, breaking the circle of poverty and unemployment that had so blighted the inter-war period. As Queen Elizabeth, wife of George VI, wrote to her mother-in-law Queen Mary during the Blitz in October 1940, 'the destruction is so awful, and the people so wonderful – they deserve a better world'.

The most influential book published during the war was the Beveridge Report, called *Social Insurance and Allied Services* (December 1942). Steve Fielding, in *From Blitz to Blair* (1997), concludes that 'this proved to be the most significant political event of the war, establishing the parameters of the debate on post-war Britain and placing party differences in stark relief'. Beveridge prefaced his report with the statement that 'a revolutionary moment in the world's history is a time for revolution not patching'. Much of the report was, however, far from revolutionary, proposing to unify pre-war social security schemes. What it did offer was a vision of a world free from what Beveridge called the 'five giants on the road to reconstruction': Want, Disease, Ignorance, Squalor and Idleness.

Aided by careful publicity the report became astonishingly influential in thinking about the post-war world. It eventually sold some 630,000 copies. Opinion polls showed that 86 per cent of the population were in favour of the report. One worker said, 'it will make the ordinary man think that the country at last has some regard for him as he is supposed to have regard for the country'. The Conservatives, however, were distinctly cool about the proposals. Churchill himself felt that Beveridge had fostered 'a dangerous optimism' out of step with the 'hard facts of life'. The Labour Party in contrast was generally supportive, but the need to sustain the wartime coalition meant that their support was muted in public.

There were many reports and proposals published during the war years, from town and country planning to health. However, only one measure was passed, the 1944 Education Act put forward by the Conservative R. A. Butler, which raised the school leaving age to 15 and introduced secondary schooling for every child.

From the summer of 1940 the state quickly became involved in spheres of activity that would have been unthinkable a few years before. Rationing,

Herbert Morrison (1888–1965)
Morrison joined the wartime coalition as Home Secretary 1940–45. He served in the postwar Labour government as Deputy Prime Minister and Lord President 1945–51, and Foreign Secretary during 1951. He was Deputy Leader of the Labour Party 1951–55.

Home Front: Aspects of the Second World War that directly affected civilians.

Mobilisation of labour:
Conscription of men and women and sending them to work where there were shortages of labour.

economic controls, and the mobilisation of labour all became acceptable. This use of state power was very much in tune with the electorate, who had seen that life had become very much fairer, and conditions for the poorest in society improved. It became accepted that the state should play a major role in post-war reconstruction. The two main political parties had radically different views of the state, with Labour accepting that government power could be used to better the lives of the people. Douglas Jay, a senior Labour minister, wrote in 1947 that 'the gentleman in Whitehall really does know better what is good for the people than the people know themselves'.

It was clear that the electorate did not want a return to the miseries of the 1920s and 1930s. As James Callaghan, a newly-elected MP in 1945, points out, 'the pervading sentiment was no return to 1919 … it was the memory of the ex-servicemen with no legs displaying their medals on street corners, combined with unemployment in the thirties, that made us all say we are not going back there' (Election '45, 1995). The election campaign itself largely resolved round the need for reconstruction. The Conservatives fought a lack-lustre campaign around Churchill urging the electorate to 'let him finish the job'.

In contrast, Labour had a very clear idea of the post-war world that it wanted to create. In an election broadcast Clement Attlee, the Party leader, argued, 'we have to plan the broad lines of our national life so that all may have the duty and the opportunity of rendering service to the nation … and that all may help to create and share in an increasing material prosperity free from the fear of want'. Candidates stressed a better future under Labour. As Michael Foot told voters in Plymouth, 'We shall not have won the peace until every citizen in Devonport [a district of Plymouth] and every citizen of England has a good roof over his head, the chance to marry and bring up his children, safe from the fears of unemployment, sickness and worry'.

Although Labour's intentions were not as radical as commonly believed today, they were very much in tune with what voters felt needed to be done to create a new and better Britain. The title given to the manifesto said it all, 'Let us face the future'. In retirement Attlee summed up the result, 'I think the general feeling was that they [the electorate] wanted a new future. We were looking towards the future. The Tories were looking towards the past.' Kenneth O. Morgan argues, in Labour in Power, 1945–1951 (1985), that Labour's victory can be understood in the context of the war years, backed by the new realism of Labour domestic and foreign policies in the 1930s. Labour was uniquely identified with a sweeping change of mood and with the new social agenda emerging during the war years.

1. How important do you think the Beveridge Report was in Labour's election victory in 1945?

2. Why do you think the Conservatives did so badly in this general election? Give reasons

2.2 Building Jerusalem – How successful was the Labour government of 1945?

Clement Attlee (1883–1967)
Attlee was Leader of the Labour Party, 1935–55, Deputy Prime Minister, 1940–45, and Prime Minister 1945–51.

The Attlee administration can readily be divided into two distinct periods. The vast majority of the radical initiatives, such as the nationalisation of the coal mines and the introduction of the welfare state, were implemented before late 1947. By the end of 1947 this radicalism died away, as Britain's economic circumstances worsened and the major parts of the party's policy had been implemented. It was to be replaced by a much more cautious, pragmatic approach.

This is particularly true of Attlee's second short-lived administration between February 1950 and October 1951. The small majority – only six

The Labour Cabinet 1945: Prime Minister Clement Attlee is sixth from the left in the front row. On his right is Ernest Bevin and on his left Herbert Morrison (grandfather of Peter Mandelson). On the left hand side of the back row is Aneurin Bevan.

MPs over the other parties (see table 1) – and the illness or evident tiredness of many of the senior ministers (many of whom who had been in office continuously since 1940) led to the feeling that, in Hugh Dalton's words, Labour was in office, but was 'without authority or power'.

Historians are divided on the achievements of the 1945 government. Generally, those on the left have argued that the Labour government did not move sufficiently far down the path towards socialism. Trevor Blackwell and Jeremy Seabrook in *The Politics of Hope* (1988) wrote, 'the role of Labour was twofold. First of all to provide illusions that the new beginning actually represented a radical break from the past. The will to create a new society which would articulate the hopes and desires of their own people. And secondly, and more prosaically, to provide a scaffolding of welfare services which would both support and shroud the restoration of the old structures.'

Meanwhile, many on the right believe that Attlee should have devoted scarce resources to building up industrial recovery rather than on the welfare state – as Correlli Barnett put it in *The Audit of War* (1986), 'to them [the voters] victory in the war merited a rich reward, and they meant to have it: for the high-minded a reward in the shape of an ideal society, and for the humbler in the shape of free welfare and a secure job'.

The position lies somewhere between these two extremes. Most historians would agree with Kenneth O. Morgan's conclusion in *Labour and Power* (1984) that the Attlee government was undoubtedly the most effective of Labour governments and possibly perhaps among the most effective of all British governments.

What were the pressures on the 1945 Labour government?

Governments are subject to pressures and constraints, either of their own making – for example from party members or the resignation of ministers – or due to external forces, such as economic trends or an international incident. The Labour government of 1945 suffered as much as any other.

Internal factors
Clement Attlee was lucky in that the party was generally supportive of his administration. Unlike ministers in the Wilson and Callaghan Cabinets of

---

Table 1 Election results 1935–2007

	1935		1945		1950		1951	
	No. seats	% vote	No. seats	% vote	No. seats	% vote	No. seats	% vote
Conservative	432	54	213	40	298	44	321	48
Liberal	20	6	12	9	9	9	6	3
Labour	154	38	393	48	315	46	295	49
Others	9	2	22	3	3	1	3	1
Total	615	100	640	100	625	100	625	101

	1955		1959		1964		1966	
	No. seats	% vote	No. seats	% vote	No. seats	% vote	No. seats	% vote
Conservative	344	50	365	49	304	43	253	42
Liberal	6	3	6	6	9	11	12	9
Labour	277	46	258	44	317	44	363	48
Others	3	1	1	1	0	1	2	1
Total	630	100	630	100	630	100	630	100

	1970		1974 (Feb)		1974 (Oct)		1979	
	No. seats	% vote	No. seats	% vote	No. seats	% vote	No. seats	% vote
Conservative	330	46	297	38	277	36	339	44
Liberal	6	8	14	19	13	18	11	14
Labour	287	43	301	37	319	39	269	37
Others	7	3	23	6	26	7	16	5
Total	630	100	635	100	635	100	635	100

	1983		1987		1992		1997	
	No. seats	% vote	No. seats	% vote	No. seats	% vote	No. seats	% vote
Conservative	397	42	376	42	336	42	165	31
Liberal	23	25	22	23	20	18	46	17
Labour	209	28	229	31	271	35	419	43
Others	21	5	23	4	24	5	28	9
Total	650	100	650	100	651	100	658	100

	2001		2005	
	No. seats	% vote	No. seats	% vote
Conservative	166	31.7	198	32.4
Liberal	52	18.3	62	22
Labour	412	40.7	355	35.2
Others	27	9.3	31	10.4

Note: In the 1983 and 1987 elections, Liberals and Social Democrats fought together as an Alliance. The Liberal Party became the Liberal Democrats in 1988.

Source: adapted from David and Gareth Butler, *British Political Facts 1900–1994*, 1994.

Ernest Bevin (1881–1951)
A manual worker, Bevin had left school at 11. He became an official of the Dockers' Union. He organised the amalgamation of 18 unions into the Transport and General Workers' Union and was its General Secretary, 1921–40. Elected to Parliament for the first time in 1940 he went straight into the Cabinet as Minister of Labour. He was Foreign Secretary from 1945 until a month before his death in 1951.

the 1960s and 1970s, personal relationships were generally good. There was however deep personal animosity between Ernest Bevin and Herbert Morrison. It was once suggested to Bevin that Morrison was his own worst enemy. 'Not while I'm alive, he isn't', Bevin growled.

To an extent this unity was the result of careful party management. As Kenneth O. Morgan in *Labour in Power* argues that 'the Cabinet and leadership were in control at all levels of the party hierarchy'. Complaints from local parties, particularly about Labour's defence and foreign policies and the expulsion of MPs for Communist sympathies, such as Konni Zilliacus and John Platts-Mills, were brushed aside. Indeed these protests only came from a small number of constituencies; most members remained happy with their government's policies and achievements.

Despite some grassroots complaints about wage restraint, the trade unions remained very supportive of the government. The leaders of the big three unions, Arthur Deakin (Transport and General Workers' Union), Tom Williamson (General and Municipal Workers' Union), and Will

Lather (National Union of Mineworkers) were all firmly on the party's right and were aggressively hostile to the left and the Communists. They ensured that the Trades Union Congress (TUC) remained supportive of the government's work.

Only during 1950 and 1951 was there a hint of the divisive left-right split which would so damage the Party in years to come. This mainly centred around the massive rearmament programme proposed by the Chancellor of the Exchequer, Hugh Gaitskell, as a result of the outbreak of the Korean War in June 1950. The programme led to the introduction of prescription charges and other cuts to the welfare state, causing the resignation of three left-wing cabinet ministers Aneurin Bevan, Harold Wilson, and John Freeman in April 1951.

For all its radicalism it should be remembered that the majority of ministers were essentially conservative figures. Paul Addison in *The Road to 1945* (1975) called them 'moderate social patriots'. They had come to political maturity in the inter-war period, and their responses were conditioned by their experiences then. This helps to explain why they were relatively uninterested in constitutional reform or in regenerating British industry, yet keen to maintain Britain's position as a great world power. They preferred to address the very real evils of poverty that they and their constituents had experienced during the 1930s, rather than plan ahead for a post-war world.

Tripartite division of secondary education: The Education Act 1944 proposed to divide secondary education into three types of school – grammar (for academically minded children), technical (for the scientifically minded) and secondary modern (for the rest).

In education the ministers responsible, Ellen Wilkinson and George Tomlinson, were happy to accept the arguably socially divisive **tripartite division of secondary education** and resisted demands from teachers and educationalists for comprehensives, which indeed had been party policy since 1942. Instead Wilkinson persuaded the Cabinet to raise the school leaving age to 15 in 1944 and to maintain the expensive programme of rebuilding schools and training new teachers, undoubtedly considerable achievements at a time of economic difficulty. Kenneth Morgan, however, concludes that 'it is hard to avoid the view that education was an area where the Labour Government failed to provide any new ideas or inspiration'.

Economic circumstances

If Attlee was lucky in having a united party and experienced and disciplined ministers behind him, he was much less lucky with the economic circumstances. The Second World War bankrupted Britain. Victory had been achieved at enormous economic cost. In particular, Britain had become dependent on American loans to keep fighting. Within a week of the surrender of the Japanese in September 1945, the Americans abruptly ended their financial support, thereby destroying British hopes for a lengthy transition from war to peace – and putting the implementation of the policies of the new government in jeopardy. As Lord (John Maynard) Keynes, the government's financial adviser, wrote, Britain was facing an 'economic Dunkirk'. After tough negotiations a further loan of $3.75bn for five years was secured, albeit with many uncomfortable strings attached. Despite these problems the government remained committed to its programme. Hugh Dalton, the Chancellor of the Exchequer, declared in November 1945 that Labour ministers were 'determined to advance along the road to economic and social equality.'

Hugh Dalton (1887–1962)
Dalton joined the war-time coalition as President of the Board of Trade 1942–45. Under the Labour Government he became Chancellor of the Exchequer 1945–47, and was later Minister of Town and Country Planning, 1950–51.

Balance of payments crisis: A situation when a country imports more than it can export thus causing a loss of confidence in its finances by the international markets.

The next economic crisis occurred two years later with a rapidly worsening **balance of payments crisis** and the outflow of British gold reserves. Eventually the introduction of import controls and other tough measures in August 1947 improved matters. Although the crisis was dangerous in the short term, it probably did most harm to the self-confidence of the government and the reputation it had built up for financial management. This reputation was to be tested again in the crisis over the devaluation of the pound sterling: in September 1949 a further 'dollar drain' from Britain forced a 30 per cent devaluation against the dollar from $4.03 to $2.80 to the pound. (The exchange rate in August 1999 was $1.60 to the pound.) This was accompanied by much dithering by ministers. The cumulative effect of these crises was pressure on social spending such as on the National Health Service, and to give credence to the accusations of incompetence levied by the Conservative opposition. However, historians such as Kenneth O. Morgan give credit to devaluation for reinvigorating the economy as devaluation meant that British goods were increasingly competitive in a world slowly recovering from the effects of the war.

Domestic circumstances

By the late 1940s British people were becoming increasingly restive. They had endured nearly a decade of rationing, shortages, and intrusive state control. This feeling is perhaps best summed up by the **Ealing Comedy** *Passport to Pimlico* released in 1949, where a London community discovers itself to be part of Burgundy, thus enabling the residents to free themselves of rationing that 'perfectly caught the public mood'. (The message of the film was, however, that they were better off as part of Britain.)

1946 saw the rise of the British Housewives League campaigning against rationing, which at its peak claimed to have 100,000 members. Although it received much attention in the newspapers the League had little effect on ministers. Indeed the League soon became discredited in the public eye because of suspected links to the Conservative Party.

Knowing the economic knife-edge on which Britain teetered the government reacted cautiously to the new mood. The new President of the Board of Trade, Harold Wilson, announced 'a bonfire of controls' in November 1948 to a broad welcome. During 1949 and 1950 rationing was gradually relaxed. Bread rationing, which had been introduced in May 1946 at the worst time in Britain's economic fortunes, was ended in July 1948. Rationing of clothes finished in March 1949, and a month later saw the freedom to buy sweets and chocolate.

The government also encouraged the **Festival of Britain**, which was held on London's South Bank in 1951 to show how the nation had recovered from the war and was ready to face the challenges of the future. Herbert Morrison sold the idea to the Cabinet by saying 'we ought to do

Ealing Comedies: A series of films made at the Ealing Studios between 1948 and 1952. The best known films were *Kind Hearts and Coronets* and *The Man in the White Suit*.

Festival of Britain: Like the Great Exhibition of 1851, the centenary of which it marked, aimed to show the world British technological and artistic skills.

In what ways was the Festival of Britain similar to the Millennium Dome of 2000?

The Festival of Britain, 1951, on the South Bank of the Thames

something jolly … we need something to give Britain a lift'. Although ridiculed by the press and the Conservatives it proved immensely popular with the public and had major impact on many fields, especially design, for nearly two decades.

What were the achievements of the Attlee administration?

Despite at times desperate economic circumstances the achievements of the 1945 government are astounding. Apart from the many new initiatives, some of which are discussed below, it should not be forgotten that the government was faced with a shattered economy and in many places a physically shattered environment as well. During the war 750,000 houses were destroyed or damaged as well as hundreds of schools and hospitals. Yet the government set about with a will to repair this damage and to build new homes and schools of a quality better than anything seen before the war. It also successfully achieved the demobilisation of the armed forces and the reintegration of ex-servicemen into the economy. Indeed, the demand for labour was so great that the period saw the first arrivals of migrants from the West Indies to fill vacancies, with the arrival of the *Empire Windrush* from Jamaica in May 1948.

The welfare state

The greatest achievement of Attlee's government was undoubtedly the National Health Service, which offered free health care. Before July 1948, health care had to be paid for by individuals, private insurance or charities. About half the male workforce were entitled to free treatment through various insurance schemes, although their wives and dependents did not qualify. Many families had no such insurance and in times of illness had to rely for support on friends and neighbours or local charities. Hospitals also varied tremendously. There were few modern hospitals. Most had begun as either Victorian workhouse infirmaries – totally unsuited for the sick – or charity hospitals, which increasingly were unable to meet needs. It was generally agreed, both before and during the war, that health provision was unsatisfactory.

> **Aneurin Bevan (1897–1960)**
> A miner's son, Bevan was Minister of Health, 1945–51, Minister of Labour 1951. In 1959 he became Deputy Leader of Labour Party and held the post until 1960. He and his wife, Jenny Lee, (also an MP) were considered by some to be the socialist soul of Labour.

Clement Attlee chose Aneurin Bevan, a leading left-wing rebel who had spent the war years on the backbenches, to be Minister of Health with responsibility for establishing the new health service. Bevan became an exceptional minister, combining considerable charm with a steely determination to succeed. His first act was to take local and charity hospitals into public ownership. This seemed a natural development, because by the end of the war, some 90 per cent of their finance came from the state. Bevan's problems, however, began when he began to establish the new National Health Service. He faced increasing opposition from the British Medical Association, representing doctors who feared that their livelihoods would be threatened by the new system. One doctor wrote in 1946 that 'I have examined the bill and it looks to me uncommonly like the first step, and a big one, towards National Socialism as practised in Germany'. As the start of the new Service approached, the doctors intensified their opposition. Eventually their fears were eased when Bevan agreed that doctors could remain outside the salaried structure of the rest of the Health Service. For the first time everybody was now entitled to free health care.

The new service was rapidly overwhelmed by the demand. The extent of health problems among the population had not been realised. It would soon have very serious consequences because the NHS budget rose from the £134 million predicted for its establishment in 1948 to £228 million in 1949, and £356 million in 1950. With increasing total NHS costs, and other demands on the national budget (such as rearmament) the principle of a free service was breached in 1949 with the introduction of a charge of one shilling (5p) per prescription. Bevan resigned from the Cabinet in 1951 over the principle of cuts to the service he had created, although by then he was no longer Minister of Health. For all the changes since 1948 it remains his memorial because as Kenneth O. Morgan says, it is the finest of monuments to his talents and his beliefs (*Labour in Power*, 1984).

Related to the National Health Service was the establishment of the welfare state to provide support to those who needed it. The minister, James Griffiths, simplified existing provisions, abolished the hated 'means testing' whereby people seeking assistance had to prove their eligibility, and introduced family allowances paying allowances for children to their mothers. The key principle of assistance for people of working age was its universality; as Griffiths later said 'it was to be all in: women from sixteen to sixty and men to sixty-five'. Pensions and allowances were also increased, in some cases for the first time in many years. In 1946 the old age pension for a single person rose to 26s (£1.30) a week, the first increase since 1920 when it had been fixed at 10s (50p).

Housing

Bevan was also responsible for housing policy. It came first among concerns of the British electorate, many of whom could remember the promise made by Lloyd George, the Prime Minister at the end of the First World War, of 'Homes fit for Heroes', which was broken in the inter-war years. This concern was not surprising because not only had some many hundreds of thousands of houses either been destroyed or damaged during the war, but many millions of people lived in slum dwellings without even basic amenities. A White Paper published in March 1945 estimated that 750,000 new houses would be needed after the war 'to afford a separate dwelling for every family desirous of having one'. During the campaign Ernest Bevin promised 'five million homes in quick time.'

To meet Bevin's target would have required a supply and organisational miracle. Even the White Paper's estimate turned out to be beyond the reach of Attlee's administration. Raw materials were in short supply. The problem was compounded by a bureaucratic nightmare. *Picture Post* magazine in 1946 estimated that it took ten ministries in Whitehall to approve any new building project from the Ministry of Health to the Board of Trade and Ministry of Works.

Two short-term solutions were adopted to cure the housing shortage. The first was the provision of pre-fabricated houses (prefabs). By the end of 1948 nearly 125,000 had been produced largely by aircraft factories as the demand for their usual output eased. The second was squatting. Incited and encouraged by the Communists, the homeless occupied many empty properties, especially army bases. By October 1946 it was estimated that nearly 50,000 people were occupying over a thousand military properties. The authorities generally turned a blind eye, glad to have some kind of safety valve that eased the pressure on housing stock.

New council houses were slowly being built: 55,400 in 1946 rising to 217,000 in 1948. Thereafter there was a slow decline as the economic crisis further affected the provision of raw materials. Even so a million houses were built by 1951, of which four out of five were built by the state. Building private housing almost stopped as priority for scarce resources was given to council houses. Bevan insisted on good quality, well-designed houses, arguing that 'we shall be judged for a year or two by the number of houses we build. We shall be judged in ten years time by the type of house we build'. He increased the space allocated to each family from 750 square feet to 900, with lavatories upstairs as well as down.

Nationalisation: The taking over and subsequent control of an industry by the state.

Nationalisation

Some 20 per cent of British industry, much of it suffering from years of neglect and under-investment, was nationalised (see table 2). Nationalisation of the coal mines had long been a central plank of Labour's programme as the result of pressure from the mining unions, although resolutions in favour of the takeover of other industries by the state was passed at the 1944 party conference despite opposition from the leadership.

Nationalisation, however, has long been proclaimed as being one of the key successes of the Attlee government. Kenneth Morgan in *Labour in Power* argues that nationalisation was essential to sustain the morale and impetus of the 1945 Labour government. To members of the party and the movement nationalisation was the government's ultimate justification. It was a defining moment of the administration when on 1 January 1947, signs appeared outside the mines declaring, 'This colliery is now managed by the National Coal Board on behalf of the people'. In many industries – coal, electricity, gas and the railways – it made sense to establish a national monopoly rather than the patchwork of municipal and private companies that had existed before the war. Some industries, particularly coal and the railways, had suffered decades of poor management and bad labour relations. Only the nationalisation of the iron and steel industry provoked much opposition.

Yet looking at the subsequent history of these industries it is easy to query the reasons behind nationalisation. The government was often uncertain about what the nationalised industries should do, except to act as non-profit-making utilities. It was hoped that nationalisation would encourage efficiency and investment as well as improve working conditions. Critics, such as Correlli Barnett in *The Lost Victory* (1995), have claimed that 'nationalisation turned out in all respects to be not so much a revolution as a prolonging of the *ancien regime* by bureaucratic means'.

In certain cases, particularly with the mines and railway, nationalisation was probably the only solution to the otherwise certain collapse of these industries. The record of the nationalised industries proved to be patchy, but most turned out to be competently if conservatively run.

Table 2 Nationalisation measures 1945–1951

Industry	2nd reading of bill	Vesting day	Numbers employed
Bank of England	29 October 1945	1 March 1946	6,700
Coal	29 January 1946	1 January 1947	765,000
Civil aviation	6 May 1946	1 August 1946	23,300
Cable and Wireless (telecommunications)	21 May 1945	1 January 1947	9,500
Transport (railways, canals, road haulage)	16 December 1946	1 January 1948	888,000
Electricity	3 February 1947	1 April 1948	176,000
Gas	10 February 1948	1 April 1949	143,500
Iron and steel	15 November 1948	15 February 1951	292,000

Source: Kevin Jeffrey, *The Attlee Government*, 1992.

What were the failures of the 1945 Labour government?

Certainly the 1945 'revolution' was curiously patchy, reflecting the interests of the Cabinet and to a lesser degree the wider party. In nationalising the mines, railways and other industries, the government was generally content to leave the existing managers in charge, and resisted attempts to appoint representatives of the workforce to their boards. Attempts to plan the economy were less than successful, and this from a party that had proclaimed the benefits of planning before the outbreak of the Second World War. This anomaly may be due in part to the fact that very little work had been done on the practicalities of actually implementing these measures. Planning was virtually still-born, as ministers and their advisers adopted a voluntary approach towards industry, which had been commonplace during the war, encouraging rather than directing effort.

In foreign and defence policy the Attlee administration was also very conservative. In this they received considerable criticism from the Labour Party and backbench MPs. Attlee and his ministers had grown up at a time when the British Empire was at its height. One of his colleagues described Ernest Bevin, the Foreign Secretary, as a man who 'at heart was an old-fashioned imperialist keener to expand than contract the Empire'. The departure from the Indian sub-continent, although often portrayed as a great triumph, actually came about as ministers realised that British forces could no longer control mounting communal strife, which indeed occurred with great ferocity in the months after the granting of independence to India and Pakistan in August 1947.

Closer to home the need to remain a great power distorted economic recovery. This desire persuaded the government in 1946 to build the atomic bomb. At the Cabinet meeting that decided to proceed with the development of the new weapon, Bevin exclaimed, 'we've got to have this thing over here, what ever it costs … We've got to have a bloody Union Jack flying on the top of it.' The financial crisis of 1947, caused largely by a drain on Britain's financial reserves, was in part due to the burden of a world role that in the view of many observers 'obviously exceeded the country's economic capacity'. Four years later the ambitious rearmament programme, designed to help the United Nations in Korea, derailed Britain's economic recovery, at the very time when Germany and Japan were successfully rebuilding theirs. According to Kenneth O. Morgan the budget of April 1951, which announced this plan, was a political and economic disaster (Labour in Power, 1984). The Conservatives had to scale down the rearmament programme once they took power in October 1951 for they could see the danger it was doing to the economy.

Conclusion

There is no doubt that Attlee's administration was one of the great reforming administrations of the 20th century. It succeeded despite tremendous economic problems and an increasingly fraught international situation, not forgetting the frailties of the members of the government themselves.

The 1945 Labour government was effective in three important ways. Firstly, in contrast to Lloyd George and the Conservative administration between 1918 and 1922, it successfully saw the return of the nation to a peacetime economy with no dislocation of industry or mass unemployment. Secondly, it achieved a transformation of British society which improved the lives of millions of people, male and female, young and old. For the first time the uncertainties caused by unemployment and serious illness were banished by the welfare state, and a start was made in providing decent housing and education for everyone. Thirdly, and perhaps most importantly, many of the policy assumptions, particularly the central importance of the mixed economy, containing both state controlled and privately-owned industries, and the need to maintain the welfare state and the National Health Service, were wholeheartedly adopted by politicians of all parties. Certainly Winston Churchill's incoming Conservative government in October 1951 made no attempt to

1. What do you think the greatest achievement of the Attlee administration was? Explain whether you think the government was successful and why.

2. What constraints were there on Attlee's government? Of these which do you think was the most important?

reverse any of the achievements of the previous administration. With the exception of the return to the private sector of the iron and steel industry, the nationalisation of which in February 1951 had been widely opposed even within the Labour Party, they left well alone.

This 'post-war consensus' built around a shared belief in Keynesian economics, the welfare state and the mixed economy would remain until the economic difficulties of the mid-1970s forced the rethinking of ever-increasing state spending. However, it took the election of Margaret Thatcher in 1979 to rigorously challenge these beliefs by privatising the nationalised industries and shaking up the National Health Service. Even today no politician could seriously call for the National Health Service to be broken up and welfare provisions to be totally abandoned.

2.3 Lessons in failure? – The Labour governments of 1964–70 and 1974–79

Labour under Harold Wilson and then James Callaghan was in power between 1964–70 and 1974–79. Historians have long been critical of the performance of the administrations. The left bemoans the lack of progress towards social equality. Critics like Ralph Milliband in *Parliamentary Socialism* (1973) felt that 'the government could have had all the support it required from trade unionists had it been genuinely engaged in the creation of a society marked by greater social justice'. The left-wing MP and NEC member, Ian Mikardo, thought '1974–9 was a greater disappointment than 1964–70. The rich got richer under Callaghan.' While the right, both in business and within the Conservative Party, were confirmed in their prejudices that Labour was incapable of running the economy.

In discussing these governments however it is important to remember that they were constrained by three factors:

● Between October 1964 and March 1966, and for the whole duration of the 1974–79 administrations, Labour either had a very small majority (six in 1964; three in October 1974) or no majority at all (February to October 1974 and 1977 to 1979). This meant that ministers could have difficulties in getting measures through Parliament.

● Both governments suffered major economic crises. Harold Wilson during 1966 and 1967 had to grapple with problems brought about by an over-valued pound. Ten years later his successor James Callaghan had to accept large cuts in public expenditure as a condition of a loan from the International Monetary Fund (IMF) to prop up the economy.

● Dissension was growing within the party and the wider Labour Movement. Party members increasingly became frustrated at the ineffectual performance of both governments. Between 1964 and 1970 150,000 members left the party. A decade later party activists were much more confident about using the machinery at their disposal, especially the **National Executive Committee** (NEC), which the left controlled, to make their feelings known. Trade unions were also increasingly estranged from the party by the actions of Labour governments, particularly perceived attacks on living standards of members, and attempts to curtail wage increases.

National Executive Committee (NEC): 'The administrative authority' of the Party, made up of trade unionists, constituency delegates (mostly MPs), as well as the leader and deputy leader. It is responsible for both administrative and election organisation, and also for much policy research.

The Labour Governments, 1964–70

The new Labour government was swept into office in October 1964 in a wave of enthusiasm. Harold Wilson was, at 47, the youngest Prime Minister since 1812. He contrasted well with the patrician Conservative leader Sir Alec Douglas-Home. Peter Shore, later a senior figure himself within the Party, says, 'what Harold Wilson offered was not just an image but to some extent also the reality of a modern man, a competent man – none of the old Labour business of lumbering along … He was on the move. He knew what the modern world was all about.' Harold Wilson played on this image by talking about the need for planning and the opportunities offered by, in his phrase, 'the white heat of technology'. In this the Party had caught the mood of the moment.

In practice neither planning nor new technology received a high priority within the new administration. Responsibility for planning was given to the mercurial George Brown at a new ministry – the Department of Economic Affairs. Although industry, the trade unions and the government signed what was grandly called the National Plan in September 1965 it was clear, as Kenneth O. Morgan comments in *The People's Peace* (1990), that it had no real regulation or procedure for raising production or exports. The Department itself suffered from the hostility of the Treasury, which resented another ministry having influence over economic matters.

Investment in research and development of new products was largely swallowed up by the arms industry. What remained tended to be used for a few high-profile projects such as **Concorde** or **nuclear energy**. The government, however, encouraged the merger of companies to enable British industry to compete worldwide. One of these new companies was International Computers Ltd (ICL), still a leader in computing today.

What dominated the government for the nearly six years of its existence was the economy. When the new Chancellor of the Exchequer, James Callaghan, arrived at the Treasury in October 1964, he was greeted with the news that the economic position of the country was much worse than the previous administration had let on. The need to maintain the pound's strength in the international money markets, encourage exports and restrict imports limited what the new administration could do. As a result, certain key manifesto pledges had to be abandoned or curtailed. In particular the government failed to build as many houses as had been promised, the raising of the school leaving age to 16 in 1968 was postponed, and ambitious plans to restructure state pensions had to be abandoned.

As a reaction to the economic situation the government cut back public spending and increased taxes in an emergency budget in July 1966. Many observers see this as a turning point in the government's life. The severity of the cuts stunned the party and helped to fuel the growing atmosphere of distrust among party members and the public in general about the resolve of the government.

The real problem faced by the government was the high value of the pound against foreign currencies, particularly the dollar. This made British exports very expensive while imports, in comparison, were cheap. Despite mounting pressure, particularly on the money markets, the government refused to devalue the pound until November 1967. The delay in **devaluation** was largely due to the opposition of Harold Wilson to the measure. There are three reasons for this: he had been a key part of the decision to devalue the pound under Clement Attlee in 1949; he believed that devaluation would damage Britain's prestige in the world; and lastly there were good economic arguments for why Britain need not devalue. Peter Shore witnessed the Prime Minister's private response when the decision to devalue had been made, 'that was terribly damaging to him personally. He felt it, and it was damaging to him politically as well, and to the whole coherent reputation and authority of the Labour government.'

Roy Jenkins (1920–2003)
Jenkins held the posts in Labour governments of Home Secretary 1965–67, Chancellor of the Exchequer 1967–70, and Home Secretary 1974–76. He was Deputy Leader of the Labour Party 1970–72 and, following his split with the Labour Party, was Leader of Social Democratic Party 1982–83.

Barbara Castle (1911–2002)
Castle was Minister of Overseas Development 1964–65, Minister of Transport 1965–68, Secretary of State for Employment 1968–70, and Secretary of State for Health, 1974–76.

Anthony Crosland (1918–1977)
Crosland held the posts of Secretary of State for Education 1965–67, President of the Board of Trade 1967–69, Secretary of State for Local Government 1969–70, Secretary of State for the Environment 1974–76, Foreign Secretary 1976–77.

Devaluation and careful management of the economy by the new Chancellor of the Exchequer, Roy Jenkins, however, led to a much better position by the time of the general election in June 1970.

Another difficulty faced by the government was industrial relations. Paradoxically as Kenneth O. Morgan points out, in *The People's Peace* (1990), this was the government's particular claim to understanding and authority, and in the end its most disastrous failure. Relations with the trade union movement soon became strained as the new government continued the Conservative freeze on pay increases. Matters were made worse by a rash of strikes, of which perhaps the most extraordinary was the seamen's strike between May and July 1966. On 20 June Harold Wilson startled the House of Commons when he attributed the strike to sabotage perpetuated by 'a tightly knit group of politically motivated extremists', although there is little evidence of such a group.

In 1968 Wilson appointed Barbara Castle as Secretary of State for Employment and Productivity. Although on the left of the Party, Castle had long believed that order was needed in industrial relations. With the support of Wilson and Roy Jenkins she published a White Paper, optimistically entitled 'In Place of Strife', in January 1969 in which she proposed fairly mild controls, by the standards of legislation in the 1980s and 1990s, over unions and their right to strike. She called it a 'charter of trade union rights'. Although popular with the public it met a lot of opposition not just from within the trade unions but across the Labour Party. James Callaghan, the Home Secretary, led much of this opposition. Even with a majority of a hundred it soon became clear that there was no chance of getting the legislation through Parliament. Eventually Wilson and Castle had to back down and signed a 'solemn and binding undertaking' with the Trades Union Congress (TUC) in June 1969 that stated that the Congress would monitor strikes and attempt to mediate in industrial disputes.

The whole episode was a humiliation for the government and the Prime Minister in particular. Philip Whitehead, in the *Writing on the Wall* (1985), noted that 'The government had lost both trade union support for being too tough and some public support by appearing in the last analysis to be too weak'.

The government had many achievements to its name. It may not have had the impact of those of the Attlee administrations, but Clive Ponting in *Breach of Promise* (1989) believes that it 'had a significant impact on social attitudes and the lives of ordinary individuals'. The one that Wilson himself had most time for was the establishment of a 'University of the Air' (or Open University as it became known) to enable working adults to receive a university education at home. Meanwhile Anthony Crosland, as Secretary of State for Education, began to introduce comprehensive schools, replacing grammar and secondary modern schools.

The 'swinging sixties' and 'the permissive society' had an effect on ministers and resulted in some notably liberal measures. Theatre censorship and the death penalty were abolished in 1965. Two years later came the legalisation of abortion and homosexual acts between consenting adults in private. And 1968 saw the granting of votes to 18-year-olds.

The Equal Pay Act, 1970, although not fully introduced until 1975, secured the principle of equal pay for equal work. It is an important step on the path towards equality for women, because up to that time women were generally paid less for doing the same work as men. Race relations acts in 1965 and 1968 established the Race Relations Board and made illegal many forms of racist behaviour. To a certain extent this work was made harder by the Commonwealth Immigration Act 1968, which restricted the right of entry of certain groups, particularly Asians from East Africa, who had been granted British passports in the early 1960s.

Possibly the greatest achievement of all, and one in the words of Clive Ponting that was achieved 'in the face of an awful economic legacy, economic difficulties throughout the period and considerable opposition from the Treasury' was a narrowing of the gap between the richest and poorest in society. This was largely achieved by an increase in benefits, rather than in direct redistribution of wealth through higher income tax. When taking the broadest measure of disposable income (after tax but including benefits) individuals on the highest incomes suffered a fall of a third, whereas lowest incomes went up by 104 per cent (see table 3).

Table 3 Increase in spending 1964–70

% of Gross Domestic Product (GDP) spent on

	1964	1970	% increase
Education	4.8	6.1	12.7
Health	3.9	4.9	12.6
Social security	16.0	23.0	14.3

There has always been an air of failure attached to the Labour government of 1964 to 1966. The achievements are overlooked and perhaps too little is made of the economic problems which the government tackled and over-came. Labour had been elected in October 1964 with such high hopes and yet few of these hopes had come to fruition. David Marquand in *The Progressive Dilemma* (1991) feels that 'no modern British government has disappointed their supporters so thoroughly'. He sums the period up as being one of 'lost innocence and of hopes betrayed'.

Much of the blame must be laid at the feet of the Prime Minister himself. Harold Wilson was a consummate politician, but it soon became clear that he did not believe in anything very much. This was coupled with an almost paranoid belief in plots and threats against him, which destroyed much of his credibility not just among his colleagues, but in the country in general. According to Denis Healey, one of his closest colleagues as Minister of Defence, between 1964 and 1970, 'he had no purpose of direction, and rarely looked more than a few months ahead. His short-term opportunism, allied to a capacity for self-delusion which made **Walter Mitty** appear unimaginative, often plunged the government into chaos. Worse still, when things went wrong he imagined every one was campaigning against him. He believed in demons, and saw most of his colleagues in this role at some time or other.'

Walter Mitty: A character in a short story by the American humorist James Thurber who lives his life in ever greater daydreams.

The government went into the 1970 general election campaign with a clear lead in the opinion polls. But weeks of complacent campaigning and a poor set of economic figures a few days before the election secured victory for Edward Heath. Harold Wilson put the Conservative victory down to the weather, 'I think what really did us in was the heat. It was very hot weather … the combination of the heat and the opinion polls did us.' Tony Benn, however, was shrewder when he pointed at voter apathy, 'power slipped through our fingers because we were saying nothing very useful to people'.

The Wilson and Callaghan years, 1974–79

Unlike in 1964 few people had high expectations of the Labour government which came to power in February 1974. The election produced an inconclusive result (Labour 301, Conservatives 297, see table 1 page 23). After a half-hearted attempt by Edward Heath to form a coalition with the

Harold Wilson on his way to Buckingham Palace to hand in his resignation to the Queen, 5 April, 1976.

Michael Foot (1913–)
Foot was Secretary of State for Employment 1974–76, Lord President 1976–79. During this time he was also Deputy Leader of the Labour Party 1976–80. He became Leader in 1980 and was succeeded by Neil Kinnock in 1983.

Liberal Party, Harold Wilson, who (just) had the largest number of seats, became Prime Minister. The immediate cause of the election, the Miner's Strike, was settled within two days of Wilson becoming Prime Minister. The October 1974 election produced the narrowest of majorities: three seats, which were soon whittled away in a series of poor by-election results for the government.

The new administration was in some ways very different from the one that left office in 1970. Wilson himself was happier to take less of a leading role, acting as he described as a 'deep-lying centre-half' encouraging rather than leading ministers. His cabinet reflected the increasing left-right split within the Party. The veteran left-winger Michael Foot was appointed as Secretary of State for Employment, a popular choice with the trade union leadership. Tony Benn became first Secretary of State for Industry, where his attempts to introduce radical policies were effectively blocked by Wilson and departmental civil servants, and from July 1975 Minister for Energy. The great offices of state were however reserved for those on the right of the Party: Denis Healey became Chancellor of the Exchequer, James Callaghan Foreign Secretary, and Roy Jenkins returned to the Home Office where he had been Home Secretary a decade before.

Wilson remained as Prime Minister, until he suddenly resigned in March 1976. Subsequently there has been much speculation as to the reasons why. The answer simply seems to be that he had long promised his wife that he would leave politics when he reached sixty. His birthday occurred a few days before he resigned. In the leadership contest James Callaghan easily beat Michael Foot. Callaghan was a rather different leader to Wilson. He had close personal links with the trade unions and had an avuncular, common-sense approach which a number of commentators have compared to the Conservative inter-war Prime Minister Stanley Baldwin. Kenneth O. Morgan in *The People's Peace* argues that he was the most effective Prime Minister since Harold Macmillan. One of his colleagues, William Rogers, (referring to Callaghan's wartime service in the Navy) thought that Callaghan saw himself as 'the able seaman, the man who understands the common man'.

The most important task of the government, under Wilson or Callaghan, was to survive, because it could be defeated at almost any time in the House of Commons. It had to endure many amendments to

Whip: MPs of a party responsible for ensuring MPs support that party's position in the House of Commons.

Referendums (or referenda): National vote on whether a policy should be adopted or approved. In 1997 referendums were held in Scotland and Wales to approve the establishment of a Scottish Parliament and Welsh Assembly.

Denis Healey (1917–)
Deputy Leader of the Labour Party, 1980–83, Healey's earlier career had been as Minister of Defence 1964–70 and Chancellor of the Exchequer 1974–79.

legislation that it would have preferred not to accept. Joe Ashton, a Labour **Whip**, recalled, 'the 1974–79 government did a magnificent job with hardly a majority … You had to be in government to know how thin the thread was. We never revealed the wheeling and dealing to secure a majority.'

For 18 months from the spring of 1977 a lifeline was thrown to the government in the form of a pact with the 13 MPs of the Liberal Party. At the time both Labour and the Liberals were doing badly at by-elections and the pact brought a respite for both sides. In practice, however, it made little difference to the running of the government, as the Liberals asked for very little in return for their support.

The 1974–79 government's achievements were pretty modest. In part this stems from the precarious situation in which it found itself, but also the October 1974 party manifesto was a pretty cautious affair. Their achievements, however, do include the Health and Safety Act (1974), which aimed to make the workplace a far safer place. Race discrimination and equal opportunities legislation was also strengthened.

Referendums to set up regional assemblies in Scotland and Wales were held in March 1979, but support for devolution did not meet the 40 per cent of the total population threshold required by the Act. The threshold was inserted by rebellious backbench MPs opposed to devolution, including Tam Dalyell and Neil Kinnock, into the legislation. This is an example of the weakness of the government in Parliament.

Possibly the greatest achievements relate to the economy. Callaghan bequeathed to the Conservatives a more promising inheritance than the utter disaster that Harold Wilson had inherited from Edward Heath. When Labour was returned to power in 1974, inflation was running at 30 per cent, but by mid-1978 this had been reduced to 7 per cent. Although unemployment undoubtedly rose over the five years that Labour was in power, and despite a memorable Conservative policy claiming that 'Labour isn't working' (see page 73) the unemployment rate in May 1979 was 5.5 per cent. No government of the 1980s or 1990s could claim so few unemployed.

One reason for this was that the revenue from the North Sea oilfields was beginning to flow into the Treasury. By the end of 1978 Britain was well on the way to becoming self-sufficient in oil and gas, thus reducing imports considerably.

The defining moment of the government was the International Monetary Fund (IMF) loan crisis of the autumn of 1976. As so often in the past the crisis was caused by a run on the pound, leading to a drain in Britain's foreign reserves. Foreign bankers, especially from America, put increasing pressure on the British Government to make severe cuts in public spending to satisfy the markets. Despite measures taken in July designed to satisfy the markets it was not enough. By the end of September 1976 the situation had deteriorated. In a dramatic move the Chancellor, Denis Healey, on his way to Heathrow Airport for a meeting in the Philippines, received a message that the position had worsened. He went instead to Blackpool where the Labour Party was having its conference. There Healey discussed the position with the Prime Minister and, in his words, 'decided the only thing to do was to announce we were going to the IMF [for a loan] because that was the only thing that would hold the markets, which it did'. They decided to ask for a loan of $3 billion.

The IMF insisted on severe terms in return for the loan, including large cuts in public expenditure. This was resisted by many of the Cabinet, not just left-wing members. Tony Benn put forward an alternative strategy to Cabinet, but Healey remembered, 'he didn't have alternative proposals. I think on many of the big issues of the time he was simply agin it'. During a series of 23 Cabinet meetings in the autumn of 1976, Anthony Crosland, Tony Benn and other critics were persuaded that the very severity of the crisis made the loan essential. According to Benn, Crosland eventually told Cabinet, 'it is mad but we have no alternative'. The Cabinet agreed the terms and announced £2.5 billion of cuts in public spending.

Ironically it seems that the loan wasn't actually needed. The whole exercise was done on false figures. Healey concluded, 'the virtue of the whole thing, even though it wasn't necessary, is the sentiment internationally completely switched round'. Ultimately, as Martin Holmes, in *The Labour Government 1974–1979* (1985), suggests 'both Healey and Callaghan knew that the IMF medicine, while tasting foul, would benefit the patient in economic terms'. However there was a price to pay. Many within the Labour movement were disgusted by what they saw as a sell-out to international **capitalism**. Martin Holmes believes 'the most valuable contribution of the 1974–79 government was arguably not in any specific policy at all but in the change of intellectual direction in the latter months of 1976 away from **Keynesian economics** towards what is known as monetarism'.

Part of the medicine administered by the IMF was the slow abandonment of Keynesian economics, which no longer seemed applicable for the position Britain found itself in. James Callaghan sounded the death knell of the old ways when he told the 1976 conference, 'we used to think you could spend your way out of a recession and increase employment by cutting taxes and boosting spending. I tell you in all candour that the option no longer exists, and in so far as it ever did exist, it only worked by injecting a bigger dose of inflation into the system.' The public expenditure cuts of 1976 and the subsequent recovery in the economy demolished the post-war consensus, and showed the way for Thatcher and the Conservative governments of the 1980s and 1990s.

For many people the abiding memory of the Callaghan administration was the so-called 'Winter of Discontent'. Three years of agreed pay deals between unions and the government had cut many workers' living standards. The 5 per cent maximum pay rise proposed by Callaghan did not please the unions or their members, as they felt entitled to greater increases to make up lost ground. Alan Fisher, leader of the health service union **NUPE**, complained, 'you know what percentages do for the lower paid. It gives least to those who need it most and most to those who need it least.'

Government ministers repeatedly ignored warnings from friends in the labour movement that the figure proposed was too low. Denis Healey remembers, 'I'm convinced now that if we had said we wanted settlements in single figures, we'd have probably come out with something like 12 per cent overall and retained the support of the unions, avoided the Winter of Discontent, and won the election. But **hubris** tends to affect all governments after a period of success, and by golly it hit us.'

The TUC, with the support of many within the Labour Party, decided to ignore the government's recommendation. The round of pay settlements began with the Ford workers receiving a rise of 15 per cent. This set the pattern for other rises. When the government tried to enforce moderate pay rises it found it couldn't. Callaghan was reluctant to take on the unions, with whom he had had close links for many years. By the end of January 1979, however, many public sector workers were on strike. Roads went ungritted, rubbish uncollected, and in one macabre twist the dead on Merseyside were left unburied. The **tabloid press**, most of which supported the Conservatives, had a field day with screaming headlines 'Has Everyone Gone Mad?' 'No Mercy' 'Target for Today – Sick Children' with graphic photographs of picket lines, unoccupied graves and closed

Capitalism: The economic system prevalent in Britain and western society, sometimes called the free market or private enterprise economy. Economic decision-making is highly decentralised with a large number of companies selling goods and services and consumers choosing which services and goods most suits their needs.

Keynesian economics: Argued that a government could spend its way out of an economic crisis.

NUPE: National Union of Public Employees now part of the union UNISON.

Hubris: A feeling of self-confidence, that nothing can go wrong.

Tabloid press: Mass circulation newspapers such as the *Sun*, *Daily Mirror*, *Daily Express* and *Daily Mail*. Only the *Daily Mirror* was traditionally a Labour-supporting newspaper.

Why did scenes such as this discredit the Labour government of the time?

Uncollected rubbish in Leicester Square, London, during the 'Winter of Discontent', 1978–79

hospitals. NUPE, many of whose members were the least well paid in the country, were at the forefront of the action. Eventually many pay deals were signed with employers giving rises far higher than had been anticipated.

The damage, however, had been done. In the short term the images of militancy were a gift to the Conservatives under Margaret Thatcher. The government was finally put out of its misery when it lost a vote of no confidence in March 1979. The memory of picket lines and unfilled graves would linger for many years, damaging Labour's electoral prospects and the reputation of the unions themselves.

The resulting election marked a decisive break in British history. Callaghan himself recognised this when during the campaign he confided to a friend that he sensed 'a sea change' in British society, as great as the one that had first taken him to Parliament in 1945. Yet to an extent, with the adoption of monetarist policies and severe cutbacks in public spending, Callaghan had already anticipated Thatcherism.

How successful was the Labour government between 1974 and 1979? Eric Shaw, in *The Labour Party since 1945* (1996), feels that 'one is left with the impression of a government struggling to do its best in extremely bleak conditions, where the familiar landmarks were vanishing and where few of the levers used in the past to control events any longer worked'.

Although the record of the government has long been attacked within the Labour Party, and indeed its perceived failure fuelled the civil war which engulfed the Party after 1979, it is difficult not to come to the conclusion that – unlike the 1964–70 government – it did its best under nearly impossible circumstances. Economically it left the country in a much healthier position than it inherited. Despite cuts it did its best to protect the least well-off. Ultimately it failed however because it could not control its own supporters, particularly within the trade unions. It would take almost 20 years for the lesson to be learnt by the Party.

1. How successful do you think the Labour governments of 1964–70 and 1974–79 were?

2. Identify the constraints on Harold Wilson and James Callaghan as Prime Ministers. Why do you think they acted as they did?

2.4 Why did the Labour Party spend so much time in opposition after 1951?
A CASE STUDY IN HISTORICAL INTERPRETATION

Many political commentators in the 1940s and late 1960s predicted that the Labour Party was the 'natural party of government'. The reality however has been very different, with the party in opposition for 35 of the 55 years since the end of the Second World War. The reason for being in opposition for so long depends not just on the effectiveness of Conservative governments, but also on the failure of Labour in opposition to modernise its policies and to present a united face to the electorate.

The 1950s and 1960s

Cast into opposition in 1951 Labour went through a similar, if unfinished, period of modernisation of its policies. As James Cronin wrote in *Labour and Society in Britain 1918–1979* (1984), 'in the 1950s the Labour Party's problem was not that it had become the natural party of government but that it seemed incapable of presenting a sufficiently coherent face to the electorate to recapture power at all'.

The left-right split was mainly centred within the Parliamentary Labour Party and was fuelled by intense personal rivalry. The left wing was led by Aneurin Bevan, and the right by Hugh Gaitskell. Ideologically the left, always in a minority, called for a fresh extension of the public sector, while the right supported Herbert Morrison's call for a period of 'consolidation' to digest the accomplishments of the post-war administration and concentrate on administering the new welfare state.

Renewal within the party began with the election of Hugh Gaitskell as leader after the 1955 general election, and his cautious rapprochement with Aneurin Bevan. Gaitskell was an enthusiastic **revisionist**, believing that it was vital that the party should be educated in the new realities of post-war Britain and that its programme should accordingly be renewed.

In this Gaitskell was helped by Anthony Crosland, his close friend and ally. During 1956 he published *The Future of Socialism* described by Eric Shaw in *The Labour Party since 1945* (1996) as 'the most important work of post-war British social democracy since the war'. In it Crosland argued that the need for public ownership and the replacement of the market economy was outdated. Socialism was about values – above all, equality and social justice, in Crosland's words 'the most characteristic feature of socialist thought'.

The high point of revisionism was Gaitskell's failed attempt to remove Clause IV at the 1961 Party conference (see page 45). He urged the party to accept that there had been 'a significant change in the economic and social background in politics' that required Labour to abandon its old doctrines and slogans. He told the conference, 'let us remember we are a party of the future, not of the past … It is no good waving the banners of a bygone age.' Gaitskell failed to persuade the conference and the wider party of the advantages of making the change, largely because he could not provide a satisfactory alternative. A chance was missed to update Labour's core doctrine to meet the aspirational needs of those in the newly 'affluent society'.

A decade of internal debate and bitter factional rivalry was in the end remarkably unproductive in terms of revising and updating the party programme. A saviour, however, appeared in the form of the scientific revolution, which was, as James Hinton argues in Labour and Socialism (1983) 'a compromise based more on torpor than on genuine agreement'. The claim that Labour would revive the economy by harnessing science emerged as a major theme with the party's 1960 document 'Signposts to

---

Hugh Gaitskell (1906–1963)
Gaitskell was Chancellor of the Exchequer 1950–51. He was Leader of the Labour Party from 1955 until his sudden death in 1963. Many regarded him as the great lost leader of the Party.

Revisionist or revisionism: In this context the term given in the 1950s to those who wished to revise the Party's policies, and ultimately its aims and objectives. In some ways they were not dissimilar to the modernisers of the 1990s.

Richard Crossman (1907–1974)
Crossman published a diary of his time as a Labour minister, during which he was Minister for Housing 1964–66, Lord President 1966–68, and Secretary of State for Social Services 1968–70.

Platform: The policies on which a party stands.

the Sixties'. Scientific managerialism was an idea that both right and left could agree on. As Crossman put it, 'here was an new creative socialist idea needed to reconcile the revisionists of the right with the traditionalists of the left'.

Harold Wilson, who was elected leader of the party in early 1963 on the sudden death of Hugh Gaitskell, enthusiastically took this theme up. Wilson played on the image by talking about the need for planning and the opportunities offered by new technology. It was best expressed in Wilson's speech to the 1963 Party conference, in which he talked about 'the white heat of technology'. The idea of the scientific revolution was popular with the electorate. The experience of the 1964 and 1966 Labour governments, however, was disillusioning. The emphasis on the scientific revolution was largely forgotten in the economic crises that beset the new administration.

Neither Gaitskell nor Wilson saw fit to really challenge the post-war consensus because it largely grew out of the achievements of the Attlee administration to which they had contributed. Gaitskell did not have the support successfully to challenge the consensus, while Wilson was uninterested in doing so. A wholesale reform of the party's **platform** had not been made and this would considerably damage the Party in the decades to come. As Keith Middlemass in *The Politics of Industrial Society* (1979) said, 'what really occurred ... resembled the dosing of a malarial patient with quinine: the symptoms disappeared, but the Party wasn't really strengthened, nor were its ideological fevers cured'.

The rise of the left 1970–87

The 1970s and early 1980s saw the rise of grassroots activism, which moved the Labour Party considerably to the left. The reasons for this grassroots revolt are threefold:

- Dissatisfaction within the party at the performance of the Labour governments of 1964 and 1974, which promised much but seemingly delivered very little in the way of socialist measures let alone reduced the inequalities within society;

- Frustration at the unresponsiveness of MPs and ministers to the concerns of ordinary members;

- A changing membership which brought into the party younger, better educated people, largely from the public services such as teaching and social work, who were less prepared to be deferential to senior figures within the party.

Matters were made worse by an antiquated party structure. In particular there was conflict and uncertainty over the powers of conference, the National Executive Committee (NEC), the Parliamentary Labour Party (PLP), and the Leader. Michael Foot, leader of the party between 1980 and 1982, pointed out in *Another Heart and other Pulses* (1984) that 'many of the internal rows ... have revolved around this theoretically impractical constitutional arrangement'.

Until the 1960s the system worked reasonably well, partly because the membership was in general in agreement with the policies of the party promulgated by the leadership. The leadership could usually also count on the support of the trade unions at conference, where their voting strength would defeat motions with which the leadership disagreed. Trade union support became less certain in the late 1950s as a new generation of left-wing trade union general secretaries, notably Jack Jones (Transport and General Workers' Union) and Hugh Scanlon (Amalgamated Engineering Union) was elected. The trade unions were also increasingly estranged

Trotskyists: As the name suggests, they follow the teachings of Leon Trotsky (1879–1940) one of the leaders of the Russian Revolution who increasingly became critical of the development of Communism in the Soviet Union under Joseph Stalin. They seek to use working-class organisations, particularly trade unions, in order to ferment socialist revolution.

Constituencies: The Constituency Labour Party (CLP) is the organisation of the Labour Party locally. Its boundaries are identical to those of a parliamentary constituency. Each constituency is divided into a number of smaller wards, based on local authority ward boundaries. CLPs are run by General Committees comprising delegates from local trade union branches and ward branches. Until 1992 the General Committee also selected the Parliamentary candidate.

Anthony Wedgwood Benn 'Tony Benn' (1925–)
A peer, Benn succeeded in renouncing his peerage in 1963 to sit in the Commons. He held the post of Minister of Technology 1966–70, Minister of Trade and Industry 1974–75, and Minister of Energy 1974–79. He contested Deputy Leadership in 1981 and 1988.

---

from the party by the actions of Labour governments, particularly attempts to curtail wage increases through prices and incomes policies.

The party machinery in the country was also increasingly in a poor way. In the mid-1950s Harold Wilson described it as being 'a penny-farthing machine in the jet age'. Membership in particular declined dramatically. In the early 1950s there were about a million members of the party. By the early 1980s this had declined to 250,000. (In 1997 it was about 400,000.) The loss of members was due in part to disillusionment with Labour government. The decline was particularly steep between 1964 and 1970 when 150,000 people left the Party. The party leadership, however, remained complacent, believing that as election campaigns were increasingly fought on television, the need for local electioneering and other activities were, in the words of Anthony Crosland, 'now largely a ritual'.

It was easy for small groups of left-wing activists to take control of moribund local parties. The real importance was that control of local parties gave influence to **Trotskyist** and other extremist groups, way beyond their actual strength within the Labour movement as a whole. The most active group engaged in these activities was the Revolutionary Socialist League, better known as the Militant Tendency. In 1975 Militant stated, 'we must consciously aim to penetrate every **constituency** in the country .... A citadel in every constituency, a base in every ward'. The influence these groups exerted is not clear. According to Eric Shaw in *The Labour Party since 1945* (1996) 'the influence [of Militant] was often wildly exaggerated'. Many party officials, however, were less sure.

The pain of Labour's dismissal from office in 1970 was not eased – as it had been 20 years previously – by pride in its accomplishments. Indeed the mood was one of disillusionment. This made party members resentful of the leadership who had been ministers in government. As Clive Ponting suggests in *Breach of Promise* (1989), 'the 1964–70 government sowed the seeds of much of the grassroots revolt in the 1970s with its demands for greater accountability within the party'.

The early 1970s saw Anthony Wedgwood Benn's (Tony Benn as he increasingly wished to be known) move to the left. Kenneth O. Morgan, in *Labour People* (1987), says, that having been a centre, even right-wing member of Labour cabinets, Benn became the pied piper of almost every available left-wing cause. In opposition, Benn increasingly felt that the Party's defeat in 1970 had been brought about by the government's drifting too far from the wisdom of its supporters.

By 1974 Benn was increasingly perceived as leading the left and articulating the views of many party members. His Cabinet colleague, Peter Shore, thought that Benn 'had a special claim to be architect and custodian of Party policy' at this time. Benn was helped by the fact that the NEC was dominated by the left, which initiated a number of policy reviews leading to the adoption of left-wing policies, particularly in connection with planning and nationalisation. The result of this work appeared in the 1973 policy paper *Labour's Programme 1973*, parts of which significantly were rejected by Harold Wilson and other senior Labour figures. Wilson denounced the adoption of the proposal to nationalise 25 key British companies, telling reporters, '... the shadow cabinet would not hesitate to use its veto ... It is inconceivable that the party would go into the general election on this proposal'. Activists, however, were horrified by the way in which the leader ignored the democratic will of the party. Attitudes like this by senior ministers would come back to haunt them in years to follow.

The election of a Labour government in February 1974 curtailed feuding within the party. The truce was not to last long. The perceived poor performance of the government, particularly relating to the International Monetary Fund (IMF) loan negotiated in the autumn of

1976 and continuing industrial relations problems, led to renewed criticisms. In particular the government's handling of the various public sector industrial disputes which made up the 'Winter of Discontent' during the winter of 1978–79 was heavily criticised by many within the Party. Peter Hain, a cabinet minister under Blair and Brown in the 2000s, but a leading political activist in the 1970s, was one critic: 'above all [the government was] not seen by party members such as myself as really seriously putting forward a socialist economic strategy. They were seeking to manage capitalism in crisis … So I think there was tremendous disillusionment and a feeling of betrayal. That was a word often used – that lots of these Labour leaders didn't actually believe in the policies upon which they had been elected.'

Peter Hain and his fellow critics failed, however, to take into account the precarious position of Harold Wilson and James Callaghan, who found themselves without a workable Parliamentary majority for most of the five years Labour were in power. This severely hampered the government's room for manoeuvre and ability to introduce controversial legislation.

Much of the infighting, which erupted from 1979, concerned internal party matters, particularly how the Party Leader should be elected, the mandatory reselection of MPs, and who was responsible for the election manifesto. These measures, it was argued, should ensure that activists had some control over the Parliamentary Labour Party and Shadow Cabinet that had so often ignored the views of the membership. The left's triumph over reselection and the election of the leader, Benn recorded in his diary in January 1981, had wrought 'an enormous change because the PLP, which has been the great centre of power in British politics, has had to yield to the movement that put members there'.

Much of the campaign to introduce these policies was masterminded by the Campaign for Labour Party Democracy. It was always a small body with only 1,200 members at the height of its influence in 1982. But what it lacked in size the Campaign more than made up for in its skill in using internal party procedures to forward its agenda.

Callaghan stepped down as Party leader in November 1980, and Michael Foot was elected as his replacement. Foot had impeccable left-wing credentials and was widely respected within the party as a man of honour. But he was no match either for opponents of the Labour leadership, or his Conservative opponents in Parliament and the media. Eric Shaw, in The Labour Party since 1979 (1994) argues that 'Foot proved to be an ineffectual leader who lacked either the power base or the political gifts to stamp his authority on the party'.

The turmoil eventually led to the first major split within the party since 1931 as Roy Jenkins, David Owen, William Rogers, and Shirley Williams – four former cabinet ministers – left in January 1981 to form the new Social Democratic Party (SDP). Eventually 25 Labour and 1 Conservative MPs joined the new party. They believed that the SDP could replace Labour as the party of the centre-left. In the words of the Limehouse Declaration, which launched the SDP, 'we believe that a realignment of British politics must now be faced'. This realignment resulted in an alliance with the Liberal Party in 1982. The two parties formally merged after the 1987 general election to become the Liberal Democrats.

The greatest battle of the civil war within the Labour Party was the election for the Deputy Leadership in 1981. Tony Benn launched a challenge for this largely honorific post against Denis Healey. It was perceived as being a battle for the soul of the Party, and the campaign was conducted with increasing vehemence. In the end Healey won, but his margin of victory was less than 1 per cent, and was largely secured by the fact that four MPs, including Neil Kinnock, abstained in the final vote.

David Owen (1938–)
Becoming Foreign Secretary at the age of just 38, Owen held the post 1977–79. Disillusioned with the Labour Party he was one of the 'gang of four' to leave and set up the Social Democratic Party. He was Leader of the SDP from 1983 until its demise in 1990.

Unilateral disarmament: A policy abandoning Britain's nuclear weapons. The Labour Party had famously adopted nuclear disarmament for a short period in the early 1960s. Increased fear of nuclear war in the late 1970s saw the rebirth of the pressure group Campaign for Nuclear Disarmament (CND) and increasing demands for the Labour Party to get rid of Britain's nuclear weapons when it returned to power.

Neil Kinnock (1942–)
Leader of the Labour Party 1983–92, European Commissioner 1995–2004.

The left also became increasingly influential in the policy-making procedures through its control of the National Executive Committee. As a result the party adopted **unilateral disarmament**, agreed to withdraw from Europe, and proposed further nationalisation of industry. These policies, especially nuclear disarmament, were used by the media, especially newspapers, to portray Labour as an extremist party, out of touch with the needs of ordinary voters. The myriad policies were combined into the 1983 election manifesto, subsequently memorably described by Peter Shore as being 'the longest suicide note in history'.

The 1983 general election was a disaster for the Labour Party. Its campaign was amateurish and largely irrelevant, especially when compared with the slick media-friendly Conservative performance under Margaret Thatcher. The result showed deep disillusionment with Labour and its policies, especially among the expanding social groups of skilled workers and white collar workers and the south east. As Philip Gould, in *The Unfinished Revolution* (1998) writes, 'the point could not be clearer – there was a new majority in Britain – new working class, new middle class voters. And yet Labour and this new majority were parting company. Labour dragging its feet, they surging ahead. Labour had lost its purpose.'

The total vote and number of MPs were the lowest since 1935 (see table 1 page 23). It just avoided coming third behind the Liberal-SDP Alliance in the popular vote. Michael Foot resigned shortly after the election. A much younger man, Neil Kinnock, replaced him. Kinnock was on the left of the party, but was essentially a pragmatist who was determined to rebuild Labour as a credible political force whatever the cost.

Neil Kinnock was helped by the fact that Tony Benn had lost his seat at the general election and so could not contest the leadership. Even when he was returned to Parliament in a by-election in 1984, observers such as Kenneth O. Morgan, in *Labour People,* sensed that Benn seemed more and more marginalised and was a spent force. In addition the left-wing coalition, which dominated the party up until the deputy leadership contest, slowly disintegrated, as members preferred to engage in internal disputes rather than unite for further potential gains.

Even so Kinnock did not have an automatic majority in the National Executive Committee, let alone at conference, so he had to tread very carefully, and such reforms as he made were necessarily piecemeal. He soon discovered that he could not rely on loyalty to the leader, but had to build convincing majorities for change. His first task, as advisers told him, was to establish unquestionable control. That finally came in 1985 with his conference speech attacking the Militant-run council in Liverpool for its dogma, reminding them, 'you can't play politics with people's jobs and with people's services and their homes'. Neil Kinnock was praised by the media: The *Guardian* commented that it was 'the bravest and most important speech by a Labour leader in a generation'.

During 1986 Peter Mandelson was appointed the Party's Director of Communications, significantly under the leader rather than the NEC. He made various changes to the presentation of the Party, but it was not enough to prevent an election defeat in 1987 almost as bad as that of 1983. This time, in the words of Colin Hughes and Patrick Wintour, in *Labour Rebuilt: the new Model Party* (1990), 'it was the defeat with excuses: there had been no winter of discontent, no Falklands War, no ageing leader, on which to blame the electorate's refusal to embrace Labour'. It was increasingly difficult to avoid the conclusion that the party was out of touch with the electorate.

Table 4 Election of leaders and deputy leaders of the Labour Party 1980–83

1980 – Election of Leader
Electorate: MPs

1st ballot

Michael Foot	83
Denis Healey	112
John Silkin	38
Peter Shore	32

2nd ballot

Michael Foot	139
Denis Healey	129

1 September 1981 – Election of Deputy Leader
Electorate: electoral college with trade unions having 40% of the vote, constituency parties and the Parliamentary Labour Party 30% each

1st ballot	Trade unions %	Constituencies %	MPs %	TOTAL %
Tony Benn	6	23	7	36
Denis Healey	25	5	15	45
John Silkin	9	1	8	18
2nd ballot	%	%	%	%
Tony Benn	15	24	10	50
Denis Healey	25	6	20	51

1983 – election of leader
Electorate: electoral college with trade unions having 40% of the vote, constituency parties and the Parliamentary Labour Party 30% each

	Trade unions %	Constituencies %	MPs %	TOTAL %
Roy Hattersley	11	1	8	19
Eric Heffer	0	2	4	6
Neil Kinnock	29	27	15	71
Peter Shore	0	0	3	3

Source: David and Gareth Butler, *British Political Facts, 1900–1914*, 1994.
All discrepancies in percentages are due to rounding.

Explain how the election of Michael Foot and Neil Kinnock affected the development of the Labour Party.

Roy Hattersley (1932–)
Hattersley was Secretary of State for Prices 1976–79, later becoming Deputy Leader of the Labour Party 1983–92.

The triumph of New Labour, 1987–1997

The 1987 election made it clear that the party could not remain as it was. Policies had to be updated to meet the challenges of the 1980s and 1990s. The instrument to change these policies was the Policy Review that took place during 1988 and 1989. Its conclusions formed the basis of a policy document, *Meet the Challenge Make the Change*, published in 1989, which in turn formed the basis of the platform upon which the Party fought, and lost, in 1992. The review led to the Party gingerly embracing market forces, abandoning most public ownership, general acceptance of the industrial relations legislation introduced by the Conservatives, and, most controversially of all, the abandonment of a unilateral defence policy. The critics, left and right, proclaimed that the Party had deserted its socialist roots. Ivor Crew claimed that the Review was the 'least socialist policy statement ever to be published by the Party'. Others, like David Marquand in *The Progressive Dilemma* (1991) argued that the Review had been 'opinion-survey-driven' rather than 'doctrine-driven.' But Tudor Jones in *Remaking the Labour Party* (1996) is surely right in saying that 'it offered

Tony Blair during the 1997 general election campaign.

John Smith (1938–1994)
Smith was Secretary of State for Trade, 1978–79. He was Leader of the Labour Party 1992–94.

more modest, if arguably more realisable objectives and aspirations and as a result lower aspirations'.

Organisationally the party was becoming much more professional, increasingly focused on presentational matters and preparation for the forthcoming election. Much power and influence was increasingly centred around the leader taking control of policy-making. In this Kinnock and his advisers hoped to by-pass the NEC and other potential centres of opposition to the modernisation that was sweeping the party. Considerable improvements were made to Labour's relations with the media, and in the campaigns conducted in the country, professional marketing and advertising techniques were being used.

Yet, all this was not quite enough to win the 1992 general election campaign (Conservatives 336, Labour 271, see table 1 page 23). It was clear that further change had to be made. As one of the key modernisers, Philip Gould described in *The Unfinished Revolution: How the modernisers saved the Labour Party* (1998), 'Labour had failed to understand that the old working class was becoming a new middle class … They had outgrown crude collectivism and left it behind in the supermarket car park.'

It was clear, as David Hill, communications director of the Party, told the NEC in December 1992, that the Labour Party had no clear identity with the electorate, which still associated it with a poor economic record, trade union dominance, and the so-called 'loony left'. He concluded that 'the greater the prospects of a Labour government the more fearful the public were of that prospect'.

John Smith, who took over from Neil Kinnock in July 1992, was sceptical of the need to alter to any great degree party policy. However, he pressed ahead with reforms within the party, giving ordinary members a greater role in electing the leader and parliamentary candidates.

Tony Blair, who became leader on the sudden death of Smith in May 1994, had no such doubts about the need for change. He and his supporters believed that the party had not adapted sufficiently rapidly or wholeheartedly to new social, and economic realities. Since 1994 the Labour Party has portrayed itself as being almost a new political movement, distancing itself from the policies and many of the politicians who had made the party unelectable over the previous 20 years. In his speech to the Labour Party conference in October 1995, for example, Blair used the word 'new' on 59 occasions, 16 with reference to 'New Labour'. In contrast he referred to socialism just once and to the working class not at all.

The pace of change in the policies and structure of the party was bewildering. Symbolically Blair started with **Clause IV** of the party's constitution, which Hugh Gaitskell had failed to replace 35 years previously. A referendum of members overwhelmingly approved a more modern statement of the party's aims. It was the changing of Clause IV that is widely seen as the moment at which the Labour Party became New Labour.

> **Clause IV**: of the Labour Party constitution sets out the aims and values of the Party. Its direction has been argued over throughout much of the Party's history.

> **Gordon Brown (1951–)**
> Brown was chancellor of the exchequer in the Blair Cabinet from 1997 to 2007, when he replaced Blair as Labour leader and prime minister.

> The original version of Clause IV, drafted by Sidney Webb, 1917:
>
> > To secure for the workers by hand or by brain the full fruits of their industry and the most equitable distribution thereof that may be possible upon the basis of the common ownership of the means of production, distribution and exchange, and the best obtainable system of popular administration and control of each industry or service.
>
> The new version, adopted in 1995, after an internal Labour Party debate:
>
> > The Labour Party is a democratic socialist party. It believes that by the strength of our common endeavour we achieve more than we achieve alone, so as to create for each of us the means to realise our true potential and for all of us a community in which power, wealth and opportunity are in the hands of the many, not the few, where the rights we enjoy reflect the duties we owe, and where we live together, freely, in a spirit of solidarity, tolerance and respect.

Labour increasingly focused on the aspirations of the floating voters, reassuring them about the party's tax and economic plans which had caused doubt among many in 1992. In particular, economic policy was rather different than before 1992. Gordon Brown, the Shadow Chancellor, made it clear that 'spending is no longer the best measure of the effectiveness of government action in the public interest'. Unlike in 1945, New Labour was not offering the public a radically new political economy. Thatcherite policies and assumptions would remain in place. The 1997 election manifesto, New Labour, New Britain, stressed that 'we are pledged not to raise the basic or top rates of income tax throughout the next Parliament'.

The work of Blair and his allies came to fruition with the general election of 1997. The result (Labour 419, Conservatives 165, see table 1 page 23) gave the Labour Party its biggest majority ever; indeed the biggest majority for any political party in Parliament since 1832. The result is in part a reflection of the poor performance of the Conservative government under John Major, but it was also an emphatic sign that after nearly 20 years in the political wilderness the electorate finally trusted the Labour Party to provide policies that met its needs and concerns.

> 1. Using information on Clause IV, in what ways did the 1995 version differ from the original?
>
> 2. What factors do you think contributed to the Labour Party being in opposition for so long?
>
> 3. Of these which do you think was the most important? Give reasons to support the answer.

2.5 The Blair years, 1997 to 2007

History is for historians. For today, it is extraordinarily difficult to assess Tony Blair. To his admirers he is already one of the great prime ministers of modern times, the man who not only made Labour electable again, but who reshaped Britain through devolution and put Britain at the heart of the European Union. To his critics, he is a shallow politician with a talent for self-promotion and gaining support from uncritical political followers (Tony's cronies) who took him into government, but who had little profound to say once there. Between these two extreme views there remained a very skilful politician, easily underestimated by his opponents. During his ten years as prime minister, Blair clearly had achieved remarkable success.

Blair's first term, 1997–2001

Tony Blair was blessed with two major advantages during his first term in office. First, the main opposition party, the Conservatives, were in complete disarray. They had suffered their worst election defeat since 1832 and were bitterly divided over Europe. They elected a new leader, William Hague, who could not match Blair's popularity in the country. Early on in his administration, for example, Blair clearly hit a chord with the public by his reaction to Princess Diana's death, describing her as the 'People's Princess'.

Secondly, Britain benefited from the continued growth and stability of the world economy. Blair's government aided the process, in 1997, by declaring that the Bank of England was to be free from direct government interference. Instead the Bank of England was free to set interest rates as it saw fit, to ensure stable, low inflation – which was achieved throughout Blair's first term in office. Another important economic reform was the introduction of a statutory minimum wage.

Under the leadership of Gordon Brown, at the Treasury, the Labour government maintained strict spending controls – mirroring, often, the policies of its Conservative predecessors. It did engage, however, in major capital improvement programmes for building hospitals and schools.

In many ways Blair's policies on the economy and trade unions were similar to the Conservatives. There was no plan to reverse Conservative laws on trade unions and the general running of the economy. Indeed, some critics called Blair's first term in office 'Thatcher's fifth term', as most of her legacy was left undisturbed.

However, major changes occurred in the political make-up of the United Kingdom. The 1998 Good Friday Agreement on Northern Ireland was one of Blair's most impressive achievements. Although it looked fragile on a number of occasions between 1998 and 2007, the Good Friday Agreement endured. (For a more comprehensive coverage, see Chapter 8.)

Changes also occurred in Scotland and Wales, with laws passed in 1998 allowing for devolution. Scotland received its own parliament and government, while Wales received less local control with the creation of a Welsh Assembly and Executive. Both forms of devolution became operational on 1 July 1999. Devolution raised a number of important questions. Scotland, and to a lesser extent Wales, could legislate on their own affairs but could also influence UK law. England, however, did not have the same privilege, which led to the desire for devolution to the English regions. Although Labour was supportive of English regional assemblies this idea had only a marginal effect on how Britain was governed.

Having been an anti-European party in the early 1980s, New Labour were firmly pro-European under Blair. But Blair decided not to join the new 'Euro currency zone', nor would he contemplate a referendum on the issue.

By 2001 Blair had experienced considerable success in his major policies. Where problems did arise – over party funding and ministerial indiscretion – Blair seemed to raise above them with relative ease, which gave him the nickname 'Teflon Tony'. The first problem involved a U-turn on banning tobacco advertising in motor racing, which suggested that he had bowed to pressure from a major Labour sponsor, the Formula 1 businessman, Bernie Ecclestone. The other problem concerned financial irregularities involving Peter Mandelson, a Cabinet minister who was forced to resign.

Perhaps the most serious challenge to Blair came with a fuel-price revolt by lorry drivers and haulage companies, which temporarily threatened to bring the country to a halt in 2000.

In the 2001 general election Blair experienced a second landslide victory, and within twenty-four hours of his defeat, the Conservative leader, William Hague, resigned.

Blair's second term, 2001–05

During his second term the Labour government embarked on a major programme of spending on the public services, most notably health and education. Health service workers (doctors in particular) and teachers received generous pay settlements. Blair also launched his programme of raising standards in socially deprived areas with his 'academy' programme – secondary schools partly financed by private sector sponsors with considerable autonomy from local education authorities. However, Labour did have problems with one former nationalised industry, the railways. Railtrack, the private sector rail operator, suffered severe financial problems in 2001, which led to the company being taken under government control, under the new name, Network Rail. In the process, transport secretary Stephen Byers was forced to resign in May 2002.

Yet Blair received very little pressure from the Conservatives. They chose Ian Duncan Smith to replace Hague as leader. But he proved to be no match for Blair either, and such was the Conservative disillusionment that he was forced to stand down as leader in 2004, to be replaced by former home secretary, Michael Howard.

The main opposition to Blair came from within his own party. The most serious issue in his second term was the crisis over Iraq and the decision to go to war, along with the USA, in March 2003. Blair was able to persuade the House of Commons that Iraq was a major military threat to Britain and the Middle East because it had acquired 'weapons of mass destruction'. The failure to locate any weapons of mass destruction after the invasion of Iraq and the continuation of warfare after the fall of its leader Saddam Hussein undermined Blair's credibility. There was even an attempt by a Plaid Cymru MP to impeach Blair for 'lying' to Parliament.

However, in April 2005, Blair went to the country for a third time as leader. Although Labour lost some ground to the Conservatives and Liberal Democrats – losing 57 seats – it still had a commanding majority over all other parties after the election. One casualty of Blair's third victory was Conservative leader, Michael Howard – the fourth Conservative leader during the Blair years.

Blair's third term, 2005–07

An enduring 'story' in the Blair years was an alleged meeting, in 1994, in the Granita restaurant in London, between Blair and Gordon Brown. At the meeting it was suggested that Brown would stand back to allow Blair to replace John Smith as Labour leader, and in return Brown would be allowed to run the British economy, as chancellor of the exchequer. In addition, Blair suggested that he would then hand over to Brown as leader after two terms in office. For virtually the entire length of Blair's third term the Labour Party was faced with two governments. One was Blair's actual government, and the other was Brown's 'government in waiting'. In early 2007 Blair announced his decision to retire later in the

Cartoon by Martin Rowson

What does this cartoon tell us about the Labour Party during Blair's third term?

year, and by September 2007 he had stood down to be replaced by Brown, his unopposed successor.

How will history judge Tony Blair? Perhaps, one verdict was made by Blair himself in his farewell speech:

> Now in 2007, you can easily point to the challenges, the things that are wrong, the grievances that fester. But go back to 1997 … Think about your own living standards then and now … There is only one government since 1945 that can say all of the following: more jobs, fewer unemployed, better health and education results, lower crime, and economic growth in every quarter – this one.
>
> Decision-making is hard. Everyone always says 'Listen to the people'. The trouble is they don't always agree … And, in time, you realise putting the country first doesn't mean doing the right thing according to conventional wisdom or the prevailing consensus – it means doing what you genuinely believe to be right. Your duty is to act according to your conviction.
>
> All of that can get contorted, so that people think you act according to some messianic zeal. Doubt, hesitation, reflection, consideration and reconsideration – these are all the good companions of proper decision-making. But the ultimate obligation is to decide.
>
> I decided we should stand shoulder to shoulder with our oldest ally. I did so out of belief. So Afghanistan and then Iraq – the latter, bitterly controversial. Removing Saddam and his sons from power, as with removing the Taliban, was over with relative ease. But the blowback since, from global terrorism and those elements that support it, has been fierce and unrelenting and costly. For many, it simply isn't and can't be worth it.
>
> For me, I think we must see it through. They, the terrorists, who threaten us here and round the world, will never give up if we give up. It is a test of will and of belief, and we can't fail it.
>
> Great expectations not fulfilled in every part, for sure. Occasionally, people say, as I said earlier, 'They were too high, you should have lowered them'. But, to be frank, I would not have wanted it any other way. I was, and remain, as a person and as a prime minister, an optimist.

Politics may be the art of the possible but, at least in life, give the impossible a go.

So, of course, the vision is painted in the colours of the rainbow, and the reality is sketched in the duller tones of black, white and grey.

But I ask you to accept one thing – hand on heart, I did what I thought was right. I may have been wrong. That's your call. But believe one thing if nothing else – I did what I thought was right for our country.

This country is a blessed nation. The British are special, the world knows it, in our innermost thoughts, we know it. This is the greatest nation on earth. It has been an honour to serve it. I give my thanks to you, the British people, for the times I have succeeded, and my apologies to you for the times I have fallen short.

What do you regard as the major successes of the Blair years?

Source-based questions: Labour Party manifestos

SOURCE A

Britain's coming election will be the greatest test in our history of the judgement and common sense of our people. The nation wants food, work and homes. It wants more than that – it wants good food in plenty, useful work for all, and comfortable labour-saving homes that take full advantage of the resources of modern science and productive industry. It wants a high and rising standard of living, security for all against a rainy day, an educational system that will give every boy and girl a chance to develop the best that is in them … The nation needs a tremendous overhaul, a great programme of modernisation and re-equipment of its homes, its factories and machinery, its schools, its social services. All parties say so – the Labour Party means it. For the Labour Party is prepared to achieve it by drastic policies of replanning and by keeping a firm constructive hand on our whole productive machinery; the Labour Party will put the community first and the sectional interests of private business after … the Labour Party is a Socialist Party and proud of it. Its ultimate purpose at home is the establishment of the Socialist Commonwealth of Great Britain – free, democratic, efficient, public spirited, its material resources organised in the service of the British people.

From the Labour Party's 1945 Manifesto, *Let us Face the Future*.

SOURCE B

The world wants it and would welcome it. The British people *want* it, *deserve* it, and urgently *need* it. And now, at last, the general election presents us with the exciting prospect of achieving it. The dying months of a frustrating 1964 can be transformed into the launching pad for the New Britain of the late 1960s and early 1970s. A New Britain:

Mobilising the resources of technology under a national plan;

Harnessing our national wealth in brains, our genius for scientific invention and medical discovery;

Reversing the decline of thirteen wasted years*;

Affording a new opportunity to equal, and if possible surpass the roaring progress of other western powers while Tory Britain has remained sideways, backwards but seldom forwards.

The country needs fresh and virile leadership. Labour is ready. Poised to swing its plans into instant operation. Impatient to apply the New Thinking that will be the end of chaos and sterility …

The Labour Party is offering Britain a new way of life that will stir our hearts, rekindle an authentic patriotic faith in our future, and enable our country to re-establish itself as a stable force in the world today for progress, peace and justice.

From the Labour Party's 1964 Manifesto, *Let's Go with Labour for the New Britain*.

*Thirteen wasted years: The Conservative administrations between 1951 and 1964.

SOURCE C

I [Tony Blair] believe in Britain. It is a great country with a great history. The British people are a great people. But I believe Britain can and must be better: better schools, better hospitals, better ways of tackling crime, of building a modern welfare state, of equipping ourselves for a new world economy.

I want a Britain that is one nation, with shared values and purpose, where merit comes before privilege, run for the many not the few, strong and sure of itself at home and abroad. I want a Britain that does not shuffle into the new millennium afraid of the future, but strides into it with confidence …

The Conservatives' broken promises taint all politics. That is why we have made it our guiding rule not to promise what we cannot deliver; and to deliver what we can promise. What follows … is not the politics of revolution, but of a fresh start, the patient rebuilding and renewing of this country – renewal that can take root and build over time …

We have modernised the Labour Party and we will modernise Britain. This means knowing where we want to go; being clear-headed about the country's future; telling the truth; making tough choices; insisting that all parts of the public sector live within their means; taking on vested interests that hold people back; standing up to unreasonable demands from any quarter; and being prepared to give a moral lead where government has responsibilities it should not shirk.

From the Labour Party's 1997 Manifesto, *New Labour because Britain deserves better.*

---

1. Study Sources A, B and C.

What are the similarities and differences between the three manifestos? Explain your answer.

2. Study Sources A and B.

Of what value are these sources to a historian writing about the Labour Party after 1945?

3. Study Sources A, B and C and use information contained in this chapter.

How far did the Labour Party achieve its electoral aims between 1945 and 2007?

Further Reading

Texts designed specifically for AS and A2 students

The Attlee Government, 1945–1951 by Kevin Jefferys (Longman Seminar Studies, 1992)

The Labour Party since 1951: 'Socialism' and Society since 1951 by Steve Fielding (Manchester University Press, 1997)

Never Again: Britain 1945–1951 by Peter Hennessy (Jonathan Cape, 1992)

The People's Peace: British History 1945–1990 by Kenneth O. Morgan (Penguin, 1990)

More advanced reading

Blair by Anthony Selden (Free Press, 2005)

Blair's Britain 1997–2007 by Anthony Selden (Free Press, 2007)

The Blair Years by Alistair Campbell (Hutchinson, 2007)

Breach of Promise: Labour in Power 1964–70 by Clive Ponting (Penguin, 1989)

Election '45 Reflections on the Revolution in Britain by Austin Mitchell (Fabian Society, 1995)

From Blitz to Blair: A new history of Britain since 1939 edited by Nick Tiratsoo (Weidenfeld & Nicolson, 1997)

Generating Socialism: Recollections of life in the Labour Party by Daniel Weinbren (Sutton Publishing, 1997)

The Labour Party since 1945 by Eric Shaw (Blackwell, 1996)

The Labour Party since 1979: Crisis and Transformation by Eric Shaw (Routledge, 1994)

Labour in Power 1945–1951 by Kenneth O. Morgan (Oxford University Press, 1985)

Labour People: Leaders and Lieutenants, Hardie to Kinnock by Kenneth O. Morgan (Oxford University Press, 1987)

Remaking the Labour Party: From Gaitskell to Blair by Tudor Jones (Routledge, 1996)

The Writing on the Wall: Britain in the Seventies by Philip Whitehead (Michael Joseph, 1985)

In addition, Tony Benn, Barbara Castle and Richard Crossman have all published diaries of their time as ministers. They offer illuminating insights into the Labour governments of the 1960s and 1970s.

3 The Conservative Party, 1945–2007

Key Issues

- What factors have affected the success of the Conservative Party since 1945?

- To what extent did Conservative policies change between 1945 and 2007?

- How important were Conservative leaders to the development of Conservatism in the period 1945 to 2007?

3.1 What factors explain the revival of Conservatism after the general election defeat of 1945?

3.2 To what extent does the affluence of the 1950s account for the Conservative election victories in 1955 and 1959?

3.3 Why did the Conservative Party lose the general election of 1964?

3.4 To what extent is it fair to criticise Edward Heath's government of 1970–1974 for its 'U-turns' on policy pledges made in opposition?

3.5 What factors account for Margaret Thatcher's election to the leadership of the Conservative Party in 1975?

3.6 How far did Margaret Thatcher achieve the aims of 'Thatcherism' between 1979 and 1990?

3.7 What factors account for the decline of Conservatism in the final decade of the 20th century?

3.8 Historical Interpretation: The myth of consensus

3.9 The Conservative Party in opposition, 1997 to 2007

3.10 In-depth study: Did Thatcher really bring about a social, political and economic revolution?

Framework of Events

1945	July: Conservative defeat under Winston Churchill
1947	Publication of *The Industrial Charter*
1951	October: Conservative victory returns Churchill to power
1955	Churchill retires, Anthony Eden becomes party leader
	May: Conservative victory under Eden
1957	Eden resigns over Suez, succeeded by Harold Macmillan
1959	October: Conservative victory under Macmillan
1962	'Night of the Long Knives' – Cabinet reshuffle
1963	Macmillan resigns
1964	October: Conservative defeat under Sir Alec Douglas-Home
1965	July: Edward Heath becomes first elected leader of the Conservative Party
1970	June: Conservative victory brings Heath to power
1974	February: general election returns Heath to power in minority government
	October: Conservative defeat under Heath
1979	May: Conservative victory brings Margaret Thatcher to power
1983	June: Conservative victory under Thatcher
1987	June: Conservative victory under Thatcher
1990	Thatcher resigns as Prime Minister and party leader
1992	April: Conservative victory under John Major
1997	May: Conservative defeat under Major
	William Hague defeats Kenneth Clarke to become Conservative Party leader
1998	Conservatives make gains in local government and EU elections
1999	Criticism of Hague's leadership and policies leads to defection of Shawn Woodward, MP, to Labour Party. Conservatives still trail the Labour Party badly in opinion polls
2000	Michael Portillo joins the Shadow Cabinet as Shadow Chancellor of the Exchequer

2001	Conservatives suffer another major general election defeat
	William Hague resigns and is replaced by Iain Duncan Smith
2003	Iain Duncan Smith is forced to resign as Conservative leader
	He is replaced by Michael Howard
2005	The Conservatives suffer their third successive general election defeat, the first time in the party's history
	Michael Howard resigns as leader and is succeeded by David Cameron.

Overview

THE years covered in this chapter feature two landslide defeats for the Conservative Party. In both 1945 and 1997 the rules of politics seemed to have shifted significantly in favour of the Labour Party. But there were important differences in the circumstances of these elections. In 1945 the mood of the country had swung decisively towards the left and in favour of socialism. Influenced by the sacrifices of the war and the desire to build a new and better society, voters in 1945 were primarily interested in social reform and welfare. Labour was widely viewed as more likely to deliver these objectives. This was especially the case given memories of the interwar years. Conservative dominated governments had retreated from promises of social reform after the First World War, and led the country during the Depression years. Few people wanted to see a return to that era, and the Conservatives after 1945 had to convince the electorate that they could be trusted with this new set of priorities.

The defeat of 1997 was quite a different matter. This time it was Labour that had shifted towards the right. Bruised and battered by the popular successes of the Thatcher administrations of the 1980s, New Labour under the leadership of Tony Blair set a very different agenda from Labour under Clement Attlee. Whereas the Conservatives after 1945 could gather a broad base of support, particularly from middle-class voters grown weary of high taxation and rationing, in the late 1990s Labour had managed to capture and hold the middle ground of political debate with an agenda that bore a close resemblance to Conservatism in the 1950s. It proved more difficult in these circumstances for the Conservatives to find their feet again.

Paradox: A statement that sounds absurd but is nevertheless true.

The **paradox** of the situation in which the Conservative Party found itself at the end of the century was that it was largely the victim of its own success. The intervening years had seen two long stretches of successful and popular Conservative rule. Between 1951 and 1964, and again between 1979 and 1997 the Conservatives had set the agenda of British politics. At times slowly and at times rapidly, the party in government shifted the country away from the values of 1945. So many Conservatives and political commentators have highlighted the contrast between the Conservatism of the 1950s and the 1980s, that the differences between these eras have been exaggerated. In fact, the continuity in the party's policy has been far more significant than its differences. While it is true that tactics and strategy have changed with different circumstances, the general determination to promote widespread property ownership and to challenge the socialism of the left have been the overwhelming and consistent goals of Conservatism, not only since the war, but since the beginning of the 20th century.

Conservative Party Leaders since 1940

Date became leader

9 October 1940	Winston Churchill	(Prime Minister 1940–45 and 1951–55)
21 April 1955	Sir Anthony Eden	(Prime Minister 1955–57)
22 January 1957	Harold Macmillan	(Prime Minister 1957–63)
11 November 1963	Sir Alec Douglas-Home	(Prime Minister 1963–64)
2 August 1965	Edward Heath	(Prime Minister 1970–74)
11 February 1975	Margaret Thatcher	(Prime Minister 1979–90)
28 November 1990	John Major	(Prime Minister 1990–97)
19 June 1997	William Hague	
12 September 2001	Iain Duncan Smith	
6 November 2003	Michael Howard	
6 December 2005	David Cameron.	

As of 2008, William Hague, Iain Duncan Smith, Michael Howard and David Cameron are the only Conservative leaders since Austen Chamberlain (1922) never to have been prime minister.

In these objectives the party has been strikingly successful.

However, during the Blair Years, 1997 to 2007 the party was more concerned with internal party politics than winning back the central ground of British politics. During this period, the party suffered three successive heavy general election defeats – for the first time in the party's history. Another first was the fate of Conservative leaders William Hague, Iain Duncan Smith, Michael Howard and David Cameron. These leaders are the first since 1922 never to be prime minister. None of these leaders proved a match for Tony Blair. Nor did the party develop policies that were sufficiently popular and different from Labour to make a major impact on the UK electorate.

Groups within the Conservative Party

● The **1922 Committee** was founded in 1923 to assist and inform backbench Conservative MPs. It meets weekly and provides a forum for the frank exchange of views between the backbenches and the party leadership.

● The **Bow Group** was founded in 1950 by former Conservative students to provide a forum for new ideas from young members of the Conservative Party.

● The **One Nation Group** was founded by a small number of new Conservative MPs in 1950 to promote a progressive and modern approach to policy-making.

● The **Suez Group** was formed in 1954 to protest against the government's decision to withdraw from British military bases in Egypt.

● The '**No Turning Back**' group of MPs was founded in 1985 to support Thatcherism.

1. Which of the factors in the mind map helped the Conservative Party to be successful in national politics? Give reasons for your answer.

2. Which of the factors do you think contributed to Conservative decline after 1997?

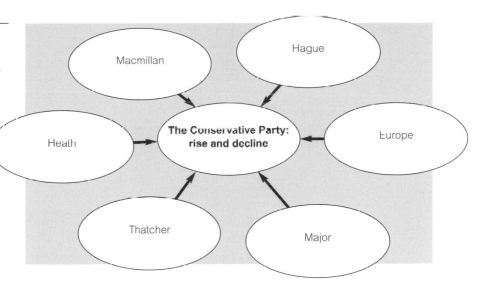

3.1 What factors explain the revival of Conservatism after the general election defeat of 1945?

The outcome of the general election of 1945 should not have come as a complete surprise to the leaders of the Conservative Party. There had been clear indications in opinion polls taken during the latter stages of the war, that social and economic reform at home would be a key issue. Most voters believed that Labour was better at domestic issues like housing, health care and maintaining full employment than the Conservatives. Furthermore, the Conservative-dominated National Governments after 1931 were associated in many people's minds with the mass unemployment and hardship of the Depression. While Winston Churchill was universally agreed to have been a great war leader, attention was now focused on rebuilding Britain.

But the defeat came as a crushing blow. Labour won an overall majority of 146 seats in the House of Commons and won 8 per cent more votes than the Conservatives. The Conservative share of the vote had dropped by 5.9

Churchill addressing the 1945 Conservative Party Conference

per cent from that of the last election, which had been held in 1935. There seemed to be an enormous job to do in reorganising the party's structure and policies to have a fighting chance when the time came to go back to the polls, and few would have predicted that the party would recover as quickly as it did. But by 1948 the Conservatives had regained their confidence and were looking like a serious party of Opposition. In the general election of 1950, the Conservatives gained 85 seats, and the Labour Party's overall majority was reduced to only five. Over the following year, the party's front and backbenchers tirelessly harassed the exhausted and increasingly divided Attlee administration. When a new election was called for October 1951, the Conservative Party was fighting fit, only six years after its humiliating defeat.

How was this recovery accomplished so quickly? There are four basic factors that contribute towards an answer: structural reorganisation and recovery, policy development and propaganda, domestic economic problems, and the political and cultural atmosphere that accompanied the Cold War.

Structural Reorganisation and Recovery

Lord Woolton (1883–1964)
Became a household name during the war as Minister of Food 1940–43 and Minister of Reconstruction 1943–45. He served as Chairman of the Conservative Party 1946–55 and is credited with the revival of the party's organisation and finances after the war. As a member of the 1951–55 Churchill government he served as Lord President of the Council 1951–52 and Chancellor of the Duchy of Lancaster 1952–55.

Patron: A financial supporter.

The professional and efficient local and national organisation of the Conservative Party, which had set it apart from other parties in the interwar years, had disintegrated during the war. The 1945 campaign had been run on a shoestring with almost no professional staff. After the election, the party had to be built up again almost from scratch, and much of the first 18 months was spent recruiting new staff for the Central Office in London as well as in the regions. Even the most basic tools of a political party, such as lists of members, or handbooks for party workers, had to be reconstructed, and it was not until 1947 that these basic operations had been restored. Lord Woolton's appointment as Party Chairman in July 1946 was an important step in this process, although important steps had been taken by his predecessor. Between 1945 and 1950 nearly 300 people qualified as constituency agents for the party, and many more than that began their training.

The membership and fundraising drives initiated by Lord Woolton were very successful. By the beginning of the 1950s the party in England, Wales and Scotland had a combined membership approaching 3 million, making it easily the largest organisation of its kind before or since. Woolton's Fighting Fund restored the party's depleted finances through small member donations, as well as sponsorship from industry and wealthy **patrons** in Britain and abroad. This money enabled him to expand the party's staff and public relations machinery.

The party attempted after the war to project a more youthful and democratic image. The Young Conservative movement, which got underway in 1946 and grew rapidly, operated in many communities as a social club rather than as a political movement, but was nevertheless a key aspect of the revival of the party's grass roots. Democratisation of the party's structure was the main aim of the Maxwell-Fyfe Report of 1949, which attempted to open and democratise the party's selection procedures. By 1950 the party had been fully restored and had the finances and the organisation to fight from a position of strength.

Policy development and propaganda

The second factor in explaining the party's recovery after the war involves policy-making and presentation. The Labour government's domestic programme stressed the nationalisation of key industries and the implementation of a welfare state which was *universal* (social services for

Richard Austen ('Rab') Butler (1902–1982)
Remembered as one of the most influential Conservative politicians of the century, and came close on three occasions to becoming Prime Minister. He was responsible for the development of Conservative policy after the defeat of 1945, and served as Undersecretary of State at the Foreign Office 1938–41; President of the Board of Education 1941–45; Minister of Labour 1945; Chancellor of the Exchequer 1951–55; Lord Privy Seal 1955–59; Home Secretary 1957–62; First Secretary of State 1962; and Foreign Secretary 1963–64.

Enoch Powell (1912–1998)
Served as Minister of Health 1960–64 but is chiefly remembered for his increasingly inflammatory right-wing political views on issues such as European integration and immigration, which ultimately led to a break with the Conservative Party in 1974.

Iain Macleod (1913–1970)
Remembered for his efforts to adjust Conservative policy after the war to the changing nature of British power and society. He served as Minister of Health under Churchill 1952–55; Minister of Labour 1955–59; Colonial Secretary 1959–61; Chancellor of the Duchy of Lancaster 1961–63. He resigned from government in protest over the undemocratic way in which a new leader was chosen to replace Macmillan. When Heath came to power in 1970, Macleod served briefly as Chancellor of the Exchequer before his sudden death in July.

Laissez-faire: French for 'let do': used to mean that the economy works best when governments leave it alone.

Manifesto: A written statement of a party's policy.

everybody rather than just for the poor). The Conservatives opposed all of this, but had to face up to the fact that much of Labour's programme was very popular. Devising an effective Opposition policy was therefore no easy matter. That is one reason why Winston Churchill, who remained leader of the party after 1945, initially opposed making any specific policy commitments.

By the end of 1945, however, there were already signs of life in the party's policy making machinery. Richard Austen ('Rab') Butler, author of the 1944 Education Act and chairman of the party's wartime policy committee, was appointed leader of a new Advisory Committee on Policy and Political Education in November 1945. This was served by a Conservative Political Centre to promote policy education and propaganda. Early the following year Butler became chairman of the revived Conservative Research Department, which acted as a think tank on policy development. Under Butler's leadership, these organisations attracted a number of talented young and ambitious Conservatives, including Reginald Maudling, Enoch Powell, and Iain Macleod. Gradually, some meat was put into party policy and strategy as these bodies became established. Catchy but rather vague phrases such as 'property-owning democracy' became increasingly well defined around the notion of individual ownership and enterprise.

Churchill was forced to approve further policy development when a resolution calling for a clear statement of policy was passed almost unanimously at the October 1946 Party Conference. This led to the establishment of a committee, also chaired by Butler, to consider industrial policy. The ownership and structure of industry was given first priority because of the strength of feeling aroused by Labour's programme of nationalisation. The committee's work resulted in the publication of *The Industrial Charter* in 1947, which is seen as a landmark in the party's road to recovery. *The Industrial Charter* was not by any means a revolutionary document. Nor did it mark a dramatic break with past policy. It placed great emphasis on the need for cooperation within industry, and acknowledged the valuable role that trade unions had to play in a democratic society. It called for the reduction of taxation and public expenditure, but conceded that government economic policy should be used to encourage high levels of employment. It attacked monopolies and restrictive practices and supported schemes of 'co-partnership' and profit sharing in industry on a voluntary basis. The document was written in a style that seemed progressive and in tune with the aspirations of individuals and people of all class backgrounds. Above all, *The Industrial Charter* made it clear that Conservatism did not stand for *laissez-faire* as many people believed, but rather for a reduction in the role of the state and a greater part for individual enterprise in society.

The Industrial Charter was followed up with a series of charters on other aspects of policy including women and agriculture. In 1949 the first general statement of party policy was produced under the title *The Right Road for Britain*. This acted as the basis for the **manifesto** in the 1950 campaign, and stressed that the Conservatives would protect the welfare state and not undo the reforms of the Attlee years. In subtle ways, however, the party did not conceal its desire to lower taxes and make people in work responsible for a greater share of the cost of services such as health care and housing. At the Party Conference in 1950, a resolution was passed which pledged a future Conservative government to building 300,000 houses a year, which was claimed to be possible in free market conditions. This was a powerful weapon with voters, many of whom had been waiting for new homes for many years.

Domestic economic problems

The third factor that contributed to the rise of Conservatism after the war concerns the continuing economic problems faced by the Labour government after 1945. In spite of the fact that Britain was a victor in the Second World War, this was accomplished at an enormous cost, and the country was virtually bankrupt by the end of hostilities. Although still much wealthier than its neighbours on the continent of Europe, the country's spending commitments were also far greater – in defending and developing the Empire and Commonwealth, in paying for the occupation of Germany, in undertaking to construct a welfare state, and in the costs of rebuilding ravaged city centres and damaged housing.

The Labour government was determined that the 'fair shares' policy which had characterised the war years should not be abandoned in peacetime. Indeed this was extended in some respects. This was the postwar '**age of austerity**'. Labour hoped that by restricting individual consumption money could be diverted into industrial production as well into the new social services. Many middle-class voters, women in particular, soon became tired of this. It was one thing to put up with queuing during the war, but quite another once the war was over. The Conservatives took advantage of these circumstances by promising that if elected they would drastically reduce the controls and bureaucracy that had grown during the war.

Age of austerity: The period after 1945 when rationing was still in force.

The impact of the Cold War

A final factor which contributed to the postwar recovery of Conservatism was the changing political climate at home and abroad which accompanied the early Cold War. Conservatives had been placed on the defensive when life during the war seemed to justify socialist claims that the state could provide efficiently and more fairly the employment and services which had been so conspicuously absent during the Depression. The Soviet Union, after all, was a wartime ally, and wartime propaganda had portrayed socialist approaches to the economy and society more favourably than had been the case before. The opposition to Labour which emerged after the war was in essence an anti-Socialist alliance. Not only Conservatives, but Liberals too were disturbed by the apparent ease with which wartime high taxation and expansion of the role of the state seemed to have been continued into peacetime.

When the Cold War began to emerge in the spring of 1946, the language of politics began to change. This was true first and foremost of course, in Britain's dealings with the Soviet Union and communism. That debate stressed freedom and democracy versus repression and dictatorship; enterprise and opportunity versus planning and bureaucracy; individualism and justice versus collectivism and injustice. This language with which Britain, the United States and their allies attacked the Stalinist Eastern bloc, fed usefully into domestic debates at home. Even though Labour's version of socialism bore little resemblance to the Soviet system, the same language could be and was adopted by the Conservatives to persuade voters to reject policies aimed at increasing equality in society. Capitalist free enterprise no longer had the negative associations linked with the 1930s that it had in 1945. By 1950 such concepts had gained a far more positive meaning as a result of the changing international climate.

1. Why do you think that so many women voted for the Conservatives in 1950s and 1951?

2. Why is the Industrial Charter remembered as a milestone in postwar Conservative history?

3. To what extent did the Cold War assist the Conservative recovery after the war?

Source-based questions: The recovery of the Conservative Party after the 1945 general election

SOURCE A

In my opinion, we owe our defeat not to anything which happened during the election campaign itself, but to a persistent and ably-conducted campaign of socialist propaganda which extended from the last general election in November 1935 until July 1945 with no let-up whatsoever during the war.

We Conservatives (wrongly I think) interpreted the political truce as barring us from all propaganda efforts. The Socialists, on the other hand, interpreted it as a by-election truce only … It would require a good deal of investigation to assess the value of the various forms of Socialist propaganda, but there can be no doubt that the following had their part:

● The appointment of a prominent member of the Workers' Educational Association to direct the Army Bureau of Current Affairs, and the clever use made by the Socialists of many of the lectures. Many paid lecturers were Socialists, and made full use of their opportunities.

● The persistent use of the BBC broadcasting service granted to prominent left-wing writers and politicians, and the left bias of many of the news reports and talks.

● Widespread newspaper propaganda in the columns of left-wing national daily papers, such as the *Daily Herald*, *Daily Mirror*, *News Chronicle*, *Daily Worker*, *The Star*.

● On top of this widespread press campaign, we had regular week-end speeches by leading Socialists, invariably well reported not only by the press but also by the BBC.

From *The Next General Election* by Sir Joseph Ball, acting Chairman of the Conservative Party, 1940–45. He was acting Chairman during the 1945 general election.

SOURCE B

The organisation of the Conservative Party was the most topsy-like* arrangement that I had ever come across. It had grown up amidst conflicting and – it seemed – almost irreconcilable claims. I faced up to the fact that whilst as the Chairman of the Party I had received an enthusiastic welcome from the associations, I had, on paper, no control over their activities; they selected their candidates; they selected their agent and employed him … I depended on their goodwill, I relied on Central Office earning the goodwill and confidence of all these diversified bodies which troubled my business instincts.

I rejected caution and decided to ask for a fund of one million pounds, thereby demonstrating my faith in the willingness of the Party to make sacrifices in order to convince the electors of the country of the rightness of the Conservative approach. These were shock tactics. This bold demand created an infectious and compelling enthusiasm. People went out for this apparently unassailable goal, and the stimulation of this widespread effort among all grades of society of which the Conservative Party is composed not only produced the millions of pounds that I asked for, but it gave the Party a sense of accomplishment. Their hopes revived; they found that people believed in them in spite of the recent electoral defeat.

From the *Memoirs of Lord Woolton*, 1959. Lord Woolton was Chairman of the Conservative Party from 1946 to 1955.

* Topsy like – it just grew.

SOURCE C

At the age of 77 Churchill returned to power, and his own instincts and the narrowness of the margin ensured that his ministry followed a moderate line in home affairs. The Conservative dominance of 1951–1964 was founded upon this and three other factors which remained constant until the early 1960s: the public appeal of successive moderate Conservative leaders, the growth of consumer affluence over which they presided, and the persistent disunity in the Labour opposition. An effective combination of 'progressive' Tory domestic policy and 'world power' foreign policy characterised the governments of Churchill and his successors from 1951 to 1964. Only after this did a different agenda emerge in part under Heath, with 'Selsdon Man' and the entry into Europe, and later and more completely with Thatcher's crusade to roll back the state and shatter the post-war 'consensus'.

From *The Conservative Party and British Politics, 1902–1951*, by Stuart Ball, 1995.

SOURCE D

The reasons for this considerable success must be analysed. Some of it was certainly the result of favourable economic circumstances that the Conservatives had been able to exploit to party advantage; whatever government had been in

---

Source-based questions: The recovery of the Conservative Party after the 1945 general election

power through the 1950s such factors would have helped them to give a great measure of prosperity to the electorate. But it is not as easy as that. It was the consistent policy of Conservatism, at least since Disraeli, to improve 'the condition of the people' in the sure knowledge that such a policy was both wise and popular. Macmillan in the 1950s portrayed his party as the believers in material well-being and other parties as believers in moral changes and structural reforms. It has been a Conservative belief that politics is not the whole of life but that economics is much nearly so.

From *The Conservatives* by John Ramsden, 1977. He refers to the reasons for Conservative electoral success in the 1950s.

1. Study Sources B and C.

Using information contained within this chapter explain the meaning of the phrases highlighted as they applied to the Conservative Party 1945–2000.

a) 'Chairman of the Party' (Source B)

b) 'Selsdon Man' (Source C)

c) 'The post war consensus' (Source C)

2. Study Source A.

How reliable is this source as evidence for the Conservative defeat in the 1945 general election? Explain your answer.

3. Study Source B.

Of what value is this source to a historian writing about the Conservative revival after the 1945 general election defeat?

4. Study Sources B, C and D, and use information contained within this chapter.

Do the three sources fully explain why the Conservatives were able to recover from their electoral defeat in 1945 to dominate national politics between 1951 and 1964? Give reasons to explain your answer.

3.2 To what extent does the affluence of the 1950s account for the Conservative election victories in 1955 and 1959?

Indian Summer: A period of very warm, summer-like weather when in fact autumn is about to begin. In this context a final success in a long career.

The Conservative Party won the general election of 1951, bringing Winston Churchill back to power for an '**Indian Summer**' period of office. But the circumstances of that victory were by no means comforting for the party's leadership. The overall parliamentary majority was less than 20. The economic crisis sparked by the costs of the Korean War made it seem for the first year that things could only get worse. The Cabinet was under constant pressure to cut back expenditure, and yet feared that unpopular cuts in education or the housing programme would lead to defeat and another long period of Labour government.

Harold Macmillan (1894–1986)

MP 1924, one of a group of progressive Conservatives called the YMCA. Follower of the ideas of the economics J.M. Keynes when this was unusual among Conservatives. Critic of Munich Agreement of 1938. Minister of housing 1951–54. Then briefly in turn Minister of Defence, Foreign Secretary and Chancellor of the Exchequer. Became Prime Minister 1957.

The end of austerity

The fortunes of the government began to change by the end of 1952. Improving economic conditions and relatively rapid rates of growth in the middle of the 1950s undoubtedly helped to ensure the party's re-election in 1955, and again in 1959. The health of the economy was claimed to be the work of Butler, who served as Chancellor of the Exchequer between 1951 and 1955. In fact, the turnaround was largely the product of international economic conditions after the war in Korea had ended. The economy grew fast enough for Butler to reduce taxes and increase spending on welfare at the same time, keeping voters happy. Full employment continued to characterise this period, spreading the gains of growth widely throughout society. Harold Macmillan, who served as Minister of Housing between 1951 and 1954, was able to fulfill the '300,000' houses a year pledge in 1953, a year earlier than promised. Although this was accomplished largely through the local authority housing programmes (and partly by reducing the size of council houses) the government made a concerted effort to encourage home ownership and made it much easier to purchase a home in the private sector. The housing drive was a big source of popularity for the government, and contributed towards Macmillan's personal rise to power later in the decade.

The Churchill administration was able to end rationing and many of the controls which had characterised the war and early postwar years. Britain moved from an era of austerity into an era of affluence.

The primary source of disquiet within insider circles of the party and the government after 1951 was actually Winston Churchill's leadership. The Prime Minister's disintegrating health (he suffered at least two strokes in this period) accentuated his already eccentric behaviour. Churchill's almost mythical stature at home and abroad was established in these years, making it especially difficult to ease him out of office. This was a source of frustration for his expected successor, Anthony Eden. Finally, he resigned in April 1955; a new election was held at the end of May.

It was, on the whole, a quiet campaign. The Conservatives made the most of prosperity, contrasting 'socialist meddling and muddling' with the improved conditions since 1951. Divisions in the Labour Party between the Bevanites and Gaitskellites was a further factor in explaining the party's poor performance. There was never much doubt that the Conservatives would win the election. The only question in 1955 was the size of the majority. That was increased to a much safer 58 seats, while the Conservative share of the vote rose by nearly 2 per cent. Perhaps the most interesting aspect of the entire campaign was the extent to which television was used in addition to radio broadcasts. 1955 was indeed the first election fought on television, although it was not until 1959 that television took the place of radio as a medium of communication for the parties.

Eden and Suez, 1956

Eden had been confirmed as premier by the voters, but those around him in the party had deep reservations about his fitness for the job from the outset. He was emotionally unsuited for leadership, nervous and prone to sudden mood swings. Eden certainly did not have the confidence of his colleagues and it did not take long for these doubts to be confirmed. He was an indecisive and interfering Prime Minister. Conservative fortunes were flagging well before the Suez Crisis. Butler's famous quip to journalists that he was 'the best Prime Minister we have' summed up the lukewarm support he commanded in the party by the beginning of 1956.

Signs of discontent were evident as well among the voters by this time, allowing the Liberals to make surprising inroads in by-elections. Middle-class frustration over taxes and inflation was particularly evident, as shown by several short lived lobby groups that sprang up in this period such as the Middle Class Alliance. Higher interest rates hit homeowners hard at the same time that employers seemed to be raising industrial wage packets above the rate of inflation. This is the kind of atmosphere in which resentments were bound to arise, and furthered Eden's image problems.

The end was in sight, therefore, by the time that the Suez Crisis erupted (see section 4.6 and page 137) in the autumn of 1956, and in fact Eden's weak position may well have influenced his decision to take such a risky course of action. This worked while the country was at war, and the party regained its sense of unity during the crisis. The American response to the Anglo-French invasion of Egypt made it inevitable, however, that Britain would have to withdraw. This simply capped the impression of Eden as a Prime Minister without authority or sound judgement. On the advice of

Anthony Eden (1897–1977)
MP since 1923. His career was closely associated with Foreign affairs. Seen as a champion of collective security through the League of Nations, becoming minister for League of Nations Affairs in June 1935. He became Foreign Secretary in December 1935. Churchill's Foreign Secretary from December 1940. After 1945 often led the Conservatives in Parliament in Churchill's absence. Returned to the Foreign Office in 1951. Became Prime Minister on Churchill's resignation in 1955. Career effectively ended by the Suez Crisis.

his doctors, he flew to Jamaica for a rest on 23 November. There was no question that, having been unable to stand the strain of defeat, he would be allowed to resume office upon his return.

The question that remained was who would succeed him, Butler or Macmillan. Butler was the senior figure in the party, but Macmillan had several advantages over him. Butler was viewed within the party as a rather academic and aloof figure. He had been an appeaser before the war, and a bad arm had prevented him from serving in the armed forces after 1940. As Chancellor he had started out strongly, but after the 1955 election the economy had dipped, and he bore the blame. Moreover, Butler had kept quiet during Suez. Macmillan was the more confident of the two. He had built up a solid portfolio of ministerial posts after 1951 and during Suez had at least been a strong supporter of action, even if he was one of the first to advocate pulling out. There was no formal mechanism for the selection of the Conservative Party leader at this time. When Eden resigned on 9 January, Lord Salisbury, the **Lord President of the Council**, invited Cabinet Ministers into his office one by one to get their view. Almost all selected Macmillan. This advice was passed to the Queen, and he was summoned to the Palace the following day.

It is remarkable that the Suez Crisis made such a small impression on domestic politics in Britain. Compared to France, for example, where the colonial wars of the 1950s in Indochina and Algeria were to cause upheaval leading to the fall of the regime in 1958, in Britain the retreat in Egypt did not even occasion a general election. This can partly be explained by the fact that Conservative leaders were defiant in the face of defeat – there was no apology for the events of November, and indeed, the crisis was not even mentioned in the 1959 election manifesto. Part of Macmillan's genius as leader in these years was in the way that he managed to turn his back on these events, and focus the country's attention around a new agenda.

Lord President of the Council: The title given to the member of the Cabinet who is leader of the Privy Council (all former members of the Cabinet).

'Supermac' and the affluent society

The years 1957–59 tend to be remembered as the high point of the decade's affluence, while in fact it was only in the particular circumstances of the first half of the decade that the party was able to deliver lower taxes and higher public spending without serious consequences. When Macmillan

What is the message the cartoonist is trying to get across about the reasons for the 1959 Conservative electoral victory?

A cartoon published following Macmillan's victory in the 1959 general election. He is surrounded by consumer items: a fridge, car, washing machine and television.

Macmillan: Well gentlemen, I think we all fought a good fight.

delivered his well-known speech in Bedford in July 1957 declaring that 'most of our people have never had it so good' he was not welcoming an age of affluence but trying to warn the country that high public spending, rising standards of living, full employment and low inflation were not simultaneously possible. The economic difficulties which had begun in the second half of 1955 had made the Cabinet acutely aware of the underlying problems in the economy.

In fact, the harsh realities of economic management would soon culminate in an argument within the government which led to the resignation of the entire Treasury ministerial team at the beginning of 1958. The Chancellor, Peter Thorneycroft felt so strongly on the principle of economic orthodoxy that he resigned over his colleague's refusal to cut the last £50 million off the budget reduction targets that he had believed necessary to deflate the economy. The resignations, followed by a series of by-election defeats in the spring, were the low point of the administration.

But the tide turned for the government in the spring, as Macmillan became more confident, and as the government faced down the unions in the London Bus Strike. Furthermore, in 1958 the economy entered into another period of boom. In spite of the foreign and colonial record of doubt and uncertainty – as Britain lost her empire and sense of purpose in the world order – the domestic record was the one that mattered to most voters in the run-up to the election. This created a feeling of affluence and well-being sufficient to carry the party through the general election of 1959. But the concerns which had been identified by Thorneycroft had not gone away and would soon resurface.

These were the years of 'Supermac', the nickname coined by the cartoonist Vicky, and cultivated by the Prime Minister. Macmillan was a clever politician. He mastered television and understood the importance of addressing his own image in the age of visual media. His personal approval ratings rose steadily in the polls: from less than 40 per cent at the beginning of 1958 to nearly 70 per cent when the election was called. During the chairmanship of the popular Lord Hailsham between 1957 and 1959, the party adopted new methods of campaigning in the late 1950s which paid far more attention to opinion polling and modern methods of public relations. Campaigns in the national press designed by commercial advertising firms signalled a new standard in political communication.

The party was thus well prepared for the election, when it was called for October 1959. In spite of Suez and the internal divisions of only two years previously, the Conservatives entered the campaign with an advantage in the polls which dipped slightly over the first two weeks, only to recover by the end of the campaign. This was to be the third successive victory, which saw the Conservative majority in the House of Commons increase to 100 seats. It was unprecedented in modern politics, and Macmillan's star continued to rise in 1960. No Prime Minister at least, had ever had it so good.

1. What were the main domestic reforms made by the Conservatives in the 1950s?

2. What factors explain Harold Macmillan's rise to the leadership of the Conservative Party in 1957?

3. Why did the Conservatives win the general election of 1959?

3.3 Why did the Conservative Party lose the general election of 1964?

The success of the Conservative administrations of the 1950s rested in large part on the material conditions of those years. With hindsight the 1950s have been criticised as a period of missed opportunity and growth that was sluggish by comparison to its competitors. At the time, the record of the party in office was strong. But with great speed, the party lost its way after 1959. By 1964 no one was surprised when Labour came back to power. The Conservatives now looked out-of-date and uncertain. How did this happen so quickly?

Sir Alec Douglas-Home (Lord Home) (1903–1995)
Served briefly as Prime Minister 1963–64 following the resignation of Harold Macmillan and was an influential figure in British politics for a remarkably long time, first entering Parliament in 1931 as MP for South Lanark, and still taking an active role in the House of Lords after Margaret Thatcher came to power.

Old Etonians: Men who had been educated at the privileged public school at Eton.

The Establishment: The ruling elite.

The establishment factor

For one thing, Macmillan was tired. Sixty-five in 1959, he had spent ten years in Cabinet and led the party and the country through the tense international and economic climate surrounding Suez. He also seemed to be increasingly out of touch with the socially mobile affluent age that the party had been at pains to cultivate in the previous decade. Half of his Cabinet after 1959 were fellow **old Etonians**. The promotion of a peer, Lord Home, to the Foreign Office in 1960 was criticised as highly undemocratic, and in general Macmillan did not hesitate to use politicians from the Lords to an extent that was difficult to reconcile with a modern democracy. He and his government were thus easy targets for satire, as shown to devastating effect by the young comedians of the day. Suddenly, the Conservative leadership became labelled as 'the **Establishment**'.

Educational background of Conservative MPs

Year	Public School followed by Oxford or Cambridge University
1945	48%
1955	50%
1964	48%
1974 (Feb)	48%
1983	42%
1992	32%

Source: *Dod's Parliamentary Companion*, 1945–1992

Equally worrying was the extent to which the party's organisation lost its sense of momentum after 1959. Lord Hailsham was not reappointed by Macmillan (who found his popularity something of a threat). Butler took on the Chairmanship, but as Leader of the House and Home Secretary as well, could not spend the time necessary to keep on top of the party. After so many years in office it would in any case have been difficult to maintain the sense of passion for doing voluntary work for the party that is needed for a healthy grass roots organisation. Macleod replaced Butler as Party Chairman in the autumn of 1961, and he proved to be a more dynamic and younger-minded leader. But by that time the government's downturn had become more obvious, and that made the job of rescuing the party organisation far more difficult to achieve.

The problem of affluence

Affluence too brought its own problems for the government. Party officials sensed that the voters had come to expect too much and grew angry when these objectives could not all be met. And it was becoming increasingly clear in the early 1960s that the country's economic performance was hitting some serious problems. Selwyn Lloyd, who became Chancellor of the Exchequer in July 1961, imposed an unpopular series of deflationary policies over the following months, which contributed to the poor local and by-election results at this time. At a broader level, Britain seemed to be losing a sense of purpose and place in the world. Decolonisation in Africa was speeding up and the days of empire were ending quickly. There was increasing disquiet on the right of the party and among many voters over West Indian and Asian immigration to Britain, forcing the government to pass the Commonwealth Immigration Act in 1962. Factors such as these, combined with economic problems, contributed to a sense of unease in British society in these years.

Macmillan fights back

In politics, these problems were reflected in a series of by-elections from the middle of 1961. The Liberal Party benefited most from the government's problems, and in March 1962 actually won the previously safe Conservative seat of Orpington, Kent, on a **swing** of 27 per cent. Conservative Party strategists became preoccupied with winning back 'Orpington Man'. There were several strands to the recovery strategy that emerged in response to these problems.

The Cabinet's decision to apply for membership of the EEC in July 1961 should be seen in this context, for example. European integration, it was hoped, would set a new and modern agenda in British politics and economic policy which the Conservatives could take a lead on. This would force a cold shower of modernisation and competition on industry that the government could not impose in isolation. In the meantime, Macmillan was convinced that economic policy was the basic problem for most voters. He told his Cabinet in May 1962 that trying to maintain full employment, low inflation, the balance of payments and high rates of growth all at the same time was like trying to juggle too many balls. Under his direction the Cabinet agreed an economic strategy in the early summer of 1962 that was far more interventionist than anything the Conservatives had ever tried previously, hoping that voters could be convinced that the government was back in control. Macmillan gambled on the idea that controlled expansion of the economy could revive the party's fortunes in the following year, and that the prospect of membership of the European Community would inspire and rejuvenate the party's fortunes at the next general election.

The 'Night of the Long Knives'

If this 'New Approach' to economic policy was the first element in Macmillan's plan to regain popularity, a radical reshuffle of the Cabinet was the second. In July 1962 he announced abrupt and radical changes to the composition of the government, which involved alterations to 39 out of the total of 101 ministerial posts. This move, which is remembered as Macmillan's 'Night of the Long Knives', was intended to create the impression of having appointed virtually a new government in an attempt to inject an air of freshness into an administration which had come to seem old and stale. But it proved to be an enormous miscalculation. Macmillan caused great offence by dismissing so many of his colleagues without adequate warning or ceremony. This only served to make the low morale in the party worse, as there was widespread anger at the way so many loyal and experienced Conservatives had been treated. The affair did little to enhance Macmillan's personal reputation. The Liberal MP, Jeremy Thorpe, famously quipped afterwards that the Prime Minister had 'laid down his friends for his life'.

The night of the long knives is often cited as an important example of the Prime Minister's prerogative, or power. By dismissing so many senior members of the government simultaneously, he was wielding one of the most important tools that the executive has in the British system of government. It was clear, however, that Macmillan was not acting from a position of strength, but rather out of an increasing sense of political desperation. On the other hand, the long-term damage that the reshuffle caused has probably been exaggerated. It is true that the Conservatives failed to recover sufficiently to win the election in 1964. But it could be argued that the defeat might have been worse had such radical action not been taken. Significantly, the reshuffle cleared the way for Macmillan's economic ideas to be implemented. Expansion after 1962 was certainly an important factor in drawing votes back to the party, even in numbers insufficient to retain overall control of the House of Commons.

Swing: The shift in votes between two elections when comparing the results for each party in percentages, i.e. an increase in votes from 45 per cent to 50 per cent is a 5 per cent swing.

Why did Macmillan decide to reshuffle his government so drastically in July 1962?

Europe, scandal and the fall of Macmillan

Macmillan's New Approach took a series of beatings in 1963. In January, General de Gaulle famously said '*non*' to the British EEC application. Party strategists had not planned for this possibility, and the Conservative case for voters had depended heavily upon the ability to contrast the efficiency and modernisation of EEC membership that they promised, in contrast to Labour's increasingly anti-European, insular line. Moreover, in the same month Harold Wilson was elected to lead the Labour Party following Hugh Gaitskell's sudden death. At 46, Wilson found it easy to contrast his youth with the old and 'square' Macmillan (and also his successor, Alec Douglas-Home).

The news on Europe left the government reeling for several months. By the late spring, however, there were signs of renewed confidence. The new Chancellor, Reginald Maudling, unveiled his 'dash for growth' budget, attempting to implement the New Approach developed the previous summer. There were signs that expansionist policies were beginning to bear fruit. By May, the Conservatives were back on their feet, planning for the forthcoming election campaign in a style reminiscent of 1958.

Meanwhile, however, the government was rocked by the Profumo scandal, and by June, the Prime Minister was fighting for his political life. John Profumo, the War Minister, was rumoured in the press to have had an affair with a woman named Christine Keeler in 1961. She was in turn said to have also had an affair with a Russian diplomat. The government had had to handle a spy scandal in the autumn of 1962, which had been the subject of hysterical press coverage. At first, Macmillan was determined to face down this new round of gossip. In March, the Cabinet backed Profumo, who denied the rumours in the House of Commons. But the scandal would not go away. Profumo, it emerged, had lied about his actions. In June, he was forced to admit this and resign. The Profumo scandal certainly weakened Macmillan's already battered position as premier.

The 'changing of the guard'

In these circumstances, it was inevitable that speculation grew about Macmillan's position as leader of the party. Macmillan himself was undecided about whether to resign in time for a new leader to take charge of the general election campaign. Part of this indecision was due to the fact that the succession was uncertain. These questions were brought to a head in a sudden and dramatic fashion, when Macmillan was taken ill at the beginning of the week of the Conservative Party Conference in early October. On the advice of his doctors, Macmillan resigned, and, in an fit of bad judgement, made that decision known while the Conference was in full-swing. The week degenerated into one of undignified jostling between the contenders. Macmillan, who initiated a process of formal consultation to find a successor in the week following the Conference, was sobered by this performance. As the opinions of Cabinet Ministers, MPs and peers, and the constituencies were canvassed over the next several days, it became clear that opinion was sharply divided between Butler and Hailsham. It was in this context that Lord Home emerged as a compromise candidate, even though he was hardly anyone's first choice. It was for this reason that Macmillan advised the Queen to invite Home to form a government.

The selection process in 1963 was highly controversial. Macleod, in particular, would later charge that it had been undemocratic, governed by a 'magic circle' of old Etonians around the Prime Minister. In the short term, the bitter aftertaste of the selection process gave a public impression of division within the party which would be a further hindrance in the election campaign. In the longer term the episode demonstrated how important it was to have an open and clearly democratic leadership selection process.

Sir Alec Douglas-Home (who renounced his peerage upon becoming Prime Minister) was never going to have enough time to stamp his mark in office before a general election had to be called. He was hampered from the outset by his aristocratic background, at a time when the Conservative Party was already vulnerable to the charge of being led by the upper class and out of touch with the concerns of middle- and working-class voters. Wilson's Labour Party had a soft target against which to offset its modernising agenda. In spite of the Conservative Party's attempt to run an effective and sophisticated campaign along the lines of 1959, these were handicaps which proved difficult to overcome.

The timing of the election was postponed as long as possible to give the government the maximum amount of time to gather support in 1964 and to recover from the series of disasters of the previous year. Finally, in September the vote was announced for 15 October. Home did not prove to be an effective campaigner. He was no good on television, and did not handle hecklers well. In the circumstances, it was almost surprising that the defeat was not more convincing. Although the Conservative vote dropped by around 1.75 million, Labour was sent to power with a majority of only four seats.

1. Why was Sir Alec Douglas-Home's appointment as Conservative leader controversial?

2. What 'image problems' had the Conservative Party developed by 1964?

3.4 To what extent is it fair to criticise Edward Heath's government of 1970–1974 for its 'U-turns' on policy pledges made in opposition?

Edward Heath (1916–2005)
He became an MP in 1950 and joined a group of Conservatives with an interest in social policy. As chief whip held the party together during the Suez crisis in 1956. Minister of Labour 1959. At Foreign Office from 1960 and involved in negotiations to join Common Market. Became leader in 1965 while party were in opposition. First leader to be elected. Lost 1966 election but came to power in 1970. Led the opposition from 1974 until the election of Thatcher in 1975.

Edward Heath, who led the Conservative Party for the decade 1965–75, has often been condemned for failing to carry through the promised tough programme of economic and industrial reform on which the Conservatives had won the general election of 1970. These charges were highlighted particularly by the Thatcherite wing of the party that rose to prominence following the fall of Heath in 1975. Indeed, Margaret Thatcher deliberately and effectively contrasted her leadership of the country when she famously declared that 'the Lady's not for turning'. Were the actions of the 1970–74 government the product of weak leadership or of the extraordinary and unstable domestic and international problems with which it was faced?

Heath in opposition

Edward Heath became leader of the Conservative Party in July 1965. The first leader to be elected democratically by a ballot of Conservative MPs (Home had introduced this new system in February), he was judged to have the tough, bullish qualities required of an Opposition leader. Unlike his predecessors, moreover, he was a product of the state education system, and came from a solid middle-class background. Heath was from the outset viewed as a professional, technocratic moderniser, devoted to the cause of good and efficient government. He proceeded to promote a generation of younger politicians, many of them, like himself, from suburban, middle-class backgrounds. This was an important departure in the character of the Conservative Party, which was no longer perceived to be dominated by products of a privileged, upper class elite. But Heath was, nevertheless, a difficult personality. He was never an easy-going leader, and his abrasive character led him to become an isolated party leader, particularly in the years after he became Prime Minister.

The party's top priority after the election defeat of 1964 was to undertake a complete review of its policies, initially at least in preparation for the next generation which was bound to come quickly in view of the narrow majority of the Wilson government. Already by the time that a new election was called in 1966, a new emphasis was noticeable in British Conservatism. In its manifesto of that year, the party stressed tax reform, competition, trade union reform, and more means testing in the welfare system. All of these policies were designed to increase competition and efficiency in the British economy in order to prepare it for membership of the European Economic Community of which Heath was, throughout his career, a strong advocate.

'Powellism' and 'Selsdon Man'

These policies were developed further between 1966 and 1970, as the party prepared for an election which it stood a reasonable chance of winning. As the Wilson administration faced a whole series of crises – from the failure of trade union reform to the devaluation crisis of 1967 (see chapter 2) – the Conservative Opposition moved steadily to the right. This can be partly explained by the success of Enoch Powell's increasingly extreme pronouncements, beginning with his vocal advocacy of the free market in the mid-1960s, and reaching a climax with his infamous series of speeches on race relations and immigration beginning in 1968. This latter development led to his sacking from the front bench, and the beginning of his role as maverick outcast on the right fringe of British politics. But Heath, in spite of the fact that he personally detested Powell, could not ignore his views, which had strong support within the party and among a significant section of the electorate. The rise of the right was a foretaste of the Thatcherite movement which would emerge in the following decade. In the second half of the 1960s, it could be traced by the growth of organisations such as the **Monday Club**, whose membership grew to around 2,000 by 1970. Heath had to take this influence into account in formulating policy, as it was his duty to maintain party unity in the run-up to the election.

The Conservative shift to the right got a big publicity boost as a result of the weekend strategy meeting of the Shadow Cabinet held at the Selsdon Park Hotel just south of London in January 1970. Harold Wilson's subsequent jibes about 'Selsdon Man' – meant to poke fun at Heathite policies – had the effect of giving coherence to the Conservative platform, which it had not previously had. In the public mind, Selsdon Man stood for a return to free enterprise and values of hard work, for a tough approach to the trade unions, and a more efficient and independent industry independent of government control. None of this was a new departure for the party in 1970, but by the time that the general election was called for 18 June, there was a widespread perception that the Conservatives were offering a new alternative to Wilson.

Heath in power

Heath started out determined to carry through a Conservative 'quiet revolution' by reducing the scale of the public sector and government intervention in the economy. But as premier, he was always better at the details of policy and the business of government than at communicating a message to the public or at keeping focused on the 'big ideas'. He also became quite isolated in office, and unwisely dependent upon the advice of his civil servants. The Heath Administration was beset with a series of problems from the outset, but it must be said that these were compounded by tactical errors of judgement. It is easy to forget, however, that the government was learning bitter lessons that the next Conservative administration did not repeat. For example, in industrial relations, Heath, in his

Monday Club: The extreme right-wing Conservative group founded in 1961 to protest against the loss of Empire.

Industrial Relations Act 1971: The basic terms of the act were: unions had to register; secret ballots had to be held of union members to agree to a strike; the National Industrial Relations Court ensured that the Act was obeyed; the Commission for Industrial Relations would iron-out conflicts between unions.

determination to get the trade unions under control, made the mistake of legislating too quickly, without sufficient consultation. The **Industrial Relations Act 1971** was so broad in scope that it became an obvious target for the hostility of the labour movement. The good aspects of the Act became lost in the general bitterness over the method of its passage. The general refusal to comply with its terms meant that it never became a credible part of the legal culture of Britain, and was inevitably repealed by the next Labour government, in spite of the fact that a large majority of the voters continued to approve of its basic provisions.

It is also true that the Heath government was beset by a series of problems not of its own making. The Ugandan Asian Crisis of 1972, for example, inflamed public hostility towards New Commonwealth immigration. Politics in Northern Ireland were an added problem, because Heath continued to rely upon the support of the Unionist MPs in the House of Commons. Rising violence in Northern Ireland led inevitably to the imposition of direct rule from London in March 1972. This precipitated the loss of Unionist support, and hampered Heath's political position at a critical moment.

But in other respects, the Heath administration made determined efforts to carry through its manifesto commitments. Taxes were cut, and radical reform of the tax and benefits system was well advanced by the time that the government fell. The government stopped subsidising house-building and increased council rents in face of strenuous opposition. It also continued and extended the rights to buy council houses – although as in the 1950s this was obstructed by Labour local authorities. Again, this was a lesson learned by Margaret Thatcher, who understood that an extensive sell-off of public housing would depend upon central government control of local housing policy.

The U-turns

Heath's policy reversals of 1972 are what the government has been chiefly criticised for. Although Rolls Royce had been nationalised in 1971, this could be explained as a special circumstance for a firm on the brink of bankruptcy with an international reputation and operations of strategic importance to the country. The decision, after a year of refusal, to bail out the Upper Clyde Shipbuilders in the spring of 1972, on the other hand, was a climb down in the face of the threat of public disorder. Rising unemployment, combined with the determination to speed the rate of growth before entry to the EEC led to deliberate economic expansion – 'the **Barber boom**' – which flew in the face of Heath's previous commitment to solve the problem of inflation. Voluntary wage control proved impossible to maintain in the face of rising inflation, and when tripartite talks between the government, employers and the unions broke down in 1972, Heath announced that prices and wages would be controlled by law. This was the ultimate U-turn, and no amount of qualification and explanation from the Prime Minister could get away from the fact that the government had strayed far away from its claims at the Selsdon Park Hotel. By the end of its period in office then, the Heath government had failed dramatically in its attempt to impose a quiet revolution.

Barber boom: The name given to Anthony Barber's policies as Chancellor of the Exchequer under Heath.

---

1. What was different about Edward Heath's rise to the leadership, compared with previous Conservative leaders?

2. Why did Enoch Powell and Edward Heath dislike each other?

3. Why was the Heath government forced to reconsider its policies in 1972?

3.5 What factors account for Margaret Thatcher's election to the leadership of the Conservative Party in 1975?

Powellism: The ideas associated with Enoch Powell.

Margaret Thatcher's emergence as party leader in 1975 was a landmark in the history of British Conservatism. As a supporter of the New Right thinking that had become increasingly influential since the appearance of **Powellism** in the previous decade, it was clear even at the time that her leadership would mark a real break with Heath and the moderate pragmatism for which he stood. Moreover, in the history of gender politics, this was also a milestone. Thatcher had been only the second woman to achieve a position in a Conservative Cabinet. Her election to lead the party thus took nearly everyone by surprise. No one had considered her campaign as a serious one until it was all over.

Why Thatcher hated Heath

In order to explain her rise to power, it is important to recall the increasingly bitter divisions in the party which had emerged after 1970. The U-turns of 1972 had caused widespread disillusionment at a grass roots level. The get-tough policies associated with 'Selsdon Man' had fizzled out, and by the beginning of 1974 Heath was involved in a miners' strike that threatened chaos. The February election, called on the issue of 'who governs Britain?' did not, as Heath had hoped, indicate that the country wanted strong government action. Within the party, the election brought out even further some of the simmering resentment that had been building for several years. Enoch Powell, a strong opponent of EEC membership, was so disgusted that he resigned his seat in the House and announced his intention to vote Labour, which was also anti-Europe. That election resulted in a hung Parliament, and the lowest number of votes for the Conservatives since the 1920s. Heath clung on for several months, even though the Conservatives actually had fewer MPs than Labour. The election called in October returned a small Labour majority. It had become clear that Heath's days as party leader were numbered. But Heath was reluctant to give up the position.

Changes in the party

The general gloom within the party at this point was evident on a number of levels. Membership levels had fallen dramatically since the 1950s, and once thriving organisations such as the Young Conservatives had almost collapsed. Meanwhile, the character and profile of the party was changing. Whereas in the days of Macmillan, the typical Conservative MP had been to a public school, had a private income, and a paternalist sense of civic responsibility, by the mid-1970s a Conservative backbencher was far more likely to have been educated at a grammar school, to come from a middle-class suburb, and to have a more professional and ideological approach to politics. There was an increasing frustration among this group with the Front Bench approach to economic and social policy. As British society became characterised by industrial militancy and rising levels of social discontent, many Conservatives began to question the moderate approach which the party had adopted since the 1950s. Heath and the 'Heathmen' seemed to be following a kind of domestic appeasement when what was needed was a strong and principled leadership.

It was in this atmosphere that the ideas of the right-wing thinkers began to gain widespread support. Whereas Powellism had been confined to a marginal group, by the mid-1970s New Right thinking was becoming far more respectable – and as traditional approaches to governing Britain

Keith Joseph (1918–1994)
Senior Conservative Minister in the Heath and Thatcher administrations. He served as Minister of Health and Social Security 1970–74; Minister of Industry 1979–81; and Minister for Education and Science 1981–86.

coup d'état: An unexpected change of leadership.

seemed to fail, this radical alternative seemed increasingly plausible. In March 1974, two Cabinet Ministers, Keith Joseph and Margaret Thatcher, founded the Centre for Policy Studies, a party research unit to promote these ideas. Joseph was at this point the senior figure, and a series of high profile speeches in these months attracted much publicity. Joseph, Thatcher, and those around them were arguing for what they believed to be an entirely new approach, which would break with the 'consensus politics' that had dominated public life since 1945. In their view, past Conservative governments had compromised their principles in order to reach a consensus with Labour on broad areas of policy. Joseph argued famously that this had led only to a 'ratchet effect', as Labour's demands moved further to the left.

Margaret Thatcher's *coup d'état*

Heath was reluctant to resign the leadership after the October election defeat, on the grounds that he would be delivering the Conservative Party into the hands of right-wing extremists. But in November, bowing to the inevitable, he called a leadership election for February. The exercise became, in effect, a vote of confidence in Heath. In spite of the fact that there was a widespread feeling in the Parliamentary Party by this time that Heath had to go, there was no obvious contender for the job. Joseph himself was too prone to making gaffes, and ruled himself out; Enoch Powell had given up his chance during the February election, just as the party had begun to move firmly in his direction; other possible candidates were either too inexperienced or otherwise inappropriate.

It was in these circumstances that Margaret Thatcher put herself forward. With the benefit of hindsight, it is difficult to appreciate how extraordinary this situation seemed at the time. She had a personal score to settle with Heath, who had patronised her in Cabinet. The two clearly disliked each other from the moment that they had to start working together. Heath, along with many others, underestimated her chances essentially on the grounds that the party would never elect a woman to be leader. But although Thatcher had been kept down in Heath's Cabinet before 1974, she had made a strong impression as Minister for the Environment from February, and as Shadow Finance Minister in the autumn. Thatcher was clearly a fighter, with strong and passionately-held Conservative beliefs. Her conduct in these weeks soon took on a legendary significance. It had taken a woman to stand up to Heath, and Thatcher had shown the courage and determination that her male colleagues lacked. In this way, she gathered admirers and was able throughout her subsequent career, to turn her gender to her political advantage.

Her success was not entirely due to luck and grit, however. Thatcher's campaign was skilfully managed by the MP Airey Neave, who came on board in January. Neave's tactics, which deliberately fostered the impression that Thatcher would not get enough votes to challenge Heath's leadership sufficiently to go to a second ballot, was effective in persuading wavering backbenchers to vote for her. When the votes were counted on 4 February, she came a wholly unexpected first with 130 votes to Heath's 119. Heath withdrew immediately. In the second ballot several substantial candidates entered the fray. But Thatcher was in a strong position, and admiration for her grew dramatically as a result of her stand against Heath. It was in these circumstances that she won the second ballot and was elected leader of the party. Heath's fear that the party would be taken over by his enemies had come to pass.

1. Why was Conservative morale so low by the beginning of 1975?

2. What factors explain the increasing influence of the right wing of the Conservative Party by the middle of the 1970s?

3. In what ways did Margaret Thatcher's gender affect the leadership election of 1975?

3.6 How far did Margaret Thatcher achieve the aims of 'Thatcherism' between 1979 and 1990?

Margaret Thatcher stands apart from other modern leaders of the Conservative Party to such an extent that many commentators have argued that she was not really a Conservative at all. Conservative government has traditionally placed stress on 'conserving' the status quo, and on reforming only where it is necessary to preserve and strengthen British society and its institutions. Baldwin, Chamberlain, Churchill, Macmillan and Heath were all party leaders in that mould. Thatcher, by contrast, embarked upon a series of reforming measures which seemed so radical that by the middle of the 1980s the term 'Thatcherism' was commonly used to describe her approach.

Thatcherism

'-Isms' – Marxism, Socialism, Fascism – are normally associated with a coherent set of ideas or an ideology. The term Thatcherism would therefore imply that Margaret Thatcher entered office with a clearly thought out plan of action for putting into practice her deeply-held beliefs. This assumption is misleading, however, because there is little evidence that this was the case in 1979. Much of what we have come to associate with Thatcherism was not part of a premeditated plan, but rather a set of responses that evolved as a pragmatic reaction to circumstances as they arose. In that sense, it is not strictly accurate to think of Thatcherism as an ideology. It is more useful to think of Thatcher's outlook as one based upon a set of moral values accompanied by her belief in strong and authoritative leadership. These values included a faith in individual responsibility, the importance of hard work and the right to enjoy the fruits of success, the central importance of the traditional family, the need to limit the role of the state, the importance of patriotism, and an utter revulsion against socialism. All of these beliefs were firmly held from the time that she became active in politics. Upon becoming Prime Minister, Thatcher was determined to *restore* these moral values to the centre of British political culture. In that sense, she was not a radical reforming Prime Minister. Rather than introducing new ideas, her premiership represented a period of *reaction* against the reforms of the previous generation. This is what she believed would be required to rescue Britain from what she saw as an economic and moral decline, the roots of which went back to the Second World War.

Thatcher comes to power

When she came to power Thatcher's more moderate colleagues hoped that she would be tamed by the pressures of office. There were several grounds for this. The election manifesto of 1979 was not particularly extreme. It was based on the promise to reduce inflation through the introduction of 'monetarist' economic policy, trade union reform, the sale of council housing, the reduction of taxation and public spending, the firm handling of immigration, a stress upon law and order, and a strong defence policy. These policies had a widespread popular appeal, and proved to be particularly successful with skilled workers – who swung to the Conservatives in high numbers. It was not a particularly extreme agenda.

Secondly, the Conservatives came to office with a majority of 30 in the House of Commons. It was enough to govern comfortably, but not sufficient to survive great controversy. In Cabinet, moreover, she was surrounded by Conservative 'grandees' of the moderate centre. Between

Conservative Party poster during the run up to the August 1979 general election (which the Conservatives went on to win)

How important was the role of advertisers such as Saatchi and Saatchi and other 'image' makers in British politics during the 1980s and 1990s?

William Whitelaw (1918–1999)

A political survivor, widely respected by Conservative politicians of both right and left. First entering the House of commons in 1955 as MP for Penrith and the Border, he served as a junior minister in the Macmillan period. Under Heath, he served as Leader of the House of Commons and Lord President of the Council 1970–72; as Northern Ireland Secretary 1972–73; and Minister of Employment 1973–74. He served as Party Chairman during the stormy Thatcher leadership challenge to Heath, and subsequently served as her loyal Deputy Leader. After 1979 he served as Home Secretary 1979–83; and became Leader of the Lords after the 1983 election. He resigned from government in 1987 due to ill-health.

men like William Whitelaw, Jim Prior, Ian Gilmour, and Peter Walker and the moderating influence which the civil servants generally have on policy-making, there did not seem to be any great danger that the right wing of the party would gain the upper hand.

By 1983, however, it had become clear that Thatcher had out-manoeuvred her opponents, and was not prepared to countenance the policy U-turns that had characterised the Heath years. This was particularly surprising given the deep recession of 1979–82, which saw unemployment rise to 3 million and the collapse of the manufacturing sector. The Prime Minister's refusal to shift was a reflection of her extraordinary determination and utter belief in the policies she had endorsed. That she was able to impose her views was the result of both the power of the office of Prime Minister, and the powers conferred on the leader of the Conservative Party. As premier, she wasted no time demoting or sacking the 'wets' in her Cabinet, and promoting supporters like Norman Tebbit, Nigel Lawson and Cecil Parkinson. As party leader she, like Heath, could claim to have support for her approach to an extent that had not been true before electoral reform had been introduced in the party in 1965. Thatcher's domineering style of leadership was both criticised and admired. Her conduct of the Falklands War, in 1982, exemplified her approach to leadership. She took the decision to challenge General Galtieri herself, by-passing the Cabinet Committee system by conducting the war with the aid of a hand-picked group of advisers. It was in this period that she secured her own domination of the government and the party. Cabinet met less often and became less of a team. By the mid-1980s she had surrounded herself with her own supporters, isolating or dismissing her opponents.

Thatcherism in practice

Thatcher's strong image, assisted by the Falklands victory and the signs of an economic upturn helps to explain her decisive victory in the 1983 election. The enormous Conservative majority of 144 can only be fully explained by the weaknesses of the Opposition, and the structure of the British 'first past the post' electoral system, however. With such a large majority, Thatcher's dominance and freedom to legislate was finally secured. But it had been achieved on only 42.4 per cent of the vote. In political terms, Britain was now clearly divided geographically, and increasingly by wealth and poverty. Those areas which had been hardest hit by the recession – the north of England, Scotland and Wales – had become impregnable Labour strongholds. More prosperous areas of England went to the Conservatives, with the Social Democratic Party often taking second place.

This was evident in the second Thatcher government, when most analysts, such as Peter Riddell in *The Thatcher Decade* (1989), have traced the beginnings of what is generally understood to be 'Thatcherism'. It was in this administration that privatisation became a central feature of government policy. The revenue raised by selling nationalised industries such as British Airways and British Gas, was, like the revenue from North Sea oil and gas, absorbed into general government spending rather than **ringfenced** for a planned programme of investment. In spite of this, privatisation was a popular programme, largely because of the **windfall profits** available for investors. The government attempted to encourage more popular support for capitalism through widespread share ownership, in a similar fashion to the extension of home ownership to low income earners through the sale of council housing. Easy credit policies and the deregulation of the City contributed to a boom centred on the south of England. For the 'haves' of the mid 1980s, real wages outstripped inflation. By the time that the next election was called in 1987, Thatcher seemed to be delivering an economic miracle in the prosperous parts of the country where the Conservative vote was already focused. That victory was on a similar scale and for similar structural reasons, led to a majority of 101 seats on just 42.3 per cent of the vote.

Ringfenced: Identified as being kept for a particular purpose.

Windfall profits: An unexpectedly large profit. The shares of privatised business rose in value soon after issue and investors could then sell them on for a very quick and substantial profit.

Election night 1987: Margaret Thatcher becomes the only 20th century British Prime Minister to serve three consecutive terms of office

Poll Tax riots: Violent public demonstrations against local tax reform in the spring of 1990.

Eurosceptic: Opposed to further European integration.

Michael Heseltine (1933–)
Served as Environment Secretary 1979–83 and Defence Secretary 1983–86 under Margaret Thatcher, and came closer than any other senior Conservative figure to bringing her down, when he resigned in January 1986. While on the surface, this decision concerned his disagreement with the Cabinet's decision to allow the sale of the ailing Westland helicopter company to an American firm, Heseltine was frustrated by her increasingly autocratic and anti-European approach.

Quango: A quasi autonomous non-government organisation. Although not a government organisation these were funded by government departments and, to a certain extent, were responsible to those departments to oversee aspects of government work.

Beneath this veneer of success, however, there were profound and troubling failures associated with the Thatcher years. For those who did not directly benefit from the government's economic policies, these were years of increasing social exclusion. This was evident as early as 1981, as social unrest erupted in Brixton, south London, soon to be followed in other cities. The problems of the inner city were compounded in those parts of Britain where unemployment hit levels not seen since the interwar years as a result of industrial decline. Thatcher's handling of the miners' strike in 1984–85 may have won admirers from among those who believed that the trade unions needed to be confronted. But the extent of police powers used during the strike, and the evident weakness of the miners as a result of the new reforms convinced many that the Conservatives had tipped the balance too far in the other direction. Thatcher's Britain had little regard for civil liberties, and by the latter years of the decade, the Prime Minister seemed increasingly distant from these concerns. The disaster of the Local Government Finance Act 1988, culminating in the '**Poll Tax riots**' of the following year, was a crucial turning point. Thatcher, previously the strongest Conservative Party leader of living memory, suddenly seemed an electoral liability.

Margaret Thatcher's off-hand treatment of her senior colleagues had made her many powerful enemies by the end of the 1980s. Her judgement on a range of issues, from the Poll Tax to her **Euroscepticism** had led to increasing unease within the party. In November 1989, she became the victim of the same amended rules which she had used against Heath. Sir Anthony Meyer, a relatively obscure pro-European backbencher, challenged her for the leadership. In the ballot, it became clear that she had lost the support of one-fifth of Conservative MPs. The following November saw a more serious challenge from Michael Heseltine, openly supported by Geoffrey Howe and Nigel Lawson. This time the revolt was large enough to go to a second ballot. When it became clear that she had lost the confidence of most of her Cabinet colleagues, Thatcher had no option but to resign.

The impact of Thatcherism

How successful was Thatcherism? The answer depends upon the criteria used to measure that success. In many ways her policies had failed. It proved far more difficult to roll back the state than had been foreseen. In 1980 government spending accounted to 43.2 per cent of GDP; in 1995 the same figure was 42.5 per cent. Indeed one of the key paradoxes associated with Thatcherism was that, under Thatcher's leadership, the authority of the government became increasingly centralised and interventionist at a number of levels. Because so many of the local authorities remained Labour controlled, the governments of the 1980s imposed a series of entirely new powers over local government spending and policy-making. In education policy, the Conservatives introduced a national curriculum that set clear limits on the freedom to choose subjects and methods of teaching in state schools. The privatisation of industry was accompanied by the introduction of a bewildering series of regulatory bodies and 'quangos' staffed by unelected officials.

At other levels, Thatcher's accomplishments were more impressive, however. The power of the trade unions was drastically reduced, to an extent undreamed of a decade previously. The density of trade union membership in the total workforce dropped by nearly 10 per cent between 1981 and 1991, from 43.7 to 34.3 per cent. The number of working days lost to strikes declined steeply, from nearly 30 million in 1979 to just under 2 million in 1990. The pattern of housing ownership was also dramatically changed, in spite of the disastrous collapse of the housing market in the late 1980s. The Housing Act 1980, which gave council tenants the right to buy at substantial discounts, meant that council house sales completed rose from 1,342 in 1980 to a high of 202,558 in 1982, settling down to an average of over 100,000 for the rest of the decade. Local authorities were barred from ploughing these profits back into public housing, insuring that the structure of the market was shifted towards the private sector.

At a broader level, it could be argued that Thatcher succeeded in changing Britain's political culture. Labour's political wilderness of the 1980s was a powerful argument in favour of policy modernisation on the left. Socialism as a force in domestic politics was finished off by the clear popularity of the Thatcherite agenda, not only among middle-class voters but also with skilled workers. By the time that Tony Blair won the general election of 1997, it had become clear that her aim of killing off a socialist alternative in British politics had been surprisingly successful in the long term. The implications that this would have for Conservative fortunes, however, were bleak.

3.7 What factors account for the decline of Conservatism in the final decade of the 20th century?

John Major succeeded Thatcher as leader of the party and Prime Minister at the end of November 1990. His rise to power was sudden. He had only served as a Cabinet Minister since 1987, and he benefited from being untainted by the bitterness of those years. Initially it was hoped that he could unite the party and provide a period of consolidation. His style of leadership was far more conciliatory than his predecessor's, and he had a reputation for integrity and decency that earned him the nickname 'Honest John'. For a time this formula worked. By December 1990 the polls showed a swing of around 9 per cent in favour of the Conservatives. Moreover, Major's personal rating in the polls far exceeded Thatcher. In spite of the fact of an economic recession that he inherited (and as Chancellor of the Exchequer, was partly responsible for), Major managed to win the general election of 1992. Voters still seemed to trust the Conservatives to handle the economy more competently than Labour, and there were clear signs of recovery in the months before polling day. The tabloid press was savage in its portrayal of Neil Kinnock as untrustworthy and incompetent. Major's homespun campaigning style was popular with many voters.

The collapse of Conservatism

This victory was followed by the disintegration of Conservative fortunes, however. A series of local, European and by-elections beginning in 1993 recorded the worst results experienced by any modern British political party. In May 1993, for example, a Conservative majority of more than 12,000 turned to a Liberal Democrat margin of over 22,000. In 1994 the news was even worse than that. By the end of 1995 the Conservative Party had been wiped out in local politics throughout Great Britain. Only 13 councils in England retained a precarious Conservative majority. What factors explain this dramatic reversal of fortunes?

First of all, the Major administration lost the traditional public confidence in Conservatives being better at managing the economy than Labour. This was partly the result of 'Black Wednesday', 16 September 1992, when Britain was forced to pull out of the European Exchange Rate Mechanism and to devalue the pound (see chapter 7, section 1). The Cabinet's uncertain leadership during that crisis cost the country billions of pounds, and the consequences were clearly reflected in the opinion

Conservative general election performance 1945–2005

Date	No. of Conservative Candidates	Conservative MPs Elected	Total votes for Conservative Party	Conservative Share of Vote (%)
1945	618	210	9,972,010	39.6
1950	619	298	12,492,404	43.5
1951	617	321	13,718,199	48.0
1959	625	365	13,750,876	49.3
1964	630	304	12,002,642	43.4
1966	629	253	11,418,455	41.0
1970	628	330	13,145,123	46.4
(Feb) 1974	623	297	11,872,180	37.9
(Oct) 1974	622	277	10,462,565	35.8
1979	622	339	13,697,923	43.9
1983	633	397	13,012,316	42.4
1987	633	376	12,760,583	42.3
1992	645	336	14,092,891	41.9
1997	611	165	9,602,989	30.7
2001	643	166	8,357,613	31.7
2005	644	198	8,772,598	32.3

1. How does the information in the source above highlight the lack of fairness in the single majority system of voting which is used in British general elections?

2. In what ways did John Major's Conservative government differ from Margaret Thatcher's last administration?

polls. The Labour lead grew by around 14 per cent in the weeks that followed. This disaster was compounded by unpopular tax increases, particularly the proposal to impose of VAT on fuel in 1994. Higher taxes seemed particularly hypocritical in view of Conservative warnings of Labour tax plans in the 1992 election.

Secondly, the Major government was plagued by a 'sleaze factor' which easily surpassed the scandals which plagued the final years of the Macmillan government. A series of sexual revelations involving both ministers and backbenchers contrasted sharply with the government's moralizing postures on subjects like single motherhood and 'back to basics'. In November 1992 Major announced the formation of the Scott Inquiry into the sale of arms to Iraq between 1984 and 1990, against government guidelines. Most damaging of all, in October 1994, the Nolan Committee on standards in public life was established in response to a 'cash for questions' scandal which implicated a number of MPs in the improper acceptance of money and other perks from wealthy individuals and corporations in return for political favours. The party seemed to have been corrupted by its years in power, and even Major's personal high standing could not overcome that impression.

Thirdly, the Conservative Party, which traditionally presented a unified public face, was split throughout the 1992–97 Parliament. Europe was the most divisive issue, and as Euroscepticism swept through the party and the Cabinet, it became increasingly difficult for Major to maintain party discipline. He was forced to contend with a small but defiant group of Eurosceptic rebels on the backbenches who wielded power out of proportion to their numbers as a result of the slim majority on which the government depended. The debate on Europe hardened over the ratification of the Treaty of Maastricht (see chapter 6, section 9) and policy towards a single currency. By 1995 only 12 per cent of the public identified the Conservatives as a unified party.

Major's problems took place in the context of the revival of the Labour Party, which was transformed under the leadership of Tony Blair from 1994 into a unified, confident and disciplined party. For once, the voters had a clear and convincing alternative to vote for by the time that the election was called for 1 May 1997. Certainly, the press was convinced. The hostility of traditionally pro-Conservative newspapers towards the

John Major and Tony Blair after New Labour's landslide victory in the 1997 general election.

The Murdoch press: The group of newspapers owned by the Australian tycoon, Rupert Murdoch, including *The Times* and the *Sun*.

government from the mid-1990s was wholly unprecedented in modern history. In particular, the **Murdoch press** swung in favour of New Labour – providing the greatest election publicity for any party at the time.

In spite of the evidence of a likely heavy Conservative defeat, the extent of Labour's victory in the May 1997 election was unanticipated. In what is likely to be remembered as the worst defeat in Conservative election history, the party lost 178 seats, retaining only a rump of 165 on a swing of 10 per cent towards Labour. Major seemed relieved to hand over the burden of managing a disintegrating party. At the end of the century, William Hague, who succeeded Major as leader, did manage to manufacture greater unity in the party. He proved to be effective and confident in Parliamentary debate, but lacked the charisma necessary to provide a convincing alternative to Blair with the voters. Unable to challenge the Blair ascendancy on law and order, the economy, or foreign policy – traditional Conservative strengths – Hague took the gamble of playing to the public's fear of deepening European integration. By the end of the century, the party had become marginalised on the right wing of British politics, effectively a single issue campaigning group. This process occurred against the advice of many of the party's most experienced politicians, many of whom – like Michael Heseltine and Kenneth Clarke – had more in common with Labour's European policy. The shift to the right of Hague's Conservative Party MP was highlighted on 18 December 1999, when Shaun Woodward MP defected to Labour shortly after his sacking as junior environment spokesman over his support for gay rights. By the end of 1999 the Conservatives were becoming more disciplined than under Major, but seemed increasingly out of touch with mainstream British politics.

1. Why should the Conservatives not have been surprised by their loss of the 1997 election?

2. What factors account for the popularity of John Major between 1990 and 1992?

3. Why did the Conservative Party become so divided after 1992?

4. What impact did the shift to the right of party policy under Hague's leadership have on the party's performance after 1997?

3.8 The myth of consensus
A CASE STUDY IN HISTORICAL INTERPRETATION

When contemporary historians began to write about early postwar British society and politics the theme that emerged was one of 'consensus'. The war, it was argued, had led to an unusual degree of agreement between politicians, civil servants, and people of all classes over the shape of postwar Britain. This common agenda for the future was characterised by support for a number of goals. In economic terms, there should be a mixed economy, in which key industries – such as coal or the railways – should be nationalised, but alongside a large private sector which allowed scope for free enterprise and competition. The ideas of the economist John Maynard Keynes on the government's role in maintaining economic stability and relatively high employment levels were broadly accepted as well. In industrial relations, there emerged a broad commitment to collective bargaining between the trade unions and the employers with minimal intervention by the state. In respect of social policy, there grew a marked acceptance of the construction of a 'welfare state' that would guarantee a minimum income, access to adequate health care, education through the secondary level, decent housing, and social insurance in case of hardship to every individual, regardless of background. Taken together, these aims and objectives formed a broad common vision of the future, which was intended to establish a new Britain, more efficient and productive, more just and compassionate than that of the interwar years.

The origins of this supposed consensus have been traced most persuasively by Paul Addison, whose influential book *The Road to 1945* was published in 1975. Addison argued that a combination of factors accounted for a new sense of purpose in British politics emerging from 1942. The popular unity engendered by the shared hardship of war, the experience of coalition government, the popular pressure for social reform following the publication of the *Beveridge Report* in November, the growing power of the trade unions in the midst of labour shortages, the example of high productivity which resulted from the war economy, and memories of mass unemployment and poverty during the Depression era – all were factors in the development of consensus politics.

According to supporters of this interpretation, a basis for policy was forged during the war that was adhered to by both Labour and Conservative governments for many years afterwards. Thus the period from the late 1940s until the mid-1970s has often been described as the era of consensus. This was indeed the heyday of the mixed economy, full employment and the welfare state. But it was also a period in which Britain's economic performance was slipping relative to its competitors abroad. By the 1970s Britain was beset by a series of grave problems: widespread industrial unrest, inflation, growing unemployment, disaffected youth, and urban decay.

The period of consensus is widely perceived to have ended when Margaret Thatcher became leader of the Conservative Party in 1975. Thatcher was highly critical of the postwar consensus, accusing **'wet' Conservatism** of collaborating with the left in a series of weak policy compromises and unrealistically high levels of public welfare spending. For her, consensus meant mismanagement, and her policy advisers deliberately chose to criticise the concept in order to highlight the new approach that her brand of Conservatism could offer to cure the British 'disease'. Many commentators have argued that Thatcherism ultimately replaced the postwar Keynes/Beveridge consensus with a new set of broadly shared beliefs and attitudes that were subsequently taken up by the New Labour of Tony Blair.

The 'consensus' view of postwar Britain came under increasing scrutiny from the mid-1980s. As historians gained access to the official archives and began to test the consensus model, it became clear that there was far more division and debate both during and after the war than this interpretation allows for. Moreover, both Labour and Conservative governments pursued economic and social policy agendas that were sharply at odds, even in the forties and fifties. In simple terms, Labour was determined to develop a

'Wet' Conservatism: Inclined to compromise.

universal welfare state, paid for through direct taxation, and a greater degree of planning in order to deliver a broader range of social services, and less social inequality, arguing that only a society which delivered a social as well as a political basis for citizenship could remain stable and prosperous. The Conservatives wanted to limit nationalisation, reduce taxation, encourage the private sector, and reorient the welfare state to target those in genuine need, arguing that only a system that rewarded hard work and ingenuity could remain productive and successful. In other words, the war did little to shift the fundamental axis of British politics from its familiar poles of individualism versus collectivism. Unsurprisingly therefore, historians in recent years, such as Kevin Jeffreys in *Retreat from New Jerusalem* (1997) have begun to stress the continuities in British politics between the interwar and postwar periods, and have become increasingly sceptical of the idea that the war led to significant or sharp change.

Consensus, in the sense that it has been applied to the postwar era, seems increasingly simplistic as an historical explanation, and shows part of the celebratory tone that is typical of British memories of the war. The explanation for policy convergence on issues like welfare and full employment seems to owe more to international economic and political circumstances and constraints rather than to any deliberate series of agreements on domestic policy. Full employment, for example, was widespread throughout the West, not just in Britain. Welfare states all over Western Europe at this time are increasingly understood as having been a response to the need to stabilise capitalist economic systems during the Cold War. Labour and Conservative policies in this period were inevitably limited by the circumstances to which they were responding.

1. Why have some historians argued that there was an unusual degree of 'consensus' in Britain after 1945?

2. How have the views of historians on the question of a postwar consensus changed since the 1970s?

3. Is it possible to have a stable democracy without some sort of policy consensus between the major political parties?

3.9 The Conservative Party in opposition, 1997–2007

The Hague years, 1997–2001

In 1997 the Conservative Party suffered its biggest electoral defeat since 1832. Immediately after the election John Major resigned as leader.

The Party had been badly affected by infighting over Britain's relations with the European Union throughout Major's period as prime minister. This issue also affected the leadership contest following Major's departure.

The most senior Conservative to stand for the Party leadership was Kenneth Clarke. He had a long and distinguished career as a cabinet minister being Home Secretary, Education Secretary and Chancellor of the Exchequer. Unfortunately, Clarke was one of the most pro-European Conservatives and this cost him the leadership. He was defeated by a youthful William Hague, who had been Secretary of State for Wales shortly before the election.

Hague promised a new beginning for the Conservatives. He planned to drop the party emblem, the Torch of Freedom' and re-brand the Party. A senior Conservative, Teresa May, claimed that the Conservatives had been viewed as the 'nasty' party and it was time it changed its policies on law and order and tax.

Hague also tried to adopt a new image. An early photo opportunity saw Hague wearing a baseball cap with 'Hague' written across the front at a theme park.

During the 1998 Conservative Party Conference in Bournemouth, the tabloid *Sun*'s front page infamously referenced Monty Python's 'Dead Parrot' sketch'.

Hague's period as leader saw no real improvement in Conservative fortunes. His decision to choose Jeffrey Archer as Conservative candidate for London Mayor backfired when Archer was accused of lying in court and was sentenced to a period in prison. In an attempt to win over the right wing of his party he launched the 'Save the Pound' campaign (see page 197) even though the Labour Government had announced it was not going to join the Euro zone. Things went from bad to worse when Hague stated that the plan to keep the Pound referred only to the period of the next parliament not a permanent commitment. In the 2001 General Election the Conservatives gained only one extra seat (165 to 166 seats) over their humiliating loss of 1997. Like Major, Hague resigned immediately after the announcement of the election defeat.

The Duncan Smith and Howard years, 2001–2005

In 2001 Kenneth Clarke continued his bid for the Conservative leadership. This time he faced two major opponents, Michael Portillo and Iain Duncan Smith. Again Clarke lost out with Iain Duncan Smith winning the support of the ring wing of Conservative MPs over Portillo. Duncan Smith proved to be another poor choice as leader. He had no ministerial experience and performed poorly against Tony Blair as Prime Minister's Question Time in the House of Commons. His public image was also poor. Duncan Smith's impact was so limited that attempts to remove him from the leadership developed in late 2002. In 2003 he resigned after a series of very poor opinion poll results for the Party. His replacement was former Home Secretary, Michael Howard.

Howard's main task was to halt the party's decline. Howard brought discipline to the party. In the 2005 general election campaign he 'sacked' Conservative MP Howard Flight for speaking 'off message'. In the 2005 General Election the Conservatives gained as extra 32 seats. However, what was more disturbing was the fact that their share of the vote rose only slightly from 31.7% in 2001 to 32.4% in 2005.

The Cameron years

Howard, like his two predecessors, resigned shortly after the election result. Howard's tenure as leader was always seen as temporary, so his decision to go was not a surprise. In December 2005 the Party chose a new leader, David Cameron, who, at 40 years of age was a member of the new generation of Conservative MPs. His Shadow Cabinet reflected this new direction by including George Osborne, 35 years old, as Shadow Chancellor.

Like Blair, Cameron wanted the Conservatives to occupy the centre ground of British politics. He also planned to modernize the party. He dropped the Party emblem of the Torch of Freedom and replaced it with an Oak Tree to symbolize the Party's new green credentials. Cameron became a champion of green issues such as combating climate change and improving the environment. He also cycled to the House of Commons, but unfortunately for his image it was discovered that he was followed by his official car. Cameron's style of leadership was compared to that of Tony Blair, inviting satirical comparison (see cartoon, below).

By the time of Blair's resignation, opinion polls suggested that Cameron had made some progress. However, the task he faced was daunting; Cameron took over as leader when the two other major parties were also going through change. In 2007 Blair resigned to be replaced by Gordon Brown. Also, the Liberal Democrats elected a new young leader in the autumn of 2007 when Nick Clegg replaced Sir Menzies Campbell.

By the end of 2007 David Cameron had established himself as a major political figure.

1. What problems did the Conservatives face in opposition, in the years 1997 to 2007?

2. Look at this 2006 cartoon of David Cameron and Tony Blair. What message does it give about why David Cameron was chosen as the new Conservative leader?

3.10 In-depth study: Did Thatcher really bring about a social, political and economic revolution?

■ To what extent was there an economic revolution?

■ How radical were the political and constitutional changes?

■ What impact did Thatcher have on social policy?

Framework of Events

1979	First Budget; tax cuts and VAT increase
1980	Steel strike
	'Lady's not for turning' speech at Party Conference
	First Employment Act, which reduced trade union power
	Medium Term Financial Strategy Budget
	Housing Act – council house sales start
1981	'Wets' – such as Ian Gilmour – sacked
	Appointment of 'Dries' such as Lawson, Tebbit and Parkinson in government
	Toxteth riots
	BP and British Aerospace privatised
1982	'The Health Service is safe with us' speech at Party Conference
1983	Second election victory; civil service cut by 100,000
	Inflation down to 5 per cent; financial controls on local government commence
1984	Miners' strike
	BT privatised
	Major TU Act limiting strikes
1985	Collapse of miners' strike
	3.2 million unemployed – post-war record
	Local Government Act – abolition of GLC
1986	Privatisation of Gas
1987	Third election victory
1988	Poll tax
	Local Government Act – compulsory tendering of services
	Education Reform Act – national curriculum arrives
1989	NHS reform – hospitals trusts
	Lawson resigns over Exchange Rate Mechanism
1990	Howe resigns; Thatcher resigns.

THERE are two major debates surrounding the administrations of Margaret Thatcher (1979–90). The first is whether she brought about revolutionary change – did she fundamentally change Britain, its society, its economy and its politics? The second is whether those changes were beneficial to Britain.

To what extent was there an economic revolution?

The case for arguing that there was an economic revolution between 1979–90 under Thatcher is a very strong one. Economic historians such as D. Smith in *Mrs Thatcher's Economic Legacy* (1991) make this very clear. There are at least seven major areas where there was significant change in the economy or the way in which it was managed. They are as follows:

- The role of the government in managing the economy changed fundamentally. Market forces directed the economy, and not the government.

- Thatcher imposed a new economic 'philosophy' – monetarism – on Britain.

- Inflation was radically lowered.

- She reintroduced an 'enterprise' culture into Britain.

- High personal taxation, public spending and borrowing by the government ended.

- The role of trade unions in the economic life of the country was substantially reduced

- Huge sections of industry which were owned by the state, such as Telecommunications and Electricity, were sold off to private ownership.

To what extent did the role and influence of the trade unions change?

Several of the principal writers of the period, such as P. Jenkins in *Mrs Thatcher's Revolution* (1987) and D. Smith, argue that it is in her reduction of the power of the trade unions that Thatcher had the greatest impact on the economy. They argue that breaking union power brought real benefits to the UK. Critics in her own party, such as Ian Gilmour in *Dancing with Dogma* (1987), argue that her trade union policy brought only confrontation and unemployment. This was also the line taken by critics on the left, such as Tony Benn, who referred to it in Parliament as 'pure fascism'.

Before she became Prime Minister in 1979, trade unions had had a huge and possibly damaging influence on the economy. They were felt to be responsible for driving up wages and prices and making UK industry unmanageable by its managers. Many felt that trade unions were a key factor in causing the economic decline of the UK.

Trade union actions had largely led to the collapse of Edward Heath's Conservative government in 1974. Unions were also largely held responsible for fuelling the inflation of the 1970s. The public was unsympathetic to trade unions and was likely to support attempts to control them and reduce their economic muscle.

By 1984, Thatcher had achieved this objective, and trade unions had ceased to play a significant role in public life. By a series of key Acts of Parliament and decisive government action, Thatcher reduced trade union power. She was helped also by rapidly rising unemployment, which acted as a major disincentive to many workers to going on strike or pressing too hard for higher wages.

There were three very important Acts of Parliament dealing with trade unions in 1980, 1982 and 1984. They helped to limit trade union power and influence by:

Secret ballots: when trade union members were able to vote secretly, and therefore were less likely to be pressurised into strike action.

Picketing: where those involved in a strike protest outside their place of work and try to stop anyone else from working there.

Secondary picketing: where those not directly involved in a strike picket in support of those who are.

- ending many of the legal immunities (privileges) of trade unions – unions could now be sued by employers for damages caused by illegal strikes

- requiring that **secret ballots** (votes) be held by a union before strike action took place

- ending the 'closed' shop – this required anyone working in a particular factory to join the trade union, which of course gave that union considerable power

- controlling **picketing** and **secondary picketing**

- making the dismissal of employees by managers easier

Thatcher took three main actions to reduce trade union power:

1 She played a key role in defeating the miners' strike of 1984. It was a 359—day strike, led by the miners' socialist leader, Arthur Scargill. This strike was a serious confrontation over the right of the Coal Board to try and place the industry on a realistic economic footing. The state would no longer subsidise out of taxation uneconomic pits. They were to close, throwing thousands of miners onto the dole queue. In a way, Thatcher deliberately provoked this strike in order to show who 'ran' Britain. Large coal stocks were collected first so that the vital coal-fired power stations could keep generating electricity. The police were organised nationally, for the first time, to deal with miners' picketing. Thatcher successfully presented the strike as a threat to the rule of law. Defeating the miners was seen as a huge victory by Thatcher and was a clear symbol that she had defeated union power and reduced its influence on the economy.

2 She encouraged Rupert Murdoch, owner of *The Times* newspaper, to resist the Printing Unions over the move of the newspaper's headquarters to Wapping and the adoption of new 'high-tech' methods of printing, which inevitably cost many *Times* employees their jobs.

3 She banned trade union membership at **GCHQ**.

Her supporters see the Acts of Parliament and the actions listed above as vital in her struggle against the trade unions. A 'new' trade unionism emerged in the late 1980s, which largely seemed to accept Thatcherism. These unions were prepared to sign 'no strike' agreements with employers. Trade unions became much more democratic organisations. By 1990 there were more workers who owned shares than there were trade union members. The number of working days lost by strike action went from 29.5 million in 1979 to 1.9 million in 1990.

Other factors helped Thatcher 'defeat' the unions. There was increasingly high unemployment. Thousands of jobs were lost in manufacturing industries, always strongholds of trade unions. There was growing employment in areas that tended not to be unionised, such as the service sector. It was felt to be a huge victory. The **corporate state** was dead.

Union leaders before 1979 had been national figures, regularly seen in Downing Street playing a central role in the management of the economy. Now they were marginalised. Thatcher regarded it as a vital step in her regeneration of the UK.

How significant was the privatisation programme?

Some writers, such as Peter Riddell in *The Thatcher Era* (1983) argue that Thatcher's most radical innovation was her privatisation programme. Again she was opposed by her own party, with former Conservative Prime Ministers Edward Heath savaging it in the Commons, and Harold MacMillan accusing her 'of selling off the family silver' in the Lords.

Privatisation involved the government selling off a huge range of state-owned industries, such as Electricity, Telecommunications and British Airways. The reasons for the state originally taking over this vast range of industries were varied. Some had been nationalised (taken over by the state from private owners) by Labour governments, as it was part of their socialist beliefs. Others, such as British Rail, had been taken over by the state because the damage done to them in the Second World War meant that only the state had the resources to get them back on their feet again.

By 1979, many Conservatives and the public at large strongly criticised these vast state-owned **monopolies**, such as Electricity, for many

---

Arthur Scargill (1938–)
A Communist – and later socialist – miner, Scargill became President of the Miners' Union in 1972. He played a key role in the strikes that brought down Heath's government in 1974. He led the miners in their last great strike in 1984, but failed to attain his objectives of preventing the closure of pits.

Rupert Murdoch (1931–)
Australian-born Chief Executive of News International, a vast multi-national media group that owns Sky TV, *The Times*, the *Sunday Times*, the *Sun* and *News of the World*, and HarperCollins Publishers. He was a strong supporter of Thatcher and notoriously required all his editors to support her.

GCHQ: the government's secret intelligence gathering centre in Cheltenham.

Corporate state: where the economy was managed by an alliance between government, management and the unions.

Monopolies: industries where there is only one supplier or manufacturer.

reasons: they were over-manned, inefficient and poorly managed; they tended to be heavily subsidised by the taxpayer; the majority of their workers were involved in the 'over-powerful' unions, such as the Miners' Union; they were too subject to political control by Ministers and civil servants who were unqualified to run such industries efficiently; they lacked investment.

Rolling back the state

Part of Thatcher's aim was to reduce the role of the state in managing the economy. She argued that, 'privatisation is at the centre of any programme of reclaiming territory for freedom', and it was part of her broader campaign to stop the damage done to the UK by socialism.

Privatisation also proved to be very popular with the voters and their support of it played an important part in Thatcher's election victories, particularly in 1987. Privatisation also enabled her to do other, equally popular things, such as cut taxes, as it brought large sums of money into the Treasury.

There were three main parts of the overall programme referred to as privatisation:

- Denationalisation: this was simply selling off state-owned industries, such as British Gas, to the public.

- Contracting out: other public sector areas, such as Local Authorities and the Prison Service, were required to put the services they provided out to public tender, such as transporting prisoners. If a privately owned company, such as Group 4, could transport prisoners more cheaply than the Prison Service, then they won the contract.

- Deregulation: for example, Local Authority bus services could no longer have a monopoly in a certain area – there now had to be competition.

There was a limited amount of privatisation in the first administration (1979–83). The programme aroused virtually no opposition, was clearly popular, and in 1980–1 raised £405 million for the Treasury – that was £405 million less to be raised in taxation.

The main period of privatisation came after the successful 1983 election. Playing a key part in the programme was the new Chancellor of the Exchequer, Nigel Lawson, and the Energy Secretary, Cecil Parkinson. Both were keen supporters of the 'market forces/anti-socialist' ideas of Thatcher and the **New Right** in British politics.

New Right: a section of the Conservative party which supported Thatcher and wanted an end to the consensus politics of the past and clear new policies, particularly in areas such as race, immigration, law and order and the economy.

The wish to privatise was also accelerated by the crisis facing BT, the state-owned telephone monopoly, which needed billions to invest in a new system to modernise telecommunications. Nigel Lawson was determined to cut taxation, inflation and public spending. He was not prepared to give BT billions of taxpayers' money to modernise. To solve the crisis facing BT, Thatcher's government decided to privatise. They would simply sell off BT. There was a brilliant marketing campaign and an official policy designed to create a new type of small investor in stocks and shares. This would give more of the public a stake in industry. It enabled people to buy shares easily.

BT was sold off with speed and success. Thatcher's dream of a property-owning and share-owning democracy was becoming reality. Gas, Electricity, British Airways, Sealink and Jaguar (the list is a long one) followed BT into the private sector. In 1987–8 alone the Treasury received over £5.1 billion from the proceeds of privatisation. In this area, Thatcherism has become permanent. It deservedly merits being seen as a key part of the Thatcherite 'revolution'. The state was getting smaller and government was being 'rolled back'.

The privatisation debate

The programme can certainly be criticised, however. Public monopolies became private monopolies, and there simply was no, or not enough, competition. It created a 'casino' mentality about stocks and shares. Share-owning was all about quick and easy profits, and not about long-term and wise investment for the future. The huge sums raised by the sales were 'wasted', and not used to improve the country's infrastructure, such as roads. Those industries that were left, such as the rail industry, would always be a huge drain on the taxpayer, and not balanced by the profitable ones. Furthermore, the government had lost a very useful tool of social policy (for example, it could not order a power station to be built in an area of high unemployment to create jobs). The programme failed to reduce public spending enough and the industries were sold off too cheaply. Most of the shares went quickly from the hands of the small shareholders into those of the big organisations, such as the banks. Privatisation played a major part in causing a rapid rise in unemployment as these industries shed their workers. How such monopolies were to be controlled and competition introduced had not been properly thought through.

The defenders of privatisation argued that there was now much more scope for effective management of these industries, and industries such as Gas and Telecommunications became much more efficient. The need for the taxpayer to subsidise on a large scale was gone. Taxes and government borrowing could be reduced. There was now much greater awareness within these industries of the need to provide a quality service, and make a profit. British Airways went from being a huge drain on the taxpayer to a highly successful and profitable organisation by 1987.

The privatisation of large sections of British industry forms, along with her trade union changes, a central part of the Thatcher's economic 'revolution'.

To what extent did Thatcher attain her hoped-for 'revolution' in the areas of taxation, borrowing and public spending?

As with every aspect of Thatcher's work, there is controversy in this area. There are two schools of thought. The first line comes from the economists/economic historians, such as D. Smith, in *Mrs Thatcher's Economic Legacy* (1990), or Martin Holmes in *Thatcherism* (1989), who broadly argue that her impact in this area is profound. More 'conventional' historians, such as Denis Kavanagh in *Thatcherism and British Politics* (1987) or Robert Skidelsky in *Thatcherism* (1987), tend to minimise it.

When it came to taxes, government borrowing and spending, Thatcher had simple but clear views. She wished her governments to tax, borrow and spend less. She took great care to appoint Chancellors of the Exchequer– Geoffrey Howe, Nigel Lawson and John Major – who shared her views. She certainly aimed at a revolution in this sphere, and tried for a real change of direction.

As far as income tax was concerned she attained her objectives. There were in fact tax cuts in every annual Budget between 1979 and 1990, bar one, and National Insurance contributions dropped as well. This was naturally, extremely popular with the voters and played an important part in her election victories.

Between 1979 and 1990 income tax on:

the wealthy dropped from 50 per cent to 33 per cent of every pound earned

average earners dropped from 25 per cent to 21 per cent of every pound earned

below average earners dropped from 20 per cent to 8 per cent of every pound earned

---

There was still, however, what became known as a 'poverty trap'. The tax system made it difficult for those on very low wages to survive, and wages could be so low that it was not worth while going off unemployment benefit to get low pay which was also taxed.

There was still the expectation that the government would provide very expensive services, such as healthcare and education, so there were large increases in indirect tax such as VAT (for example, on services and petrol) to pay for them. The Budget of 1979, for example, cut income tax – a direct tax – by a total of £4.5 billion but increased VAT – an indirect tax – by £4.2 billion.

By 1988, income tax was down from 33 pence in the pound to 25 pence in the pound for normal taxpayers, and it was cut from as high as 95 pence in the pound for the highest earners to 40 pence in the pound. There was also a substantial cut in **corporation tax**.

Corporation tax: the tax on business profits.

Thatcher and her Chancellors argued that this change in taxation increased incentives for workers, encouraged enterprise and hard work, encouraged investment and savings, lowered the **black economy** and helped keep wages down.

Black economy: where earnings are not declared and tax is not paid on them.

Economists disagree as to whether it actually encouraged more hard work and provided incentives. Most argue that under Thatcher only the rich got richer and the poor did not really benefit.

Did the Thatcherite revolution spread to public spending and borrowing?
Another central part of the intended Thatcherite revolution was to cut government spending. She failed in the long term. Initially she was able to reduce it marginally, and then it became a struggle just to hold it steady. In the end it became a fight to try and simply reduce the rate of growth of spending by the government.

The aim behind this programme was to contain inflation, as well as to reduce taxation and borrowing and the role of the government generally. Initially there would be some increase in taxation and spending, mainly because of her earlier commitment to raise **civil service** pay, which had been promised by the previous government. There were also 1979 Conservative Manifesto promises to spend more on defence and law and order, especially police pay.

Civil service: responsible for the public administration of the government of a country. Members of the civil service have no official political allegiance and are not generally affected by changes of government.

Spending on healthcare and social security was to be maintained. There were cuts in spending by the government on overseas aid, the arts, subsidy to industry, education and housing.

Overall public spending continued its seemingly endless rise under Thatcher. Taxpayers continued to want better public services, such as education and healthcare, but were anxious to pay less for it from their taxes.

There are several reasons why Thatcher failed to contain and reduce public spending. She had to substantially increase spending on defence, in order to keep the United Kingdom as a major military power. She also had to spend more on law and order, and police pay went up considerably. Three million unemployed also had to be supported by the taxpayer. Improvements in healthcare and social services meant that people were likely to live much longer – at the cost to the taxpayer – and spending on healthcare soared, as the public demanded an improved (and very expensive) service. There was a demand for better education, and many more were going to university, subsidised by the taxpayer.

All of these factors meant that she was unable to reduce government spending. It was simply not politically possible if she wanted to stay in power. However, there was success in one area: the amount that had to be borrowed by the government – the Public Sector Borrowing Requirement (PSBR) – was much reduced, and by the time Thatcher left office the

Election—**what** election?

SOW NOW FOR BEST RESULTS

PUBLIC SECTOR

Thatcher's strategies for winning elections were always very successful.

government was not only borrowing less (and therefore not paying out interest to its creditors) but it had also embarked on a substantial debt reduction programme.

Ultimately Thatcher was unsuccessful in attaining her overall objectives with taxes. She was to feel later that she had had a real chance to attain her objectives in terms of spending and borrowing, but she had had too little support from her Ministers in the crucial 1979–83 period, when she felt that the public would have accepted radical change.

To what extent did Thatcher remove inflation from Britain?

High inflation: rapid rises in prices.

The ending of **high inflation** was a major aim of Thatcher. Unlike previous governments, which saw unemployment as a far greater enemy, she was prepared to put up with growing unemployment if it helped eliminate inflation from the system. Better some pain in the short term, she felt, in order to bring the economic 'happiness' of low inflation.

The early Budgets of her administration were dominated by the wish to lower inflation, running at over 14 per cent per annum when she came in, and soaring to well over 20 per cent in the early 1980s. She was convinced that by lowering the amount of money in circulation, keeping wages low, and cutting public spending and government borrowing, she could get inflation down.

Initially she had no success in keeping price rises down. A revolution in oil-producing Iran disrupted supplies and the price of oil soared, pushing up other prices. Furthermore, there was a wages explosion in 1979–80 in both the private and the public sectors, as she was unable to resist the demands for massive increases in wages from many groups such as teachers and miners.

Monetarism: controlling the supply of money.

However, by the end of her period in power, inflation went back down into single figures. The days of high inflation have been eliminated. Economists debate whether Thatcher's **monetarism** was in any way responsible. Some argue that the drop in the price of oil in the mid-1980s was as important. However, recession and unemployment helped to contain wage demands, and imposing very tight spending controls on normally extravagant local government also helped.

A much tighter fiscal policy certainly helped to lower inflation and keep it low. Some argue that the price paid in terms of unemployment and the running down of much of the UK's manufacturing industries was too high for reducing inflation, and that her success in this area was paid for by many thousands losing their jobs.

To what extent did Thatcher reintroduce an enterprise culture into Britain?

One of the reasons put forward by many of the New Right, or committed Thatcherites, for Britain's economic decline after the Second World War was that there was a serious lack of men and women with an entrepreneurial attitude. The way in which the economy was managed created an atmosphere hostile to entrepreneurs.

Thatcher wished to recreate a climate which in the past had enabled men of determination and vision to establish vast manufacturing industries, such as Josiah Wedgwood in the 18th and early 19th centuries who founded the potteries in Staffordshire. In the past, these industries had generated wealth and employment, and had played a central role in making Britain the 'workshop of the world'.

Just as economists such as Milton Friedman had influenced Thatcher in her desire to lower inflation, key advisers such as John Hoskyns (Policy Unit 1979–82) and Lord Young (another successful businessman) worked hard to persuade her to create a climate in Britain which would lead to greater business success. They argued that the demand for British products was there, but so were the barriers to successful business, such as high taxes on profits and income, and over-regulation by government.

Many on the right argued that business creativity was stifled by bureaucracy. Thatcher wanted to enhance the status of the successful entrepreneur, and give them the position in society enjoyed by professionals such as lawyers and doctors. She tended to regard such 'professionals' as parasites sucking the wealth off the entrepreneurs who were responsible for creating the wealth of Britain. Thatcher and her Ministers did much to try to help develop the desired entrepreneurship by putting a variety of measures forward. They were:

> **Milton Friedman (1912–2006)**
> Well-known economist at the University of Chicago, and Nobel prize winner for Economics. He is the founding father of monetarism – Thatcher was an avid fan.

- Tax cuts: there were considerable cuts in income tax, corporation tax, and tax on income from investments, capital gains taxes and capital transfer tax.

- Deregulation: government interfered less with business and imposed fewer rules on it.

- Introduction of controls on prices and dividends.

- Enterprise zones: these enabled new businesses to set up in areas free from restrictions such as planning or having to pay taxes to Local Authorities.

- Breaking up the big monopolies: the ending of monopolies in areas such as transport encouraged competition.

- Small business initiatives: a whole series of initiatives, such as cheap loans, helped small businesses get started.

- Grants: these were available for training in new technology and for technical innovation and research.

The success that Thatcher attained in this area is, as always, debated. Certainly her approach helped unemployment decline from 1984 onwards. There were many more new 'high-tech' firms and there was a considerable increase in the number of self-employed workers. There was also much more capital available for investment.

Major foreign firms, such as Honda and Toyota, were encouraged to invest in new plant and equipment in the UK, and there was a large growth in investment by the UK in both the USA and Europe. There was a growth in the number of better-qualified managers and a much greater growth of professionalism in industry.

A change in attitude is difficult to quantify, for although manufacturing had continued to decline in Britain it became much easier for the small businesses to raise capital and start a venture – and keep more of the profits. Making money was increasingly seen as a respectable occupation.

Did Thatcher impose a new economic set of ideas – monetarism – on the UK?

There are almost as many interpretations as there are writers on this issue! Strongly critical historians, such a Dennis Kavanagh, argue that she did, as do equally critical Conservative politicians, such as James Prior in *Balance of Power* (1986). Hugo Young in *One of Us* argues that she did, while the similarly liberal critic Peter Riddell in *The Thatcher Era* (1991) argues that she did not.

The principal economic thinker who influenced government prior to the arrival of Thatcher was John Maynard Keynes. Central to Keynes' ideas was the view that the government had a central role to play in ensuring a healthy economy and, above all, full employment. It was right and necessary for the government to involve itself in the direction and control of the economy. Government should play not only an active, but also a leading role in all aspects of the economy. Both Labour and Conservative governments after 1945 put these ideas into practice. Thatcher disagreed with Keynes's ideas. Governments did not seem to be solving economic problems, but causing them.

During her years as Leader of the Opposition, from 1975 to 1979, she gradually adopted a very different set of economic beliefs, which became known as 'monetarism'. Studying writers such as Friedrich Hayek and Milton Friedman gave her ideas, which reinforced her instincts. Other leading Conservatives, such as Keith Joseph and John Biffen, argued strongly in favour of monetarism. Academic Brian Griffiths, Professor of Banking at the City University, financial journalist Nigel Lawson and 'Think Tank' Alfred Sherman, also worked hard to persuade her to adopt this economic theory. She spent much time listening to such men during

Not everyone agreed on the benefits of monetarism.

her time in Opposition, and the growing economic problems facing the Labour government increasingly convinced her of the need to review the management of the British economy.

When Thatcher got into power she brought with her a fixed set of ideas and beliefs to deal with the problem of Britain's economic decline. The Keynesian revolution of the 1940s, when governments 'ran' the economy, was to be replaced by the monetarist counter-revolution.

Certainly monetarism had its critics, even in her own party, where the Keynesians, known as the 'wets', opposed it. Reginald Maudling, a former Conservative Chancellor of the Exchequer, referred to it as 'this crazy, if coherent, vision'. Thatcher certainly maintained in her memoirs that it was successful, but the economic 'jury' is still out on it.

In 1990 the British economy was very different to how it had been in 1979. There were still crises to be faced, such as in 1992, but it could be argued that they were less frequent and less severe. Living standards for the majority improved substantially from the mid-1980s onwards, and that continued through the 1990s.

The key ideas of monetarism

- The key responsibility of the government when it comes to the economy is to control inflation.
- Inflation is highly damaging to any economy.
- Inflation is caused by having too much money in circulation.
- The only economic activity the government should be involved in is in the control of the amount of money in circulation and public borrowing.
- If government involves itself in other areas, such as wages and prices, it does more harm than good.

How radical were the political and constitutional changes?

Thatcherism was not simply an economic revolution; it was also political and constitutional. She changed the British political system fundamentally. In many ways, she did not intend this revolution to happen, but in order to attain her economic objectives, she had to bring in major changes in other areas.

There is no serious historical dispute about the nature of the changes to the political and constitutional structure. The debate is whether she should have undertaken these changes, and whether they were to the benefit of the UK. Richard Rose's *Prime Minster in a Shrinking World* (2001) and also Peter Hennessey's superb *Whitehall* (1989) describe and analyse the huge changes she brought to politics and government. Conservatives such as John Hoskyns in *Inside the Thatcher Revolution* (1986) praise her, while others, such as Michael Heseltine in *Where there is a will* (1987), strongly attack her. She is accused of both improving and damaging democracy in the UK.

The changes she made during her eleven years as Prime Minister were several: the office of Prime Minister was made much more powerful; the cabinet was weakened; the role of the civil service was changed; many more quangos were set up; many more 'outside' political advisers, who were not elected, were brought in to help Ministers; the power of local government was reduced; the ideology and policies of the Conservatives were increasingly adapted.

The Prime Minister became the dominant force in the whole administration to an extent that had never happened before. The cabinet, always a key influence in policy-making, became increasingly the agent of Mrs Thatcher's wishes. The civil service was radically reduced in size and

Sir Alan Walters (1926–)
A well-known UK economist and Professor of Economics at the London School of Economics and also at other US universities. He was personal economic adviser to Thatcher 1981–4 and again in 1989. He played a key role in pushing her towards monetarism. Chancellor Lawson resigned in 1989 as Thatcher was apparently listening more to Walters than to her Chancellor.

completely restructured. Functions that had been performed by local government, such as control of the school curriculum, were given to unelected bodies only accountable to Ministers. Political advisers, such as Sir Alan Walters, became very influential in Whitehall so Ministers got advice not just from their civil servants. Local government, with its huge role in areas such as education and housing, was subjected to rigid control from London. The Conservative party developed a clear and radical ideology far removed from the broad consensus politics of the 1960s.

All those changes surveyed above were bitterly opposed by her political opponents, both inside and outside her own party, but they have all remained. In 1990, Britain was governed in a totally different way to how it had been when Thatcher first arrived in Downing Street in 1979.

What impact did Thatcher have on social policy?

'There is no such thing as society.'
Margaret Thatcher, 1984

Norman Tebbit (1931–)
An RAF and British Airways pilot, Tebbit was a Conservative MP 1970–92. He was a strong Thatcher supporter with very right-wing views. He became a Minister in 1979, and was appointed Employment Secretary 1981, where he authored many of the laws that reduced trade union power. In 1983 he became Secretary of State for Industry and was responsible for much of the privatisation programme. He was Party Chairman 1985–7 and played a key role in Thatcher's election victory of 1987.

Almost everything that Thatcher did aroused controversy, but her social policy was the area that aroused most. The only defence of what she did in the field of social policy can really be found in her own memoirs, *The Downing Street Years* (1993). Here she agrees that she did not find solutions to every problem, but at least she tried and no one had any better ideas! Members of her own party, such as Norman Tebbit in *Upwardly Mobile* (1989), criticised her for not being nearly radical enough; others criticised her for being too radical and harming society, such as James Prior in *Balance of Power* (1986). The 'economists', such as D. Smith, and Martin Holmes in *Thatcherism* (1989), indicate she did not go far enough in her changes. The normally quite sympathetic journalist/contemporary historian Hugo Young in *One of Us* focus on the social 'harm' she did in limiting welfare and causing unemployment. Perhaps the most persuasive attack on what Thatcher tried to do – and did – is written by Will Hutton in *The State We're in* (1996), which analyses her government from the viewpoint of a committed Keynesian thinker.

Britain was a very different place in 1990 than it had been in 1979, and much was due to the work of the Prime Minister. In some cases it was her policies that were enforced, in others it was policies that her Ministers put through which had had to fit into her broad ideological aims. These were in the areas of education, healthcare, welfare and social security, law and order, and crime and poverty.

In some cases, particularly education and healthcare, she did not attain what she wanted, as she would have lost elections as a result of her actions. She hoped for radical change in education, healthcare and social security. However, the British electorate did not, so she backed away from too massive a change for political reasons. She did not want to lose elections.

What impact did Thatcher have on education?
Thatcher felt the UK educational system was failing children badly. It was failing to provide the appropriately trained and skilled workforce the UK needed to compete in a modern, technological world. Levels of illiteracy were among the highest in the EU, and the number of students staying on after 16 were amongst the lowest.

Thatcher's own experience, as Education Secretary had been a formative one. She had emerged with a dislike of civil servants, teachers and teachers' unions, universities, comprehensive schools and 'professionals' generally. She felt, possibly correctly, that these 'professionals' were too concerned with their own interests and not with providing a quality education for pupils. She listened to successful businessmen, such as John Hoskyns who she put into her Policy Unit in 1979, who were deeply concerned by the lack of skills and training in the UK workforce.

Thatcher never had education as a high priority, but nevertheless she had a major impact on it. Initially she cut spending on schools as part of her policy to bring down inflation and cut government spending. However, after 1987 there was a considerable increase in *overall* spending on education, as the enthusiasm for monetarism waned. Overall, in the Thatcher period there was a considerable growth in real terms in spending on education, particularly on secondary schools, universities and polytechnics.

There were three major Acts of Parliament concerning education, in 1980, 1986 and 1988. They deserve to be viewed as an integral part of the Thatcherite revolution. Between them these Acts of Parliament:

- gave central government much greater power over all aspects of the British education system

- radically reduced local government control over education

- set up a new, centrally controlled inspection system (OFSTED) to check progress in all schools

- introduced greater central financial control over all education spending.

- introduced parental choice of schools, and parents were given much more opportunity to control schools

- offered schools the opportunity to opt out of Local Authority control totally and only be responsible to governors, parents and Whitehall

- introduced targets for schools and league tables

- scrapped the old O Level and CSE exams and introduced the new GCSE

- introduced a compulsory national curriculum

- brought in teacher appraisal and improved teacher training

- massively increased the number of students going on to, and funding for, university

- monitored and inspected universities much more tightly

The education that all pupils received and the structure of the education system, from the nursery school to the elite 'old' universities, such as Oxford and Cambridge, changed fundamentally between 1979–90.

Certainly standards did improve throughout the whole education system, and spending rose. When Thatcher came to power in 1979, spending on education was £15.9 billion (by 1988 prices) – it had gone up to £17.4 billion in 1987. Whether it was enough to meet the needs of both pupils and the economy, and whether it was spent in the right areas, is still debated. There was in fact limited interest in cabinet or in the Conservative party in educational change. There was also always strong opposition from Local Authorities who at times seemed more interested in preserving their own powers than in improving the education they delivered – so Thatcher must get the credit for most of the changes.

Welfare state: a system largely created by the Labour government of 1945–50. In it the state took responsibility for caring for its citizens by providing such things as free healthcare, pensions, sick pay, unemployment pay, maternity grants and child benefit.

To what extent was there a radical change in the provision of healthcare?
Perhaps the greatest problem and challenge that Thatcher faced, after the economy as a whole, was the National Health Service (NHS) and the **welfare state**. Created by the 'socialist' Attlee Labour government between 1945 and 1951, the welfare system and the NHS had become expensive, inefficient – and very popular.

Public expectations about what they could get in terms of healthcare and welfare benefits grew continuously. Developing technology in medical provision meant those services became much more expensive, while public willingness to actually pay for these services and benefits through taxation was declining rapidly. With a better healthcare system there was a rapid increase in the proportion of people over sixty still living – who of course cost the taxpayer more in terms of both pensions and healthcare.

Chancellors of the Exchequer before 1979, both Labour and Conservative, had been faced with the growing costs of the modern welfare state. Ideologically Thatcher did not care for the NHS and much of the welfare state. She felt that 'welfareism', as she called it, created a **'dependency culture'** which harmed innovation, risk-takers and economic attainment. She preferred the US system where the states and federal government provided a safety net for those at the bottom of the economic heap, and the rest of the population looked after themselves through their own insurance schemes.

Dependency culture: where citizens were dependent on the state and not on their own efforts.

Her right-wing advisers really pressed her for a radical change towards the American model while in Opposition in the 1970s and during her early years in government. Proposals for radical surgery on both the role of the NHS and its spending, as well as a radical shift in welfare benefits, were seriously considered for the Budgets of 1980–1, as part of her 'monetarist' policy. However, leaks to the public and the media by opponents within the government and the civil service led to such public anger, that in order to stand any chance of re-election in 1983, Thatcher had to stress publicly that the NHS and its free healthcare was 'safe' with the Conservatives.

Never one to admit defeat, she adopted a more gradual approach. Helped by one of her toughest Ministers, Kenneth Clarke, major changes were imposed on the NHS in the late 1980s. Costs were cut in many areas. Hospitals were allowed to 'contract out' and attain an independent status as schools had done. Services such as laundry and cleaning had to be put out to tender. GPs were given control over their own budgets, and these were much more tightly controlled. For the first time there were incentives for preventative medicine and health education.

As in education, central government in London controlled more. The whole idea of the internal market, where hospitals competed with each other to provide a better service, came in. She could not privatise the NHS, but there was a serious attempt to introduce competition and as many market forces as she could into it. The idea of the patient as a 'customer' with 'rights' was pushed hard. There were 18 per cent more doctors in the NHS when she left office than in 1979. It was a more efficient service treating many more people.

Her right-wing critics, such as Norman Tebbit and Nigel Lawson, criticise her for failing to radically alter the whole principle of the NHS. There was a huge increase in costs. Spending in real terms went up by over 25 per cent on healthcare in the period, but there were fewer beds and more bureaucrats. Chancellors still grapple with the eternal dilemma of rising public healthcare expectations and rising costs of the NHS to the taxpayer. However, on the other hand, the number of people actually treated grew rapidly in the period, fewer babies died and more people lived longer.

Were there changes in social security policy?

'Welfare benefits, distributed with little or no consideration of their effects on behaviour, encouraged illegitimacy, facilitated the breakdown of families and replaced incentives by idleness and cheating.'

Margaret Thatcher, 1992

With the social services it is much the same story. Thatcher had radical hopes and plans, but electoral reality dictated otherwise. Her critics on the right again argued that she had wasted the opportunity to be radical in the early 1980s. She had wished to be, but not at the price of losing an election.

The rapid growth in the number of unemployed, pensioners and those needing other benefits, such as disability pensions, meant that public spending increased rapidly. Just as spending on health increased massively in real terms, so did spending on pensions and other forms of social security. Spending was £33.7 billion in 1979 and £44.8 billion in 1989 (by 1988 prices).

Norman Fowler, the Thatcherite Social Services Secretary, adopted a gradualist approach to change. Help to individuals was much more carefully targeted to ensure only those in need gained. Benefits did not go up in line with inflation, and child benefits were gradually reduced so that the wealthy got less and other benefits were increased to ensure the children of the poor got them.

Universality gradually ended. Policy in the end was to squeeze slowly into a new shape rather than radically alter the structure. The government remained the basic provider, but there were many more incentives to provide for oneself. The private and voluntary sector was used much more to help people, and, as with the healthcare system, there were much tighter managerial controls and competition where possible.

Thatcher felt that she had failed to end the dependency culture. She felt that the social security budget was still too large and a drain on the productive sectors of society. It was an area where she felt she had failed and she would like to have been much more revolutionary. However, her period in office did mark the start of a change of attitude in government.

Thatcher started to change deeply rooted attitudes about what the state should and could do. Her attempts to reform healthcare provision and welfare benefits made her deeply unpopular, but she felt that it was vital to convince people that any government does not have unlimited money to hand out to its citizens.

In some areas of social policy she can be seen to have failed. More was spent on police and policing, but crime grew. There was serious poverty and urban deprivation in 1979 and it existed still in 1990. Racism was still a huge issue in British society and it was one in which she played no part in trying to eradicate.

> 'I was asked whether I was trying to restore Victorian values. I said straight out I was. And I am.'
>
> Margaret Thatcher, 1983

Universality: where a state benefit, such as child benefit, was given to all regardless of income.

Did Thatcher really bring about a social, political and economic revolution?

1. Read the following extract and answer the question.

'Too much of our present unemployment is due to enormous past wage increases unmatched by higher output, to union practices, to over manning, to strikes, to indifferent management and to the basic belief that, come what may, the government would always step in to bail out companies in difficulty.'

(quoted in Margaret Thatcher, *Statecraft*, HarperCollins 2002)

Using this extract and your own knowledge, consider how successfully Thatcher solved the UK's economic problems in the 1980s.

2. To what extent is 'Thatcherism' an ideology?

Further Reading

Texts designed specifically for AS and A2 students

British Domestic Politics 1939–1964 by Paul Adelman (Access to History series, Hodder & Stoughton, 1994)
The Conservative Party and British Politics 1902–1951 by Stuart Ball (Longman Seminar Studies, 1995), chapters 7 and 8
Politics UK by B. Jones and others (Prentice Hall, 1998), chapter 14

Articles

The *Modern History Review* regularly has articles on this topic
Politics Review also has articles on this topic on a regular basis including:
'Labour and Conservative Members compared' by P. Seyd and P. Whitely (No. 4, April 1998)
'The Conservative Leadership Contest, 1997' by P. Norton (Vol. 7, No. 4, April 1998)
Talking Politics also has regular articles including:
'The 1997 Election and the Conservative Party's Prospects' by D. Nicholson (Vol. 10, No. 3, Spring 1998)

For more advance reading

The Conservative Party since 1945 edited by Stuart Ball (Manchester University Press, 1998)
The Conservative Party from Peel to Major by Robert Blake (Heinemann, 1997)
How Tory Governments Fall: The Tory Party in Power since 1783 edited by Anthony Seldon (Fontana, 1996)
Conservative Century: The Conservative Party since 1900 edited by Athony Seldon and Stuart Ball (Oxford University Press, 1994

Further reading on Thatcher

Texts specifically designed for students
Holmes, M. *Thatcherism, Scope and Limits 1983–7* (MacMillan, 1989)
Holmes, M. *The First Thatcher Government, 1979–83* (Wheatsheaf, 1985)
Smith, D. *Mrs Thatcher's Economic Legacy* (Studies in the UK Economy, Heinemann 1992)

Texts for more advanced study

Adonis, A. and Hames, T. (ed) *A Conservative Revolution?* (Manchester University Press, 1994) Excellent contrast between the ideas and practices of Thatcher and Reagan.
Campbell, J. *Margaret Thatcher* (Pimlico, 2001) Probably the best of the many biographies to date.
Gilmour, I. *Dancing with Dogma* (Simon and Schuster, 1992) Lucid attack by a Tory 'wet' sacked by Thatcher.
Hennessy, P. *Whitehall* (Secker and Warburg, 1989) A superb work of contemporary history and politics which analyses Thatcher's huge impact on the structure of government.
Hoskyns, J. *Just in Time* (Aurum Press, 2000) A highly sympathetic view from a successful businessman who worked for Thatcher in No. 10.
Jenkins, P. *Mrs Thatcher's Revolution* (Cape, 1987) Less sympathetic than Young, but still an excellent work of contemporary history.
Jenkins, S. *Accountable to None* (Penguin, 1995) Probably the most wide-ranging and effective attack on Thatcherism.
Raised, R. *The Prime Minister in a Shrinking World* (Polity, 2001) Quality analysis of what happened to the Office of Prime Minister under Thatcher.
Riddell, P. *The Thatcher Era and its Legacy* (Blackwell, 1991) Excellent analysis, which is both sympathetic and perceptive.
Seldon, S. and Snowden, P. *The Conservative Party* (2004)
Thatcher, M. *Statecraft* (HarperCollins, 2002) Very readable insight into her thinking on foreign policy and the EU.
Thatcher, M. *The Downing Street Years* (HarperCollins, 1993) Highly readable narrative, which gives a fascinating insight into her approach to people and issues.
Young, H. *One of Us* (Macmillan, 1989) A superb analysis by an outstanding journalist.

4 From Empire to Commonwealth, 1945–2007

Key Issues

- Did the Second World War make decolonisation an inevitability?

- How successfully did Britain manage the process of decolonisation?

- In what ways did the end of empire affect British society and politics?

Framework of Events

1947	Partition of India into India and Pakistan
	Independence given to India and Pakistan
	Communist insurrection begins in Malaya
1948	Ceylon (Sri Lanka) given independence
	British withdraws from Palestine mandate
1949	India becomes a republic
	London Declaration allows India to stay in Commonwealth
1951	Anglo-Iranian oil company nationalised
1952	Mau Mau rebellion in Kenya
1953	Shah of Iran restored to power by Britain and United States
1955	State of emergency declared in Cyprus
1956	Suez Crisis
1958	Malayan emergency ends
1960	Nigeria given independence
1961	South Africa becomes a republic and leaves the Commonwealth
	Zambia and Malawi given independence
1962	Uganda given independence
	Tanganyika given independence
1963	Kenya given dependence
1965	Rhodesia's Unilateral Declaration of Independence
1972	End of sterling area
	East Pakistan gains independence as Bangladesh after war with West Pakistan
1979	Rhodesian Settlement in Lancaster House Agreement. Ceasefire in Rhodesian civil war
1980	Zimbabwe created – it joins the Commonwealth
1982	The Falklands war
1984	British-Chinese agreement on future of Hong Kong. Britain to hand over Hong Kong to China in 1997
1985	Britain isolated in Commonwealth over Thatcher government's attitude towards sanctions against South Africa

1987	Fiji leaves Commonwealth after military takeover
1990	Namibia becomes independent and becomes 50th member of the Commonwealth
1994	Multi-racial South Africa rejoins Commonwealth following end of Apartheid
1997	Hong Kong returns to China
1998	Mozambique, a former Portuguese colony joins Commonwealth
	Nigeria's membership of Commonwealth suspended following military takeover
1999	Commonwealth celebrates fifty years as a modern international association
	Nigeria's suspension lifted
	Pakistan suspended after the unconstitutional overthrow of the democratically elected government
2000	Fiji Islands suspended from the Commonwealth, pending the restoration of democracy and the rule of law after army overthrows elected government
2001	Fiji suspension lifted
2002	Commonwealth Committee on Zimbabwe set up following a critical report by Commonwealth observers of Zimbabwe presidential election. Committee recomends that Zimbabwe to be suspended from the Commonwealth for one year
2003	Zimbabwe's suspension extended to December 2003 which results in Zimbabwe leaving the Commonwealth
2004	Pakistan's suspension lifted
2006	Fiji's suspension from the Commonwealth comes to an end.

Dominions: By 1931 the Dominions – Australia, Canada, New Zealand, South Africa and the Irish Free State were legally independent in all internal and external matters, though economic and other ties remained. Egypt and Iran were legally independent but Britain retained control over their foreign policy and had a military presence. The rest of the countries in the Empire were colonies, not Dominions.

ALTHOUGH countries such as Australia had become self-governing **Dominions**, at the end of the Second World War Britain still had a large Empire, and even the Dominions retained strong trade links with Britain and almost all had joined Britain to fight during the war. Twenty-five years later this Empire had almost entirely gone. Decolonisation was not simply the 'end of empire'. The creation of the Commonwealth shows that Britain regarded the process as an adjustment in the nature of the relationship between itself and its former colonies while it still kept its influence over them. The Commonwealth has survived – in 1999 there were 54 member countries, all except one once part of the Empire – because it suits the interests of its member states.

After 1945 Britain's political relationships with its colonies had to change. This was due to various factors. Internally Britain faced economic difficulties. Internationally the situation was changing, as the United States and the Soviet Union became the dominant world powers. The growth of nationalist movements in the colonies also forced change. But Britain still believed that it was possible to retain a 'special relationship' with former colonies, by managing change carefully. In many ways this failed – yet the Commonwealth remains a live and often lively organisation, informal but with influence over its member countries.

Although it had to give India independence immediately after the war, Britain attempted to develop other parts of its Empire as a source of power, prestige and (more easily measured) US dollars. This caused some of the discontent that grew during the 1950s, as nationalist movements took hold in many countries. Britain had seen decolonisation as a leisurely stroll towards independence, followed by continued strong links between Britain and the newly-independent colonies. In practice the processes turned to rapid withdrawal from the colonies, for example from Africa between 1959 and 1964. White settlers, once a key part of Britain's policy of self-government, became an international embarrassment and problem to be solved. The Suez crisis of 1956 demonstrated that Britain could not act independently, when the United States and almost all the countries of the United

Nations were against its foreign policies, even when Britain was allied with another European power – France – and (secretly) with Israel.

The Commonwealth never developed into the profitable trading area that the British had hoped, and from the 1960s Britain began to turn instead towards Europe. However, the Commonwealth has, perhaps unexpectedly, survived. As an informal group of countries, which at least attempts to promote and support democracy, and allow industrialised and developing countries to meet and exchange views, it has become a useful organisation and shows every sign of continuing well into the 21st century.

Commonwealth Secretaries General

Arnold Smith (Canada) 1965–75
Sir Shridath Surrendranath Rampal (Guyana) 1975–89
Chief Emeka Anyaoku (Nigeria) 1989–2000
Donald McKinnon (New Zealand) 2000–2008
Kamalesh Sharma 2008–

---

1. Explain how each of these affected the development of the British Empire and Commonwealth in the period 1945 to 2007.

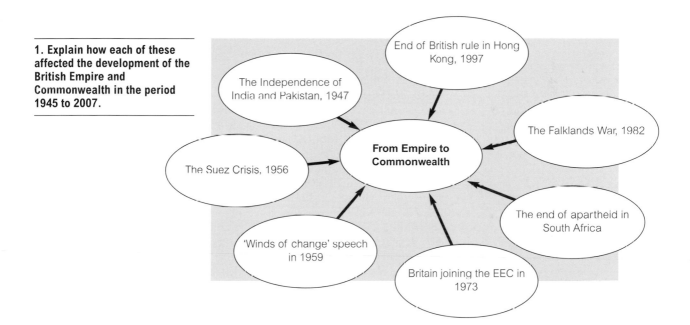

4.1 How did the Second World War affect Britain's imperial policy?

During the Second World War, it seemed possible that Britain might emerge with a much-reduced Empire. Burma, Singapore, Hong Kong and Malaya were all occupied by the Japanese in 1942, and although one of Britain's war aims was the preservation of Empire, both its principal allies, the United States and the Soviet Union, were, in principle, opposed to colonialism. The United States periodically suggested that British colonies, especially in Asia, should be placed under international control prior to independence, and was keen that the **closed imperial economy** should be opened up to **free world trade**. President Roosevelt was a committed anti-colonialist. In fact, all Britain's colonies were restored at the end of the war, and although Britain then withdrew from India and Ceylon (Sri Lanka), this was done to improve the running of the Empire as a whole and not to abandon it.

Closed economy: The deliberate protection of trade through taxation.

Free trade: A system that encourages the free flow of imports and exports.

Clinging on to the Empire was intended to support both the British economy and its influence abroad, resisting American attempts to redefine Britain as a European power only. The costs of the war had left Britain dependent on loans from the United States; by the end it was overspending by £2,000 million each year and exports had lost two-thirds of their value. An American loan of $3.75 billion was made in 1945 on condition that sterling became **freely convertible** with dollars in July 1947, which would open up imperial markets to the United States. The formation of the United Nations, although Britain was a member of the security council, reflected the new situation in which the United States and the Soviet Union were the main players in world politics. Both these countries were officially opposed to colonialism.

Freely convertible: Allowing one currency to be traded for another without restrictions.

The postwar Labour government remained committed to the Empire – in 1948 the Prime Minister, Clement Attlee, said to the House of Commons that Britain was 'not solely a European power but a member of a great Commonwealth and Empire'. Ernest Bevin, the Foreign Secretary, said in October that year, 'if we only pushed on and developed Africa, we could have the United States dependent on us and eating out of our hands in four or five years'. They saw Britain as offering a middle way between the American capitalism and Soviet communism, which were both disliked by the Labour Party. The desire to keep Britain's importance in the world is underlined by the decision in 1947 to build an independent nuclear deterrent. The development of nuclear weapons, however, was leading to a world in which possessing an empire was not the way to military greatness. This is underlined by the way that when the Soviet Union was ready to test an atomic bomb in 1949, the importance of the relationship with the United States was stressed again, and the North Atlantic Treaty Organisation was formed, linking the United States permanently with Europe.

Events in Palestine demonstrate how important US influence had become. The British, running Palestine under the UN's mandate, wanted to restrict Jewish immigration to 1,500 people a month, in order not to alienate the Arab population, thus threatening Britain's role elsewhere in the Middle East. But the Americans, responding to a strong Jewish lobby at home, suggested initially that 100,000 Jews be allowed into Palestine and then went further in support of the **Zionists**. An Anglo-American Committee of Inquiry failed to produce a solution acceptable to either Jews or Arabs, and a UN Special Committee recommended partition. In mid-1948, Britain left Palestine rather than be involved in putting the UN plan into practice; this departure was followed by the war which led to the establishment of the Jewish nation-state, Israel.

Zionists: Supporters of the creation of an independent Jewish state called Israel.

The development of the Commonwealth was one way of achieving continued British influence. Colonial policy had been redefined during the war, partly in response to American pressure, and the Colonial Office now began to talk of developing colonies' self-governing potential and guiding them along the way to independence. After independence, however, the idea was that the former colonies should join the Commonwealth and continue to co-operate with Britain in the **sterling area** and in defence.

Sterling area: The group of countries that held the pound sterling as their reserve currency after the war.

Originally the Commonwealth (then 'the British Commonwealth') had been restricted to the 'white' Dominions – Australia, New Zealand, Canada, South Africa and the Irish Free State (Eire). These recognised the King as the head of the Commonwealth (though Eire did so only as a convenience and left the Commonwealth altogether in 1949). All except Eire fought with Britain in the Second World War. After the war the Commonwealth came to be seen as a way to set up a flexible, multi-racial community through which Britain would exercise influence. For Britain to build up a 'third force' in the world, separate from the Soviet Union and the

United States, the Commonwealth needed to be as large and inclusive as possible. This meant India and Pakistan must be part of it, and since India wanted to become a republic, the Commonwealth was changed with the 1949 London Declaration to allow both Crown Dominions, which had the British monarch as their head of state, and Republican Dominions, which did not. The monarch remained the overall head of the Commonwealth. As described in a Colonial Office paper of 1950 the aim was for the new Commonwealth to be a 'circle of democratic nations exerting a powerful stabilising influence in the world'.

Within the colonies, the aim was 'to guide the colonial territories to responsible self-government within the Commonwealth in conditions that ensure to the people both a fair standard of living and freedom from oppression from any quarter' (a Colonial Office paper, May 1950). In 1946 the head of the Africa Division in the Colonial Office proposed a local government policy that would eventually transfer power to Africans, increasing democracy and bringing 'literates and illiterates together, in balanced and studied proportions, for the management of local finances and services. Failing this we shall find the masses apt to follow the leadership of **demagogues** who want to turn us right out very quickly.'

Demagogue: A charismatic and authoritarian leader.

Although the United States was officially opposed to colonialism, for both ethical and economic reasons, the development of the Cold War meant it was more worried about containing Soviet influence. Protectionist policies, such as the sterling area, were accepted because they could speed European recovery, and in a healthy economy communist parties had less influence. The American military were also anxious that British withdrawal from colonies would create instability and leave those countries open to Soviet influence. As the Cold War spread to Asia, with communist China intervening in Korea in 1950, Malaya became a frontline state. The British army went in to fight during the 'Emergency' caused by a communist insurrection, believed to be backed by the Soviet Union and China. Elsewhere, the United States and Britain co-operated in the 1953 coup in Iran that restored the Shah to power. US influence in the Middle East was increasing, but it was not particularly interested in Africa. The Bureau of African Affairs was not set up at the State Department until 1958. By the time US loans and grants were being made to African countries, British decisions on decolonisation had already been made. Nevertheless, the possibility of American intervention in colonial affairs was one of the reasons for modernising and democratising colonial government.

Elites: Ruling groups or classes.

The British attempted to nurture moderates and create **elites** within the colonies who would work to modernise them, co-operating with the British and acting against communism. These elites would be made up of the Western-educated middle class who would, according to the plan, become involved first in local government, gradually moving towards self-government modelled on the Westminster Parliament. This was what they had attempted to do in India, where their efforts were upset by the Second World War, but they were more successful in some of the African colonies.

1. How did Britain attempt to restructure the Empire after 1945 and why?

2. How did the Cold War affect British colonial policy?

Such change had to happen, partly to avoid international pressure for change, partly in order to promote social and economic development, partly in response to nationalist aims stimulated by the war and partly to block Soviet imperialism. Pressure from within the colonies could produce surprisingly quick effects; in 1948 there were riots on the Gold Coast, and by 1950 there was a new constitution, guaranteeing an African majority in the legislative council. Where there was no significant group of white settlers, it was much easier to set up this system successfully.

4.2 Why did Britain have to leave India in 1947?

The simple answer is that the Indians had been promised self-rule when the war ended. This had long been an aim – the 1935 Government of India Act had promised eventual self-government for India as a Dominion, and the new constitution, introduced in 1937, allowed the Indian National Congress, the main nationalist party (and mainly Hindu), to take control of most of the Indian provinces. Defence and foreign policies were still controlled by the Viceroy on Britain's behalf, and the army and police were still under British command.

The British government thought that India could be given self-rule as a united country, still relying on British defence co-operation and with many Britons still working there. Defence was a key issue. The Indian Army, with mainly British officers, could mobilise as many troops as the British Army and had been stationed throughout the Empire, defending the whole – so once war was declared India was vital to the British effort. After the humiliating fall of Singapore, Malaya, Hong Kong and Burma to the Japanese in early 1942, India, along with Australia, was very vulnerable to Japanese attack. At the same time the political handling of the war exposed the limits of what Britain had granted. Britain declared war with Germany on India's behalf, and the Congress Party ministers all resigned over this action being taken without consulting the wishes of the Indians. The

How does this map help show how the British Empire declined in these areas?

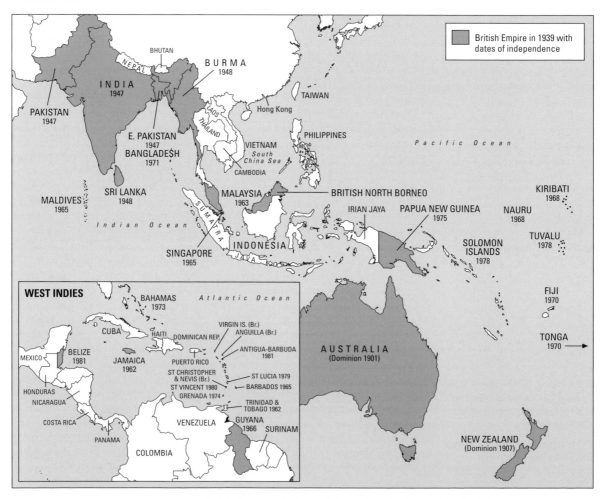

Britain's former colonies in Asia and the Pacific and the Caribbean

Gandhi, leader of the Indian National Congress since 1914 and of civil disobedience campaigns, with Lord Mountbatten, last Viceroy of India

Quit India: Led by Gandhi, this campaign of civil disruption began in 1942, and was suppressed by the British. All the Congress leaders were jailed for the rest of the war.

Visible trade: Trade in goods (e.g. cars and textiles) rather than services (e.g. insurance).

Mohammed Ali Jinnah (1876–1948)

Leader of the Muslim League and Pakistan separatist movement from 1935. Co-operated with British during the Second World War. Became Governor-General of Pakistan, 1947.

---

subsequent mobilisation, shortages, inflation and disruption of trade, as well as British defeats, meant the government became more and more unpopular. Attempts to gain co-operation from Congress in 1942 failed, despite the promise of self-government immediately the war was over and instead the **Quit India** movement was started. However, the Muslim League, committed to a separate Muslim state since 1940, did work with the British government, and so became more important in Indian politics – making partition more likely.

The promise of postwar independence remained, however, and the Labour government was committed to fulfilling it. American criticism of Britain's rule in the subcontinent had been very embarrassing, but in any case, by 1947 India was in deficit to the United States in **visible trade** and so did not bring additional hard currency to the sterling area. It was clear that Britain needed to focus on parts of the Empire that were likely to be assets, and withdraw from more problematic places. Africa was thought to be more adaptable than India.

At first, the British government hoped to establish a friendly government in India, co-operating with Britain in the Commonwealth. It was thought that Britain could retain access to military bases and manpower in India – as was agreed with Ceylon in 1947. Stafford Cripps proposed in 1946 that the Indian provinces should form a federation where foreign policy, defence, communications and finance were controlled by the centre. However, since 1940, the leader of the Muslim League, Jinnah, had been talking of the impossibility of Hindus and Muslims living together successfully in an independent India, and he feared that the Congress party wanted centralisation to reduce Muslim participation. The League refused to co-operate in making a constitution and decided on 'direct action' to obtain a separate Pakistan. In August 1946 over 5,000 people died in rioting in Calcutta between Hindus and Muslims. The violence continued, and in February 1947, Attlee announced that June 1948 was the date of withdrawal whether or not the League and Congress could reach any agreement, and sent Lord Louis Mountbatten to be the final Viceroy.

Mountbatten tried to get agreement from League and Congress to an all-India federation, but Nehru, the Congress president, was afraid that without a strong centre there would simply be more violence.

1. What difference did the war make to British policy in India?

2. Why was India partitioned in 1947?

3. How did the Indian parties campaign for nationalism and respond to British policy during the Second World War and after?

Mountbatten then proposed partition into two separate Dominions, India and Pakistan. Congress agreed to this, but only if withdrawal was speeded up, and so India and Pakistan became independent in August 1947. They immediately began to dispute the partition of Kashmir. Britain had failed to achieve a government in India with which it would maintain defence links, nor had the rights of minorities such as the Sikhs been guaranteed, but the new Dominions were members of the Commonwealth. This did not however mean they were supporters of British policy – as leader of the Non-Aligned Movement in the 1950s, India continually criticised British imperialism, and moved away from Britain in seeking allies against China. Britain has been criticised for the speed of its withdrawal. In the violence that followed at least 250,000 people died in the Punjab alone.

4.3 How did Britain attempt to make the Empire pay?

The Labour government of 1945 was committed to social policies in Britain, such as the National Health Service, which would be a significant cost to the state. There were fears that continued expenditure abroad might damage Britain's economic stability – in 1946 the Chancellor of the Exchequer was warning that the balance of payments could not stand the cost of the 1.2 million British people serving abroad. In 1947 Britain's dollar reserves were reduced as US prices rose, and in June the Treasury warned that without American aid the dollar shortage combined with convertibility of sterling to dollars (promised to the Americans for July that year) could destroy the British economy. In fact, convertibility lasted just a month before the threat of a complete loss of the pound's value led to the reintroduction of exchange controls. In November 1947 the sterling area had a dollar deficit of £600–£700 million per year.

The sterling area was formed at the beginning of the war and consisted principally of the Empire/Commonwealth countries. After 1945 it was much more controlled, and discriminated against trade with 'hard currencies' – currencies like the US dollar which could be bought and sold anywhere – and became a way for Britain to earn dollars. Exports such as rubber from Malaya and cocoa from the Gold Coast brought dollars into the area. Britain then bought the dollars at a fixed exchange rate, crediting the country with a sterling balance – which could only be spent within the sterling area. Since Britain was unable to produce all the goods that a country like Malaya wanted to purchase, this led to shortages and therefore inflation in countries that earned hard currency. The Commonwealth Colombo Plan of 1950 partly hoped to address this by improving living standards in South-East Asia. This was also meant to prevent communism from being too attractive.

The colonies were vital to the sterling area since Britain had control over them, which it did not over the Crown Dominions, such as Australia. It was feared that if power were transferred to colonial nationalists, they might draw too much on their sterling balances and destabilise the British economy, which was another factor against allowing independence for many at this time.

The British economy was rescued by Marshall Aid. In fact, American assistance, first in 1945 and then in 1948, allowed Britain to postpone a serious reappraisal of its overseas commitments and ability to pay for the Empire. Instead, attempts were made to make the Empire pay. It was a source of cheap food (often bought below market rates) and raw materials, so the aim of British policy was to try to invest in the colonies to make them happy and productive, raising their living standards, benefiting Britain economically and so also presenting colonialism in a more positive way. The Empire also offered a secure outlet for British goods, and developing colonial economies would allow their consumers to buy more of these.

The Colonial Office recruited 4,100 new staff between June 1945 and September 1948; a 45 per cent increase on the whole period 1945–54. Colonial Development and Welfare Acts were passed during the war, intended to help pay for improving living standards in the colonies and developing their economies. The overseas technical departments expanded. The Act passed in 1945 provided £120 million for colonial development. The Cabinet set up a **Colonial Development Corporation** at the end of 1948. Projects such as the **East African Groundnut Scheme** were set up to attempt to exploit imperial economic resources better, and efforts were made to reform agricultural practices in Africa. These attempts, however, were often very unpopular with the local people, and the groundnut scheme was a spectacular failure. Britain never managed to turn Africa into a source of dollars.

The Middle East was very important economically to Britain because of oil. In May 1951 the Iranian government nationalised the Anglo-Iranian Oil Company, with its refinery at Abadan, of which the British took 85 per cent of the profits. Britain had usually put pressure on Iran by threatening to intervene in south Persia, but the Americans were afraid that this would lead to the Russians attacking the north and opposed British military action. So Britain was restricted to trying to stop Iranian oil getting to the world market. Although the Iranian regime was overthrown in 1953, with secret help from the US Central Intelligence Agency (CIA), Britain only regained a 40 per cent stake in what was now an international consortium. At the time, however, this was not a disastrous economic blow, because Kuwait and other Gulf states were producing so much oil, helping the balance of payments. Attlee had contemplated withdrawing from the Middle East after the war, because of the expense of building up British bases there again, but was persuaded by the Foreign Office and the military that Britain must stay to contain the Soviet Union, and of course to protect oil interests.

Elsewhere in the Empire Britain tried to attract American investment, but although US industry needed raw materials from the Third World, it was only the Middle Eastern oil industry which attracted serious investment – where of course they were rivals to British firms. Few US companies were willing to risk their capital in an unstable and underdeveloped empire.

Despite these attempts to make the Empire pay, during the 1950s Britain was beginning to trade less with the Empire/Commonwealth and more with other industrialised nations. Economists were also beginning to question the desirability of the sterling area, and of encouraging colonies to build up large sterling balances. The various colonial loans that were floated on the Stock Market in the 1950s were all unpopular. By the end of the 1950s it was clear that the attempt to make the Empire pay had failed: in fact it had contributed to the pressure for decolonisation.

Colonial Development Corporation (CDC): Set up 1948 to promote increased colonial production on an economic and self-supporting basis, especially of food, raw material and manufactures, which would help improve the balance of payments. It could borrow up to £100 million for investment.

East African Groundnut Scheme: In 1946 it was proposed that 1 million acres of Tanganyika be used to grow groundnuts as a solution to the shortage of edible oils and fats. The scheme was approved in January 1947 and the area increased to 3.2 million acres. By 1949 the scheme had to be closed down: almost all of the budget had been spent on clearing 1.4 per cent of the ground.

1. a) What was the sterling area?

b) Why was It Important to British imperial policy?

2. How important was the Empire to Britain's economy in the 1940s and 1950s?

3. Could the Empire be made to pay? (Give reasons to support your answer.)

4.4 What caused the growth of nationalism in so many different colonies in the 1950s?

The Second World War had an important impact on nationalism in many colonies. Local populations were mobilised to produce war materials, or to serve abroad, and economies were disrupted. Service abroad influenced many people from the colonies, as they came into contact with fellow

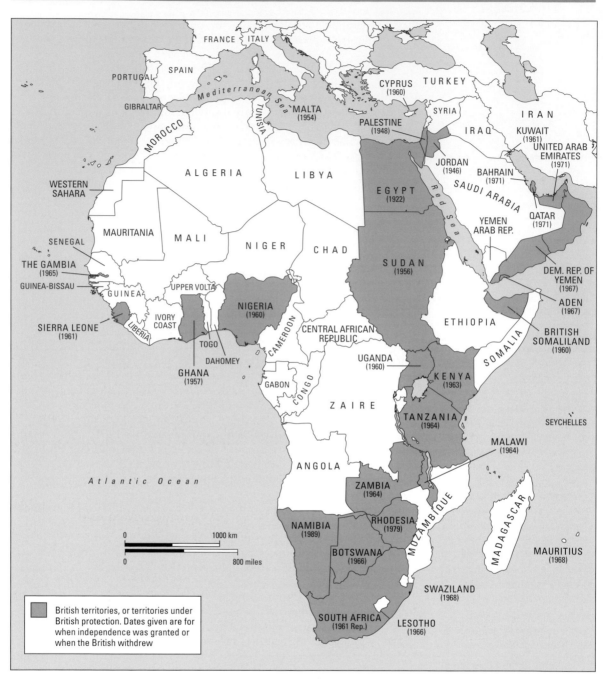

FRANCE ITALY

PORTUGAL SPAIN

GIBRALTAR

Mediterranean Sea

MALTA
(1954)

CYPRUS
(1960)

TURKEY

SYRIA

IRAN

PALESTINE
(1948)

IRAQ

KUWAIT
(1961)

UNITED ARAB
EMIRATES
(1971)

MOROCCO

TUNISIA

WESTERN
SAHARA

ALGERIA

LIBYA

EGYPT
(1922)

JORDAN
(1946)

BAHRAIN
(1971)

SAUDI ARABIA

QATAR
(1971)

Red Sea

YEMEN
ARAB REP.

MAURITANIA

MALI

NIGER

CHAD

SUDAN
(1956)

DEM. REP. OF
YEMEN
(1967)

SENEGAL

THE GAMBIA
(1965)

GUINEA-BISSAU

GUINEA

UPPER VOLTA

ADEN
(1967)

SIERRA LEONE
(1961)

IVORY
COAST

LIBERIA

TOGO

DAHOMEY

NIGERIA
(1960)

CAMEROON

CENTRAL AFRICAN
REPUBLIC

ETHIOPIA

SOMALIA

BRITISH
SOMALILAND
(1960)

GHANA
(1957)

GABON

CONGO

UGANDA
(1960)

KENYA
(1963)

ZAIRE

TANZANIA
(1964)

SEYCHELLES

MALAWI
(1964)

Atlantic Ocean

ANGOLA

ZAMBIA
(1964)

MOZAMBIQUE

MADAGASCAR

NAMIBIA
(1989)

RHODESIA
(1979)

MAURITIUS
(1968)

BOTSWANA
(1966)

SWAZILAND
(1968)

SOUTH AFRICA
(1961 Rep.)

LESOTHO
(1966)

0 — 1000 km
0 — 800 miles

British territories, or territories under
British protection. Dates given are for
when independence was granted or
when the British withdrew

**How does the map help explain
the British withdrawal from
Africa in the 1950s and 1960s?**

Decolonisation in Africa and the Middle East: the dates of British withdrawal

soldiers and with military organisation, and often developed a sense of
their national identity. Wartime measures were accompanied by talk of
postwar development and movement towards self-government, as the
reward for co-operation during the war. After the war ministers spoke of
the mutual benefits that Britons and colonial peoples would derive from
colonial development – Britain might benefit economically, but the
colonies would also gain a higher standard of living. As we have seen,
attempts to make the Empire profitable were unsuccessful, but they raised
expectations among the local populations.

Instead of development, immediately after the war there were shortages, unemployment and inflation in many colonies, such as Nigeria, Kenya and Tanganyika, leading to strikes and protests. When attempts were made, for example to develop agriculture, this often involved unacceptable interference with traditional practices by agricultural officers. They wanted to build terraces to avoid soil erosion, introduce new crops, destroy diseased animals and plants, and backed this up with penalties and compulsory labour. In Kenya, for example, the government believed that such measures would solve the problem of the Kikuyu tribe's claim to the land farmed by the white settlers, by increasing production. Although these measures might have been necessary, in countries that were still being underpaid for their products and experiencing no rise in living standards, they aroused huge resentment. Putting such policies into practice were the increased numbers of European Colonial Office administrators and experts, thus making British rule much more visible and resented. In some countries, such as Southern Rhodesia, these additional officials were accompanied by a new generation of white settlers, for whom peasant African farmers were evicted – a very unwelcome 'second colonial occupation'.

The Gold Coast (Ghana)

The attempts at political development were not always welcome, and often contributed to nationalist feeling. The Gold Coast (now Ghana), where cocoa was the main commercial product (and a major dollar earner), provides an example of this. After the war, a constitution was introduced to give greater representation to local opinion, as a first step on the gradual road to independence. During the war, income tax had been introduced and central control over local government extended. Traditionally government had been operated on a local level in alliance with the local chiefs, but the new constitution proposed to bring the whole country under one legislature. It seemed that local chiefs now needed political influence at the centre to protect local interests. The business community feared that the constitution would entrench the chiefs too closely with the colonial government, and the chiefs were conservative and opposed to western ideas of democracy. The nationalist United Gold Coast Convention (UGCC) was formed in 1947 by a lawyer, J. B. Danquah. Meanwhile, the war had led to inflation and food shortages, making the colonial government unpopular. At the same time the government was enforcing the destruction of cocoa trees attacked by swollen shoot disease, according to the Colonial Office technicians' advice. Farmers resented this – the trees could go on being productive for years – and did not believe they would receive compensation. In early 1948 a demonstration by unemployed ex-servicemen led to riots.

The riots were put down by the British, and a constitutional committee set up, which recommended a larger elected assembly and universal (though usually indirect) suffrage. Meanwhile, Kwame Nkrumah, who had returned from studying in London to help with the UGCC's campaign by mobilising trade unions and local farmers' associations, set up his own party, the Convention People's Party, and began organising strikes and demonstrations. He was imprisoned, but his party still won the election and he had to be let out to take office as chief minister of the new assembly. In fact, once in office, he co-operated happily enough with the British, and made it clear that he sought self-government within the Commonwealth and the sterling area. Britain accepted this, and the Gold Coast became independent in 1957. The nationalist movement started and developed clear aims partly because of Britain's attempts to draw up a new constitution, uniting the country more firmly, partly because of the shortages and inflation caused by the war, and partly because of the attempts to control the cocoa industry (even if for its own good). All these factors united the different interests in the local population against British rule. Colonial development, once begun, could lead very quickly to independence.

Nigeria

Similarly in Nigeria, initial plans for a gradual move towards self-government did not last. Britain wanted to draw together the very distinct parts of Nigeria – Muslim in the north, more influenced by western Christianity in the south, which was itself divided between the Yoruba in the west and Ibo in the east – into a modern state. When a new constitution was proposed, aiming to draw educated groups in all areas into developing the state, the very difficulty of getting these different groups to agree meant that independence had to be promised as a reward, and was achieved in 1960.

Kenya

British attempts to create large federations also aroused nationalist feelings and fears – part of the motivation for the Mau Mau revolt in Kenya was the proposal for a union of Kenya, Uganda and Tanganyika in an East African Federation. Given the example of the Central African Federation (see below), this did not appeal to their black populations. In Kenya, urban unemployment and housing shortages combined with rural grievances about the new development of agriculture, leading to disturbances and the creation of the underground Mau Mau movement, which was violently resisting British rule by the end of 1952 – though in fact most of its victims (14,000 compared to 95 whites) were Kikuyu. It was a war fought between those who had adopted western ideas or had benefited from colonial rule and those who believed it must be resisted in every way. Britain responded with force, declaring an emergency and eventually suppressing the Mau Mau by the end of 1956. However, at the same time the colonial government attempted to make fundamental agriculture and land reforms, consolidating holdings and creating a new class of conservative farmers. This meant that African representation had to be extended to gain moderate support for these plans, though this was a part of Britain's aim that Kenya should be run by a power-sharing group of Europeans, Asians and Africans.

Tanganyika

Attempts from 1952 to reform the Tanganyika government to fit in with the same multi-racial powersharing model were what led to nationalist resistance there. Locally government had been African, with a British district officer; now it was to include Europeans and Asians. At the same time, efforts were being made to improve agriculture, conserve the soil and raise productivity. The local chiefs used to enforce this had become unpopular, and the Tanganyika African National Union (TANU) had been formed. It became an important force of opposition to multi-racialism and in the 1958 elections, which Britain had intended to produce a multi-racial council, TANU candidates won a majority.

In South-East Asia matters seemed easier to handle. In Malaya, consideration had been given to self-government since the start of the Emergency operation against Chinese communist rebels, which lasted from 1948 until the mid-1950s. The different communities in Malaya – Chinese, Malay and Indian – needed incentives to co-operate with each other and, as elsewhere, Britain hoped for multi-racial parties to emerge.

Meanwhile, however, Britain had been left as the only major colonial power in South-East Asia, when France left Indo-China. The United States wanted the end of colonialism in the area to help contain communism in Vietnam. The leaders of two main Malayan parties, allied to each other, were keen to retain their connections with Britain, partly because they needed help in ending the Emergency, and agreed in return to remain within the sterling area. This was precisely the kind of decolonisation Britain wanted – but it was the need for continued security assistance that brought it about.

Nationalist movements were becoming troublesome elsewhere in the Empire. Aden, between Yemen and Oman, which Britain valued increasingly during the 1950s, was coveted by Yemen. Also, within the Aden colony, British rule was resented – more so after the Suez crisis of 1956, which had shown the limits of British power. Attempts to put together the Federation of South Arabia, created in 1963, which would bring together the interior with the Aden peninsula, threatened the power of local tribes, who revolted in 1963.

1. Why were British governments in favour of federations?

2. How and why did nationalist parties develop in Africa? Give examples from at least two countries.

As we have seen, then, nationalist movements everywhere grew during the 1950s. The economic problems following the war, together with increased controls that had been imposed during it, meant that local populations found British rule increasingly oppressive, while increased numbers of white officials and settlers made it more visible. Attempts to create limited suffrage as a first step on the road to independence gave nationalist parties an opportunity to gain political influence, and overturned programmes for very slow constitutional change moving very gradually towards independence – as in Ghana. Britain would hang on, for example in Kenya, fighting violent nationalist movements, but this was a very expensive option.

4.5 The problem of white settlers in Africa

There were particular problems with decolonisation in areas with significant numbers of white settlers. In Central Africa, white nationalism was a strong force – there were 300,000 whites in Southern and Northern Rhodesia, and new settlers began to arrive after 1945. Although, in theory, the British government had to approve constitutional changes and laws that affected the African population of Southern Rhodesia, in fact the country had been internally self-governed since 1923. White Northern Rhodesians aspired to the same independence, and after the war, as Rhodesian copper and tobacco were vital to the sterling area, the British government had to move carefully. White workers in the mining industry had active trade unions, and were afraid of cheap black labourers taking their jobs. Moves towards black majority rule elsewhere in Africa encouraged white nationalism, and the belief that white settlers were beneficial to African development was shared by the British government during the 1950s. The extreme poverty of most of the black Africans in Nyasaland and Northern Rhodesia meant that there was little political organisation or nationalist agitation among the black population. In Southern Rhodesia more Africans had moved to the towns during the war, and trade union and political organisation had developed (there was a strike in Salisbury and Bulawayo in 1948) but the white population there had full political control. Opposition from the British government to the white population's desire for unification was abandoned in 1949, partly influenced by fear of Afrikaner domination in the Rhodesias – there were many Afrikaners among the new immigrants, and the National Party had just won control of South Africa. South Africa later adopted a system of apartheid by which

Federation: A group of states, which retain equal status but share aspects of central policy making.

Amalgamation: Joining together.

the black and white populations were separated in every part of life, education, sport, work, transport and where they lived.

The scheme developed during 1951–53 (with a constitutional review promised for 1959) was for **federation** rather than **amalgamation**, and included Nyasaland, a poor British protectorate. The Colonial Office would continue to supervise Northern Rhodesia and Nyasaland, with responsibility for the political advancement of the Africans and for internal security, and staffed by members of the Colonial Service. However, when in 1957 the African Affairs Board, set up to do so, referred to British legislation that enlarged the Federal Assembly while keeping the number of African representatives the same, the British government approved it. The federal government pressed for further self-government for Northern Rhodesia, and in 1957 the British government began to redraw the constitution (though attempting to include measures encouraging multi-racial politics), but black opposition was by now more effective. Attempts to involve Africans in politics to preserve the constitution had increased their political awareness, but the main force behind African nationalism, uniting rural and urban, chiefs and politicians, was the fear of being trapped in a white Dominion.

Under Kenneth Kaunda, the Zambia African National Congress split from the African National Congress to promote a boycott of the new constitution in Northern Rhodesia, while Dr Hastings Banda of the Nyasaland African Congress (NAC) was leading a campaign for independent majority rule there. By March 1959 an 'emergency' had been declared in Nyasaland and a police and military operation against the NAC begun, on the pretext that the NAC planned to murder government officials, which led to the deaths of about 51 Africans. At the same time in Northern Rhodesia the Zambia African National Congress (ZANC) led by Kaunda was banned and in Southern Rhodesia 500 African political activists were arrested. Instead of crushing opposition to federation, the number of deaths and the disorder in Nyasaland meant there had to be an independent inquiry, and its report condemned the government's actions. The Monckton Commission, set up to review the federal constitution, recommended in 1960 that federation should be retained, but with, for example, parity of representation for whites and blacks in the Federal Assembly and African majorities in the Nyasaland and Northern Rhodesian assemblies. The British government was rapidly repositioning itself away from the white settlers, releasing Kaunda and Banda and pressing the federal premier to accept an African majority in Northern Rhodesia. Britain was not prepared to fight in defence of white settler claims. Attempts to negotiate a new federal constitution in 1960 were deadlocked between white and black nationalists. There were violent disturbances in Northern Rhodesia when a constitution was proposed for Southern Rhodesia weighted to give a white majority in the legislature; by March 1961 the new Colonial Secretary, Reginald Maudling, announced a new constitution that would give an African majority for Northern Rhodesia. Elections in Northern Rhodesia resulted in a majority for independence, and in Southern Rhodesia a new Rhodesian Front campaigned for separate independence there. The Federation was over. Northern Rhodesia became Zambia and Nyasaland Malawi.

Elsewhere, Britain had planned for an East African Federation of Kenya, Uganda and Tanganyika, under governments sharing power between Europeans, Asians and Africans. Kenya had been attracting white settlers since the end of the 19th century, and their community, based on exclusive use of a large area of land, the 'White Highlands', dominated Kenyan politics, sharing **executive power** with the Colonial Office administration. The Mau Mau rebellions horrified the British government and the white settler

Executive power: The power to carry out and enforce laws and decrees.

population, and meant all national organisations for Africans were banned. It appeared that the white nationalists were on the way to achieving similar status as Southern Rhodesia, but in fact, as constitutional concessions were made in Uganda and Tanganyika, it was hard to deny them to Kenya. In addition the agricultural reforms made after the Mau Mau rebellion had developed a class of rural notables who now demanded influence over government policy and were hard to resist, since they had been set up by the government and were important in getting the reform programme implemented. Kenya's white settlers lost their influence. They had had to turn to Britain for the money and men to suppress the Mau Mau. Now Britain ended the ban on African movements and held the Lancaster House Conference on the constitution in 1960, at which it was agreed that Africans would have a majority in the legislature. The Kikuyu leader Jomo Kenyatta was in detention, but the two new African parties, rivals for support at home, were demanding his release and further steps towards independence. Although one of them was considered to have British support, it could not be controlled by Britain, and at the same time its requests were difficult to refuse. Kenyatta was released in August 1961, and independence followed in December 1963.

Southern Rhodesia, normally referred to as Rhodesia, remained a problem for Britain for many years. International pressure – including that from within the Commonwealth – was firmly against giving way to white nationalism. South Africa left the Commonwealth in May 1961, ostensibly because it was a republic but really because of the violent demonstrations at Sharpeville (see section 4.7), which showed clearly Commonwealth opinion on this issue. The Central African Federation had to be ended, and Zambia and Malawi were independent, but Rhodesia was still a white-ruled colony, pressing for independence on those terms. Britain refused independence, not wishing to offend the Afro-Asian Commonwealth, and not finding Rhodesia willing to make any real constitutional gesture towards the black community there. Both the Conservative government and then the new Labour government of 1964 under Harold Wilson tried to negotiate with Rhodesia, where Ian Smith was now prime minister, but unsuccessfully. Rhodesia made a Unilateral Declaration of Independence (UDI) on 11 November 1965. Wilson had already said he would not use force, though economic sanctions were imposed, and, governing with a

Jomo Kenyatta (1889–1978)
Leader of the Kikuyu in Kenya, he was one of the moderate Africans who negotiated with Macmillan for independence in the early 1960s, after the cost of suppressing the Mau Mau rebellion became too much for Britain. Became Prime Minister of independent Kenya in 1963 and President in 1964.

British Prime Minister, Harold Wilson, meeting Rhodesian Prime Minister Ian Smith

small majority, was afraid that acting against the white Rhodesians would help the Conservative Party. But in the Commonwealth it became the most important issue between Britain and the African and Asian countries, and continued efforts were made to negotiate a solution. All these failed, even though Britain was not demanding majority rule or any quick approach to it. When the final set of proposals (which might lead to majority rule 30 years later) was put to the African population by a commission of enquiry, independence on such terms was comprehensively rejected.

What brought about black majority rule in Rhodesia were other changes in the area, including independence for Portugal's colonies of Angola and Mozambique. For South Africa, the guerrillas operating from eastern Rhodesia were a serious problem, and they used the economic and military help they gave the Rhodesians to press for a compromise with the black population. By 1976 Ian Smith had announced majority rule within two years, and reached an Internal Settlement with some of the African nationalists, which was supported in the elections by the black population. Bishop Muzarewa became Zimbabwe-Rhodesia's first black prime minister, but the 'Patriotic Front' parties, led by Joshua Nkomo and Robert Mugabe (see page 157), continued to fight a guerrilla war against the government of Zimbabwe-Rhodesia, acting from Zambia and Mozambique. Britain might have wanted to accept the Internal Settlement and recognise Zimbabwe-Rhodesia, but a large number of other Commonwealth countries were firmly opposed to this. At the Lusaka Heads of Government meeting in 1979 Britain agreed to a new constitutional conference to establish an independent Zimbabwe, and that at new elections the 'Patriotic Front' parties would be allowed to participate. Commonwealth observers would attend and report on the fairness of the elections. Additionally, as negotiations continued, a Commonwealth Monitoring Force was sent to police the ceasefire. In the elections the Patriotic Front parties, including the one led by Mugabe, won, and Zimbabwe was finally established as an independent republic, and a member of the Commonwealth – which had itself successfully influenced British policy.

1. Compare decolonisation policies in Gold Coast (Ghana) and Kenya. How far were any differences caused by white settlers?

2. When and why did Britain come to see African white settlers as a problem, and how did governments attempt to solve it?

4.6 What difference did the Suez Crisis make to the Empire?
A CASE STUDY IN HISTORICAL INTERPRETATION

On 26 July 1956 the Egyptian President Gamal Abdel Nasser (see page 137) nationalised the Suez Canal Company, in which Britain and France had previously had a majority shareholding. The Suez canal linked the Mediterranean to the Red Sea and was regarded as an essential strategic asset. Britain had continued to have a military presence in Egypt, even when it was technically independent, to defend the Middle East and its oil (which, coming through the Suez canal from sterling area companies, could be paid for in sterling, not precious dollars), and the Empire generally. Nasser's regime was hostile to Britain, and under pressure from the United States, where Eisenhower was President, Britain had signed a new Anglo-Egyptian treaty in 1954, which included British withdrawal from the Canal Zone by June 1956. When Nasser nationalised the canal, therefore, Britain no longer had the enormous Suez military base behind it.

The United States and Britain agreed in spring 1956 to collaborate on a scheme to destabilise Nasser's regime, but only through economic and political pressure, and propaganda. When Eden, after the nationalisation, began to prepare a military expedition to bring down Nasser and install a friendly government, Eisenhower was opposed to this from the start. Efforts were made to establish a negotiated solution between Britain,

France and Egypt, but in the October the French and British agreed to attack Egypt, and secretly arranged that Israel would attack also. On 29 October Israel did attack Egypt: Britain and France began to bomb Egypt on 31 October. When Britain and France entered Egypt on 5 November, they presented it as an effort to restore peace between Israel and Egypt in the Middle East.

The Americans, however, refused to support such action. They were mainly concerned with containing the Soviet threat in the Middle East, where Britain was concerned for oil and for its own long-term position there. The Commonwealth did not support Britain while India supported Egypt, and in the United Nations the vote for an immediate ceasefire was 64 to 5. As sterling came under pressure, the Americans forced an end to the invasion by withholding essential loans to prop up the pound until Britain had withdrawn unconditionally, which it did in December.

Peter Hennessy, looking at the government papers relating to the Suez crisis, notes that there were plenty of warnings to the government about the course it was taking. Lord Mountbatten, the First Sea Lord, urged Prime Minister Anthony Eden to accept the UN resolution and 'cease military operations' before the fleet reached Port Said. Sir Edward Bridges, at the Treasury, explained in September 'the vital necessity from the point of view of our currency and our economy of ensuring that we do not go it alone, and that we have the maximum United States support'.

Clearly the military expedition was a failure in its own terms and more generally as a demonstration that Britain's imperial power could not be resurrected and was dependent on US support. Historians have argued whether it was even more important than that. Hennessy said it was 'conventional wisdom' that Suez hastened the end of Empire, but that Alec Douglas-Home, then Commonwealth Secretary, interviewed in 1987, thought it had not – 'it was inevitable that the Empire should dissolve'. Brian Lapping (in *Contemporary Record*) argues that Suez did speed up Britain's withdrawal from Empire, for example in Africa in the 1960s. He points out that Suez had an effect on France as well as Britain. Algerians rebelling against French rule were encouraged by Suez, and without that defeat it is unlikely the French would have so abruptly granted independence in 1960 to colonies such as Senegal and Ivory Coast. This in turn influenced British policy. Lapping also notes that Nasser offered help to many African nationalist leaders, including offices in Cairo and access to radio broadcasts. Egypt turned away from the West, and accepted Russian military and economic advisers. At the same time, the Americans became more interested in Africa, and established their Bureau of African Affairs. Britain reduced its overseas military bases after Suez: the crisis had demonstrated that Britain and France could not make military interventions without US backing, so it was reasonable to cut back on the troops. From 1957, the numbers in the armed services fell from about 700,000 to 375,000.

Lapping argues finally that Macmillan, who succeeded Eden as Prime Minister, at first had to continue with Eden's policies in order to reunite the party, but then, having won a general election, was able to change direction, speed up decolonisation and turn towards Europe. 'Macmillan and Macleod changed policy because they saw that, in the light of all the changes speeded up by Suez, they had no choice.' Suez had shown that the British Empire was no longer supported by a superior military force.

Anthony Low (also in *Contemporary Record*) argues instead that Suez did not make much long-term difference to decolonisation. All political parties were already committed to allowing the colonies self-rule, which had already been promised to Ghana (though it would not take effect until 1957). He argues that African nationalist movements were one of the main causes of the speeded-up decolonisation programme after 1959. After the Suez crisis, in 1959, the dates considered for Kenya, Tanganyika and Uganda to become independent were from 1970 to 1975. Although African nationalists may have been encouraged by Suez, there is no evidence of this, and many other considerations, such as the consequences of Belgium's withdrawal from the Congo, and the fear of white domination in Central Africa, appear far more important.

John Darwin (in *Britain and Decolonisation*) suggests that the influence of Suez was 'subtle and diffuse', and did make clear 'the strength of the new pressures on Britain deriving, especially, from the Commonwealth', which would make themselves felt over Rhodesia. It did not, however, mean Britain was unable or unwilling to make military interventions or commit forces abroad – the Anglo-Malayan Defence Agreement came in 1957, after Suez. The most influential aspect of the Suez crisis was 'the fear that by incautious commitment and inflexible conservatism, Britain might again find herself isolated and friendless'.

---

1. How far was 1956 a turning point for the Empire? (Use examples from the whole chapter.)

2. Why have historians argued about the importance of the Suez crisis?

4.7 'Winds of Change': Why did decolonisation speed up after 1959?

Imperial preference: A system of import and export tariffs giving preferential treatment to Empire goods, constructed during the 1930s. The United States opposed it in favour of free trade.

In 1954 the Conservative Party Conference rejected **imperial preference** in favour of free trade. It was no longer true that the Empire was Britain's route to economic prosperity and world influence. When Harold Macmillan became Prime Minister in 1957, he asked for a review of the costs compared to the benefits of Empire, which came to the conclusion that Britain could withdraw from the colonies without damaging the home economy. Indeed, where once it had been believed that large transfers of sterling into other imperial countries were beneficial to Britain, the Treasury had come to think that external investment was damaging the ability to invest at home. Rather than exporting manufactured goods to the colonies in exchange for raw materials, economists had begun to look to the trade opportunities offered by other industrialised countries, such as the United States and the members of the European Economic Community (EEC). Britain's first application to join the EEC in 1961 is a key turning point in Britain's shift from imperial to regional economic interests.

Macmillan did not, however, believe that decolonisation was a complete break with the past. In early 1958 he said that in those former colonies that were now independent but members of the Commonwealth, 'though we no longer had authority, we still had great influence'.

Where before maintaining colonies had been seen as a weapon against the Soviet Union in the Cold War, by the early 1960s both the Soviet Union and China were offering moral support to anti-colonialists at the United Nations, and Britain was keen to prevent that turning into military support. Managed withdrawal, giving way to democratic government, was expected to avoid newly-independent colonies coming under Communist influence. The consequences of badly-managed decolonisation were sharply illustrated in the Belgian Congo. In January 1960 the Belgian government decided that it should become independent on 30 June, and by 5 July it had begun to sink into anarchy. The civil war there deeply worried Macmillan, who wrote in his diary that, like the Balkans in 1914, it could trigger a world war as the various nationalist groups looked to the Soviet Union for support. It seemed possible that the trouble in the Congo might extend into the surrounding countries, Uganda, Kenya, Tanganyika and the Central Africa Federation, and Britain came to believe that to pull out sooner rather than too late was the best way of maintaining goodwill towards the west in the former colonies.

The French example was also instructive. The extremely expensive war that the French fought in Algeria led to constitutional change in France itself, where the French colonists had representation. After de Gaulle came to power in 1958 France offered independence to its colonies and achieved this by 1960. There was no parliamentary representation for the white colonists in Britain, so it was under no constitutional threat, but there were of course strong links, particularly with Conservative MPs. Iain Macleod, who was Colonial Secretary from 1959–61, had a brother in the white moderate New Kenya Group, which took part in the 1960 constitutional conference.

Racism at home and the start of pressure for immigration restrictions also contributed to the speed with which Macmillan began to seek decolonisation. If citizenship of the Empire or membership of the Commonwealth meant little, and certainly not freedom of movement within the Empire, this affected Britain's ability to assume a world role. The Commonwealth was also putting pressure on Britain to deal with the problem of white nationalism. Macmillan therefore concluded that Britain needed to take a new attitude towards its colonies, and to speed up change. He appointed Iain Macleod as Colonial Secretary in 1959, and the important decisions about moving quickly towards majority rule were taken in the next two years. Macleod said that any other course would have led to rebellion and civil war, and certainly the example of Algeria, and events in South Africa, where following violent demonstrations at Sharpeville and elsewhere over 70 Africans had been shot by the police, reinforced this view. Official criticism of British actions in Nyasaland (see section 4.5) in the Devlin Report, which said it had become 'no doubt only temporarily, a police state', did the government's image no good either at home or internationally. Meanwhile, the speed of French decolonisation made Britain's ideas on gradual democratisation and independence look ridiculous, while giving France a larger block of allies in the United Nations.

All these reasons combined to change Britain's colonial policy in Africa and most of Britain's black African colonies became independent between 1959 and 1964 (including Nigeria, Tanganyika, Jamaica, Kenya, Nyasaland and Zambia). They all joined the Commonwealth. The Commonwealth was clearly a success, although not simply as a vehicle for continued British influence in the world.

In the Far East, however, events moved more slowly, confirming that Britain had not been suddenly converted to believing it had no further international role. Britain was concerned to preserve its role in the Indian Ocean, as part of opposition to the Soviet Union and communism generally. The confrontation with Indonesia, which was thought to be allied with communist China and therefore a threat to Singapore and Malaysia, absorbed a huge amount of British defence effort and only ended in 1966. At the height of the crisis a fleet of 80 ships was in the Far East, including two aircraft carriers. In January 1962 it was still believed that the main threats to Britain were in Africa and Asia, and therefore that Aden and Singapore were the most important places for British troops to be deployed overseas. The Americans were happy for Britain to maintain its role in the Far East, as part of the attempt to contain communism there.

1. In what ways and why did decolonisation speed up after 1959?

2. How did other European countries manage decolonisation? Compare Britain's situation and response.

Source-based questions: Decolonisation in Southern Africa in the 1960s

SOURCE A

In the twentieth century and especially since the end of the war, the processes which gave birth to the nation states of Europe have been repeated all over the world. We have seen the awakening of national consciousness in peoples who have for centuries lived in dependence upon some other power. Fifteen years ago this movement spread to Asia. Many countries there of different races and civilisations pressed their claim to an independent national life. Today the same thing is happening in Africa and the most striking of all the impressions I have formed since I left London a month ago is the strength of this African national consciousness. In different places it takes different forms but it is happening everywhere. The wind of change is blowing through this continent and, whether we like it or not, this growth of national consciousness is a political fact. We must all accept it as a fact, and our national policies must take account of it.

From a speech by Harold Macmillan, the British Prime Minister, to a joint session of both houses of the parliament of the Union of South Africa in Cape Town, 3 February 1960.

SOURCE B

We shall bring before Parliament a general Enabling bill to deal with the situation. It will, first of all, declare that Rhodesia remains part of her Majesty's Dominions and that the Government and Parliament of the United Kingdom continue to have responsibility for it. It will go to give power to make Orders in Council, to enable us to carry through the policy I have stated.

I think that the solution of this problem is not one to be dealt with by military intervention, unless, of course, our troops are asked for to preserve law and order, and to avert a tragic action, subversion, murder and so on. But we do not contemplate any national action, and may I say any international action for the purpose of coercing even the illegal Government of Rhodesia into a Constitutional posture.

A speech by Harold Wilson, the British Prime Minister, to the House of Commons on the Unilateral Declaration of Independence by Rhodesia, 11 November 1965.

SOURCE C

It is convenient here to mention the Wilson government's wavering over its policy towards South Africa. In Opposition, as Leader of the Labour Party, Harold Wilson had spoken with some eloquence in condemning the apartheid regime of the Republic of South Africa. He had promised that the Labour Party in office would not sell arms to South Africa. In 1963 he said: 'Under Hugh Gaitskell's leadership we condemned the supply of arms to South Africa as long as apartheid continues. That is the policy of the Labour Party today. It will be the policy of the Labour Party when we are called to form the Government of this country.'

Wilson reaffirmed this stand in June 1964. However he refused to go further, to a general boycott of trade with South Africa. The argument used was that such a policy would hit the black South Africans harder than the white minority. On paper it looked a fairly clear and straightforward policy.

From Britain Since 1945: A Political History, by D. Childs, 1992.

---

1. Study Sources A and C.

Using information contained within this chapter explain the meaning of the word and phrase highlighted in the sources.

a) Decolonisation (title)

b) Apartheid regime (Source C).

2. Study Source B and information contained in this chapter.

Given that this just refers to Rhodesia, how significant is this speech in the history of decolonisation in Southern Africa?

3. Study Sources B and C.

Of what value are these two sources to a historian writing about British policy towards southern Africa in the 1960s?

4 Study Sources A, B and C and use information from this chapter to answer the question:

'How successful was British policy towards southern Africa during the 1960s?'

4.8 How does the European Union affect the Commonwealth?

Britain first applied for membership of the European Economic Community (now the European Union) in 1961, though at that stage it believed that it would be possible to combine EEC membership with the system of Commonwealth and Empire trade preferences. When it was first planned, in 1955, Britain had not been interested in becoming involved in forming the EEC, though membership of NATO, of the Organisation for European Economic Co-operation and of the European Payments Union meant it had some connection with European integration. It was the most powerful western European nation, with close connections to the United States, but it believed that membership of a European community could not be combined with the Commonwealth. The European Free Trade Area, including Austria, Denmark, Norway, Portugal, Sweden, Switzerland and Britain – was set up in November 1959 as a way of reducing tariffs and promoting trade between these countries, without destroying Commonwealth links.

Economically, however, the Empire and Commonwealth were turning away from Britain, and Britain's exports to other industrialised nations in Europe were increasing. Overall, however, as the western economies recovered after the war, Britain's share of world exports declined (from 29 per cent in 1948 to 13.7 per cent in 1964). The United States and the EEC countries offered the best future markets for British goods. The sterling area, which had kept Commonwealth trade links strong, finally ended in 1972, following the crisis of the pound in 1967.

As we have seen, when Harold Macmillan became Prime Minister he no longer believed that the Empire was essential to Britain's economy, and instead looked to EEC membership to modernise and expand British industry and its markets. He also believed that this could revitalise British influence in European affairs, without which its importance to the United States would start to decline. This did not mean a complete turning away from the Commonwealth, or from world influence – Macmillan was determined to maintain Britain's independent nuclear deterrent – but Britain could no longer afford to remain outside a revitalised western Europe. Commonwealth interests had to be made compatible with membership of the EEC. In fact France vetoed British entry twice, but when de Gaulle was succeeded by President Georges Pompidou, and the Heath administration accepted the Treaty of Rome, Britain was able to join in 1973.

The turn towards Europe also grew out of decolonisation, as it became clear that the Commonwealth was not increasing Britain's international influence as had been expected. South Africa's exit from the Commonwealth was important to Macmillan's decision to look towards Europe. Interestingly, as the Conservative Party became pro-Europe in the late 1960s, many in the Labour Party became more attached to the Commonwealth. It was seen as a promoter of international peace and a third way between capitalism and communism, while it was feared that the EEC would restrict a Labour government's freedom of socialist action in domestic policies.

The other countries in the EEC had withdrawn from their colonies, some extremely abruptly, such as France leaving Africa at the end of the 1950s and Belgian withdrawal from the Congo in 1960. The Netherlands had lost the East Indies, but experienced economic growth in the 1950s. So maintaining colonies in New Guinea and the Caribbean came to seem unnecessary. For Portugal, during the 1950s and 1960s, European markets became more and more important to the economy, and when its dictatorship was overthrown in 1974, the new Portuguese government withdrew from Africa as it too turned towards the EEC.

Although Britain may not have seen membership of the EEC (now the European Union) as conclusive withdrawal from the Commonwealth, it was a permanent and highly important reorientation of Britain's interests, economy and world role. During the 1970s, the value of all British exports rose about five times: the value of exports to EEC countries rose about eight times. The freedom of movement of people which had once been the characteristic of the Empire was now freedom to move within the European Union. At the end of the 20th century, although Britain was sometimes a reluctant partner in Europe (as over the single currency), it had enthusiastically promoted other areas of integration, such as the Single Market. The European Union will occasionally act to try to protect trade with former colonies, as it did in the 1990s over bananas from the Caribbean, against efforts (in this case by the United States) to open up the European market completely. In recent years it has developed agreements on trade with Commonwealth countries and the former colonies of other nations, as world trade generally has opened up. Nonetheless, the importance of the European Union to Britain, and the relative unimportance of the Commonwealth, would have astonished the politicians of the 1940s and 1950s.

1. Did joining the European Community mean the end of the Empire? Give reasons.

2. Was the Empire a principal reason for Britain not joining the EEC when it was first set up? (Use information from chapter 6 as well.)

4.9 Why did Britain fight the Falklands War?

By the end of the 1970s many of the remaining British imperial territories were on the way to achieving independence. The new Conservative government seemed set to follow the well-established path of continuous shedding of overseas responsibilities over which political consensus prevailed. One of Thatcher's first acts was to move resolutely on the Rhodesian issue: after intensive negotiations in London in September 1979 Zimbabwe was created. However, the government's, or rather the Prime Minister's attitude to withdrawal from the Falkland Islands in the Southern Atlantic proved to be different.

The Falklands had been a British colony since 1833 but Argentina had continuously put forward claims. Britain had long realised the need to solve the problem as the islands were a long way away and needed good relations with the regional powers. One option had been to transfer sovereignty to Argentina in return for a long-term lease to Britain to administer the Islands: this was opposed by both the islanders, who insisted on remaining British, and Parliament. After 1979 the pressure on Britain had increased. By March 1982 there were clear signs of Argentina preparing to overtake the Islands by force, yet no British reaction was registered. What is more, the Ministry of Defence had just proposed the removal of *HMS Endurance,* which patrolled the South Atlantic.

All this was probably interpreted by Buenos Aires as lack of British resolve to fight for the Falklands. However, as soon as the Argentine invasion took place on 1 April, a cross-party consensus that Britain should react emerged. The government sent a naval task force immediately. It reached the Southern Atlantic on 25 April. One of the most controversial British acts was the sinking of the Argentine cruiser *General Belgrano* at the beginning of May. The Islands were recovered after less than two months when the Argentines surrendered on 14 June. Britain had achieved victory with a relatively low level of casualties with 255 killed (around 750 on the enemy side) and six ships from the task force of twenty sunk.

The government was accused of negligence and incompetence in handling the problem before the invasion. Indeed, Lord Carrington resigned as Foreign Secretary, although it may be claimed that he was more of a scapegoat rather than the real culprit. In fact, the Foreign Office had warned that in the spring the Islands had been left defenceless. John Nott, the Defence Secretary, also resigned. However, Thatcher came out as the eventual winner. She had been firmly in favour of war and the victory was portrayed more or less as her personal achievement. She triumphantly proclaimed that Britain had ceased to be a nation in retreat and that Great Britain had become great again. This secured her position as a Prime Minister and almost overnight increased the popularity of the Conservatives. It also raised Thatcher's profile abroad and served as an example of her determination and leadership. In stark contrast to Suez, Britain had secured support from regional powers such as Chile, from the United States and even from the United Nations.

That the Falklands War was an exception was confirmed by the relatively smooth process of negotiations regarding other dependent territories, most notably Hong Kong. The 99-year lease from China upon which it was administered was due to expire in 1997. Initially, some sort of renewed lease had been suggested but China persistently demanded the colony back. In 1984, an agreement was reached that for 50 years after the transfer of sovereignty Hong Kong would retain some **autonomy** as a Special Administrative Region whereby its social and economic system would not be altered to copy that of mainland China. However, it was increasingly difficult to believe that China's leadership would honour any Western concepts of economic and political liberalism especially after the cruel suppression of the pro-democracy movement in June 1989. After that incident, all the British governments of both Thatcher and her successor John Major could do was to broaden and speed up political reform in Hong Kong in the hope that democratic practice would be well-established before the transfer. Little could be said in reply to the criticism that Britain was preparing its colony for the biggest mass return of free people to Communism. In 1997 under the last Governor, Chris Patten, Britain handed over Hong Kong to the People's Republic of China, although it had its own self-government guaranteed until 2047.

Autonomy: Self-government.

1. Why did Argentina invade the Falkland Islands in 1982?

2. What impact did the Falklands War have on Britain?

Chris Patten, the last governor of Hong Kong, receiving the Union Flag after it was lowered for the last time at Government House, 30th June 1997

4.10 Why has the Commonwealth survived?

One of the main reasons that the Commonwealth has survived is that it has never been defined too closely and has always been flexible. For example, South Africa was expelled in 1961 officially for being a republic (and really for the Sharpeville massacre), but India is a republic and also a member: the rules were changed for it in 1949. The Commonwealth offers an extraordinary combination of countries, which would not normally have an international voice, the chance to meet and have their say. The row over whether or not there should be sanctions against South Africa over its apartheid regime may have seemed to threaten to pull the Commonwealth apart, but in fact offered the former colonies a welcome chance to make Britain listen to their views.

There is no fixed Commonwealth constitution, though now there is the Harare declaration on good government and human rights of 1991, which all members are supposed to adhere to. Decolonisation may have failed to establish democratic self-government everywhere, but the Commonwealth has worked towards this. Nigeria's membership was recently suspended when there was a military coup, and it was welcomed back when elections had been held and a civilian regime re-established. South Africa, having ended apartheid, rejoined in 1994, and the 1999 Commonwealth Heads of Government meeting was held in Durban. Like the UN and the Organisation for Security and Co-operation in Europe, the Commonwealth Secretariat sends observers to elections and attempts to encourage and enforce democracy in the member countries. In the mid-1960s the Commonwealth also kept up pressure on the rebel white minority government in Rhodesia and helped train some 4,500 Zimbabweans in the professional skills they would need on the day of majority rule.

There are economic benefits to being a member of the Commonwealth, which has funds to help its poorer members – for example, the Commonwealth Fund for Technical Co-operation (CFTC), which was set up in 1971. This supports many industrial schemes, improving output and creating jobs. Britain contributes 30 per cent of its budget, which was £25 million in 1996–97. The Commonwealth Development Corporation (CDC) is a public corporation sponsored by the UK to assist developing economies, with £1.2 billion directly invested in over 400 businesses in the 55 countries. Separately, over half of British bilateral aid goes to developing countries in the Commonwealth. The Commonwealth includes 13

Prince Charles tours a slum near Kampala during the Commonwealth Heads of Government meeting in November 2007

of the world's fastest growing economies and 14 of the world's poorest. To help developing states, Commonwealth experts advise on national debt problems, economic restructuring and other macroeconomic questions. Targeting smaller businesses, the Commonwealth Secretariat carries out feasibility studies, transfers know-how and helps with education and training.

By 2007 the Commonwealth was an enormous association, made up of 30 per cent of the world's population. It may be too large to be a trading bloc and too diverse to have a single voice in world affairs, but on some issues – such as Nigeria – it can make its views heard and back them up with sanctions. Connections between its various countries, through educational exchanges, development aid, grants and advisory commissions are encouraged, and it may have developed the links between, for example, different countries in Africa, not least through opposition to white rule in Rhodesia and South Africa. It continues to evolve, and has become a success, though not quite in the way Britain originally envisaged, to the extent that membership is prized and has even been extended to Mozambique, a former Portuguese colony. Part of its success in retaining and improving its functions has been the informal nature of many of the contacts and discussions that go on. The 1999 meeting of Heads of Government believed that the modern Commonwealth, which had then lasted 50 years, remained strong and relevant and 'renewed their commitment to the Commonwealth's fundamental political values of democracy, human rights, the rule of law, independence of the judiciary and good governance. They reiterated that fundamental political values and sustainable development were interdependent and mutually reinforcing, and that economic and social progress worked to enhance the sustainability of democracy. They called for increased international co-operation to support democracies in achieving benefits for the poor' and considered that the Commonwealth offered one important way of doing this.

1. How far does the present Commonwealth fulfil Britain's aims for it in 1947?

2. Does the present Commonwealth matter? Explain why or why not.

3. Has the Commonwealth influenced British government policies? Give examples to support your answer.

Further Reading

Articles

'Controversy: Did Suez Hasten the End of Empire?' *Contemporary Record*, (Vol. 1 No. 2, Summer 1987), Institute of Contemporary British History

'Suez – What the Papers Say', by Peter Hennessy and Mark Laity, *Contemporary Record*, (Vol. 1 No. 1 Spring 1987), Institute of Contemporary British History

For more advanced reading

Britain and Decolonisation by John Darwin (Macmillan, 1998)

British Decolonisation, 1946–97 by David McIntyre (St. Martin's Press, 1988)

Decolonisation and the British Empire 1775 to 1997 by D. George Boyce (Macmillan, 1999)

Decolonisation: The British Experience since 1945 by Nicholas J. White (Longman, 1999)

Industrialisation and the British Colonial State by Lawrence Butler (Cass, 1997)

The Lion's Share 1850–1995 by Bernard Porter (Macmillan, 1996)

The Pursuit of Greatness: Britain and the World Role 1900–1970 by Robert Holland (Fontana, 1991)

5 British foreign and defence policy, 1945–2007

Key Issues

- What factors explain Britain's decline as a world power after the Second World War?

- Why has Britain's foreign and defence policy been so closely bound with the United States since 1945?

- How far did the collapse of Communism affect Britain's foreign and defence policy?

- How did the events of September 11th, 2001 affect British foreign policy?

5.1 Historical interpretation: What caused a 'cold war' to develop after 1945?

5.2 How did British foreign policy re-adjust to political and military realities after the Second World War in 1945–1951?

5.3 How successful was Britain's search for nuclear capability, 1951–1956?

5.4 Why did Britain's dependence on the United States increase between 1957 and 1964?

5.5 How similar were the foreign and defence policies of the Labour and Conservative governments between 1964 and 1979?

5.6 How important was Margaret Thatcher's policy in 1979–1990 for the end of the Cold War?

5.7 In-depth study: Iron Lady or American Poodle – which best describes Thatcher's foreign policy?

5.8 How did the end of the Cold War affect British foreign policy after 1990?

5.9 Yugoslavia, Afghanistan and Iraq: The Blair Years, 1997–2007

Framework of Events

1945–1947	Installation of pro-Soviet Communist regimes in eastern Europe
1946	Soviet pressure on Iran and Turkey
	August: McMahon Act
1947	February: conclusion of the peace treaties with the former German satellites
	March: Truman doctrine
	March: Dunkirk Treaty between Britain and France
	June: Announcement of Marshall Plan
	September: Formation of Cominform
1948	March: Conclusion of Brussels Treaty
	June: The Berlin blockade (ends May 1949)
1949	April: Conclusion of North Atlantic Treaty
	August: First successful Soviet atomic explosion.
	October: Mao's Communist victory in China
1950	June: Start of Korean War (armistice July 1953)
1952	May: EDC Treaty signed
	October: Britain's own atomic explosion carried out
1954	April – July: Geneva conference
	September: South East Asian Treaty Organisation established
1955	May: West Germany entered NATO
1956	April: Khrushchev's visit to Britain
	July – November: Suez crisis
1957	March: Macmillan and Eisenhower meet in Bermuda
	October: Sputnik launched
	October/November: Macmillan, Eisenhower, Washington meeting. Declaration of Common Purpose

1959	September: Khrushchev makes a tour of the USA
1960	May: Paris summit collapses after U-2 incident
1961	June: Kennedy meets Khrushchev in Vienna
	October: Berlin crisis
1962	October: Cuban missile crisis
1964	October: China tests its own nuclear bomb
1967	Johnson meets Soviet Premier Kosygin
1972	Nixon visits Beijing and Moscow; SALT I signed
1979	December: Soviet troops invades Afghanistan
1981	Martial law declared in Poland
1982	April –May: Falklands War
1983	Strategic Defence Initiative launched
1984	British-Chinese agreement on Hong Kong
1985	March: Mikhail Gorbachev becomes leader of Soviet Union
1986	October: Soviet-US summit in Reykjavik
1987	February: Thatcher's visit to Moscow
1990	October: Re-unification of Germany
1991	January: The Gulf War
	August: Dissolution of the Warsaw Pact and the Soviet Union
1995	May: Paris agreement between NATO and Russia
	November: Dayton accord to restore peace in former Yugoslavia
1998	British involved in NATO Kosovo operation
	December: Operation Desert Fox
	Anglo-French agreement on defence co-operation
1999	Hungary, Czech Republic and Poland join NATO
2001	September: 9/11 attack on USA
	Britain joins US in global war on terror
	Britain participates in overthrow of Taliban regime in Afghanistan
2003	March: Britain joins USA in invasion of Iraq
2003–	British troops involved in occupation of Afghanistan and Iraq.

Overview

Marxist-Leninist: Lenin's interpretation of Marx's basic socio-economic theory which claims to take into account the development of European capitalism at the turn of the century and also to adapt it to Russia's specific conditions. It saw the current stage of the development of bourgeois society as the most advanced and therefore the last one before the imminent workers' revolution and accordingly called for the organisation of highly disciplined and militant Socialist parties to educate workers and lead their struggle.

THE Cold War was seen as a period of heightened tensions derived from confrontation after 1945 between the opposing ideologies of the supporters of free markets and democracy – the United States, Britain and the Western Allies – on the one hand and the **Marxist-Leninist** communist bloc led by the Soviet Union on the other. It is called the 'cold' war because it was not a 'hot' war fought with weapons. Instead it mainly involved propaganda, subversion and attempts at **destabilisation** of adversaries. A number of hot wars were fought between **superpower-proxies** on the periphery in the third world and never led to armed conflict between the superpowers themselves.

Although not a superpower, and seen as being in relative decline since the Second World War, Britain was not a negligible force. It was to become the world's third nuclear power maintaining numerous overseas defence commitments. It is, even now, one of the world's largest economies, with an international currency, and

Destabilisation: Undermining the existing order by creating political, social or economic tensions and unrest.

Superpower-proxies: Countries acting on behalf of the Superpowers, e.g. North Korea and North Vietnam for the USSR.

global interests. However, growth in Britain's economy was insufficient to permit the funding of an independent defence policy to underpin responsibilities that derived from Commonwealth relationships and colonial possessions. Therefore Britain chose two strategies to fight the Cold War and to project her interests. One was to operate by means of alliance diplomacy: through the North Atlantic Treaty Organization (NATO), the Baghdad Pact, later the Central Treaty Organisation (CENTO), the Australia, New Zealand and Malayan Defence arrangement (ANZAM) and the South East Asia Treaty Organisation (SEATO). The other strategy was to become the close ally of the United States. The Anglo-American relationship has fluctuated in warmth, but throughout the second half of the 20th century defence and espionage links have been developed and maintained.

Bipolar: Divided between two different ideologies.

In the context of the **bipolar** world of the Cold War, British foreign policy and defence policy formulation were closely related. After the Second World War the British government decided that Britain must retain 'a seat at the top table' in international diplomatic relations. The key to this was nuclear capability. Denied the continuation of nuclear research and development with the United States by the McMahon Act of 1946, a British nuclear capability was developed unilaterally, with the first bomb being detonated in 1952. Anglo-American research and development co-operation resumed from 1957, even though the British government and Chiefs of Staff saw independent nuclear capability as the means to influence American defence (and especially nuclear) policy formulation. Moreover, nuclear capacity was also seen as the means to compensate for the manpower reductions which were an integral part of the cost-cutting 1957 Defence White Paper. Funding problems also led to the 1960 decision to cancel the British *Blue Streak* missile and rely on the United States to provide delivery rockets for British-made nuclear warheads.

The high points of Anglo-American diplomatic co-operation were the Bevin-Truman understanding, the Macmillan relationships with US presidents Eisenhower and Kennedy and the Thatcher-Reagan partnership. It is notable that at other times, Britain's global role has been more low-key. The lowest points of post-1945 Anglo-American relations, the Wilson-Johnson and the Heath-Nixon relationships co-incided with the period when Britain was deemed to be in the greatest decline.

Nevertheless, throughout this period Britain has managed to maintain a significant international profile and has remained one of the world's major military powers.

Explain how each of these contributed to Britain's changing role in international affairs, in the period 1945 to 2007.

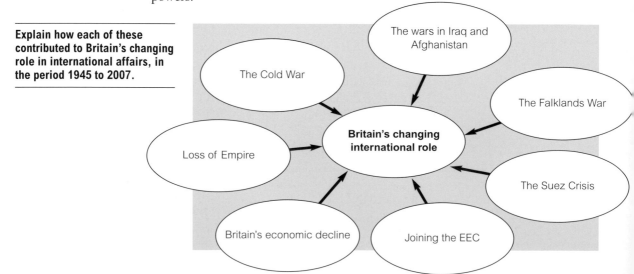

5.1 What caused a 'cold war' to develop after 1945?
A CASE STUDY IN HISTORICAL INTERPRETATION

The historiography of international relations in the post-war period has been largely preoccupied with the policies of the Three Big Allies towards each other. Historians have been predominantly concerned with a number of political developments, mostly in Europe, trying to assess their importance in the origins of the Cold War. Two schools of thought – traditionalist and revisionist – initially offered opposing views of the causes and nature of the controversy. The former developed after the Second World War and entirely blamed the Soviet Union, which was intent on world domination and motivated by its militant Marxist-Leninist ideology. Soviet behaviour in eastern Europe and the Middle East was given as evidence. This aggressive conduct was variously explained by traditional Russian strategy, the nature of the Communist regime and even Stalin's personality. The traditionalists believed that Britain and the United States only reluctantly conceded Soviet domination over eastern Europe because they recognised their own inability to prevent such a development. The West was credited with continuing to uphold the values of democracy and human rights as outlined in the Atlantic Charter and the Yalta Declaration, even after Western recognition had been granted to the Communist governments.

The revisionists who advanced their theories in the period after the Vietnam War argue that the Soviet Union had a legitimate right to dominate the countries lying to its west. They pointed out two precedents – at the end of the war Britain and the United States did not allow equal Soviet participation in the administration of Italy, and the two also insisted on exclusive control over Japan. The revisionists also argued that the tensions between the two Western Allies and the USSR were made worse by actions such as issuing the Truman Doctrine and the Marshall Plan. These were seen not only to have condemned Soviet behaviour in eastern Europe but also to have been correctly understood by the Soviet leadership as part of a campaign to force the Soviet Union out of eastern Europe.

A later trend in historiography, called 'post-revisionism', challenged both traditionalists and revisionists. It tried to introduce new sources as well as new ideas, mainly the theory of mutual misunderstanding and misconception of each other's objectives. Influential works in this category are those of Vojtech Mastny who discussed Soviet foreign policy during 1941–47 in terms of 'the intricate relationship among Moscow's military strategy, diplomacy and management of international Communism'.

Post-Communist Russian scholars attempting to analyse newly-available documents have interestingly had the same debate. Some come to the conclusion that senior Russian diplomats were guided mostly by geo-strategic considerations rather than desire for communisation of Europe. Others claim that careful examination of the interaction between the ideas of world Communism and Russian imperialism reveals that the two were not necessarily contradictory; in fact it is even possible to perceive them as complementing each other.

As the bulk of historical literature on the Cold War originated from the United States it dealt mainly with the Soviet-US controversy and treated Britain as the junior partner in the Atlantic relationship. Such a view was reiterated by the British historian Elisabeth Barker who in *The British between the Superpowers, 1945–50* (1983) described Britain's position 'between the superpowers' as being motivated by a growing concern for its own weakness and acknowledgement of its limited ability to influence world events and pursue independent policy. In contrast, Anne Deighton in *The Impossible Peace* (1993) traced the roots of British post-war diplomacy back to the patterns of wartime thinking and planning. She claimed that it was vital for the interpretation of British policy to understand that Britain regarded itself as a Great Power able to determine the course of events in Europe. Above all Britain justified its right to do so not by its military or economic strength, but because of its expertise in international affairs.

---

1. What different interpretations explaining the start of the Cold War have been made by historians?

2. Explain why historians have differed in their views.

5.2 How did British foreign policy re-adjust to political and military realities after the Second World War in 1945–1951?

In July 1945, even before the hostilities in Asia had ended, a general election took place in Great Britain. Returning a Labour majority to the House of Commons, the British public demonstrated a significant swing to the left that became characteristic across Europe. After the deprivations of the war, the Labour Party received an unequivocal **mandate** for a speedy economic reconstruction and above all for a welfare-oriented domestic policy. This caused both domestic and foreign observers to wonder whether the new government might not also follow a socialist foreign policy in tune with its welfare and nationalisation programmes. Stalin was shocked by the British electoral result when Churchill had to step down in the middle of the Potsdam conference of Allied leaders (17 July – 2 August 1945).

Mandate: Right or authority given to carry out specific policies.

Stalin, however, could confirm his distrust of any kind of socialists as both Britain's new Prime Minister Clement Attlee and Foreign Secretary Ernest Bevin were strong opponents of communism. Bevin especially had fought the communists who had tried to overtake the Labour-dominated trade unions and was suspicious of communist methods in international affairs. Both Labour leaders had been members of the wartime National Government and were aware of the tensions rising among the Allies towards the end of the Second World War. They were convinced that Britain should preserve its Empire and the Great Power status associated with it. This belief continued to be the underpinning principle of British foreign policy.

Britain faced a number of problems as a result of the Second World War, most notably economic ones. Even though the country's share in world trade had been continuously declining since the end of the 19th century, the 30 per cent decline in the value of exports between 1938 and 1945 was unprecedented. Almost all foreign assets held in Britain by private individuals and companies had been sold off to finance the war. A debt of £365 million was owed to the Empire for materials supplied in the course of the war but it was small in comparison to the £31 billion Britain owed the United States for deliveries under the Lend-Lease agreement. Combined with the huge domestic spending necessary for the implementation of the welfare reforms all this precipitated a severe **balance of payments crisis** throughout the later 1940s.

Balance of payments crisis: When the money earned from exports is less than the money spent on imports a country has a balance of payments deficit. The size or continuation of the deficit can cause a crisis.

Demobilisation: Returning soldiers to civilian status.

This situation added to the pressures for rapid **demobilisation**. Indeed, between 1945 and 1948 the number of armed forces was cut fivefold to under 1 million. The level was well above that of the inter-war period but it had to be kept up as British troops were stationed in over 40 countries across the world. To maintain the size of the army in April 1947 the Labour government introduced 12-month national service; its length was extended to 18 months in 1948 and to two years in 1950.

Why did Britain and the Soviet Union clash over Eastern Europe?

Big Three: Winston Churchill representing the British Empire, Josef Stalin representing the U.S.S.R. and F. D. Roosevelt representing the U.S.A.

Britain's wartime dealings with either of its Allies had not been easy. Relations with the Soviet Union had never approached cordiality and there had been a lack of co-operation on anything but military matters. When as early as 1942–43 various British government departments had begun planning for the post-war reconstruction of the world, they had become deeply aware of the need to take into account the global interests of the Soviet Union. Some progress had been made at the **Big Three** conferences at Teheran, Yalta and Potsdam as well as at high-level Anglo-Soviet meetings, notably the one between Churchill and Stalin in Moscow in October 1944. However, after the defeat of Germany, there remained a number of outstanding political questions with Soviet Russia. To those were added new spheres of friction, springing mainly from the Soviet Union's behaviour in its zones of occupation in Europe.

At Yalta (4–11 February 1945) the Allies had signed a joint declaration calling for the establishment of broadly representative governments and the conduct of free elections in all of Germany's ex-satellites. However, at the very moment he was assuring the West of his democratic intentions, Stalin was working towards the elimination of democracy in eastern Europe. One instrument for this was the Allied Control Commissions (ACC) set up to oversee the implementation of armistice terms with Bulgaria, Romania and Hungary: they were headed by high-rank Soviet commanders and used for the promotion of Soviet interests.

How does this show how the world was divided by the Cold War?

Throughout the war Stalin had emphasised the need for the Soviet Union to increase its security through the establishment of friendly governments in the countries along its western borders. The United States

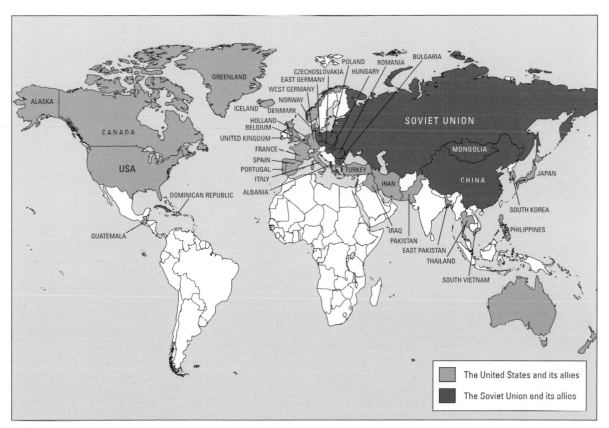

The world during the Cold War.

and Great Britain recognised this as a legitimate demand. They were prepared to accept an increased degree of Soviet influence over the external relations of its immediate European neighbours but did not consider this incompatible with the application of democratic principles in domestic politics. In contrast, in the view of the Soviet regime security could only result from the establishment of governments that shared its own ideological outlook. In consequence, the Soviet authorities backed the efforts of the local communist parties to secure a leading position in government. Across Eastern Europe, Communists had gained popularity due to their anti-German resistance but nowhere did they hold a parliamentary majority and so had to participate in coalition governments. In direct communication with the Central Committee of the Soviet Communist Party, east European communists used a range of violent methods to gain dominance over the other political parties and gradually eliminate them from effective government.

Coup d'état: An abrupt change of leadership or government, often violent or illegal.

With practically no troops in the region the British government was reduced to watching its worst fears for eastern Europe coming true. In 1945–47 the communists were continuously strengthening their hold over such institutions as the army, the police and the justice system. Already in February 1945, a pro-Soviet **coup d'état** was carried out Romania and in July 1945 a communist-dominated Soviet-backed government was installed in Poland with British and US recognition. The Polish question had been the subject of prolonged controversies between Stalin and Churchill, even though the latter was careful not to jeopardise Soviet-British relations during the war.

The fact that Britain could not stand up to the Soviet Union, even when its traditional allies were involved, demonstrated Britain's declining influence in East European affairs. This was even more clearly shown by Britain's inability to secure the formation of at least broadly representative governments in the former German ex-satellites. In September 1945, Soviet Foreign Minister Molotov went as far as to insist that the Soviet Union had the right to determine unilaterally the political complexion of the post-war governments in Eastern Europe. In Britain's understanding this was a clear breach of the terms of the Yalta Declaration. However, Britain soon realised that any argument on the subject would not change the situation while also straining further overall Anglo-Soviet relations. That is why after the conclusion of the Peace Treaties in 1947, the Labour government chose to recognise the communist regimes in eastern Europe, which effectively meant that Britain was resigned to Soviet dominance in the region.

What was the nature of the Soviet threat?

From the British perspective, the consolidation of Communist power transformed eastern Europe into a Soviet stronghold, which could be used as a springboard for the extension of Soviet influence in the adjoining areas. This raised suspicions as to how far Soviet actions were due to genuine security considerations or by traditional Great Power demands for domination over foreign territories. After 1945, both opinions had supporters in the Foreign Office. Increasingly however, British foreign policy experts subscribed to the view that the Soviet Union was intent on using its strategic gains for the spread of Communism world-wide.

Proof was easily found in Soviet behaviour in the Middle East and the Eastern Mediterranean, both areas of long-term British concern. At the beginning of 1946 Soviet forces were deliberately protracting their withdrawal from the Azerbeijani province of Eastern Persia. After Persia presented the issue for discussion in the first United Nations General Assembly, Soviet troops were finally evacuated in May 1946 but the incident loomed big in British perceptions, not least because of similar Soviet actions in Greece. In that country, historically associated with British influence in the Balkans, elections had been carried out under British supervision in March 1946. The electoral success of the right-wing Populist Party spurred insurgence from Communist-led forces. As in October 1944 Churchill had obtained an undertaking from Stalin not to meddle in Greece, the Soviet Union had no direct involvement in the Greek Civil War. Nevertheless, the Soviet Union continued to voice public criticism of Britain's handling of Greek affairs and even raised the question in the United Nations General Assembly in a move mirroring that regarding Persia. Archival evidence has shown that Stalin had little hope in the victory of the Greek Communists and was therefore reluctant to associate with them.

Simultaneously, just as during the war, the Soviet Union was exerting pressure on Turkey throughout 1945. Soviet demands focused on a revision of the existing friendship treaty between the two countries that would have given the Soviet Union increased influence over the regime of the Straits not only in war but also in peacetime. When Turkey refused, the Soviet Union denounced the treaty and even prepared to invade the country but was dissuaded by the British and US support for Turkey. The Soviet move could be interpreted as nothing but a clear challenge of Britain's strategic interests. This impression was confirmed by a number of subsequent Soviet actions affecting the Eastern Mediterranean such as a demand for a share of Italy's North African territories.

How did Britain react to the Soviet challenge?

Even before the end of the Second World War the British government had realised that it had very limited means with which to counteract growing Soviet domination in Eastern Europe. Therefore, despite frequent public protests to the violent methods of the Soviet-sponsored East European Communists, the Labour government chose not to clash directly with Russia on account of the political developments in the region.

On 6 February 1946 Stalin seemed consciously to exacerbate tensions by declaring at an election rally that capitalism and communism were incompatible and therefore war between the supporters of these doctrines was inevitable. Churchill responded in his speech delivered on 5 March 1946 in Fulton, Missouri, USA, warning that 'an iron curtain' divided the European continent. Churchill's opinion was only that of the leader of the British Opposition. However, as nothing was done in London to refute Churchill's accusations against the Soviet Union, Stalin had to believe them to be also representative of British official views.

In the meantime, the British government continued to support the anti-Communist forces in Greece with measures such as the financial maintenance of the Greek Army. However, Chancellor Hugh Dalton demanded that this stop by March 1947 in view of the deteriorating economic situation at home. In the midst of an extraordinarily severe winter, the British government decided to reduce its imperial and foreign commitments, which were a drain on its limited resources. One consequence was that on 21 February 1947 the British government informed the US Department of State that British aid to Greece and Turkey would end in six weeks.

In 1945–46, the American government had itself increasingly recognised the danger to democracy and capitalist economies from the Soviet Union. However, the American demand for quick demobilisation and gradual disengagement from European affairs created uncertainty as to how far the United States would be willing to support Britain in its deepening conflict with Soviet Russia. This was all the more true for areas of traditional British strategic involvement. On the other hand, Soviet actions in eastern Europe combined with the continuing Soviet pressure in the Middle East had led a number of US diplomatic and military officers to express growing fear of the spread of communism. The announcement of Britain's ending of responsibilities alerted the American administration to the need to contain the Soviet Union within its present zone of influence. As a result, on 12 March 1947 President Truman asked the US Congress to approve $400 million in aid to Greece and Turkey and thus 'support free peoples who are resisting attempted **subjugation** by armed minorities or by outside pressures'.

Subjugation: To place under the control of someone.

What was Britain's role in the division of Germany?

Germany was another area where a major confrontation between the Soviet Union and the western Allies occurred in 1947–48. At the Potsdam Conference (17 July – 2 August 1945) the Allies had decided to share the burden of administering Germany after the war and so each of them as well as France had a separate zone of occupation. It was agreed that food deliveries would be made to the western zones from the predominantly agrarian Soviet zone in exchange for industrial goods. The Western Allies had also agreed to reduce the production levels of German industry.

Occupied Germany and Austria 1945–48

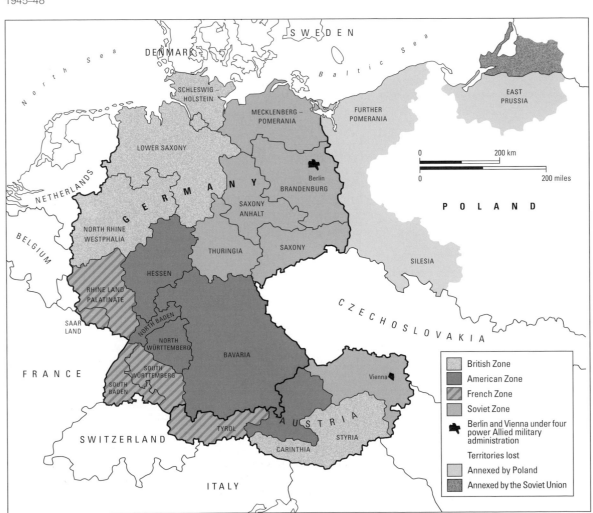

Soviet policy was to extract as much reparations as possible from Germany as compensation for the huge Soviet wartime material losses. Such an approach, although also aiming at reducing Germany's long-term war potential, had the immediate effect of total disruption of what was left of the economy after the devastation of the war. Britain occupied the Ruhr which was the worst damaged part: its maintenance cost the British budget around £120 million in 1946. However reluctantly, Britain and the United States agreed that they should reintegrate their zones and encourage the regeneration of German industry so that Germany could at least partially pay for its needs. On 1 January 1947 the British and American zones were merged into what became known as bi-zonia and later in the year the French zone was added.

The Soviet Union did not approve and accused the West of not honouring its obligations for the treatment of defeated Germany. Moreover, Soviet actions in the eastern part of Germany aimed at securing a dominating role for the communists: clearly Stalin intended to follow the pattern of political developments in Eastern Europe and transform the country into another **Soviet client**.

Soviet client: A country under the influence of the USSR, e.g. East Germany or Poland.

The stalemate over Germany's settlement was a major impetus for the declaration of American economic aid to Europe by American Secretary of State General George Marshall on 5 June 1947. This became known as the 'Marshall Plan'. For Ernest Bevin this was 'like a life-line to a sinking man' and within days he had managed to co-ordinate the positive West European response to the US offer. This however accelerated problems with the Soviet Union, which after some initial hesitation decided against participation in the European recovery programme and also imposed the withdrawal from it of the eastern European countries. Eventually, when the scheme began to function in the spring of 1948, Britain received the largest single share, $3.2 billion, of the $12 billion allocated to Europe by the US Congress.

Throughout 1947 and the first half of 1948, the Soviet Union and the western Allies had continued to work at cross purposes in Germany. Each side was supervising the economy and making separate preparations for the establishment of German government while claiming to be following previous wartime agreements. On 18 June 1948 as a step towards the reconstruction of Germany a new currency was introduced in the Western zone; within four days the Soviet authorities introduced their own new German currency. Next, the Russian troops blocked land access to Berlin (itself deeply into the Soviet zone). Realising that the abandonment of West Berlin would have deep political and psychological consequences, without much initial expectation Britain and the United States hastily organised an airlift of essential supplies. It lasted until 12 May 1949 when both sides lifted the blockade.

How did the European and Atlantic circles of British policy interact?

Cominform: The Communist Bureau of Information which existed between 1947 and 1956. In addition to the Soviet Communist Party it included the Communist Parties of the USSR's Eastern European satellites except Albania and those of Italy and France. Yugoslavia was expelled in 1948. This was an instrument for the co-ordination of the domestic and foreign activities of the members and for their subjugation to Stalin's interests.

In the final stages of the Second World War, the British Chiefs of Staff had concluded that, although not in the position to begin an immediate war, Soviet Russia was the only potential military threat for Britain. Initially this belief had not been fully shared by the Foreign Office, which worried that if the view became known to Stalin this in itself would precipitate hostility. By April 1946 the Foreign Office was convinced that the Soviet Union sought domination of Europe and would put pressure on Western governments, not least through the strong West European Communist parties. This view was sealed by every next Soviet move – the formation of the **Cominform** in September 1947, the Communist coup in Czechoslovakia in February 1948 and the events in Germany later that year.

As it had become increasingly clearer that the post-war world order would not be based on co-operation among the wartime Allies, Britain explored alternative principles for its security. One possibility was to work closer with the West European states, which in the event of Soviet aggression would provide the first line of defence. Another option would be to co-ordinate strategy primarily with the United States, which was the only power capable of facing the Soviet Union on equal terms. In the immediate post-war period the British government had some doubts about the depth of the American commitment to Europe. After the Truman Doctrine and the Marshall Plan, it became more evident that the two circles of British foreign and defence policy – the European and the Atlantic one – were not mutually exclusive. On the contrary, they influenced each other.

In March 1947 Britain signed the Dunkirk Treaty with France: the two countries pledged mutual assistance against Germany and also economic co-operation. After this Bevin continued to seek closer links between the European countries and in March 1948 Britain, France and the Benelux countries signed the Brussels Treaty committing themselves for fifty years to collective defence against any attack. Britain was convinced that the western European countries' initiative to provide for resistance to a possible Soviet attack could only be successful if underwritten by the United States. Days before the conclusion of the Brussels Treaty the US administration began negotiations with a view to placing US involvement in Europe into a definite military and political framework. The United States' growing conviction that its own interest lay in the provision of material support for any regional security organisation in the West which sought to oppose Communism culminated in the conclusion of the North Atlantic Treaty in April 1949. The new alliance, which also included the United States and Canada provided the foundation for British defence policy for the larger part of the next half a century.

British-American post-war relations were already following a particular direction before the formation of NATO. In the economic sphere they had been coloured by the abrupt termination of Lend-Lease in September 1945. However, the US government decided to demand the repayment of only about one-fiftieth of the full amount (£650 million out of £31 billion).

More controversy was caused by the US McMahon Act of August 1946 which put an end to collaboration with Britain on atomic research and development. This was a severe blow to Britain: the atomic bomb had been developed during the war as an Anglo-American project and agreement for consultation and full collaboration had been secured from both Roosevelt and Truman. After the atomic bomb had been used against Japan in August 1945, the very idea of a Great Power was inextricably bound with the possession of nuclear weapons. Immediately after the war, despite its grave economic difficulties, Britain had not lost its self-perception as a world power that had the right to a say in almost every corner of the world. Moreover, unlike the United States, Britain lay within range of Soviet bombers and this was probably the crucial factor that precipitated Britain's decision in January 1947 to develop its own bomb. The necessity for this could only be confirmed when in August 1949 the Soviet Union performed its first successful atomic explosion.

What were the causes and consequences of Britain's involvement in the Korean War?

Containment: A policy aiming to prevent the expansion of Communism and therefore keep Soviet influence within its current boundaries.

The emphasis Britain laid on the US guarantee for the security of Europe presupposed some co-ordination on issues outside that continent. Indeed, the United States retained a generally negative attitude to Britain's ambitions to keep the Empire. In the later 1940s the doctrine of **containment** meant high level of overseas involvement by the United States and its allies. Therefore the United States agreed that Middle East was important. Britain's imperial decline should not allow its former possessions to be infiltrated by Communism: moreover, through its network of military bases from North Africa to Iraq Britain was capable of launching long-range bomb attacks on Eastern Europe and the Soviet Union itself.

In contrast to this understanding was the disagreement on the treatment of China after Mao's communist victory in October 1949. The United States, following a rigid policy of anti-communism refused early diplomatic recognition of the new regime. The British Foreign Office was prepared to shelve its ideological beliefs in the name of good trade with China and also for the benefit of the British colony of Hong Kong. British attitude was additionally shaped by the consideration that normal relations with China could to a degree counter Russian influence there and therefore hinder the enlargement of the Soviet bloc. In January 1950 Britain officially recognised China.

The British-US relationship was finally tested in the Korean conflict of 1950–51. In 1945 Korea had been divided along the 38th parallel where American and Soviet forces had met at the end of the war. In the course of 1949 both the Soviet and the US occupying armies withdrew although the border situation was steadily deteriorating. Additionally, while US attention was preoccupied with developments in Europe and elsewhere in the Far East, in the beginning of 1950 both President Truman and Secretary of State Dean Acheson made speeches implying that South Korea was not included in the American defence perimeter. On 25 June 1950 with Stalin's sanction North Korea invaded the South. South Korea appealed to the UN Security Council. As this body was at the time boycotted by the Soviet Union, American troops were sent in support of the South under UN supervision. Fighting went on for a year and the **38th parallel** was twice crossed first by American and then by Chinese troops, which had entered the war on the side of the North. Although the Soviet Union had not got involved in direct action, it was actively supporting North Korea in the UN Security Council. Although fighting ended in 1951 an armistice was only reached on 27 July 1953.

38th parallel: The political border between North and South Korea.

Western governments believed that the conflict had been started by the Soviet Union and demonstrated Soviet aggressiveness and intention to uproot democratic influences from Asia. Thus, the Korean war assumed the proportions of a clash between communism and liberalism on a global level. In July 1950, British ground and naval troops were sent to Korea. By January 1951 these were more than 10,000-strong, the largest non-American element in the UN force. If Britain strove for continued US involvement in Europe it too had to back the United States in those parts of the world that mattered to the latter. Finally, the British government reasoned that its own participation would have a restraining influence on the United States. Indeed, when in October 1950 the Chinese army overran South Korea, there was a widespread fear that the United States was about to order a nuclear attack. Attlee visited Washington and received a reassurance from Truman that this would not be done without prior consultation with Britain.

The Korean war started the Labour government's plans for massive rearmament which were announced in early 1951. The Chiefs of Staff made the grim prediction of war with the Soviet Union in 1952 or even in 1951. For the first time since the end of the Second World War the total numbers of the armed forces rose. The cost of defence also increased as there was renewed emphasis on research and development, especially in air defence and anti-submarine combat. As a result, defence spending, which had constituted 8 per cent of GDP in 1950, rose to 14 per cent in 1951. This became one of a number of factors that brought a balance of payments crisis.

1. How did the Cold War develop in the years 1945 to 1953?

2. Explain how the growth and development of the Cold War affected British foreign and defence policy.

5.3 How successful was Britain's search for nuclear capability, 1951–1956?

Peaceful co-existence: The possibility for two opposing systems built on clashing ideologies to exist simultaneously without seeking domination one over the other. This is largely associated with the changes in Soviet foreign policy after the death of Stalin when the new leadership took a less confrontational line towards the West.

In October 1951, the Conservative Party returned to power and once more Churchill became British Prime Minister with Anthony Eden his Foreign Secretary. The problems inherited from Labour in the international field by far exceeded the worst fears of 1945. Not only did it seem that communism was on the rise world-wide but Britain's capacity to carry out an independent foreign policy was reduced. The British position was further complicated when in November 1952 General Eisenhower won the US presidential elections on a anti-Communist Republican agenda. Just two months after Eisenhower assumed office Stalin died on 3 March 1953. When Stalin's successor Malenkov spoke of the possibility for **peaceful co-existence** between different socio-political systems, Churchill saw an opening to present Britain as the mediator between the two superpowers.

What was Britain's contribution to the resolution of the conflicts in Asia?

The immediate concerns of the Conservative administration were those of its predecessor. While Britain was experiencing difficulties in maintaining its imperial positions in Asia, it seemed that this part of the world was at the forefront of the Cold War.

The Korean crisis was still unresolved: in October 1951 armistice talks had begun in earnest but were painful and prolonged as both sides used any excuse to resort to minor shows of force. When in early 1952 Churchill visited Washington, he discussed this situation with Truman and declared that 'prompt, resolute and effective' measures would be taken if either side in Korea broke the truce. It was on 27 July 1953 that finally hostilities ended.

Among the conflicts in Asia those in British Malaya and French Indo-China were similar in that the two imperial powers were struggling against communist insurgents. The United States had already supplied the French with over $1 billion worth of military aid, transport aircraft and military advisers. In early 1954 the militant new Secretary of State, John Foster Dulles, considered the use of nuclear strikes in Vietnam. Such a step however required strong support from the United States' allies and Britain for one was not prepared to extend it. After this opposition, Eisenhower himself decided against using 'those awful things against Asians for the second time in less than ten years'. After the French collapse in Vietnam, Eden became the leading international politician to campaign for a multilateral peace conference on Asia. It never took the form intended by him as the **belligerents** and their protectors could not agree on the agenda or even who should be represented. Nevertheless, in Geneva between April and July 1954 some steps were made towards the resolution of the conflicts in Asia. All troops should be withdrawn from Laos and Cambodia: the 17th parallel was confirmed as the line of cease-fire in Vietnam. No solution was found for the political future of Korea. Partly, the success of the conference lay in the fact that it had met at all. On the other hand, the conference was yet another reminder that the issues of the Cold War in South East Asia, the Far East and Europe had become inextricably merged. In the wake of the Geneva conference, in September 1954 the South East Asian Treaty Organisation (SEATO) was established as a defensive alliance, jointly guaranteed by the United States and Great Britain.

Belligerents: Participants in war.

How did Britain influence the defence of Europe?

A number of proposals were set in motion towards the strengthened defence of the western part of the continent. The initiative never came from Britain but often the British attitude influenced the outcome. The Labour government had been sceptical towards the Council of Europe – set up in 1949 as a forum for the debate of human rights, individual freedoms and the rule of law – as it had no legislative powers. Britain had more sympathies for the Schuman Plan put forward by the French Foreign Minister in mid-1950 but had not joined the European Coal and Steel Community to which it led in April 1951.

Churchill's peacetime government became more entangled in the fortunes of the Pleven Plan produced in October 1950 by the French Defence Minister. It saw the foundation of a European Defence Community (EDC) with a European parliament and defence minister. The crucial element was that this organisation would have its West European Army which would also include a West German brigade. It had been for some time widely recognised by all European governments, including the French and the British, that because of its rapid economic recovery and central geographic position Western Germany would play an important role in the defence of Europe. Even so, when in May 1952 the EDC treaty was signed by six west European countries, Britain abstained. Britain's reservations towards the process of European economic and military integration sprang from the perception that an overwhelming commitment to Europe might have a limiting effect on British global responsibilities. Furthermore, as the United States was assuming more burdens world-wide and closely guarding its nuclear programmes, Britain was worried about the strength of the US commitment to Europe.

Indeed, it was under US pressure that Britain had to reconsider its decision regarding the EDC. Yet just when Eden had negotiated treaties of British association and agreed to place a British division in the EDC corps, in August 1954 the French National Assembly refused to ratify the EDC treaty and thus effectively put an end to the whole idea. This pleased the Soviet Union which had tried by resuming negotiations over Germany and Austria to slow down if not to prevent their reintegration on the Western sphere. At the same time the United States had made its desire for the rearmament of Germany clear and had reached an agreement with Britain to this effect. In September the British government initiated consultations regarding German rearmament. Eden proposed that after renouncing its right to nuclear weapons West Germany should be admitted to NATO and to a newly constituted Western European Union. Additionally, in November 1954 Britain signed an agreement committing to the defence of Europe through the same framework, immediately assigning 50,000 British troops for the purpose. The achievement of these efforts was the fact that finally US participation in the defence of Europe was firmly secured with the stationing of more than 300,000 US troops in Europe. In response West Germany entered NATO also in May 1955.

Was there an Alternative to Nuclear Strategy?

Since the final stages of the Second World War the plans for Britain's defence had recognised the importance of the alliance with the United States. However, it was evident that Britain itself was heavily dependent on the United States. Furthermore, while Britain could portray itself as holding the ring between Europe and the United States, it could be argued that for the United States Britain's main value was as a base for European defence.

The Berlin crisis of 1948 had seen the return of American bombers to Britain, some of them with nuclear capability. This made it essential that the air bases in Britain should be used as a result of joint decision and in January 1952 Churchill extracted a sort of a promise from Truman to that effect.

The major issue, however, was related to the production and use of the nuclear deterrent itself. President Eisenhower favoured closer links with Britain but was able to convince Congress to make only minor amendments to the McMahon Act. It seemed that Britain had little choice but to follow an independent nuclear strategy. This had bipartisan support and was obviously enhanced by the first successful test of Britain's own atomic bomb on the Monte Bello islands in the Pacific in October 1952. By then Britain had also acquired its own nuclear strike force as long-range V-bombers came into service.

However, soon afterwards Britain was once again left behind in the arms race by the superpowers: by 1953 both the Soviet Union and the United States had built **H-bombs**. In 1955 Britain announced its intention to produce the new weapon. Defence strategists argued that because it made the stakes so high, the new deterrent significantly reduced the risk of war on a major scale. Churchill and Eden also thought that with the invention of the H-bomb a turning point had been reached and the moment had arrived for practical schemes for disarmament. For this there was also pressure from public opinion increasingly concerned with the possibility of a nuclear accident and the consequences of nuclear tests.

A major factor bearing on the government's defence policy was the strains it placed on the budget. Britain had to commit to funding for NATO's infrastructure such as airfields, communications and headquarters. Throughout the period the cost of defence was steadily rising, and although atomic energy research was mentioned for the first time in a Defence White Paper in 1953 its costs were not included in the announced spending figures. In 1954–55 the cost of rearmament began approaching the levels at the end of the Second World War.

Churchill believed that at this stage in the development of the nuclear deterrent *détente* was possible. This seemed all the more likely since the new Soviet leadership had made conciliatory gestures to the West in the late spring of 1953 after Stalin's death in March. In April and May 1953, Churchill called for a conference between the leaders of the rival powers. No doubt he was inspired by the example of the wartime meetings of the Big Three, of whom he was now the only survivor. There was little domestic or international support for the initiative – both the Foreign Office and the US administration disliked it. The Soviet Union replied positively but the conditions it placed on the agenda made the conference impossible. Nevertheless, in January 1954 a four-power meeting took place in Berlin discussing the Austrian and German questions. The outcome was an agreement to convene a conference in Geneva that dealt with the South-East Asian settlement.

This momentum for negotiations was also captured when in early 1954 conferences on disarmament were restarted. Judging by the proposals put forward, each side was treating these occasions more as propaganda forums at which public opinion could be courted. Some relaxation in East-West relations did follow, especially after the conclusion of a Peace Treaty with Austria in 1955.

Churchill did not drop the idea of a summit in July 1954 and even suggested the possibility of a personal visit to Moscow. Finally, a high-level four-power conference was held in July 1955 in Geneva but by

H-bombs: The hydrogen bomb was the second generation of nuclear weapon and was more powerful than the first, atomic bomb.

Détente: Decline of tensions between generally hostile countries or blocs of countries. Most often this refers to the period of the mid-1960s and 1970s when better diplomatic relations were established between the Soviet Union and the West

How important was the H-Bomb for British defence policy?

The explosion of Britain's first H-Bomb near Christmas Island in the Central Pacific, 15 May 1957

then Anthony Eden had become Prime Minister. The views represented highlighted the opposed positions of the major participants regarding the security of Europe. The Soviet Union repeated well-rehearsed propositions for a European security treaty and a disarmament programme: Eisenhower outlined a plan for aerial inspection of each other's territory. Trying to bridge the gap, Eden proposed the progressive limitation of forces in Central Europe and a system for the inspection of forces. Essentially the summit failed as did a Foreign Ministers conference also in Geneva in October the same year. This stalemate did not change when in April 1956 Khrushchev visited Britain. The fact that the Soviet Union was claiming a right to be represented in discussions on the Middle East did little to bring it closer to Britain.

How did Britain embark on the Suez debacle?

The Middle East had a central role in Britain's post-war strategy. Not only did it abound in oil and provide traditional routes for British trade but it also linked the two non-communist parts of the world. Military bases there could threaten the Soviet zone in Europe and the Soviet Union itself. In this respect the Suez Canal Zone was of the greatest value with its network of air and naval bases. Although Egypt had been independent since 1936, around 40,000 British troops were stationed there in 1951. After the war Britain had gradually accepted the necessity to withdraw but prolonged negotiations to that end had yielded little progress as Egypt was reluctant to continue to co-ordinate its defence with Britain.

In October 1954 an agreement for a phased, 20-month British withdrawal from Egypt was reached: the Suez base itself would be maintained in peace and in war Britain had the right to re-enter the country. Britain also hoped to draw Egypt to the Baghdad Pact of Middle Eastern countries signed in April 1955 but Nasser opposed it and discouraged other Arab countries from joining on the grounds that it was an instrument of continued imperial influence. It is also certain that the Baghdad Pact challenged the Soviet Union to pay a closer attention to Middle Eastern politics. Nasser established closer relations with the Soviet Union and most significantly began purchasing weapons from the **Warsaw Pact**. In Western eyes this amounted to attempting to turn in the balance of power in the Middle East. Fears of Soviet intentions to make Egypt the starting point for overtaking the whole region resurfaced.

In the long run Egypt's association with the Soviet Union forced the United States and Britain to cancel the Aswan High Dam project, a favourite scheme of Nasser's that they had been funding. In turn Nasser nationalised the predominantly French-owned Suez Canal Company on 26 July 1956. While mediation by Australia and the United States as well as discussion of the question at the UN Security Council failed, urged by Britain and France, Israel attacked Egypt on 25 October 1956. When Britain asked each of the two belligerents to withdraw 10 miles of the canal and Egypt did not comply, the British bombarded Port Said and sent parachute troops in. However, on 6 November Britain had to order a cease-fire and on 29 November it withdrew forces. The reasons for this quick change of heart came when the United States refused to support Britain both politically and economically. The United States voted in condemnation of British actions in the UN General Assembly and did even more damage by putting pressure on Britain's gold and dollar reserves. In addition, the negative attitude of the international community to Britain extended even to all members of the Commonwealth except Australia.

The Suez crisis had been largely of Britain and France's own making. Indeed, the policy of intervention in Egypt had been agreed as early as

Gamal Abdel Nasser (1918–1970)
In 1945 founded the Free Officers movement, which aimed to overthrow the Egyptian King Farouk. Organiser of the successful *coup d'etat* in 1952 and became President of the Interior. In 1954 became President of Egypt.

Warsaw Pact: (1955–91) The military alliance of the Communist countries in Europe and the Soviet Union.

March 1956 and the nationalisation of the Canal Company was only the pretext used to bring the downfall of Nasser. This demonstrated a gross miscalculation of Britain's capacity to influence events in the Middle East. It also had exactly the opposite effect of asserting Nasser's position in Egypt and in the Arab world. The Suez debacle impaired Britain's standing in the United Nations and strained relations with the United States. It alienated the French who claimed that their trust in Britain had been betrayed and questioned the integrity of NATO.

In the long run the Suez adventure came to be seen as the outward expression of Britain's difficulties in accepting the contraction of its empire. Moreover, since there was some Soviet military presence in Egypt the episode could have led to Great-Powers confrontation. The fact that it did not is accepted as a sign that they deliberately restrained themselves. On the other hand, the globalisation of the Cold War was once again highlighted by the unfolding of the Hungarian uprising at the same time as the Suez crisis. The gradual **liberalisation** of the regime in Hungary had taken cue from the Soviet Union's own attempts at **de-Stalinisation**. However, when Hungary proclaimed withdrawal from the Warsaw Pact, Soviet tanks rolled into the country to bring it back in line. After the British intervention in Egypt, the West was in no moral position to criticise Soviet actions. The condemnation of the United Nations had no effect whatsoever on the Soviet attitude.

Liberalisation: Relaxation of political control over economic activities and/or freedom of the individual.

De-Stalinisation: The attempts by Stalin's successors, especially Khrushchev, to put an end to the worst atrocities of Stalin's rule.

1. In what ways did British foreign and defence policy change between 1951 and 1956?

2. To what extent did Britain's international position decline in this period?

Source-based questions: The Suez Crisis 1956

SOURCE A

The Cabinet agreed that our essential interests in the area must, if necessary be safeguarded by military action and that the necessary preparedness to this end must be made. Failure to hold the Suez Canal would lead inevitably to the loss one by one of all our interests and assets in the Middle East.

From the minutes of the British Cabinet on the issue of the Suez Canal, 28 July 1956.

SOURCE B

TOP SECRET

I have given you only a few highlights in the chain of reasoning that compels us to conclude that the step you contemplate should not be undertaken until every peaceful means of protecting the rights and the livelihood of great portions of the world had been thoroughly explored and exhausted. Should these means fail, and I think it is erroneous to assume in advance that they must fail, then world opinion would understand how earnestly all of us had attempted to be just, fair and considerate, but that we simply could not accept a situation that would in the long run prove disastrous to the prosperity and living standards of every nation whose economy depends directly or indirectly on East-West shipping.

From a letter from the President of the United States, D. Eisenhower, to Anthony Eden, British Prime Minister, 31 July 1956.

SOURCE C

The Foreign Secretary said that in his judgement the economic considerations were now even more important than the political. We could probably sustain our position in the United Nations for three to four weeks; but, so far from gaining anything by deferring a withdrawal of the Anglo-French force we should thereby risk losing the good will of public opinion, while all countries wished the clearance of the Canal to proceed as rapidly as possible. On the other hand, if we withdrew the Anglo-French force as rapidly as was practicable, we should regain the sympathy of the United States government; we should be better placed to ask for their support in any economic measures which we might need to take.

From the Minutes of the British Cabinet, 29 November 1956, following the Anglo-French attack on the Suez Canal.

SOURCE D

Worldwide Britain, France and Israel were under intense verbal fire – from friends as well as their usual adversaries. Most of the Commonwealth condemned the invasion. Especially severe was India's President Nehru, who was normally counted on as a good friend of Britain.

In any case after such a colossal defeat for [Eden's] personal policy in his central area of interest, it is hard to see how the [Conservative] party could have allowed him to stay on. Britain really needed a new captain on the bridge to convince world public opinion of its renewed sanity. Added to this Eden was a very sick man. After his holiday in Jamaica, he resigned on 9 January 1957. At the end, in the Cabinet, he had broken down in tears and cried 'You are all deserting me, deserting me'. He was in total collapse weeping unashamedly. Then he went upstairs to compose himself. For such is the agony of power when it denies you. Eden's tragedy was that. He was obviously the victim of history, caught between the old Imperial might of the Empire and its total collapse as a world power.

From *Britain Since 1945: A Political History*, by D. Childs, 1992.

1. Study Source A and use information contained in this chapter.

Why did Britain decide on military action against the Egyptian government?

2. Study Sources B and C.

How far do these two sources agree on the likely impact of a military action by Britain and France to take control of the Suez Canal?

3. Study Sources B and D.

Which of these sources is more valuable to a historian writing about the Suez Crisis? Give reasons for your answer.

4. Study Sources B, C and D and use information contained in this chapter.

To what extent was the Suez Crisis a turning point in British foreign and defence policy in the years 1945 to 2000?

5.4 Why did Britain's dependence on the United States increase between 1957 and 1964?

The Suez affair ultimately removed Eden from office. The Conservative Party, however, retained office under the leadership of Harold Macmillan who became Prime Minister in January 1957. Despite the Conservatives' unpopularity in the wake of the Suez debacle, under Macmillan they consolidated their domestic support and won the October 1959 general election. The new administration certainly felt the effects of Britain's reduced standing in the Middle East, all the more so since Macmillan had previously been Eden's Foreign Secretary. Interestingly enough, Suez did not bring about a major foreign policy review.

That there was no abrupt withdrawal from east of Suez after 1956 did not mean that Suez was an exception or that Britain could hold its imperial positions. However, none of the small regional crises that followed approached the proportions of Suez. Britain's record in the Middle East was chequered. On the one hand, there was a wave towards the termination of general defence agreements or permission to use specific bases, for example in Iraq, Libya and Jordan. The Iraqi government went as far as to suggest publicly that Britain should be expelled from the Baghdad pact, while Syria and Saudi Arabia broke off diplomatic relations with London. On the other hand, British positions in the Persian Gulf were still upheld.

Britain was soon involved in the Middle East again – this time by invitation. During 1957 and 1958, Egypt was successively accused of meddling directly or through Syria in Jordan, Turkey and the Lebanon. The West believed that behind Egypt stood the Soviet Union so when King Feisal of Iraq was overthrown on 14 July 1958, American marines landed in the Lebanon and British troops were sent to Jordan shortly afterwards. Indeed, Khrushchev declared the Middle East to be on the brink of disaster and demanded a summit but his attention was soon diverted elsewhere and at the end of September 1958 the situation had stabilised enough to allow for the Western troops to be pulled out. In 1961 Britain intervened in Kuwait against Iraq but this was a brief expedition that could not overturn the general trend. The logic of the ongoing Cold War demanded that Britain should not voluntarily leave positions which, if transferred to the Communist bloc, would increase its strategic and economic strengths. However, this was accompanied by the belief that caught between domestic difficulties and unable to compete with the economic might of the two superpowers, Britain only stood to benefit from quickly cutting its losses and concentrating on the defence of Europe.

How did Britain's nuclear strategy influence relations with the United States and Europe?

The Suez setback had not occurred because of insufficient military power and after 1956 Britain continued to be an important member of a number of defensive alliances, notably the Baghdad Pact, SEATO, ANZAM (Australia, New Zealand, Malaya) and above all NATO (see map on page 141). However, at the time and during the Suez crisis there had been an ongoing controversy around Britain's defence budget. Each of the three services claimed an increased share of the budget, asserting the centrality of its contribution in the event of an armed conflict. The strategic doctrine of the time still attributed an important role to conventional warfare despite increasing attention to nuclear deterrent. In the five years before 1957 defence had accounted for no less than 10 per cent of GDP, engaged 7 per cent of the working population and used around 12 per cent of the output of metal industries.

Macmillan's administration was intent on introducing changes in defence: it justified them with the state of the economy and recent scientific advancements rather than with the trauma of Suez. The new thinking appeared in the White Paper on Defence, *Defence: Outline of Future Policy*, issued by the new Defence Secretary Duncan Sandys in April 1957. The central proposition was that Britain's military power sprang above all from the possession of nuclear technology, therefore Britain's strategy should also place greater stress on nuclear weapons. The first successful British hydrogen bomb-test had occurred earlier in 1957. As the availability of the new deterrent was also believed to make another global war unacceptable, it was judged that Britain only needed a small central reserve to be able to fight. From the public point of view, the need for conscription and conventional forces was substantially reduced. National service would be gradually phased out by 1960 and the number of troops would be cut by 45 per cent over the next five years, including the British contingent in Germany.

The White Paper pointed out that Britain's economic weakness meant that staying in the arms race would bring bankruptcy. For that reason it considered pooling resources with the continental powers so that a united European force became comparable to both the United States and the Soviet Union. Simultaneously, the centrality of the United States for European defence and above all for British defence was also maintained. President Eisenhower also wanted to mend relations with the British. Both

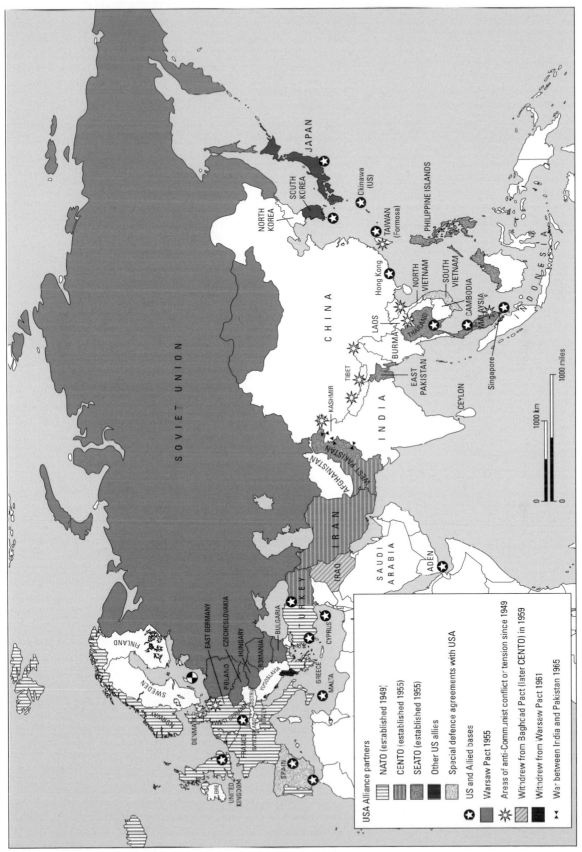

European and Asian alliances 1949–1965

Rapprochement: An increase in friendly international relations.

countries expected **rapprochement** with France as well as drawing West Germany closer. However, at the time France was at war against rebels in Algeria and the reduction of British forces on the continent was causing suspicion towards Britain's European loyalties; Franco-US relations had also suffered in the course of the Suez fiasco. Consequently, the strengthening of the Atlantic alliance seemed like the natural first step towards adjusting Britain's international position.

One lesson of Suez was a need for Britain to retain an independent nuclear deterrent capability which would also enable Britain to influence American defence and foreign policy formulation. In March 1957 Macmillan and Eisenhower met in Bermuda to repair the relationship damaged at Suez. Agreements were signed on intelligence and joint targeting. Sixty American Thor intermediate-range ballistic missiles were to be based in Britain. This had been necessitated by the fact that the V-bombers would become obsolete by 1970 and the supersonic bomber Avro-730, on which the RAF had concentrated, had been cancelled by Sandys. Not only did Macmillan secure the latest technology, he could also claim that Britain had an equal share in the control of the missiles: they would be operated by a dual key, one held by the British, the other by the Americans. Aware of Britain's progress in nuclear fission (nuclear bomb) technology, Eisenhower set up a meeting in Washington. On 3 November 1957 Macmillan and Eisenhower signed agreements providing for exchange of information on design and manufacture of nuclear weapons through the Agreement on Co-operation on the Uses of Atomic Energy for Mutual Defence Purposes, ratified by Congress on 3 July 1958. This had been to a great extent influenced by the successful Soviet launch of Sputnik, the first man-made satellite, on 4 October 1958. This demonstrated that Russia had built intercontinental missiles, a development that had a profound impact on the global balance of power. To drive the message home, in November the Soviet Union launched another larger satellite while a month later an American rocket failed to take off the ground.

The 1957 Washington agreements improved British security. Britain's chief problem was in financing the production of nuclear warhead delivery systems. In 1960 the Blue Streak missile, approved by the 1957 Defence White Paper, was cancelled. Escalating R&D costs did not square with the professed reductions in the defence budget; even more damaging to British confidence was the realisation that the Blue Streak, to be housed in vulnerable land silos, was no longer adequate in comparison to improved soviet anti-ballistic missile defences. In March 1960, meeting with Eisenhower again, Macmillan secured the purchase of Skybolt, an air-to-ground missile to prolong the life of V-bombers. Skybolt could be used with Britain's own nuclear warheads (Britain was – and still is – self-sufficient in nuclear warhead production). The President also promised that in a real emergency the British Navy could have Polaris, a submarine-launched missile. In return Macmillan offered a British base for Polaris at Holy Loch on the Clyde. In 1961 the new US Defence Secretary, Robert McNamara, cancelled the production of Skybolt due to the heavy cost and questionable reliability. Macmillan met with the new US President, John F. Kennedy, at Nassau in the Bahamas in December 1962 to warn him that unless the United States provided a substitute for Skybolt, Britain's participation in NATO would be affected. Macmillan secured Polaris but the whole episode showed that Britain's defence would rely heavily on US delivery vehicles (although Blue Streak technological development continued for satellite launcher purposes, thus enabling Britain to make a timely re-entry into large rocket development – at a later stage – for military purposes if necessary). Kennedy insisted on assigning Polaris to NATO but acknowledged

1968: HMS Revenge, Britain's fourth Polaris submarine is launched from the Cammell Laird yard in Cheshire. The city of Liverpool can be seen across the Mersey.

Britain's right to use Polaris independently where 'supreme national interests' were concerned.

What was Britain's role in the *détente* process?

Parallel to the development of its own deterrent and to Anglo-US nuclear co-operation the British government was also determined to pursue a policy of limitation of nuclear arms referred to as *détente*. The 1958 Defence White Paper took the view that while fear of mutual destruction might preserve peace a preferable option was that the nuclear race should not continue. A system of international control and inspection of nuclear weapons was suggested. Even though a resolution had been approved by the United Nations against Soviet objections, the pace of nuclear tests increased in 1958.

In the late 1950s and early 1960s the superpowers were determined not to let a war spark between themselves. Until 1963, however, the test ban negotiations went on slowly and were interrupted by a series of international crises. That they continued at all was due to the dedication and perseverance of Harold Macmillan. This was especially evident with the onset of the Berlin crisis.

After 1957 Britain had continued to adhere to the idea of a summit. Increasingly the Soviet leadership had linked this with its own insistence on the resolution of the German question by handing over West Berlin to East Germany. As in late 1958 there were signs that the Soviet Union was contemplating the occupation of the city, US Secretary of State Dulles gave a guarantee to fight for it. In turn, Khrushchev forwarded a proposal for making Berlin a free city and when this was not accepted he threatened that the Soviet Union would sign a separate peace treaty with East Germany. As the United States prepared for a potentially nuclear war, the alarmed British Prime Minister visited Moscow for ten days in February–March 1959 and agreed to a **communiqué** calling for arms limitations in Europe. Although Macmillan reduced tensions, his visit sparked off hostility from both West Germany and the United States which accused

Communiqué. An official diplomatic statement, especially one issued to the media.

Britain of appeasing the aggressive Soviet Union. The one positive outcome of the Moscow visit was that it led to a conference of the Foreign Ministers in Geneva, lasting between May and August but totally unproductive. However, it prepared the ground for an exchange of high-level Soviet-US visits – in July Nixon went to Moscow and in September Khrushchev made a tour of the United States. Naturally, this showed some relaxation of East-West tensions and thus corresponded to Macmillan's overall agenda. On the other hand, relations between the superpowers improved. The trend was confirmed when the summit arranged to take place in Paris in May 1960 collapsed after the Soviet Union brought down a US U-2 reconnaissance plane.

In June 1961 Kennedy and Khrushchev met in Vienna but got off to a very bad start and ended up threatening each other with the consequences of a war over Berlin. In the next three months the situation quickly deteriorated. As every week thousands of East Germans were fleeing to the West, the Communist leadership resorted to fencing off West Berlin first with barbed wire and then with a concrete wall. The Soviet occupation troops increasingly obstructed the free movement of Allied personnel across Berlin and the situation worsened until on 27 October Soviet and American tanks faced each other at the line between their sectors. For the 16 hours of the stand-off the danger of a nuclear war was real and although both sides quickly realised that they had overreacted, developments were already under way that precipitated a second nuclear crisis within a year.

In July 1962 the installation of Soviet missiles in Cuba began. Khrushchev's plan was to place short- and medium-range missiles in the United States' backyard and thus create parity with the US long-range weapons. On 22 October President Kennedy informed Khrushchev of a decision to introduce a naval blockade on Cuba in order to prevent the complete equipment of the Soviet nuclear bases there. The US Chiefs of Staff ordered all US forces world-wide to go to a heightened state of nuclear alert, which was substituted to the highest state on 24 October. Khrushchev made it clear that he would resist US actions and was prepared to strike. On 28 October, after an exchange of messages between Kennedy and Khrushchev and after intensive diplomatic activity, the Soviet government announced that it had ordered the dismantling of the sites in Cuba.

Britain's role in the two crises was small. Britain had sought a diplomatic solution to the Berlin question but was forced to follow the United States. At the time of the Cuban crisis, through the British Ambassador Ormsby Gore, Macmillan advised Kennedy to limit the blockade and publish photographic intelligence to prove the Soviet threat to the world. This however cannot obscure the fact that Britain had played only a small part in the overall conduct of the crisis even though Kennedy telephoned Macmillan far into several nights to discuss the issues, regarding Macmillan as his connection to the United Nations and the British Commonwealth. The US decision to remove US missiles from Turkey was again unilaterally taken by the United States even though it directly affected NATO. Nevertheless, Britain remained America's most reliable ally, the third of only four nuclear powers, and with global interests and commitments exceeding those of all states, but the superpowers. Britain and the US co-operated in intelligence operations, foreign and defence policy planning and joint targeting of weapons. Moreover, Britain could claim that throughout 1959–63 it had been the power whose initiative had kept the Geneva negotiations on disarmament going. At the height of the Cuban crisis Macmillan had written to Khrushchev to ask him to reconsider the possibility for a nuclear test ban treaty. Macmillan pursued the treaty with both Kennedy and Khrushchev to the point where, in July 1963, such a treaty was finally concluded.

1. In what ways did Britain's dependence on the United States increase between 1957 and 1964?

2. How successful do you see British foreign policy between 1957 and 1964 as being? Explain your answer.

5.5 How similar were the foreign and defence policies of the Labour and Conservative governments between 1964 and 1979?

How did Britain's withdrawal from east of Suez influence the global balance of power?

When Harold Wilson took office in 1964, he insisted that unless Britain remained a world power it would be 'nothing'. Such a statement was rooted in the understanding that the status of Great Power presupposed the possession of overseas territories. Britain's military presence abroad was justified by obligations undertaken to assist the defence of allies under the Baghdad Pact, SEATO and bilateral agreements with a number of Arab states. The logical outcome of such thinking was that Britain should not give up its role east of Suez. Wilson's views were enhanced by those of the new US President Lyndon Johnson who was keen to maintain Britain's bases east of Suez as the first line of defence for the United States. Indeed, in the summer of 1965 a secret Anglo-American deal was concluded to that effect.

Johnson also hoped for British participation in Vietnam but that was something the British government would not afford. In addition, Britain was faced with a precarious situation in the Far East where in September 1963 68,000 troops had been sent in aid of the Malaysian Federation in its border dispute with Indonesia. The strategic implications of the conflict were immense in view of the rapidly growing threat of Communism in Indochina. Similarly, Britain had been confronted with the serious internal subversion of Bahrain and Kuwait and a prolonged armed insurrection in the South Arabian Federation. If this pattern continued Britain would need to preserve substantial military capabilities overseas. Quite apart from the question of whether Britain's presence was sustainable in the long run in the face of growing nationalism, it was also a constant burden on Britain's financial resources.

The 1966 Defence Review saw the overstretch of Britain's defence capabilities as unjustifiable. It called for a reduction in defence spending from 7 to 6 per cent of GDP. It also emphasised British commitment to NATO as the core of Britain's defence strategy. The first sign was the announcement of a decision to withdraw from Aden within a year. The trend was confirmed by the 1967 Defence Review which stated that a withdrawal from Simonstown was a matter of months, while only core responsibilities would be maintained in the Gulf. However, the government's own schedule was speeded up by the devaluation of the pound caused by the six-day Arab-Israeli war in 1967. Aden was evacuated immediately and it was announced that British forces in Singapore and Malaysia would be halved in 1971 and removed in mid-1970s. As economic problems grew, in January 1968 the Cabinet agreed that spending overseas was the central problem and ruled that defence would suffer further cuts with British forces totally withdrawn from the east of Suez – Singapore, Malaysia and the Gulf – by the end of 1971.

One reason for withdrawal was that it was the end in a long-term process of cutting of imperial engagements caused by rising budgetary pressures. In addition, there was a strong political element reflecting the changes in the government's own attitude. In fact, Britain had turned down the offer of Saudi Arabia and other Arab states to fund continued British presence and the United States had suggested a number of economic measures to support the value of the pound in exchange for continued British commitment. All these proved politically unacceptable.

Heath, as Leader of the Opposition, publicly did not agree with this when in 1969 he pledged himself to maintaining a British presence in the Gulf states, as well as Malaysia and Singapore. This was partly an attempt to distinguish the Conservatives from Labour at least on one issue of foreign policy. Heath believed that he was deriving domestic political benefits by stressing the need to honour international obligations. He also had in mind the threat to stability in the Gulf from the numerous territorial disputes there. Finally, this was the moment when an enormous build-up of the Soviet navy seemed to point to a renewed Soviet militarianism.

The realities of office were however different and having assumed power in June 1970, Heath did not reverse the withdrawal. Indeed, some token commitments were undertaken as for example the sending of a military contingent to Singapore. A presence in Malaysia was also secured and such an arrangement met with the approval of the United States which saw it as an alternative to British involvement in Vietnam.

By 1971 Britain also withdrew from the Persian Gulf. The few remaining facilities were geared towards the protection of Kuwait against Iraq. Until mid-1970 Britain had played the role of a facilitator in exploring the possibility of the smaller states pulling together in some sort of regional defence arrangement. This lost the support of Bahrain and Dubai. In addition, Britain chose to support the United States which preferred Iran as the most reliable local power. This speeded up British withdrawal.

How did defence cuts affect Britain's nuclear deterrent?

Throughout 1964–79 two themes were central in British defence policy: the importance of the nuclear deterrent and the need to control defence expenditure. One of the electoral promises in Labour's 1964 campaign had been that of major reduction on defence spending. Once in government however, Wilson made little change. In turn, the two governments upheld the principles of cost-effectiveness and independent deterrence which had cross-party support in the post-war period.

In Opposition Wilson had called for re-negotiation of the Nassau agreement on terms more favourable to Britain. In December 1963 President Johnson had put forward a proposal for the creation of a multilateral West European force which would include Britain's deterrent. The new Labour governments reacted with underlined coolness. In November 1964 the British tabled a counter-proposal for an Atlantic nuclear force which would combine the entire nuclear forces of the UK and France with those of US nuclear submarines. This was unacceptable to the United States. So just like Macmillan before him, in 1964 Wilson successfully withstood US pressure for making the Polaris missiles based in Britain a part of a NATO nuclear force. This happened at a moment when the danger of **nuclear proliferation** became especially obvious: in October 1964 China had tested its own nuclear bomb. As China was a Communist state, despite its political and ideological differences with the Soviet Union, its acquisition of nuclear weapons was seen as another aspect of the world-wide clash between Communism and democracy.

Nuclear proliferation: The increase in the number of countries possessing nuclear weapons.

Labour completed the reorganisation of the services merging the War Office, the Admiralty and the Air Ministry into one Ministry of Defence headed by Denis Healey. He attempted to introduce cost-effectiveness to the defence budget. In addition, he aimed to reduce defence spending to 6 per cent of GDP. Coupled with the consequences of inflation that made the production and maintenance of military equipment even more expensive, all this led to the cancellation of three major aircraft programmes – a new fighter and transport aircraft, a new strike and reconnaissance aircraft and a new aircraft carrier. In each case a replacement with the American alternative followed and special importance was given to the purchase of the land-based F-111. As far as the nuclear deterrent was concerned, only one out of the five ordered Polaris submarines was cancelled. Against such a background it was not surprising that Healey announced that Britain would not undertake any major war operations except in co-operation with allies.

To the extent that a number of British commitments overseas were maintained in the latter half of the 1960s, Britain's ability to honour them was seriously limited by the substantial cuts in defence after 1964. Even so, further reductions were in order after the November 1967 devaluation of the pound by 14 per cent. The trend was not altered by the Heath government under which defence spending fell to 5.5 per cent of GDP. As the defence commitments in the Far East and South Africa were abandoned, manpower levels were reduced. The navy – most closely associated with imperial presence – lost about one-seventh of its surface fleet. By 1974–75, Britain's strategy was reoriented towards the protection of the Eastern Atlantic and the English Channel as well as contributing significantly to the European Central front mainly by maintaining the British army in Western Germany. This required new naval equipment and new RAF fighters – partially met by the introduction of mini-carriers for helicopters and vertical take-off jet fighters.

However, in the 1974 Defence Review Labour – striving to devote more resources to health, education and social services – once again supported a cut in the defence budget. The announced target was that defence should account for no more than 4.4 per cent of GDP by 1985. Such control of expenditure clashed with the Labour government's acceptance of the centrality of the nuclear deterrent for British security. The issue presented itself with some urgency as Polaris had become obsolete with the technological innovation in the form of multiple nuclear warheads and especially with the improvement of the Soviet anti-ballistic missile systems. Labour had been pledged not to acquire a new generation of missiles but in secret the government approved an updating programme including the deployment of 96 cruise missiles in Britain, something revealed only in 1980. In effect, Labour's decision also renewed Anglo-American co-operation in testing information. Under Heath there had been some controversy regarding Britain's position in the defence of West Germany: Britain needed West Germany to absorb more British military equipment while West Germany's needs were fully covered by US deliveries. A proposal for West German payments to the British Army on the Rhine were politically unacceptable as this would turn British soldiers into mercenaries. In addition, Britain was suspicious of the Soviet-American disarmament talks as they might lead to the scrapping of its own forces under a bilateral superpower deal. This was seen to compromise not only Britain's security. In 1979 Prime Minister James Callaghan agreed to increase Britain's contribution to NATO by 3 per cent annually. Accordingly, new tanks and artillery were ordered while manpower cuts were frozen.

Did relations with the United States decline as a consequence of increased attention to Europe?

Coming to office in 1964 Harold Wilson rejected the 'special relationship' and talked instead of merely a 'close relationship' with the United States. Edward Heath in turn insisted on the existence of a 'natural' rather than special link between the two nations, which should not obscure British involvement with Europe. Throughout the period co-operation with the United States continued on such important matters as intelligence and nuclear collaboration.

The most serious issue dividing Britain and the United States was that of the war in Vietnam. After the Geneva agreements of 1954, the country had failed to reunify and the North was governed by communists with Chinese and Soviet help: the South was also under a dictatorship but an anti-communist one. Communist infiltration in the late 1950s and early 1960s led to growing guerrilla activities in the South that appealed for American aid. Just emerged from the Berlin and Cuba crises, the United States was intent on not allowing the establishment of a Communist stronghold in South-East Asia from which the adjoining countries in the region could also be subverted. After 1961, first President Kennedy then President Johnson sent an increasing number of US troops as 'military advisers'. After the Tonkin Gulf incident in August 1964, the US Congress authorised full-scale US involvement in what was a Vietnamese civil war. This continued until 1973 when the United States signed the Paris Peace accords to disengage from Vietnam with the last US advisers pulling out in 1975 practically defeated. Vietnam played a crucial role in the shaping of subsequent US policy. Throughout the war a source of constant American irritation was the fact that the United Kingdom together with the United States' other European allies failed to contribute a single soldier.

In 1965 when the Americans looked set for further deployment in Vietnam, Harold Wilson requested an audience with Johnson to counsel against further US military involvement. His efforts were deeply resented. The United States failed to understand the British government's position. Labour's anti-American constituency and its thin majority in Parliament accounted for its stubborn resistance to American pressure. 'When the Russians invade Sussex, don't expect us to come and help you', was US Secretary of State Dean Rusk's warning to the British.

A further serious blow to Anglo-American understanding was British behaviour in the Middle East. Following the British decision to withdraw from east of Suez the United States had no choice but to step in so that Britain's place would not be filled by a Communist power. The development was best shown when Britain handed over to the United States the extensive military facilities of **Diego Garcia**. Not only did this increase the American burden but the timing was also awkward. As if all this was not enough, Britain and the United States differed with regard to the ongoing Arab-Israeli conflict which in 1973 erupted in a new war. Egypt and Syria attacked Israel on 6 October, the Day of Atonement (Yom Kippur), the holiest day of prayer and fasting in the Jewish calendar. The Arab countries were seeking to reverse the results of the previous war in 1967 when Israel had captured the Sinai peninsula.

Their initial successes were quickly turned back when Israel recovered from the surprise, rallied its forces and received US support. The latter was severely hindered by the firm refusal of Britain – again together with the other European countries – to allow American forces to use British bases or even fly over its territory to supply Israel. Britain was sensitive to the possible effects on its economy of disturbances of the oil imports from the Arab states, an attitude that did not shelter it from the shocks of the quadrupled oil prices in the wake of the war. The British government also considered that the United States had not shown sufficient interest over the previous three years so that a settlement between the opposing sides was reached. But the all-time low point of relations was caused by the order given on 24 October by President Nixon, or rather his National Security Adviser Henry Kissinger to place US forces at a state of high nuclear alert. Indeed, this was done in response to signals that the Soviet Union was preparing to send forces to the Middle East to help Egypt. However, none of the United States' European allies were consulted even though they would have been the prime target for Soviet retaliation. British Foreign Secretary Alec Douglas-Home was placed in the uncomfortable

Diego Garcia: Part of the British Indian Ocean territory leased to the United States. It eventually became a US airbase.

position of having to defend in the House of Commons the right of the US government to alert its forces without himself being consulted. Finally, the United States and Britain had completely different approaches to the Arab-Israeli settlement after the war: Heath insisted on multilateral talks overseen by the UN, while Kissinger preferred bilateral Arab-Israeli deals overseen by the United States so that the Soviet Union was denied the right of veto.

Britain also played an important secondary role in the continuing process of East-West *détente* in the second half of the 1960s and the 1970s. This was driven by the dual development of improving relations between the United States and China, and West Germany's own **östpolitik** aiming at rapprochement with Eastern Germany, Poland and Eastern Europe and ultimately the Soviet Union. A complicating circumstance ensued from the fact that in 1966 Charles de Gaulle took France out of the military structures of NATO and tried to pursue a relatively independent policy to the Soviet bloc. Although the successive British governments were strongly in favour of measures that would reduce tensions between the two opposing blocs, Britain could rarely take the initiative in this respect. Indeed, Britain was a willing participant in multilateral negotiations but could not fail to realise that the decisions were taken by the United States and USSR. In 1967 Johnson met with Soviet Premier Kosygin and even though the two states were in conflict over Vietnam, the possibilities for starting an arms control process were sounded. This was underpinned by the increased sense in the US Congress that US troops should pull out of Europe. In order to maintain the US military commitment in Europe Johnson had to seek to reduce it by negotiation with the Soviet Union. This made Britain uneasy about America's continued engagement in Europe.

However, as a nuclear power Britain was genuinely committed to a nuclear non-proliferation treaty. The first Wilson government engaged in considerable efforts both to smooth over differences within NATO and to convince West Germany that such a treaty would not either discriminate against it or endanger its security. It was probably this attitude that made the United States at least consult Britain in the course of the preparation for an anti-ballistic missile treaty under the acronym SALT I (Strategic Arms Limitation Treaty). It was signed in May 1972 after Nixon visited first Beijing and Moscow. It limited the deployment of anti-ballistic missiles as well as freezing the deployment of intercontinental ballistic missiles. Britain also played a positive role in the preparation and conclusion of the Helsinki treaties of 1975 which recognised European borders, introduced control of armaments and started a steady growth in trade and cultural links between Communist and democratic countries.

To a great extent the shifts in the Anglo-American relationship were determined by Britain's firm intention to seek increased co-operation with western Europe and aim at entry in the European Community. The process had been influenced by the deteriorating state of the British economy. This was in turn related to a change in defence strategy most evident in the 1969 Defence White Paper which argued that Britain's defence should concentrate on Europe. Moreover, the doctrine of mass retaliation was now being overtaken by that of a flexible response, which in Britain's case required maintenance of small conventional forces, especially in Europe.

Interestingly enough, for its own reasons the United States also approved of Britain's efforts to join the European Community. Both the Johnson and Nixon administrations saw Britain as a useful mediator between Europe and United States. But it was exactly the calculation that made the Europeans, especially France, suspicious of a Britain whose close Atlantic link might disturb the relative harmony of the EEC. In November 1967 de Gaulle made his second veto on British membership

Östpolitik: Foreign policy associated with West German Chancellor, Willy Brandt. It involved an attempt to improve diplomatic relations between West and East Germany.

---

1. In what ways did British foreign and defence policy change between 1964 and 2000?

2. To what extent was British foreign and defence policy still dominated by relations with the United States?

---

in the EEC. That was why Heath, in his successful bid for European membership was doubly careful about the United States. To prove his European credentials Heath responded with caution to Nixon's call in April 1973 for a new Atlantic Charter – he accepted to negotiate only from a common position with the other European powers and was prepared to contemplate French leadership in the matter. He even explored the idea of Anglo-French nuclear co-operation but French abstinence from NATO's integrated command was a hurdle. Therefore, after Britain joined the European Community in January 1973, its foreign policy became more European.

5.6 How important was Margaret Thatcher's policy in 1979–90 for the end of the Cold War?

1979 marked a turning point in British foreign policy with the election of a majority Conservative government headed by Margaret Thatcher. The new Prime Minister with her strong ideological convictions and forceful style had an impact on foreign policy.

Was anti-Communism the focal point of the renewed special relationship?

One of the most distinctive aspects of Thatcher's foreign policy was her dealing with the Soviet Union. In the late 1970s Britain's role in *détente* had diminished while the process itself had also waned. Disarmament had been increasingly handled through bilateral Soviet-American channels but whatever progress had been made lately was abruptly halted by the Soviet Union's invasion of Afghanistan. Military and financial aid had been supplied for months to the indigenous Communists who were themselves divided and faced with serious internal Muslim opposition. Finally, in December 1979, Soviet troops stepped in at the request of local Communists and among Soviet fears that China was involved in the intensifying civil war. In the following years the situation in the Middle East deteriorated further with the outbreak of the Iran-Iraq war in 1980 and the Israeli invasion of the Lebanon in 1982. To the West all these were cases in which the Soviet Union's expansionist aspirations could be detected.

In response to the Afghanistan crisis, President Carter withdrew the SALT II agreement on arms control, which had been worked out the previous year, from the process of Senate ratification. In addition, the United States imposed trade sanctions on the Soviet Union and even tried to co-operate with China in supporting the anti-Soviet rebels in Afghanistan. Amongst the European Allies, Britain was the only one which stood firmly by the United States. In 1981, the new US President Ronald Reagan went much further in that he made anti-Communism the pillar of his policies. Calling for a new-era crusade against the 'Evil Empire' Reagan set about defeating world Communism by economic and military competition. Reagan's outlook, and pro-active leadership made an immediate connection with Thatcher. She shared all the ideological convictions of liberal capitalism. Moreover, she was convinced that NATO was the linchpin of European and British defence and to strengthen it a revival of the special relationship was necessary. The outcome was – in accordance with NATO's decision to modernise its intermediate nuclear forces in Europe – the purchasing of the American Trident C4 missiles, the next generation after Polaris. When the **Pentagon** decided to develop the D5 version of Trident, Britain had little choice but to accept. This certainly illustrated British nuclear dependence on the United States, a

Ronald Reagan (1911–2004)
The 40th President of the United States, Reagan had already had a successful career as a film actor, and then as Governor of California, when he came to power. He was President of the United States from 1981 to 1989. A strong conservative and admirer of Thatcher, he had a similar agenda of tax cutting and 'rolling back the state'. He also believed in 'peace through strength' and hugely increased defence spending in America. A key reason for the collapse of the USSR in the late 1980s was the Russian attempt to catch up with US defence spending.

Pentagon: The headquarters of the US Department of Defense near Washington DC. It takes its name from the outline of the building as seen from above.

Thatcher ensured a strong relationship with Ronald Reagan and the United States, but was it at the expense of Britain's relationship with Europe?

point highlighted by the simultaneous deployment of cruise missiles in Germany in response to the Soviet SS-20s.

The new phase in nuclear rearmament started the recovery of the Campaign for Nuclear Disarmament in Britain, a civil movement that had been dormant since 1960s. It was best known for the women's tent camp at the US air base at Greenham Common. As elsewhere in Europe, where a wave of anti-nuclear movements sprang up, the British protesters adopted a distinctly anti-American outlook. They were also encouraged by the Soviet Union in the hope that the struggle to cope with domestic popular hostility would pose severe strains on the NATO alliance. In Britain, under the influence of the trade unions the Labour Party had already swung far left. In the run up to the 1983 elections Labour made the nuclear issue the central point in its campaign demanding not only the cancellation of Cruise and Trident but also a completely non-nuclear Britain. However, public opinion in Britain was generally less hostile to the deployment than in Europe.

Thatcher also supported Reagan's Strategic Defence Initiative (SDI) launched in 1983. This was a vastly ambitious research project to develop an anti-missile system on the ground and in space to act as a nuclear shield over the United States. The idea was that by intercepting Soviet missiles in space the United States would be able to survive a nuclear attack. The huge resources committed to the programme, known as 'Star Wars', had the immediate effect of increasing the arms race with the Soviet bloc, as the Soviet leadership declared that it would never allow military superiority over the USSR. Thatcher was extremely unhappy about the manner in which SDI had been announced – without consultation with the United States' Allies. After all, the shield over the United States would not extend to the other side of the Atlantic and Britain and Europe would be even more than usually exposed to a Soviet attack. The reservations were publicly expressed by British Foreign Secretary Geoffrey Howe. On her part Thatcher had a stormy meeting with the President at which she secured a joint statement that any stage of implementation of SDI beyond research would have to be negotiated in advance with the Allies. While voicing the worries of the other west European powers, Thatcher again seemed to be demonstrating unique influence over Reagan and such closeness with the United States served to complicate Britain's own relations with Europe. Soon afterwards, Reagan's anti-communism brought huge domestic political embarrassment for Thatcher when in October 1983, without consulting Britain, the United States attacked Grenada, a member of the Commonwealth, to overthrow a Marxist regime. Nevertheless, after a furious telephone conversation between Thatcher and Reagan the 'special relationship' was again patched up. It was forcefully illustrated when in April 1986 US F-111s used British bases to bomb Libya.

After the 1983 re-election the Conservative government increased attention to the Soviet zone. Under the influence of the Foreign Office a policy of differentiation between the members of the Soviet bloc was adopted, which aimed at cultivating the more open regimes of Central Eastern Europe. In fact the trend had appeared as early as 1981 when martial law was declared in Poland in a desperate bid from the local Communist leadership to suffocate political turmoil caused by striking workers and prevent a Soviet invasion. Publicly, Thatcher supported Reagan in imposing sanctions on the Polish government but the practical British measures were relatively mild. On the other hand, the British government openly disagreed with the American policy of forbidding companies to participate in the building of a Soviet gas pipeline from Siberia to Western Europe as this encroached on private and public West European economic interests.

Thatcher's dislike of Communism was combined with a practical approach. The Prime Minister approved of the relative liberalisation measures undertaken by the Communist leadership of Hungary and was openly supportive of the anti-Communist trade unions in Poland. Howe was the first British Foreign Secretary to tour all the capitals of the Warsaw Pact countries in 1985–86. Crucially, Thatcher succeeded in establishing a working relationship with Mikhail Gorbachev, who assumed power in the Soviet Union in March 1985. Over the next years there was a lot of Soviet-British activity in the diplomatic and economic field culminating in the Prime Minister's visit to Moscow in February 1987. All this placed Britain in the position of mediator between the United States and the Soviet Union serving Thatcher's need for a higher profile at home and enabling her to be presented as the supporter of peace, successfully negotiating from a position of strength.

However, for the Soviet Union facing multiplying economic and social problems under the burden of all-out competition with the West, the need for resumed *détente* was a matter of survival. It needed to be taken up with the United States, the protagonist of the Western bloc. Reagan and Gorbachev met in Geneva in November 1985 when they agreed in principle to work towards the Strategic Arms Reduction Treaty to cut their nuclear arsenals in half. After a stream of private communications, the Soviet-US summit in Reykjavik in October 1986 confirmed the agreement in principle to scrap all intermediate-range missiles from Europe, both NATO's Cruise and Pershing and the Soviet SS-20s. Further progress was made when attention was turned to the elimination of tactical and battle-field nuclear weapons and eventually conventional forces. The final agreement was reached in Washington in December 1987.

The Reykjavik agreement disturbed the Europeans in that the proposed elimination of all nuclear weapons would expose Europe to the larger conventional Soviet forces. As it would affect missiles deployed in Britain and Eastern Europe, while leaving SDI for the moment it would also make clear the limitations of the British independent deterrent. Meeting Reagan, Thatcher did indeed speak on behalf of all of Europe when she demanded that the reductions would be limited to intermediate-range missile and no more than 50 per cent cut in strategic weapons. Despite this, it was obvious that – as on previous occasions – the momentum of superpower *détente* pushed Thatcher out of the way.

The speed of events on the international scene in the last years of Margaret Thatcher's premiership was breathtaking. One by one the countries of Eastern Europe each underwent their own revolution leading to sweeping domestic changes and an effective end of Soviet domination over them. The process of slow but steady erosion of Communism that had been most notable in the events in Hungary in 1956, Czechoslovakia in 1968 and Poland in the early 1980s reached its culmination in the overthrow of the eastern European regimes within six months in 1989. The commitment of the Soviet Union to disarmament had made certain that it would not intervene to support any of the old Communist guard in Eastern Europe. And one of the crucial elements in the Soviet position was the realisation that the USSR would never be able to outspend the United States in the field of rearmament and technological innovation. By 1991 the Warsaw Pact was dead and the Soviet Union itself ceased to exist with the proclamation of independence by a number of its former republics. Aside from the moral victory that Britain could claim to share with the rest of the NATO countries, this shattered the whole framework of British foreign policy. The disappearance of Communism as the eternal enemy suddenly meant also the dismantling of the stability and security of the bipolar world.

Thatcher's apprehension of what might succeed was demonstrated in her attitude to the transformation of Germany. The changes across eastern Europe had led to the pulling down of the wall around West Berlin in November 1989 after which an unstoppable movement towards the reunification of Germany began. In March 1990 the Christian-Democrats won the elections in East Germany, in July 1990 a currency union between the two German states took place, and that led to a political union in October 1990. Before the announcement of the latter, Gorbachev had struck a deal with Chancellor Helmut Kohl under which, in return for financial help to the struggling Soviet Union, there would be German re-unification and NATO membership for the new country. This was not to Thatcher's liking. Firstly, she feared how the reappearance of a big and strong Germany would affect the European balance of power. Secondly, understanding that it would be difficult to withhold the momentum for reunification, she preferred to see it delayed while political and economic reforms in Eastern Europe were completed.

Did Britain's defence strategy change under the Conservatives?

The Prime Minister's anti-communism meant that in office, just like in Opposition the Conservatives were fully committed to maintaining and enhancing Britain's defence capabilities. The government strove to highlight the importance attached to this issue by making one of its early measures the 33 per cent pay-rise for the armed services in an attempt to arrest decline in morale and shortfall of skilled personnel. As under previous governments, the Conservative's defence strategy focused on Britain's nuclear potential which in turn required a close link with the United States and NATO.

However, the government was soon under simultaneous conflicting pressures. On the one hand, Britain was bound by and undertaking together with the other NATO countries to an annual 3 per cent increase in real terms of contributions to the Alliance's budget. NATO had also decided to modernise its INF in Europe with Pershing II and Cruise missiles, 160 of which were to be stationed in Britain. As a result Britain was spending on defence a proportion of GDP greater than any European power. On the other hand, the state of the domestic economy called for reduction of defence expenditure. In 1981 in the Defence review 'The Way Forward', the Ministry of Defence seemed to have found the solution in savings from a proposed 25 per cent cut of the surface fleet of the Navy, including vessels cruising the Southern Atlantic. This was however overturned by the Falklands War.

Nuclear deterrence was largely unchallenged in government circles. 'The Way Forward' had made a point of maintaining Britain's nuclear submarines and already in December 1980 it had been decided to purchase the Trident submarine-launched missiles. The June 1983 re-election of the Conservatives ensured that the plans would go ahead while the ascendance of Chancellor Kohl in Germany confirmed the deployment of Pershing there. Despite the controversial fashion in which Reagan had announce the SDI, Thatcher acquired a US guarantee that Britain's own nuclear deterrent would continue to be supported through Trident. Their availability to Britain was also confirmed in the wake of the Reykjavik summit. Even when NATO agreed in principle to remove its short-range nuclear forces, it was Thatcher who made sure that only partial changes would take place. As a result, Britain's defence expenditure 1981–86 amounted to an average 5.2 per cent of GDP and registered an overall increase by 21 per cent in real terms. As late as 1990, Trident was one of the few pieces in the British arsenal not suffering continuous reductions.

1. In what ways did British foreign and defence policy change under Margaret Thatcher?

2. To what extent did Margaret Thatcher change Britain's international position?

5.7 In-depth study: Iron Lady or American Poodle – which best describes Thatcher's foreign policy?

■ To what extent did she have a clear foreign policy?

■ What was the importance of the Falklands conflict?

■ How successfully did she solve the Rhodesian crisis?

■ Did she allow US interests to dominate UK foreign policy?

Framework of Events

1979	Lusaka meeting of Commonwealth leaders; settlement of Rhodesia/Zimbabwe crisis
	Russia invades Afghanistan
1980	Reagan elected US President
1981	Ottawa G7 meeting (heads of major world economic powers); first long meeting with Reagan as US President
1982	Invasion of Falklands and Falklands War
	Thatcher's first visit to Far East and Communist China
1983	Reagan announces SDI
	US invasion of Grenada
	Cruise missiles arrive at Greenham Common US base in the UK
1984	Series of meetings with rising USSR 'star' Mikhail Gorbachev
1985	Thatcher address to US Congress on 'special relationship'
1986	USA bomb Libya, using UK bases
	London meeting of Commonwealth heads of state over South Africa
	Long visit to Russia and Eastern Europe
	INF Treaty in Washington – nuclear missile reduction planned
1988	Bruges speech
	Extended visit to Poland
	Visit of Mikhail Gorbachev to UK
	Iron Curtain comes down across Europe; collapse of Communism
1989	Extended visit to Eastern Europe.

To what extent did Thatcher have a clear foreign policy?

Unlike in economic and many areas of domestic policy, Thatcher came into power with few foreign policy objectives. It was to be an area where she was not only required to spend a great deal of her time, but also where she was to make considerable impact.

She had had no early interest in foreign affairs. The advisers she surrounded herself when Leader of the Opposition, from 1975 to 1979, were primarily economic specialists. It was the British economy, not international affairs, that interested her. She had had little experience of foreign travel until she became Leader of the Opposition. She was always a strong anti-Communist and anti-socialist, and brought little more than those views to foreign affairs.

She disliked the civil servants in the Foreign Office, and felt that they regularly betrayed UK interests instead of fighting for them. She dismissed Reginald Maudling, her first Shadow Foreign Secretary, as she felt he did not have strong enough pro-British and anti-Communist views.

She liked being branded the 'Iron Lady' by the Russian Communists. They intended it as a criticism, but she felt it gave her just the image that she ought to have. It certainly raised her status in the UK and abroad. If the more gentlemanly Foreign Office did not approve, she did not mind at all. She was always much happier using the language of the battlefield than the traditional polite language of diplomacy She was totally indifferent as to whether she offended others, as long as she defended the UK in the process.

She was determined to raise the status and profile of the UK in the world. She believed in NATO as the defender of world peace and Western values. She was a firm believer in a nuclear deterrent. She was a strong British nationalist. 'Patriotism and anti-Sovietism' were the main themes of her foreign policy speeches before becoming Prime Minster, and they did not change much when she became Prime Minister.

To what extent was her policy towards the USSR simply militaristic and hostile?

To see Thatcher simply as a fanatical anti-Communist is to miss the point. Certainly she was unflinching in her dislike of Communism. No sooner had she moved into Downing Street than she condemned Russia's invasion of Afghanistan. She fully supported the United States in its attempts to arm Afghans fighting against the Communist rulers in Afghanistan and their Russian allies. As she wrote in her memoirs, *The Downing Street Years* (1993), 'I regarded it as my duty to do everything I could to reinforce and further President Reagan's strategy to win the Cold War …. I was his principal cheerleader in NATO'.

She appointed Lord Carrington as her Foreign Secretary. He was able and experienced and Thatcher respected his judgment and was prepared to follow his advice on foreign affairs.

She very publicly met leading Russian opponents of the Russian government. Thatcher was also very keen to increase spending on UK defence and arms. She insisted on a strong British nuclear deterrent, and welcomed American nuclear missiles in the UK. She was always suspicious of any attempt on the part of the Russians to try and 'deal' with the West. She wrote, 'Détente had been ruthlessly used by the Soviets to exploit Western weakness'.

When the Communist government in Poland in 1981 ruthlessly crushed the **Solidarity Movement**, she did all she could to assist them. She viewed brutal treatment of democrats as typical Communist behaviour. In her meeting with President Reagan in 1983, she ensured that the uncompromising hard line against Communism was maintained. She also

Lord Carrington (1919–)
Experienced Conservative Minister who had served under Heath (as Defence Secretary 1970–4) and Macmillan (as government Minister 1951–64). A member of House of Lords, he was a key adviser to Thatcher while in Opposition 1974–9, and one of the few 'old' Tories who rallied to her support. He was Foreign Secretary from 1979 to 1982, but resigned over the Falklands, as he was held to be responsible for the UK's lack of preparedness. He later became Secretary General of NATO.

Solidarity Movement: a group trying to win greater liberty and democracy for the Polish people.

ensured relations never got too bitter so that if the Communists wished to change, relations could easily improve. By the end of 1983, both Thatcher and Reagan were aware that Russia was close to total bankruptcy because of the cost of the Cold War.

How did she establish dialogue with Russia?

Her hard line attitude changed as soon as she sensed change in the USSR. The arrival in power of Mikhail Gorbachev in Russia in 1984 led to a rapid change of policy on her part. She sensed that he was a very different type of Russian leader: 'one we could work with'. He felt that the Cold War was a war which Russia could not win, and that the arms race with the West was bankrupting the USSR. Thatcher was able to enter into a good dialogue with him at a vital visit to Moscow in 1984, and really worked at getting a sensible and peaceful working arrangement between the two countries. She persuaded Gorbachev to visit the UK, also in 1984, and this helped to reduce the Russians' deep suspicion of the Americans and their 'Star Wars' initiative (see page 151).

Thatcher tried to focus on doing business with Russia, and not making war. She talked to Gorbachev regularly, but always from a position of strength. The result was that she soon became an important bridge, a channel of communication, between Russia and America. This more peaceful dialogue between the capitalist West and the Communist East played an important part in ending the Cold War.

The Cold War, with its endless arms race leading to both the USSR and the West possessing enough nuclear weapons to ensure '**MAD**', eased while Thatcher occupied Downing Street. She had played a major role in the final push. To see Thatcher as an aggressive anti-Communist and no more is wrong. She had several successful meetings with Gorbachev, particularly in 1986, so that a good working relationship was established with the new forces emerging in post-Communist Russia. She convinced him that the UK was not another enemy, but a possible partner in the development of a modernised Russia in a more peaceful world.

She also took great care to visit Eastern Europe as much as possible. These countries, such as Hungary and Poland, had always been under Russian Communist rule. With the collapse of the USSR, these 'colonised' countries gradually gained their freedom from Russian rule. Thatcher was very keen to open up relations with the 'new' Eastern European countries, and have the EU expand into them. She saw these countries as a counter-balance to an aggressive and expansionist Germany, as well as likely future markets for the UK and allies.

Her basic approach as far as Russia and Communism was concerned was simple. She did not like Communism, but she quite liked Russians. Britain had to be armed, in NATO, and had to protect herself. She did not trust most other EU countries to be prepared to stand up to the Communists. Once she felt that Communism was weakening, she did all she could to encourage its end. She never went to extremes, so that she could be always seen as a friend of the Russians (or Poles) once they had overcome their unfortunate Communist beliefs. She wanted Britain to be able to do business with them, and make money out of them, so she avoided generating too much hatred on their part.

Her policy toward Russia initially caused considerable controversy (although when the Communist government later collapsed she had no critics!) Two particularly strong critics had been her own Ministers, Ian Gilmour in *Dancing with Dogma* (1984) and James Prior in *Balance of Power* (1986). Both felt that she was much too aggressive towards Russia and should have adopted a much more conciliatory approach towards Communism with less of a focus on NATO and the American alliance.

Mikhail Gorbachev (1931–)
Trained as an economist, Gorbachev rose rapidly through the ranks of the Communist Party and government in Russia. By 1971, he was the youngest member of the Central Committee of the Communist Party. He became a key figure in Russian economic and foreign affairs, and from 1985 to 1991 he was the effective ruler of Russia. He was responsible for withdrawing Russian forces from Afghanistan and was a key figure in negotiating the end of the Cold War with Reagan and Thatcher.

'**MAD**': Mutually Assured Destruction, both sides being able to wipe out each other and all mankind.

Thatcher was also strongly opposed by much of the liberal press, such as the *Guardian*, and of course by the much more pro-Communist Labour party, which in 1983 was advocating nuclear disarmament and leaving NATO.

How successfully did Thatcher solve the Rhodesian crisis?

The former British colony of Rhodesia, now the independent country of Zimbabwe, was a serious problem, which Thatcher had inherited. The British white minority there had refused in the 1960s to give majority rule to black Africans. Rather than hand over power to the black majority, the minority white population had simply broken away from British colonial rule and declared independence. Rhodesia became an illegal state run by the white minority leader Ian Smith (Prime Minister of Rhodesia 1965–79) and was accepted (recognised) by no other state. The state managed to continue with support from neighbouring South Africa, with its similarly racist **apartheid** regime, and the willingness of Western oil companies to supply it with oil illegally.

The black majority of the Rhodesian population was split between various groups. Some were prepared to work with Ian Smith towards black involvement in government, but others, led by the Marxist Robert Mugabe, started a campaign of violence in order to attain a democratic solution. Just like the BBC, which was known to refer to Mugabe's soldiers sometimes as 'freedom fighters' and sometimes as 'terrorist guerrillas', Thatcher had mixed views on the subject.

It was not an area in which Thatcher had much interest, but she had to deal with it. By 1980 over 20,000 had died in the fighting. It was a former colony of the UK and the UK had to take responsibility for it. The Commonwealth, with its large number of new black nations in Africa, was badly divided on the issue. Many of Rhodesia's Commonwealth neighbours openly supported Mugabe and pressed the UK to impose tight economic sanctions on the rebel regime of Ian Smith, to 'starve' it out.

Thatcher naturally disliked Communist Mugabe, and probably shared Ian Smith's and the white minority's views that black majority rule would lead to chaos. The right wing of the Conservative party was also strongly sympathetic to Smith. However he was a rebel and thousands were being killed.

Whatever policy she adopted was bound to be controversial. Right-wing Conservatives, such as Norman Tebbit (see his *Upwardly Mobile*, 1989) wanted full support for Ian Smith's illegal government. More liberal Conservatives, such as James Prior, wanted black majority rule and settlement with the 'rebels'. The British press was also divided between support for Smith, in the *Daily Telegraph*, to demands for British military action to oust Smith in the more liberal *Guardian*.

Thatcher sensed that backing Smith was backing a loser. Carrington advised her to use the regular meeting of the leaders of the Commonwealth nations in Africa in 1979 to work for a settlement. She also used well the calming influence of the Queen who attended the opening session of the meeting. There were many Commonwealth nations, with black leaders, who felt that the UK had been both racist and incompetent in its 'soft' treatment of Smith, and passions were running high.

However, agreement was reached over Rhodesia in Africa, with Carrington preparing the ground carefully. A decision was taken for all the relevant parties – including the Marxist terrorists/freedom fighters – to meet in London. Agreement was reached (to the anger of the Tory 'right' who saw it as a betrayal of British values) and Rhodesia became the new nation of Zimbabwe under the leadership of Robert Mugabe.

The history of that country since independence may well have

Apartheid: a system where blacks were denied the right to vote, and most human and civil rights as well.

Robert Mugabe (1924–)

Born in what was then Rhodesia and educated at Catholic mission schools and at university in South Africa, Mugabe became a committed Communist in 1960. He was arrested and imprisoned by the British in 1964, and founded ZANU (Zimbabwe African National Union) in 1975, a group committed to gaining black majority rule and an end to colonial rule in southern Rhodesia. He started guerrilla warfare, backed by Communist China, to attain freedom for Zimbabwe. He became the first Prime Minister of independent Zimbabwe in 1980 after playing a key role in negotiations with Lord Carrington for gaining independence.

confirmed Thatcher's fears about the way in which Rhodesia might go after black majority rule, but she had the sense to realise that it was the only solution in the circumstances. She had been open and direct and had proved to be a tough bargainer, standing up to both right and left and finding a workable solution.

What was the importance of the Falklands conflict?

The effect that the Falklands War had on Thatcher personally and her future administrations was considerable. She may well have won the election of 1983 without the Falklands victory, but military defeat in the Falklands could well have ended her career. Winning the war also gave her a huge psychological boost and added to her confidence and status. It gave her the determination to continue with her programme of internal reform and to enhance the status of the UK in the eyes of the rest of the world.

The invasion by Argentina of a small group of rocky islands deep in the South Atlantic had huge implications for British politics. The causes of the Falklands conflict go back many years. The islands (see map, below) had become part of the British Empire centuries before. They had no military or strategic value. A private company largely administered them at a small

The Falkland Islands

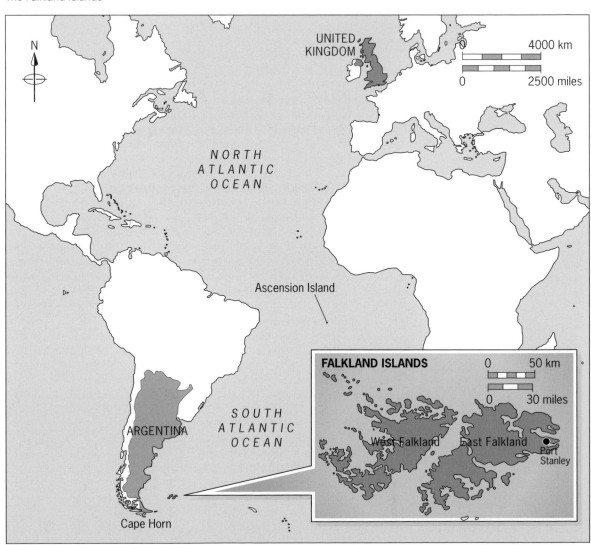

cost to the British taxpayer. There were inhabited by a few hundred islanders of British origin and a huge number of sheep.

Argentina had long resented British rule over islands so near to its coast, although none of the islanders were of Argentine origin. The islanders were determined to remain British. It was another embarrassing colonial legacy for the government.

The Argentines had made several attempts in the 1970s to gain control of the islands. Negotiations between the Argentines and the Foreign Office had taken place, with the Foreign Office indicating that it was prepared to consider some sort of agreement with the Argentines over the sovereignty of the islands.

Military junta: small, unelected government of soldiers.

In 1981, two important changes happened. The first was that a right-wing **military junta**, led by General Galtieri, seized power in Argentina. The second was that the UK, anxious to save money, started to withdraw its very limited defence forces in the area. The junta was disliked because of its failure to solve the huge economic problems in Argentina, such as inflation and unemployment, so was anxious to offer military successes to the Argentine people to gain popularity. Convinced that the UK government had neither the will nor the ability to defend the Falklands, the Junta ordered the invasion of the islands in 1982. They drove out the tiny British forces easily.

Later investigation and analysis of the build-up to the war indicates that the UK government had been both incompetent and negligent. Intelligence had come in about the Argentine intentions and the threat to the Falklands. The UK should have acted sooner. Lord Carrington, the Foreign Secretary, resigned, as he felt that he had to take the blame for this incompetence. One analyst said the war was caused by 'British indifference, indecision and lack of foresight'.

How important was Thatcher's role in the conduct of the war?

Once the islands had been invaded, Thatcher decided to retaliate. Her decisiveness and willingness to take risks and responsibility impressed all. The military thought she was marvellous. She listened and she acted. Her willingness to stand firm and take tough decisions proved to be a great strength. Attempts to negotiate a settlement with the Argentines failed. She used to the full her strong links with US President Reagan and his **Secretary of State**, Alexander Haig.

Secretary of State: the US equivalent of Foreign Secretary.

The minute the news came in of the Argentine invasion, she set up a small war cabinet, which ran the war. She ordered at once a naval and military 'task force' to assemble and go direct to the Falklands. Initially this task force was intended as a bargaining factor. When negotiations failed, she ordered the reinvasion of the Falklands by British forces in spite of the huge risks of operating so far from home.

When tough decisions were needed, such as the sinking of the Argentine cruiser, the *General Belgrano*, by a UK submarine, she took them. When disaster struck in the form of the sinking of British warships such as the *Sheffield*, by Argentine missiles, she stood firm. The whole war was a huge risk, and it paid off.

Whether the lives of so many British soldiers and civilians should have been risked, can be debated. As Thatcher put it, she was 'damned if she had a war and damned if she did not'. Public opinion was highly supportive, but may well not have been if there had been higher causalities – or defeat.

During the conflict, 255 British solders died, and many more Argentines. The Falklands were remote islands of limited value, and they have proved to be a huge drain on UK resources ever since, as naturally a large military presence has been retained there. Public opinion endorsed her stand against unprovoked military aggression and there were many

Various headlines from the London daily newspapers, 15 June 1982, following the Falklands ceasefire.

who approved of her principled and uncompromising policy. Victory in the Falklands certainly helped her win an election in 1983 and helped raise the status and prestige of the UK.

Many nations doubted the ability of the UK to mount such a difficult military operation successfully thousands of miles from base. US help was invaluable in many ways, ranging from intelligence and missiles to moral support. **The Franks report** after the war condemned her administration for incompetence in letting the war happen in the first place, but by then there had been victory and electoral success. The public approves of winners.

The Franks report: independent enquiry to investigate the causes of the war.

Public opinion at the time, and since, largely backed Thatcher. However there are two broad criticisms of her policy towards the Falklands. The first, again coming from critics within her own party such as Ian Gilmour, and also from journalist/historians such as Peter Jenkins in *Mrs Thatcher's Revolution* (1987), argue that she failed to focus on the looming crisis and take preventative action to stop the Argentines invading in the first place. The second strand of criticism comes from the left in British politics. Look at Tony Benn's *Diaries* (1995) where he argues that Thatcher did not take seriously enough the attempts of the United States, and South American countries such as Chile, to bring about a peaceful settlement. One of the best and most recent accounts, P. Clarke's *Hope and Glory* (1996) tries to look at the issue with some balanced perspective, and concludes that Peter Jenkins may well have been right, and Tony Benn very wrong.

Did Thatcher allow US interests to dominate UK foreign policy?

In her relationship with the United States, Thatcher caused huge controversy and was severely criticised. Her first three Foreign Secretaries, – Lord Carrington, Francis Pym and Geoffrey Howe – all criticised her pro-American policy, both in their memoirs and in public after their departure. The leader of the Labour party, Michael Foot, regularly criticised her as well. One of the best analyses of Thatcher American policy is Tim Hames *The Special Relationship* (1994), where he agrees that while her support for the United States was unpopular; it certainly did the UK no harm at all. With the collapse of Communism, writers on British foreign policy, such as P. Clarke, have tended to be much less critical of Thatcher once events proved her to be right!

Thatcher wrote in 1991 that, 'the US and GB together have been the greatest alliance in defence of liberty and justice that the world has ever seen'. She believed very strongly indeed that a close alliance with the United States was of fundamental importance to Britain's security. She believed it was in Britain's commercial, strategic and security interests as well. She felt that only with a very public bond between the United States and the UK could the Communist threat be resisted. She placed a good working relationship with America much higher on what she felt to be UK's list of priorities than a close relationship with the EU.

However, she was not prepared to sacrifice what she felt were essential UK interests in order to benefit American ones. Her critics, particularly those on the left who tend to be more pacifist and would have preferred a more accommodating policy towards the Communists, argue that she did, but there is no hard evidence of this.

History in the end proved Thatcher right, and her policies were vindicated when Communism in the USSR and Eastern Europe fell apart in 1990. She felt that her determined stand against the Eastern bloc and its aggressive Communist ideas had paid off.

A 'special relationship'?

She had had limited dealings with the previous US President, Jimmy Carter, who left office in 1981. She saw him as too much of a compromiser and pacifist with his policy on **SALT**, which she regarded as giving in to Communist pressure. She felt that such a compromising view had led to the Soviet invasion of Afghanistan. Co-operation with the Russians only encouraged their aggression.

SALT: Strategic Arms Limitations Talks with the Russians.

In 1981, Ronald Reagan, the conservative Republican became President of the United States. She had met him before and was to form a very close, and highly significant, working relationship with him. Personally they got on particularly well, and she utilised that friendship to try and rebuild what she felt ought to be a special relationship between the United States and the UK. This special relationship actually meant much more to her than it did to the USA. The USA was more interested in Germany and in Europe, and Reagan was far too clever a politician to be seen as sacrificing American interests for British ones. The special relationship had really died at the end of the Second World War – it was now a marriage of convenience resurrected when it was in the interest of both countries to do so.

Thatcher really only had any impact on American policy when US opinion was divided – mainly when the President disagreed with his Secretary of State. By 1979, the 'special relationship' was long gone, but a complex interdependence remained. Being a very strong anti-Communist, Thatcher naturally assumed that keeping on good terms with America was automatically in the interests of the UK. She was anxious to retain US forces in Europe and in the UK as a barrier against Communism.

By 1985, she publicly described the relations with Reagan and the USA as 'very very special'. There was close co-operation over military and intelligence matters – it was in the interests of both sides to do so. She acquired **Trident** on very generous terms in 1981 and had lots of help over the Falklands crisis, especially in terms of spare parts and military intelligence, as well as the use of Ascension Island (see map page 158).

Trident: a US nuclear missile system.

However on some issues, such as the West Indian island of Grenada, the UK was simply ignored by the USA. When the United States felt that 'Communist' influence was too strong in Grenada, they simply invaded it, even though it was a member of the Commonwealth and a former British colony. The UK was neither consulted nor informed and Thatcher was furious. When it came to defending what they perceived as their interests, the USA had no hesitation in simply ignoring their closest ally.

SDI: Strategic Defence Initiative, a huge anti-nuclear missile system based in space, also known as 'Star Wars'.

Soviet conventional weapons: non-nuclear weapons, for example infantry and tanks.

Thatcher's relationship with the US was controversial, and she was widely criticised for what many felt was pro-American policy.

Iron Lady or American poodle – which best describes Thatcher's foreign policy?

1. Read the following extracts and answer the question below.

'The United States and Britain have together been the greatest alliance in the defence of liberty and justice that the world has ever known.'

(from Margaret Thatcher, *Statecraft*, HarperCollins, 2002)

'Throughout the eight years of my presidency, no alliance we had had been stronger than the one between the United States and the United Kingdom.'

(Ronald Reagan, *An American Life*, Simon and Schuster, 1990)

Using your own knowledge, how adequately do the extracts describe UK–USA relations between 1979 and 1990?

2. How justified is the view that Thatcher's policy towards the USA damaged the interests of the UK?

Thatcher was able to have some influence over US arms control policy, particularly as the US government was badly divided on the issue. Thatcher used her influence as a restraining factor over the **SDI**, which Reagan hoped would lead to the abolition of nuclear weapons and reduce the number of atomic warheads in the world.

Most European countries, including the UK, were appalled by the SDI, as this would leave them exposed to the huge number of **Soviet conventional weapons** in Europe. But the technological failings of 'Star Wars', as the SDI became known, and the hostility of the US Congress made it unlikely to happen. Unlike the rest of Europe, Thatcher opposed 'Star Wars' quietly and offered nominal support to keep on good terms with Reagan. She ensured that British industry got several of the research contracts to develop the SDI. She helped to persuade Reagan to use it more as a bargaining tool with the Russians than anything else. Her regular visits to the United States had a moderating, but declining, influence.

How far did UK policy shift to support the USA?

Thatcher really had limited influence over US policy outside specific areas and no influence on economic policy at all. She was successful in helping retain the US military in Europe as a deterrent against the Soviets, and that was very much to the UK's advantage. Thatcher and Reagan both shared right-wing views, and they agreed on Russia and economics. Both were anti-elitist and anti-establishment, and they shared a crusading missionary spirit, based on right-wing politics.

The time when she was most strongly criticised for 'toeing' the US line was when the Americans, tired of having its citizens killed by what it was sure were terrorists controlled by the government of Libya, decided to bomb Libya in retaliation. Initially she would not cooperate with the USA and and refused permission for their bombers to use bases in the UK. Her cabinet opposed this, as did Labour. However, she felt that the Americans were going to bomb Libya anyway, so there was little point in offending an ally, and if it discouraged international terrorism so much the better. She also knew that the Libyans were helping arm the IRA in Northern Ireland, so deserved it! Although the British press was angry with her, the public were not.

Overall there is no sign that UK policy shifted radically to a pro-US stance under Thatcher, or that she sacrificed 'British' interests to support the United States. She made the UK go very much its own way in Africa and in Eastern Europe.

She felt that the Foreign Office were 'Euro freaks' and unaware of the critical importance of the US relationship to the UK. She could be quite emotional about America, but she remained essentially practical. The Foreign Office certainly felt that Thatcher was America's 'poodle' and her successive Foreign Secretaries felt she was too anti-EU and too pro-USA.

When she left office in 1990, she felt she had achieved a great deal in her foreign policy. Communism had collapsed and the status of the UK had risen sharply. The UK was on good terms with both the USA and with the newly emerging regimes in Russia and Eastern Europe. There was a strong possibility that these countries in Eastern Europe would join the EU and be valuable markets for UK goods and services.

It was not just the Russians who saw Thatcher as being ruthless.

5.8 How did the end of the Cold War affect British foreign policy after 1990?

The changes in British foreign policy after 1990 certainly reflected Thatcher's stepping down from government. To a greater extent however, they were a consequence of the radically-altered international situation. With the end of the Cold War, a new British foreign policy had to be found. Britain's position in the world and security at home had to be safeguarded in a way that would not strain further the country's continuously tight resources.

British governments in 1990–2000, both Conservative and Labour, had to lead a cautious foreign policy mainly because this was an extremely volatile period for world affairs in general. The old bipolar system was unexpectedly quickly dismantled unleashing previously suppressed tensions like nationalism. In the meantime, Britain also had to respond to the increased foreign policy integration of Europe and clarify its own view on the link between institutions such as NATO and the European Union in the field of international relations.

How did Britain react to the crises in the Persian Gulf?

One of the major tests for Britain's role in the post-Cold-War world and for the new government of John Major was in January 1991 when it participated in the Gulf War. The previous August Iraq, under its president Saddam Hussein, had invaded Kuwait. Iraq wanted to annex Kuwait because the country's position greatly hindered Iraqi access to the Persian Gulf. Kuwait, which had been under British protection also had the support of the United States and some other Arab states opposed to the Iraqi regime. The United Nations Security Council had called on Saddam to withdraw and had also imposed economic sanctions on him. The Soviet Union did not veto these measures even though it had interests in Iraq and preferred a diplomatic solution. In the following months US military presence in the Gulf region amassed and around 35,000 British troops were also sent to the zone of the conflict.

In accordance with an UN ultimatum for the withdrawal of Iraqi troops from Kuwait, on 15 January 1991 operation Desert Storm began against Iraq. Although under operational US command, it was carried out under the United Nations, the only precedent being the Korean War. Five weeks of air war were followed by a ground campaign until on 28 February 1991 Iraq accepted a cease-fire. Throughout the war, the RAF had played a prominent role on equal footing with the US Air Force and British forces had also been essential in the co-ordination of naval movements. Britain's unequivocal support of the United States through the crisis did a lot to reinvigorate the 'special relationship' for which there had been fears after both Thatcher and Reagan were gone from politics. It proved especially important against the background of limited German involvement and disconcerted response from the European partners among which France was conspicuous with a last-minute initiative to prevent the strikes. One side-effect for Britain was that relations with Syria and Iran were restored leading to the release of a number of British hostages from across the Arab world. Additionally, there occurred better opportunities for the presentation of the British position on the Arab-Israeli conflict: since 1980 Britain had consistently worked for settlement on the basis of guarantees for Israeli security in turn for some sort of a Palestinian homeland.

One of the aims of the United States and Britain had been to eliminate Saddam, but to pursue that to the end meant continuing armed action on Iraqi territory leading to the seizure of the capital Baghdad. The United

States did not feel justified in carrying out such an undertaking. President Bush believed it would break up the coalition against Iraq which had been committed to liberating Kuwait only. Moreover, it did not want to challenge either China or the USSR both of whom had reservations. In this Britain again followed the American lead. However, Iraq's effective defeat had increased instability within Iraq. The Iraqi regime turned its full military potential against the Kurds and the Shi'ite Arabs of Southern Iraq. With the humanitarian situation deteriorating steadily, the international community had to step in. Upon largely British initiative, safe havens were created in Northern and Southern Iraq over which non-fly zones for the Iraqi air force were imposed. International troops, including British were sent to monitor Iraqi observation of the rules. Britain was breaching its long-standing policy of non-intervention in other countries' domestic affairs – however just the humanitarian cause. In implementation of this new policy, in 1993 Britain participated in strikes aiming to enforce no-fly zone and secure Iraqi co-operation with the UN observers. In the following years Saddam alternated between co-operation and obstruction, backing down only when western forces were deployed in the Gulf in support of UN resolutions. Such behaviour precipitated the bombing of Iraqi military installations in December 1998 – operation Desert Fox – aiming to reduce Iraq's military capabilities. In this Britain again fully supported the United States.

How did Britain's defence priorities change at the end of the Cold War?

The elimination of the Soviet Union as the main enemy did not mean that relations became smooth and easy. On the one hand, the British government stood for the principle of self-determination and saw its interest in the promotion of democracy and market economy in the former Soviet republics and Russia itself. This determined the positive British attitude to the independence proclaimed by the three Baltic republics in August 1991. On the other hand, Britain – and indeed the other European powers and the United States – were worried in case a number of regional conflicts, similar to those in former Yugoslavia for example, emerged after the withdrawal of Moscow's control. Indeed this was already the case in the Caucasus and Moldavia. So, the UK seemed to agree that Russia should police some of the less stable former republics. Another source of potential threat was the nuclear potential of the former Soviet Union which should not fall into extremists' hands. That is why in an attempt to maintain the status quo Britain continued to support Gorbachev's presidency almost to its end even though Gorbachev seemed unable to carry through the very reforms he had initiated. Once Boris Yeltsin was established in power as the new Russian President, Britain switched support to him spending diplomatic and financial resources to boost him against Communist and nationalist opponents. Even so, on a number of occasions Britain, together with the United States, and Russia emerged on the opposite sides, the most notable example provided by Russian moral support for Serbia in the Kosovo conflict.

Despite the fact that Russia could still create trouble on the international scene, it was economically feeble and demoralised by the loss of its superpower status. Barely in a position to maintain order in the outskirts of its own territory, Moscow could hardly harbour any aggressive intentions. Such reasoning precipitated a major reappraisal of the government's defence policy which had already begun under Thatcher. In 1991 the government brought the level of defence spending to 4 per cent of GDP, the lowest in the whole post-war period. This was improved further in 1992 to

2.7 per cent of GDP. All three services experienced reduction. The biggest cuts occurred in the British European forces which were halved but participated in NATO's Rapid Reaction Force newly created and placed under British command to deal with dangers in Eastern Europe. Upon pressure from the Treasury cuts worth £3 billion over ten years were initiated. One-quarter of the Navy's ships were put into less intensive roles, the number of warheads of the Trident force was to be reduced and the RAF was gradually to be phased out of a major nuclear role. The Army suffered less due to its newly-found peace keeping role but the Territorial Army was to be reorganised for possible use in front-line operations. A new round of reductions was announced by Labour in July 1998 affecting submarines, frigates, aircraft carriers and tank regiments in Germany. All this was based on the two major assumptions that any future fighting would be carried out away from home and that battlefield has given way to battle-space dominated by air force and intelligence. Simultaneously, after 1995 the governments acknowledged that the defence budget should reflect the emphasis on highly flexible forces to meet a peacekeeping role. However, should the need arise, the existing structure of the armed forces should enable them to participate in high-intensity war and should also easily and quickly render to expansion, if necessary.

After 1989 and especially after 1991 Britain was also engulfed in debates about the future structure of European defence. One aspect was the changing nature of the relationship among the NATO countries underlined by divisions during the Gulf War and the tests for the alliance posed by Balkan nationalism in Yugoslavia. At closer inspection this is the old unresolved question of whether Britain should adhere to predominantly Atlantic or predominantly European priorities. A pro-NATO position would benefit from US participation in European defence; simultaneously in the mid-1990s Britain moved to accepting increased co-operation in foreign policy within the European Union. The idea of giving the West European Union some sort of defence identity was also mooted but for Britain this could only be as a bridge between the EU and NATO. Finally in 1995 the Conservative government stated that NATO would continue to be responsible for defence while the EU would increase security. In December 1998, when an Anglo-French agreement was signed on defence co-operation, it seemed that this could be a first step to an EU military structure to take care of occasions such as the Bosnian war where EU-member troops operated under NATO command.

A second aspect of defence policy was that related to the enlargement of NATO to include some former members of the Warsaw Pact. In October 1993 Yeltsin signed an agreement with Polish President Lech Walesa that Russia did not object to Poland joining NATO, but under pressure from the Russian military Yeltsin reversed his attitude. However, in May 1995 in Paris, an agreement between NATO and Russia was signed. This stated that Russian nuclear weapons targeting NATO would be dismantled while attention would be paid by the Alliance to Russia's views without its having a veto. The agreement paved the way for its eastward enlargement starting with negotiations with Hungary, Poland and the Czech Republic in July 1997. NATO also undertook not to deploy nuclear weapons on these territories of former Soviet satellites, which formally joined in 1999 just before the war in Kosovo. Throughout the discussions the position of the British government had been in favour of enlargement.

1. How did the end of the Cold War affect British foreign and defence policy?

2. What do you regard as the most important issues facing British defence policy between 1945 and 2007? Explain your answer.

3. How far have the aims of British foreign policy changed between 1945 and 2007?

4. To what extent has Britain's international position been one of steady decline between 1945 and 2007?

5.9 Yugoslavia, Afghanistan and Iraq: The Blair Years, 1997–2007

When Tony Blair became prime minister in 1997, he maintained the British presence in the peacekeeping operations in the former Yugoslavia, in Bosnia and FYR Macedonia. By 1998 the military situation in the Yugoslav province of Kosovo had deteriorated rapidly as the Yugoslav army occupied a province dominated by ethnic Albanians. In a bid to bring peace to Kosovo, the British, along with US and other NATO forces, launched air attacks on Serbia–Montenegro. The intervention led to a ceasefire, the withdrawal of Serbia–Montenegrin forces and the installation of a peacekeeping force in Kosovo. The operation finally brought to an end the warfare that had engulfed Yugoslavia since 1991.

In 2001 the Islamic terror group, al-Qaeda, launched an attack on the US which saw New York's World Trade Center destroyed and the Pentagon, in Washington DC, attacked. Almost 3000 people lost their lives. Blair immediately offered support to the USA and played a major role in the US-led war on terror. In 2001 the main thrust of this strategy was the removal of the Taliban regime in Afghanistan which had offered a safe haven to al-Qaeda. By January 2002, the Taliban had been removed and a new pro-Western regime under Hamid Karzai was created. However, since that time the British, along with other NATO troops, have become engaged in a guerrilla war against the Taliban and al-Qaeda, and by February 2008, 89 British service personnel had been killed in the fighting.

The most controversial aspect of British foreign and defence policy since 1997 has been the invasion and occupation of Iraq. Blair stated that:

> So far as our objective, it is disarmament, not regime change – that is our objective. Now I happen to believe the regime of Saddam is a very brutal and repressive regime, I think it does enormous damage to the Iraqi people … so I have got no doubt Saddam is very bad for Iraq, but on the other hand I have got no doubt either that the purpose of our challenge from the United Nations is disarmament of weapons of mass destruction (WMDs), it is not regime change.

In 2003 Blair told the House of Commons that Britain faced an immediate threat from the weapons of mass destruction in Iraq. On the basis of this allegation, the House of Commons voted for military action against a back-drop of public protest and condemnation from key political figures, most notably former Foreign Secretary, Robin Cook, who resigned from the Cabinet at the vote. In March 2003, UK forces joined US forces in Operation Enduring Freedom, and within five weeks the Saddam Hussein regime had been overthrown. President George W. Bush even flew to the Persian Gulf in May 2003 to congratulate his troops, on board US aircraft carrier *Abraham Lincoln*. Behind him was a huge placard claiming 'Mission Accomplished'.

Unfortunately, for both the USA and the UK, the mission had not been accomplished. Following Saddam's fall, Iraq descended into internal chaos, with guerrilla forces fighting the US and UK forces – and each other.

The failure to locate any weapons of mass destruction following the invasion undermined Blair. He now stated that the war was aimed at removing a tyrant, Saddam, but that was not the issue on which Parliament gave its support. In addition, Kofi Annan, the UN Secretary-General claimed that the war was illegal. By February 2008, 179 UK military personnel had lost their lives.

An important debate in foreign and defence policy in the Blair years was the replacement of the Trident nuclear submarine fleet. Many members of the Labour Party voiced their opposition to a programme estimated to cost approximately £20 billion over a thirty-year period. However, both Blair

Tony Blair addresses troops in Basra, May, 2003

1. Why has Blair's foreign and defence policy been regarded as controversial?

2. What message does the cartoon, below, give about the relationship between the USA and Britain at the time of the Iraq War?

3. Both the photograph and te cartoon suggest that the war was not popular. Are they reliable representations of the British views about the war? Explain your answer.

and his successor as prime minister, Gordon Brown, committed themselves to Britain's nuclear deterrent.

By 2007 British troops were fighting long-drawn-out guerrilla wars in Afghanistan and Iraq (although in Iraq Britain had been withdrawing troops steadily since 2005). Britain's support for US policy, under George W. Bush had alienated many states against Britain, especially in the Islamic world.

One of the unfortunate side-effects of the Blair's foreign policy, in particular the war on terror, was the alienation of some British Muslims. Concerns about Islamic fundamentalism in the UK had been growing since 9/11.

Anti-war protest march in London, February 15, 2003

Steve Bell cartoon from the *Guardian*, 2005, after the US had given up the search for weapons of mass destruction.

On 7 July 2005 four suicide bombers attacked the underground rail network in central London, killing themselves and 52 commuters. Approximately 700 people were injured. As well as being Islamic fundamentalists, all four bombers were British citizens. It was the deadliest attack in London since World War II. On 1 September, the news network Al Jazeera aired a tape featuring Mohammed Sidique Khan, one of the bombers (who came from West Yorkshire). In the tape he referenced the war on terror as a motivating factor for the attacks.

The war in Iraq proved to be a costly and highly controversial undertaking, and the fighting in Afghanistan, though less costly, seemed unending by the close of 2007.

Further Reading

Article

'The Cold War 1945–49', by Derrick Murphy, *Modern History Review*, Vol. No. 10, 4, April 1999

Texts designed specifically for AS and A2 students

The Cold War by Hugh Higgins, 3rd ed., (Heinemann, 1993)
The Cold War 1945–1965 by Joseph Smith (Historical Association Studies, Blackwell, 1989)
The Cold War 1945–1991 by John W. Mason (Routledge Lancaster Pamphlets, 1996)
The Origins of the Cold War, 1941–49 by Martin Macauley, 2nd ed., (Longman Seminar Studies, 1995)
Russia, America and the Cold War 1949–1991 by Martin Macauley (Longman Seminar Studies, 1998)
The USA and the Cold War by Oliver Edwards (Hodder and Stoughton, 1997)

More advanced reading

Britain and the Cold War 1945 to 1991 by Sean Greenwood (Macmillan, 2000)
Cold War Europe 1945–1989 by S. Young (Edward Arnold, 1991)
The Cold War: The Great Powers and the Allies by J. Dunbabin (Longman, 1994)
The Cold War 1947 to 1991 by S. J. Ball (Hodder Headline, 1998)
The Cold War, 1945–87, by R. Levering (Harlan Davidson, 1988)
The United States and the Cold War, 1945–53 by R. Crockatt (The British Association for the Advancement of Science, 1989)
Blair's Wars by John Kampfner (Free Press, 2004)

6 Britain and Europe, 1945–2007

Key Issues

- Why did Britain fail to take the lead in Europe at the end of the Second World War?

- Was British membership of the EEC inevitable?

- Why did further European integration divide political parties and public opinion in the period 1979 to 2007?

6.1 Why did Ernest Bovin reject the idea of a European 'Third Force' in 1949?

6.2 How did Anthony Eden deal with the problems of West German rearmament in 1954?

6.3 Historical Interpretation: Did Britain 'miss the bus' in Europe, 1950–1957?

6.4 Why did Harold Macmillan decide to apply for membership of the EEC?

6.5 Why was Britain not able to join the EEC until 1973?

6.6 Why did the Labour governments have so many concerns about Britain's membership of the EEC in the 1970s?

6.7 In-depth study: Did Thatcher really bring about a social, political and economic revolution?

6.8 Did Margaret Thatcher's attitude towards her European partners help or harm Britain's standing in Europe?

6.9 Why was the Conservative Party so divided over the question of European integration in the 1990s?

6.10 How European were the British by 2007?

Framework of Events

1947	Dunkirk Treaty signed. Marshall Aid
1948	Brussels Pact. Council of Europe
	Communist coup in Czechoslovakia
	Berlin Airlift
1949	NATO. Division of Germany
1950	Schuman Plan for European Coal and Steel Community
	Pleven Plan for European Defence Community
1954	French fail to ratify EDC
1955	Western European Union set up
	Talks begin at Messina for a European Economic Community
1956	Talks begin on Free Trade Area – Plan G
	Suez Crisis
1957	Treaty of Rome signed, creating EEC
1958	Free Trade Area talks fail
1959	European Free Trade Area (EFTA) set up
1961	Macmillan applies for membership of the EEC
1963	General de Gaulle vetoes British application
1967	Harold Wilson applies for membership of the EEC
1972	Edward Heath successfully takes Britain into the EEC
1975	British referendum on Common Market membership
1985	The EC agrees the Single European Act
1988	Jacques Delors reports on Economic and Monetary Union and Social Chapter
1990	Thatcher 'deposed' by pro-European Conservatives. Britain enters ERM
1992	Maastricht Treaty on European Union
	Britain leaves Exchange Rate Mechanism and devalues pound

1999	Eleven countries launch Euro as trading currency.
	Britain does not join the single currency
2001	Britain signs the Treaty of Nice on reform of the EU
2004	Poland, Slovenia, Czech Republic, Slovakia, Malta, Cyprus, Latvia, Lithuania and Estonia join the EU
2007	Romania and Bulgaria admitted to EU
	Britain signs the Treaty of Lisbon on future European Union integration.

Overview

THE Second World War devastated the continent of Europe. Millions lost their lives, homes and families. Whole cities were destroyed. There were drastic shortages of food and fuel. Unlike many European nations, Britain had not been occupied by the Nazis. The war confirmed British policy-makers' belief in Britain's role as a great power: Britain had her empire, and a tradition of parliamentary government unbroken since the 17th century. British policy-makers believed that Britain would be the key player in shaping post-war Europe.

However, the war had only been won with the help of the United States and the Soviet Union. This determined the political geography of mainland Europe: the Allies decided to divide Germany, and govern it among themselves. By 1948, Marshall Aid, the Czechoslovakian coup and the Berlin Airlift showed that co-operation between west and east would not be possible. Communist regimes were established in eastern European states and in East Germany. Western European nations accepted American aid and moved towards liberal capitalist systems. The Cold War, characterised by two superpowers straddling a divided Europe, had begun.

Federation: A 'federal' Europe would have a European government, consisting of the European nations, but acting in the interests of Europe as a whole.

In western Europe, France, West Germany, Italy, the Netherlands, Belgium and Luxembourg responded by creating, in 1957, a European Economic Community, to strengthen their own economic and political power. The EEC aimed to create a political **federation** in Europe, housing France and Germany under one roof and so preventing another war. It also aimed to benefit European trade. Britain declined to participate because British politicians did not want British **national sovereignty** to be challenged. However, by 1961, the British had realised the importance of membership of such a European group, for economic benefit, and to bolster Britain's flagging political influence. However, in 1963, and again in 1967, the French leader General de Gaulle refused Britain entry to the European Economic Community. Entry was only achieved after his death in 1972.

National sovereignty: The power and independence of the British nation, Parliament and people.

Britain has often been seen as an awkward partner in the EEC. British politicians found it difficult to adjust to Britain's new role; and they saw Europe as a useful question over which to fight for their own political ends. In 1975, the Labour government held a referendum on continued membership of Europe. The people voted overwhelmingly in favour, but the Labour party moved towards a position of withdrawal from the EC, causing pro-European Labour party members to leave in 1981.

Single market: The idea that all Europe should be one single economic unit.

Under the Conservative Prime Minister Margaret Thatcher after 1979, Britain appeared to be moving towards a more constructive relationship with the EC. However, the EC wanted deeper integration and increasing political unity. Thatcher supported the developing **single market** in Europe, but was not in

Supranational: 'Above the nation'. Nations agree to give some national sovereignty to European institutions.

favour of the **supranational** institutions that accompanied it. When the Community began to debate economic and monetary union in 1988, she began to withdraw her support. The result was that Britain again found itself on the outskirts of European decision-making. The Conservative Party were driven into civil war as they failed to agree on a sensible policy towards Europe.

The political landscape of post-war Europe changed again dramatically in 1989 when the Soviet Union collapsed and the Berlin Wall came down. Germany was reunified, and increased German strength encouraged the continental states to integrate further. Europe could also expand outwards into eastern Europe, raising questions about the sort of institutions Europe needed. The Treaty of European Union, signed at Maastricht in 1991, developed European unity, adding intergovernmental structures to the existing supranational ones. The British, however, found it difficult to come to terms with the new European reality.

The victory of New Labour in 1997 increased Britain's commitment to the European Union. Blair was a committed European, but in 1999, on Gordon Brown's advice, Britain did not join the new Euro zone. But in 2001 Britain signed the Treaty of Nice, on reforming the EU, and the Treaty of Lisbon in 2007, on increasing European Union integration.

1. Explain how each of the factors in the mind map contributed to the increasing British involvement with Europe.

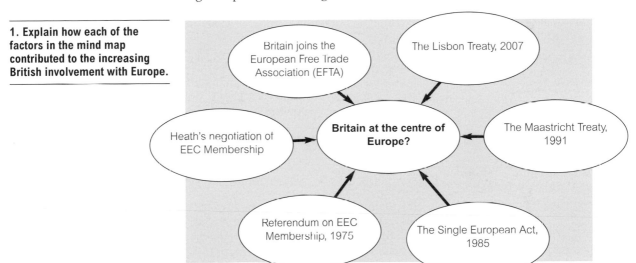

- Britain joins the European Free Trade Association (EFTA)
- The Lisbon Treaty, 2007
- Heath's negotiation of EEC Membership
- Britain at the centre of Europe?
- The Maastricht Treaty, 1991
- Referendum on EEC Membership, 1975
- The Single European Act, 1985

6.1 Why did Ernest Bevin reject the idea of a European 'Third Force' in 1949?

Ernest Bevin was one of the most brilliant politicians in Churchill's war cabinet. When the Labour government won the 1945 election, Bevin became Foreign Secretary. He was one of the more powerful members of the cabinet. A former trade union leader, Bevin was to the right of the Labour Party, and some historians believe that he was strongly anti-communist.

Third Force: The idea that western Europe could act as a powerful international political force alongside the USA and USSR and independent from them.

Did Bevin ever support the idea of a Third Force Europe?

The traditional view of historians like Lord Bullock is that Bevin was never interested in a **Third Force** Europe. Bullock argued that his whole foreign policy was aimed to attract the United States to defend Europe. Revisionist historians, however, have argued that Bevin was interested in a Third Force before 1948.

The problem facing Western Europe was how to secure a lasting peace settlement. The Versailles Peace Treaty in 1919 had clearly failed. The French wanted to crush German industrial power so Germany could not start another war, but Britain and America believed that Germany should be allowed to recover. A Third Force Europe would be one way of controlling Germany's recovery, and would offer a way of defending Western Europe if America refused to participate. It would also help to create prosperity, and so prevent the spread of communism. In 1944 the Foreign Office believed Germany to be a greater threat to peace than the Soviet Union and wanted to create a Third Force Europe. The left wing of the Labour Party also supported the idea because it would enable Europe to be independent of the capitalist United States and to pursue a co-operative arrangement with the Soviet Union.

Customs union: Nations in the union agree to remove customs duties on goods traded within the union. There is a tariff on imports into the customs union from other countries.

Bevin was certainly interested in the idea of a Third Force Europe. He spoke to his Foreign Office officials in 1945 about the possibility of close commercial, political and economic links with Europe, including Greece, Italy, France, Belgium, the Netherlands and Scandinavia. He also considered taking the industrial Ruhr from Germany and placing it under international control. In 1947, Bevin insisted that the Foreign Office study the possibility of a **customs union** in Europe. In 1948, he told the House of Commons of his vision to unite Europe with the Commonwealth. The Commonwealth's raw materials, food and resources would help to strengthen Europe. Bevin also committed British troops to the continent for the first time ever in peacetime in the Treaties of Dunkirk and Brussels in 1947 and 1948. However, Third Force proposals were only discussed once in Cabinet in 1947, and Bevin's ideas were never translated into concrete plans.

Economic recovery in Western Europe

In order to secure peace in Western Europe, it was essential that Europe's economies should recover. The immediate problem was reconstructing economic infrastructures – housing, roads and railways – which required investment of capital. After the war, Britain thought that it could provide for British and Western European recovery. However, by 1947 it was clear that Britain's economy was not strong enough, and European recovery was not possible without American help. In 1949, the Labour government had to devalue the pound, and this convinced the European countries that they could not rely on Britain to provide economic stability. It also convinced the Americans to allow Britain to concentrate on its world role in Commonwealth and Empire as the United States saw the maintenance of sterling as essential.

Sterling: The British currency.

The British government's economic departments, the Board of Trade and the Treasury, were strongly opposed to a Third Force Europe because of Britain's economic weakness. They did not think that Britain would benefit from a customs union in western Europe because of the weakness of Europe itself. A European trading bloc would also be contrary to the doctrine of free trade throughout the world, popular in the United States. They predicted that there would be a world shortage of raw materials and food, and so thought that Britain's interests lay in preserving her trading links with the Empire and Commonwealth. Furthermore, the Treasury and the Board of Trade wanted to maintain **sterling** as a world trading currency. As well as generating revenue, sterling's world role provided Britain with international prestige, and confirmed her position as head of the Commonwealth and the Empire.

Economic weakness meant that Britain had to seek economic help from the United States. In 1947, the United States offered economic aid to Europe with the Marshall Plan. The Plan had far reaching consequences. The Soviet Union refused participation for itself and for its eastern European satellites. This divided Europe into two hostile blocs, with western Europe accepting **liberal capitalism**, and eastern Europe communist ideals. Marshall Aid also forced the issue of western European co-operation, as it was necessary to set up a body to manage the four-year economic recovery programme. The French and the Americans wanted a supranational authority and customs union in western Europe. Bevin refused, and the weaker intergovernmental Organisation for European Economic Co-operation (OEEC) was set up. Bevin realised that, economically, an independent third force in Europe was impossible. Marshall Aid showed that Europe needed American money. Bevin now wanted to illustrate British strength by bridging the gap between America and Europe.

Liberal capitalism: The political and economic system based on democracy and the private ownership of businesses.

British policy towards the Soviet Union

The other main factor causing Bevin to reject the idea of a Third Force Europe was that he saw the Soviet Union as the main threat to peace in Europe. If the Soviet Union attacked, western Europe would be powerless against its superior might. America was the only power with enough resources to challenge the Soviet Union. America also had an atomic bomb, used for the first time to devastating effect in Japan in 1945. Bevin realised that only the American nuclear threat could deter the Soviet Union, and keep Europe at peace.

Historians have different views on when Bevin realised this threat. Anne Deighton, in *The Impossible Peace* (1993), argued that Bevin and the Foreign Office believed from soon after the war that the Soviet Union, not Germany, would prove to be the main threat to mainland Europe. However, the Soviet Union was an ally, and the Soviets had shown bravery and suffered huge loss of life in defeating the Germans. Bevin therefore had to hide his suspicions, while secretly working in the Council of Foreign Ministers meetings between the British, Americans, French and Russians, to attract America out of isolationism. Bullock saw the Treaties of Dunkirk and Brussels as **'a sprat to catch a mackerel'**. Europe had to show that it could defend itself, to encourage American involvement.

'A sprat to catch a mackerel': A saying where bait is used to force someone into action.

On the other hand, Sean Greenwood argues that Bevin was not completely sure until 1948 that American involvement was vital to contain the threat of the Soviet Union. That year was certainly crucial in consolidating the division of Europe: the Soviet leader Josef Stalin reacted to Czech interest in Marshall Aid by staging a coup, replacing the Czech's democratically-elected government with a pro-Soviet, communist government. He then directly threatened the west by cutting off road and rail links to west Berlin, which lay within the Soviet zone of Germany. For a whole year, the Allies had to airlift food and fuel into West Berlin to prevent the citizens from starving. In 1949, the **NATO** treaty was signed, committing America to defend western Europe. The USA promised to regard an attack against any NATO country as an attack against itself.

NATO: Established by the USA, Canada, UK, France, Iceland, Italy, Belgium, Luxembourg and the Netherlands.

Europe and federalism

British involvement with the United States both in the devaluation crisis, and in joining NATO, left France with the initiative to develop plans for western Europe. In France, ideas for a federal Europe gathered force. In 1948, at a special Congress in the Hague, the French advanced plans for a federal Europe, run by a European Parliament. Churchill raised expectations that Britain would get involved when he declared that Britain wanted

1. What evidence is there to suggest that Bevin sought to establish a European Third Force after the war?

2. How important was the Soviet Union in the formation of Bevin's foreign policy?

a 'United States of Europe'. Bevin had no intention of joining, however, as he did not want any loss of British national sovereignty. Instead he set up the Council of Europe, with a looser, intergovernmental structure. Even Churchill did not believe that Britain should surrender national sovereignty. His idea of the United States of Europe had Britain guiding Europe from the outside.

6.2 How did Anthony Eden deal with the problem of West German rearmament in 1954?

West German rearmament

After the war, an Allied Control Commission of Britain, France, the United States of America and the Soviet Union governed Germany. After Stalin annexed the eastern zone of Germany in 1948, Britain, France and America agreed to set up a German government in the west. West Germany would be allowed to govern itself: a vital step on the road to **national autonomy**. In 1950, the United States began to call for the rearmament of West Germany. The immediate reason for this was because America was fighting the communists in Korea. They saw the Korean War as evidence of Soviet aggression, which could turn next to Europe. West Germany had the potential to develop into the strongest state in Europe, and so could contribute a great deal to the defence of the continent. Britain agreed with the Americans, because of the cost of British troops in West Germany. France, however, was horrified that only five years after the end of the war, the West Germans would again be given their own army.

National autonomy: National self government, national independence.

The French solution

The French responded to this problem with the Pleven Plan for a European Defence Community (EDC). The economist Jean Monnet, who drafted the Plan, proposed a supranational army. Both France and Germany would contribute troops and military resources, which would be commanded by a joint body containing both French and German personnel. Bevin was opposed to this plan, because he thought it was militarily naïve and because it could threaten the NATO alliance. However, if the British and Americans agreed to study the Plan, the French would then agree to the principle of West German rearmament, which the British and Americans wanted.

Jean Monnet (1889–1979)
French economist and architect of European integration. Believed in supranational integration to help the French economy. One of the leading figures setting up the European Economic Community in 1957.

The British reaction to the Pleven Plan

Bevin's initial reaction was hostile, but he allowed studies of the plan to begin. Herbert Morrison, who became Foreign Secretary when Bevin died in 1950, realised that Britain would have to support the plan in order to secure West German rearmament. He believed that Britain's role should be to watch as other states moved towards supranationalism. Britain could bridge the gap between the European nations and America. In 1951 there was another change of Foreign Secretary as Anthony Eden took the post when the Conservatives won the general election. His policy has been described by John Young in *Britain and European Unity, 1945–1992* (1993) as 'benevolence towards, but non-involvement in' supranationality. Eden was anxious to see the EDC succeed, but refused absolutely to consider British participation in a supranational community. Nobody in Britain thought Britain should join a supranational community at this point. Churchill, the Prime Minister, who had been thought to have 'pro-European' attitudes, described the EDC as a **'sludgy amalgam'**.

Sludgy amalgam: Badly formed mixture.

Did the British try to wreck the EDC?

The British have been accused of trying to sabotage the EDC. The evidence for this is that Eden proposed alternative plans. For example, France, Germany, Italy, and **Benelux** – or the 'Six' – signed a treaty in May 1952 agreeing the establishment of the EDC. Eden responded with the Eden Plan for a 'bridge' to be built between the Six and those countries such as Britain, Scandinavia, Austria, Switzerland and Greece who preferred inter-governmental organisations to the Six's supranationality. Again, in 1954, Eden proposed an institutional link between Britain and the Six called the 'Council of Association'. Britain promised to commit troops to the conti-nent: roughly the same amount as demanded by the Pleven Plan. The difference, of course, was that Britain retained national control over the use of these forces. Some Conservatives, including Churchill, said in Cabinet meetings that they hoped the EDC would fail. However, records of Cabinet meetings also show that Eden appreciated the importance of the EDC to retain French goodwill in NATO, and to rearm Germany. He was concerned that Britain would appear to be trying to sabotage the EDC and worked hard to prevent this. He wanted the EDC to work, but was eager to avoid tying Britain to it. When the EDC failed, the speed with which Eden outlined his alternative proposals also raised suspicions that Britain had tried to wreck the EDC all along.

The failure of the EDC

In 1954, the French National Assembly failed to **ratify** the EDC treaty. There were many reasons for the change of French heart. Some French politicians had been opposed to the Pleven Plan from the start because they did not want to 'surrender' French forces to the Germans for nation-alist reasons. Some, including the communists, still rejected any form of German rearmament. More importantly the international climate had changed. The Korean War ended in July 1953, which meant that the need for continental forces to defend Europe was lessened. In March 1953, the Soviet dictator Joseph Stalin died. This led to a relaxation of world tension, and a belief that **détente** would follow. Furthermore, the French were now fighting a colonial war in French Indochina. The involvement of their forces there meant the German army in Europe would certainly be bigger than the French one. The French did not like the thought of being weaker than the Germans in a joint army.

Eden's proposal for West German rearmament

The British had been studying alternative plans to the EDC, and when the EDC unexpectedly failed, the opportunity was ripe for making proposals. Eden's proposal was to extend the Brussels Pact of 1948 to West Germany and Italy as well as to France and Benelux. This involved Britain further in the defence of the continent. The Brussels Pact troops would be managed in the Western European Union (WEU), set up in 1955. This was an inter-governmental organisation, meaning that forces would not be merged under one supranational authority. In return for British involvement in European defence, West Germany would be rearmed under NATO guid-ance, and, most importantly, West Germany was to regain national sovereignty and be allowed to sit in the NATO Council. Eden therefore ensured the completion of West German recovery, which was what the Americans and British wanted. In the absence of any alternative proposals, the Six agreed to Eden's plan. Robert Rhodes James, Eden's biographer, called the WEU a triumph of Eden's policy.

The consequences of Eden's solution

The acceptance of the WEU by the Six was a success for Anthony Eden. He managed to secure West German rearmament in the way the British

Benelux: Belgium, the Netherlands and Luxembourg.

Ratify: Pass into law.

Détente: Relaxing of tense relationships.

wanted, and avoided participation in supranational organisations without too much criticism of sabotage. The WEU was an example of the success of the 'three circles', with Britain mediating between the Atlantic Alliance and the European nations. However, this success may well have lulled the British into a false sense of security about their bargaining power and international role. The success of Eden's policy, and the belief that the British could get their own way in international affairs, contributed directly to Britain's failure to participate in talks to set up the European Economic Community, the most important development in European relations since the Second World War.

1. What was Anthony Eden and Winston Churchill's attitude to supranationalism?

2. Did the British try to wreck the EDC?

6.3 Did Britain 'miss the bus' in Europe, 1950–1957?
A CASE STUDY IN HISTORICAL INTERPRETATION

In 1951 the 'Six' signed the Treaty of Paris establishing the European Coal and Steel Community. In 1957, they signed the Treaty of Rome, setting up the European Economic Community, the result of talks begun at Messina two years earlier. The ECSC, originating from a Plan by the French Foreign Minister Robert Schuman, arranged supranational institutions for the Six's coal and steel industries. The EEC was an economic customs union, in a supranational political structure.

The traditional view among historians is that Britain 'missed the bus' on Europe at some point between 1945–57. The Conservative MP, Anthony Nutting, in *Europe Will Not Wait* (1964), argued that Britain threw away the opportunity to take the leadership of Europe, which was its for the taking, after the war. British policy towards Europe always developed a few years too late. For example, Britain realised only in 1961 that it would have to apply for membership. If it had realised in 1955, it could have been part of the Messina talks and the Rome Treaty. An earlier development of European policy would have been better for British interests, because it could have moulded Europe to suit itself.

Of what value is this cartoon to a historian looking at Britain's relations with the EEC in the 1960s?

"IF THEY WANT US THEY WILL HAVE TO MAKE IT EASY FOR US" —MR. MACMILLAN

Missing the bus at the Schuman Plan

The case for

- Edmund Dell, an historian and Labour MP in the 1970s, argued that Britain 'missed the bus' when Bevin failed to participate in the Schuman Plan talks. He argued that officials and ministers had a responsibility to understand events on the continent, and should have appreciated the drive towards integration. Even if ministers could not accept supra-nationality, they should have worked to encourage '**rapprochement**' between France and West Germany. Ministers should have had the imagination to sell the idea of 'Europe' to the public. Furthermore, he shows that France did want Britain to participate in the Schuman talks. Jean Monnet was frequently on the phone to Britain to ask it to join, and the French ambassador Rene Massigli was also very pro-British. The failure to participate in the ECSC, Dell argues, made failure to participate at Messina inevitable. The Six learnt they could forge ahead without Britain, and the British saw that the Six were developing in ways they did not like.

Rapprochement: Establishment of a good relationship.

The case against

- Dell and Nutting have been criticised because they assume that Britain could have taken the leadership of Europe at any point after the war. There is nothing to prove that this was the case. Britain did make initiatives in Europe, such as the Council of Europe in 1949, or the Eden Plan in 1952. Bullock shows that Britain did establish leadership, through the OEEC and NATO. However, the French preferred to pursue supranationalism in 1950 through the Schuman Plan, and the Eden Plan was ignored.

- Revisionist historians like John Young in *Britian and European Unity* show that Whitehall did not just dismiss the Schuman Plan out of hand, but seriously contemplated it, and decided that membership was not in British interests. The Plan demanded that participants agree to lose sovereignty before they began discussing the Plan. This was contrary to the British desire to develop political structures slowly. Accepting supranationality in advance would be, in Bevin's words, 'putting the roof on before you have built the house'. The Foreign Office also thought that the Schuman Plan, without British participation, had only a limited chance of success.

- The British also had domestic political reasons for not getting involved. Foreign Secretary Herbert Morrison told the Cabinet that 'the Durham miners won't wear it'. Britain had the strongest coal and steel industries in Europe and saw no reason to share this around. Coal and steel were also politically important to Labour. British industrialisation had been built on the back of coal and steel, and Labour had only recently nationalised the industries, a popular socialist policy.

- Roger Bullen argued that the French made it hard for the British to participate. They did not inform the British when Schuman first developed the plan, although they had undertaken to do so. In May 1950, Bevin wanted more time to consider the British position and whether or not Britain could 'associate' with the ECSC. Schuman, however, gave Britain twenty-four hours to decide whether or not to attend the talks. This attitude persuaded the British to say no. Whether or not the French invited the British, it was clear that the

Schuman Plan did not require British membership. Bevin may have felt snubbed. He told the junior MP James Callaghan that Britain could not join because 'the French don't want us'.

Missing the bus at Messina

The case for

● Bevin's biographer Lord Bullock argued that real opportunities were not missed until Messina. John Young agreed. Young argued that when the Six were discussing the EEC, the British fully understood the dangers of exclusion from a successful customs union on the continent. Ministers should therefore have re-evaluated the importance of Europe, and should have appreciated that federalism would not harm British interests. They knew by 1955 that the Commonwealth trade preference was less important to British interests than it had been, and they were no longer preoccupied by the Soviet threat. However, they failed to think seriously about Britain's future role in the world. Britain should have had the foresight to re-evaluate its world position.

The case against

● A second main criticism of the school of thought that says that Britain 'missed the bus' is that it judges British policy from a pro-European viewpoint. Both Nutting and Dell were strongly pro-European. They therefore assume that supranational, political integration was the correct and natural course for Europe to take after the war. During the war, resistance movements fighting the Nazis dreamed that federalism would replace nationalism. If nation states were dead, another nationalist war would be impossible. Nutting and Dell assumed that the EEC was a bus that Britain should have caught.

● Revisionist historians have suggested that perhaps Britain did not want to catch the bus. Firstly, the economic historian Alan Milward examined the nature of the EEC in *The Reconstruction of Western Europe 1945–51* (1984), and concluded that the Six joined the EEC because it was in their national interests. France wanted to share in the strong German industries, and control the development of the German state, to ensure that Germany could never again invade France. The West Germans wanted to prove their peaceful intentions by accepting limits on their national sovereignty. They could then rebuild the German economy and state. For the smaller states, membership of the EEC would give them privileged access to the large German economy, as well as increasing their political voice. Britain did not have such an obvious reason for joining the EEC.

● Miriam Camps in *Britain and the European Community 1955–1963* (1964) shows that the British felt that the EEC was against their national interest in some ways. The Foreign Office did not want join a supranational community in 1957, as it did not want to surrender national sovereignty. The Treasury and the Board of Trade still felt that British interests lay in trading with the world at large. They also thought that western European economies were weak, and could adversely affect the British economy. Politicians were also wary that the public would not support the idea of going into Europe. The idea of Empire and Britain's Great Power status was popular. As Lord Douglas-Home said, 'the British public was still too near to the glory of Empire to accept the role for Britain of just another country in Europe'. Wolfram Kaiser argued that politicians deliberately clung onto the myth of Britain's Empire and greatness, in order to emphasise how different from Europe Britain was. They used patriotic language because it was popular with the public, and so helped their own interests by helping them stay in power.

- A further criticism of the 'missed the bus' school of thought is it concentrates on what British policy should have been, rather than on what British policy actually was. James Ellison shows how Britain tried to influence the course of European integration. In 1955, Britain tried to sabotage the EEC by encouraging the Six to use the intergovernmental OEEC. The Six refused. The Treasury and Board of Trade realised that if a customs union developed on the continent, it would not be in Britain's national interests to be stuck outside. In 1956, Britain developed Plan G proposals for a **free trade area**. Between 1957 and 1958, Britain negotiated with the Six to develop a free trade area alongside the customs union. Britain therefore had a sensible response to the Messina proposals. If the free trade area talks had succeeded, Britain would not have appeared so isolated in Europe. The question was therefore less whether Britain missed the bus, but why Britain failed to change its direction.

It was not inevitable that the free trade area talks would fail. The West Germans were interested in free trade to increase markets for their exports, and there was opposition in France to supranationality. Firstly, Plan G failed because the British overestimated their bargaining power, and underestimated the strength of feeling among the Six for supranational integration. Secondly, as Miriam Camps showed, the free trade area talks failed because of the **Suez Crisis**. Suez destroyed good feeling between the French and the British. Both countries realised that they could not act alone in the world. Britain turned to America to rebuild their special relationship which would enhance Britain's power. France realised that the best way to build up its own power base was through the EEC. France could only lead in Europe in the absence of Britain. The French were therefore determined that the EEC would work, and without Britain. In 1958, the formidable French war hero General de Gaulle returned to power. He had no time for diplomatic niceties, and immediately vetoed the free trade area talks.

Free trade area: Britain wanted to encourage free trade throughout Europe, including Scandinavia. A Free Trade Area would allow preferential trade with the Commonwealth, and would not include agricultural produce. It would have intergovernmental, not supranational governance.

Suez Crisis: Conflict between the British, French and Israelis against the Egyptian leader Colonel Nasser, October–November 1956. The British, French and Israelis secretly agreed to stage Egyptian aggression in order to give them an excuse to attack Nasser. Britain could not sustain military involvement because its economy was not strong enough. It had to withdraw, internationally humiliated. The Americans were furious because they had not been consulted (see Chapter 4, section 6 and page 113).

---

1. Why have historians taken different views about Britain's policy towards European integration in the 1950s?

2. Why did Bevin reject participation in the Schuman Plan talks?

3. Why did Britain fail to create a free trade area in Europe?

6.4 Why did Harold Macmillan decide to apply for membership of the EEC?

Harold Macmillan became Prime Minister in 1957. He had been one of the Tory pro-Europeans under Anthony Eden, calling for a more constructive role with the EDC. He believed that Britain must enter the EEC, because he realised that Britain's days as a Great Power were over. Macmillan presided over some of the most radical foreign policy changes since the war. As well as the application to the EEC, he accelerated Britain's withdrawal from empire. At a famous speech in Africa, he claimed that the 'winds of change' were sweeping over that continent. By 1963, many of Britain's colonies had been granted independence. These huge changes have led historians to see Macmillan as a radical Prime Minister. Miriam Camps claimed that Macmillan's application to the EEC marked a considerable evolution in British attitudes to Europe.

It could, however, also be seen as inevitable that Britain should apply to join the EEC. The British understood, when the Messina talks began, that if a political and economic group did develop on the continent, it would not be in British interests to be excluded from it. When the free trade area talks ended in failure, Britain was left with Sweden, Denmark, Norway, Austria, Switzerland and Portugal, with whom it formed the European Free Trade Association (EFTA). EFTA could never be the political and economic force that the EEC became. Britain could not afford to remain outside the EEC, a fact it had always known.

There were several basic economic reasons pushing Britain towards the EEC. The Six were enjoying economic growth, stimulated by the removal of tariff barriers to trade among themselves in 1960. By contrast, British economic growth was slowing, and for the first time since the war, discontent was growing at home over Britain's economic policies. The weakness of the Commonwealth to provide for Britain's trading needs was also exposed as Britain's trade with Western Europe grew far faster. From 1954–60, Britain's exports to the Common Market rose by 29 per cent, compared to 1 per cent to the Sterling Area countries. EFTA did not help promote British trade, as Britain was the largest market among the EFTA countries. Big business in Britain was now in favour of British membership of the EEC, to provide a stimulus to competition, and to encourage investment.

The political reasons, however, were stronger. The Suez Crisis in 1956 dealt a severe shock to British policy makers, revealing in no uncertain terms that Britain was no longer a Great Power. The Americans were annoyed because Britain had not consulted them. Macmillan wanted to

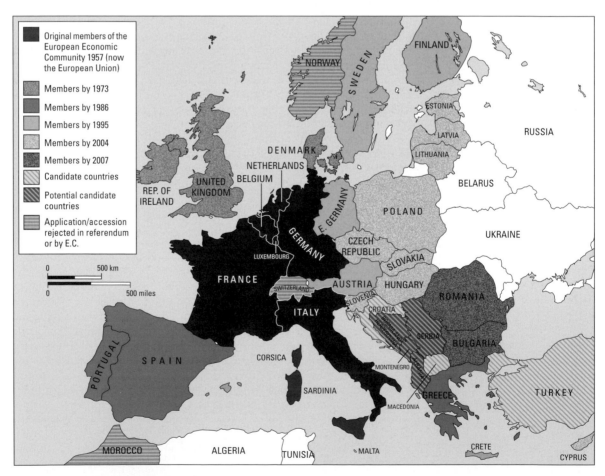

The growth of the European Union

restore the 'special relationship' with the Americans, fearing that if the EEC developed into a strong political bloc, that the Americans would prefer to deal with Germany than Britain. Britain's traditional policy in the Commonwealth was also in trouble. Economic weakness in Britain meant that the Commonwealth countries were looking to other markets to export goods and the Commonwealth was not politically cohesive. It was possible that Commonwealth countries could seek association with the EEC, as Nigeria did in 1962. Macmillan therefore saw EEC membership as a means of boosting British power and influence in the world. Rather than a radical change in attitude, Macmillan's policy could be seen as a continuation of traditional British policy. He wanted to retain British influence in the world, and wanted to use the EEC to achieve this.

Wolfram Kaiser in *Using Europe, Abusing the Europeans: Britain and European Integration 1945–63* (1963) has emphasised the positive aspects of Macmillan's policy. He argued that Macmillan's application was not just an inevitable attempt to claw back British power. Rather, the application solved some of Macmillan's short-term problems. Firstly, and most importantly, the United States wanted the British to apply for membership. When John F. Kennedy became President in 1961, he pressurised Macmillan to join the EEC. Kennedy thought it vital that the EEC developed in line with American political and security interests in Europe, and British membership would help achieve this. Britain and America wanted to avoid an independent Europe led by General de Gaulle. Such a 'Third Force' Europe could turn away from NATO. Macmillan and Kennedy wanted to keep Europe looking outwards to the Atlantic. In order to retain the 'special relationship', and to ensure that Britain retained her own nuclear capability, provided by the Americans, Macmillan had to apply to the EEC. He needed to show Kennedy that he was interested in membership, even if the application was likely to fail.

Kaiser also argues that an application would have helped Macmillan control the division in the Conservative Party over Europe. Kaiser sees this as the beginning of the problems caused by Europe in British party politics. With leading Cabinet ministers like Edward Heath, Duncan Sandys and Lord Douglas-Home now in favour of membership, Macmillan had to apply in order to show them that he too, was a 'pro' European. Influential groups in the City of London and business also wanted to join. Therefore, the application had some short-term political advantages for Macmillan.

> **General de Gaulle (1890–1970)**
> When France surrendered to the Germans in 1940, General de Gaulle led the French resistance movement, the 'Free French', setting up government in England. He returned to power in 1958, forming the Fifth Republic, and remained President until 1969. Formidably powerful.

> **To what extent was Macmillan's policy towards Europe a radical change?**

6.5 Why was Britain not able to join the EEC until 1973?

Macmillan's application was vetoed by General de Gaulle in 1963, after two years of negotiations. In 1967, the Labour government led by Harold Wilson once again applied for membership. De Gaulle vetoed it six months later, before negotiations had even begun. This time, however, Wilson left the application 'on the table'. In 1970, the Conservatives won the general election again, now led by the pro-European Edward Heath. General de Gaulle resigned as French leader in 1969, and died a year later. However, even without de Gaulle, British entry was far from inevitable.

Harold Macmillan's application

De Gaulle's vision for Europe stood in the way of British entry, and this was the fundamental reason preventing Britain from achieving entry in 1961 and 1967. Firstly, de Gaulle wanted France to lead Europe. If Britain was allowed in, Britain would also want to lead Europe, so from de Gaulle's point of view, it was better to keep her out. Secondly, he wanted Europe to be strong, and independent from American influence. He wanted French culture and language to flourish. Politically, he saw Europe as a 'Third Force' between the superpowers. Thirdly, de Gaulle was interested in pursuing détente by developing an independent French force, and by making friends with the Russians. This policy developed in the later 1960s, when de Gaulle decided he no longer wanted to participate in NATO. With these goals in mind, it is not surprising that he did not want British interference, still less did he want American influence strengthened by British membership.

Most historians agree that there was little Macmillan could do to secure British entry into the EEC in 1961–63. However, some, such as Piers Ludlow, have stressed that British policy contributed to the failure of the application. Macmillan's application said that Britain would negotiate to find out whether membership would be compatible with Britain's commitments to the Commonwealth and with British systems of agriculture. The negotiations dealt at great length with Commonwealth exports and the Community's Common Agricultural Policy (CAP). Britain would only enter 'if the conditions were right'. There was plenty of opposition in the Conservative government to the application and the Labour Party were against it. Britain did not seem to be a European nation, and this made it easier for de Gaulle to veto.

Furthermore, there was a dispute in the Community itself about the value of supranationalism. The Five – West Germany, Italy, the Netherlands, Belgium and Luxembourg – wanted to increase supranationality and move towards greater integration. France, however, preferred a '*Europe des Patries*': a Europe of independent states. This, of course, appealed to the British. In 1961, with the Fouchet Plan, the French suggested moving towards political co-operation between national governments, which would strengthen the political role of the EEC while reducing the supranational element. Macmillan believed that it was possible to put pressure on de Gaulle by emphasising that Britain could help reduce supranationality in the Community. The problem with this approach was that the Five, who supported British entry, also supported supranationalism. This again made it easier for de Gaulle to claim that Britain was not 'European' enough to join the Community.

Macmillan's main tactic, however, was to offer the French political incentives. France did not have her own nuclear weapons, and wanted them to build up French power. At a meeting at Chateau des Champs in June 1962, it is possible that Macmillan offered de Gaulle a nuclear deal with the British. After this meeting, there was some hope among French officials that de Gaulle would allow Britain to come in. However, the British were reliant on the Americans for nuclear weapons. At a meeting in Nassau, Macmillan agreed with the American President John F. Kennedy that Britain would buy Polaris missiles from the United States. Macmillan needed to do this in order to retain Britain's independent nuclear deterrent. Macmillan told de Gaulle at a meeting at Rambouillet in October 1962 that France could have these Polaris missiles as well. However, the last thing de Gaulle wanted was help from the Americans, and this gave him a further excuse to veto the application.

Harold Wilson's application

In 1967 the new Labour Prime Minister Harold Wilson decided that it was worth another attempt, and applied for membership. The economic and political reasons compelling Macmillan to take this step in 1961 were now even more urgent. Britain now had severe problems with the economy and the strength of sterling. Wilson's tactics showed that the lessons of the first application had to some extent been learnt. He kept the issues for negotiation to a minimum, mainly involving the CAP, and tried to play down the conditions for Britain's entry. Most importantly, Wilson stated that Britain was prepared to accept the Treaty of Rome. In saying this, Wilson agreed to the supranational principle behind the EEC.

Like Macmillan, Wilson may well have believed he had a chance of persuading de Gaulle to let Britain in by arguing that de Gaulle would prevent the development of Europe into a great force if he refused to let Britain in. However, he had even less bargaining power than Macmillan, and in practice had to rely on the persuasion of the Five. But it was clear that in the last resort, the Five were not willing to risk breaking up the Community and losing France just to let Britain in. When de Gaulle finally vetoed in November 1967, he stressed Britain's economic weakness, claiming that Britain only wanted to get in to help her economy. Wilson countered by leaving the application open, ready to be taken up again at the earliest opportunity. This opportunity arrived when de Gaulle resigned in early 1969.

Edward Heath's application

However, Britain could not just then enter the Community, as Britain still had certain problems with the EEC system. At an EEC meeting in 1969, the principle to negotiate for Britain was agreed, but the French insisted that agriculture must be settled first. The agricultural system then agreed was harmful to British interests, because Britain would have to pay more into it, and would get less back, than the other EEC countries. In 1970, Wilson created more obstacles by saying on television that British entry would have to be on the right terms, especially regarding agriculture. Despite his earlier concessions, he also said that there must be no federal constitution. The Europeans could see his comments as an attempt to change the nature of the Community.

In 1970, the Conservative government under Edward Heath was elected into government. Edward Heath was a committed pro-European. He even played down Britain's 'special relationship' with the United States, in order to appeal to the EEC. This was very important in the forthcoming talks. Negotiations, as set up under Wilson, began straight away. However, the talks got into difficulties in October 1970 over the question of agriculture, and the fact that the French now wanted to discuss the world role of the pound sterling. Edward Heath intervened and went to talk to the new French President Georges Pompidou. Because of Heath's pro-European attitude, Pompidou believed he could trust Heath, and it was down to these talks that British membership of the European Community was agreed.

1. How did Macmillan and Wilson attempt to achieve Britain's membership of the EEC?

2. To what extent was Edward Heath responsible for taking Britain into Europe?

3. Was French opposition the only factor keeping Britain out of Europe between 1961 and 1973?

6.6 Why did the Labour governments have so many concerns about British membership of the EEC in the 1970s?

Harold Wilson was a master politician and tactician. In his early political career, he sided with the left wing of the Labour Party. The left were mainly anti-European. When he was Prime Minister, he betrayed the left by applying to join the EEC. He continued to pretend to his left-wing allies that he did not want to go into the EEC, and told them not to worry because de Gaulle would veto the application anyway. He also outwitted the left wing. When he first considered applying to join Europe, early in 1966, he spoke about the terms and conditions Britain would have to arrange to safeguard her essential interests. The party therefore did not debate whether or not to go in, only how they would do it. The pro-Europeans, mainly on the right wing of the party, led by Roy Jenkins and George Brown, were pleased with the decision to go into Europe. However, they saw Wilson as untrustworthy, using Europe for domestic political reasons. When the Labour government fell in 1970, both sides of the party decided to give vent to their built-up anger.

Left-wing attitudes to Europe

Many left wingers, and some right-wingers such as Douglas Jay, had objections to Britain's membership of the EEC. Led by Tony Benn and Michael Foot, the left thought that Britain's national sovereignty would be threatened by the EEC. There were two threads to this fear. Firstly, and this was a fear shared by the Conservative right wing, that the EEC would erode the power of British Parliament to make law. Secondly, as more policy would be made by the government with its European partners in Brussels, rather than in London, parliament would lose the ability to keep an effective check on policy-making. Benn saw this as a threat to democracy. The left also saw the EEC as a danger to socialism. They saw the EEC as a capitalist trading bloc, which would stop Britain planning the economy. The EEC's protectionist common external tariff would also prevent international socialism and development of Third World countries in the Commonwealth. As well as these fundamental objections, the left also had specific fears. EEC membership would push up the cost of food, and harm the 'ordinary housewife'. Increased industrial competition would encourage development in the wealthy south and east, to the detriment of the poorer north and west. Farmers in the north and west would also suffer. EEC membership impeded the left's vision of a socialist solution to Britain's increasing economic problems.

The struggle between the left and right of the party to lead Labour also contributed to the strength of feeling about Europe. The right's vision for the future was much more in line with moderates in the Conservative Party. They saw that Britain had to be in Europe, and did not champion a socialist-style planned economy. Both left and right wanted to capture the hearts and minds of party members and the public, and so gain power within the party. In 1971, Heath's application was debated in the House of Commons. Heath only had a small majority, and so there was a chance to defeat the government. But the right of the Labour party – 69 MPs – voted with Heath to take Britain into Europe. The left could not believe that the right preferred to take Britain into Europe than defeat a Conservative government. The right realised that siding with the Tories over Europe was one way of ensuring that the left did not gain too much power within the Labour Party.

The question of personal political ambitions must also be taken into account. Europe was a vital issue for Britain's national interests. It was also an emotional one, and one where it was possible to influence public opinion because the public were relatively ignorant about European affairs. Tony Benn, in 1967, was moderately in favour of Britain's membership of the EEC. His conversion to anti-Europeanism could be seen as a calculation to bring maximum personal benefit. As the Labour Party became more dominated by the left in the 1970s, the best way to gain power was to support left-wing causes. Benn was the highest profile anti-European on the left, and this was a challenge to the Labour Party's leadership. The left's concerns about Europe in the 1970s therefore must be seen as a mixture of ideology and political ambition.

Wilson's response to Labour attitudes to Europe

To keep the party together, and to preserve his position, Wilson decided he had to present a more anti-European image. It is important that he never said that Britain should withdraw from Europe. Rather, he said that Edward Heath had not managed to secure satisfactory terms to safeguard Britain's national interests. Wilson now said that if he were back in power, he would renegotiate those terms with the EEC. The left, however, was not satisfied. Tony Benn claimed that Britain should have a referendum on whether or not to remain a member of the EEC. As all three of the main parties were in favour of European membership, an anti-European voter did not have the opportunity to vote for an anti-European policy. On an issue of vital national importance, Benn saw this as undemocratic. A referendum would solve this problem by allowing the public to vote. More importantly, it provided the Labour Party with a solution to their internal disputes. If the public were to decide whether or not to stay in Europe, Wilson did not have to.

Renegotiation and referendum

When Wilson was returned to power in 1974, he set about renegotiating the terms under which Britain was a member of the EEC. This has widely been regarded as a waste of time, contributing to the lack of business in the Community in the 1970s and creating bad will between Britain and Europe. Wilson did manage to slightly reduce Britain's contributions to the agricultural budget, and to extend the arrangements for importing New Zealand's butter for a further three years. These concessions did little to dampen the left's fears, and did much to annoy the right.

The referendum was a unique constitutional experience. It was the first referendum in British history. It was also the first time in British history that the Cabinet had been allowed to disagree in public. Wilson thought that this would clear the air and allow the 'pro' and 'anti' Europeans to all have their say. However, the sides were not particularly evenly matched. On the side of the pros were the leaders of the Labour party, Conservative party and Liberals, and many centre-right, moderate politicians. The pros also had the backing of big business and so their campaign was better funded. The antis on the other hand were the extremists from both parties. Left-wingers Benn and Foot campaigned with virulent right-wingers led by Enoch Powell. Powell was by this time notorious for his racist 'rivers of blood' speech, and so did not have the support of moderate opinion. The result of the referendum was a 67 per cent vote to stay inside the EEC. This was a resounding backing for British membership, but the problems causing the referendum in the first place were far from over.

The consequences of the referendum

The left wing felt hard done by because Wilson had thrown in his lot with the pro-Europeans. They saw that they had lost the centre ground of British politics and determined to win it back. Their programme was far broader than just Europe. At a time of increasing economic and industrial unrest, they wanted increased nationalisation of industries and greater welfare spending. The right wing, on the other hand, led by Roy Jenkins, saw in the referendum that they had more in common with moderate conservatives and liberals than they did with members of their own party. The referendum therefore set the scene for the split of the Labour party in 1981. Labour lost the 1979 election, and, in reaction to the right-wing Thatcher government, rising unemployment and economic recession, moved further to the left. Michael Foot was elected leader. The pro-European right, under Roy Jenkins, decided to leave the Labour party and form a new party, the Social Democratic Party (SDP).

The referendum also had long-term consequences in the development of the debate in Britain about European membership. The left did have some legitimate fears. There was a threat to British parliamentary democracy, and membership would necessitate some fundamental changes to Britain's trade and agriculture systems. However, Wilson did nothing to address these fears head on. Rather, the pro-European argument during the referendum campaign asserted that there was no alternative for Britain if it wished to retain influence in the world. While the left argued that EEC membership would increase food prices and unemployment, the right simply said that these fears were unfounded. The pro-Europeans were afraid to address the question of national sovereignty, in case it made EEC membership unpopular in the country. Pro-Europeans were anxious to play down the fact that in future, British law could be over-ridden by European legislation. Therefore, there was no serious debate about what British membership of the European Economic Community actually meant, and what changes it could bring. This had a long-term effect on Britain's ability to play a positive and constructive role in the Community.

1. Was Harold Wilson a pro or anti European?

2. Why was the left wing of the Labour party so anti-European in the 1970s?

6.7 In-depth study: Was Thatcher totally anti-European?

- Was she able to reform the Common Agricultural Policy?
- Why did she negotiate the Single European Act?
- Why did she join the Exchange Rate Mechanism?

Framework of Events

1972/3	UK joins the EEC
1979	Dublin European Council
	Thatcher raises issue of UK overpayment
1980	Cabinet backs Thatcher's EEC budget rebate demands
1981	Socialist Mitterand elected President of France
1982	Social Democrat Kohl elected German Chancellor
	Paris–Bonn axis feared
1984	European Council finally agrees to UK budget demands
1985	Delors becomes President of European Commission
1986	London European Council
	Single European Act passes Parliament
1988	Partial reform of Common Agricultural Policy
	Delors Plan for EMU produced
1990	The UK joins the European Exchange Rate Mechanism.

EU commissioners: the full-time employees of the EU, based in Brussels.

Common Agricultural Policy: the EU system for organising agriculture in the member states. A large amount of money raised by taxes went to subsidise farmers' incomes. They could be paid, for example, to produce more butter than was needed.

ONE of the most debated aspects of all of Thatcher's administration was her attitude and policies towards the European Union (then known as the EEC, but will be referred to here throughout as the EU). To many opponents of the UK's membership and the EU generally, she is seen as a heroine. She stood up to the other members, but was also a staunch defender of the sovereignty of the UK. The epic confrontations she had with other European leaders and with the **EU commissioners** over a huge range of issues, especially the UK financial contribution to the EU, but also the **Common Agricultural Policy**, are widely known. What made her even more popular with the anti-EU supporters was her speech at Bruges, Belgium, in 1988, where she attacked many of the ideas underlying

Federalist: a political system where control in some areas of public life, such as agriculture or immigration, would lie with central govenment (i.e. the EU in Brussels) with other areas, such as education, left to local government (i.e. individual countries).

Murdoch press: papers owned by Australian and anti-EU Rupert Murdoch, including *The Times*, the *Sunday Times* and the *Sun*.

EU referendum debate of 1975: when the Labour government asked the British people to vote on whether they wished to stay in the EU. They voted to stay in by a clear majority.

Bureaucracy: government by unelected officials.

Bundesbank: the German Central Bank.

the EU and the possible federalist outcomes. This has led to her being seen not only as strongly anti-European, but also anxious to leave the EU altogether.

Reality is always more complex. It must be remembered that, politically and electorally, an 'anti-foreign' and anti-EU stance was very popular, especially with right-wing voters and the important **Murdoch press**.

However, Thatcher was well aware of the benefits that membership of the EU had brought to the UK. She had no intention of the UK giving up its membership, as the country had so much to gain economically from the free movement of capital, goods and services throughout the EU. The turnaround in the UK economy in the 1980s had been in part thanks to the access the British had to the vast European market.

Thatcher actually knew little about Europe and the EU when she became party leader. She had supported it as a member of Edward Heath's government, but there was no sign of any real enthusiasm on her part, nor was there from many on the Conservative right.

She was conspicuously silent and uninvolved in the **EU referendum debate of 1975**. She much preferred to see the USA as the UK's principal ally. She saw the USA very much as 'one of us' and the EU as 'foreign'. She did not like the vision of a united Europe backed by many on the Tory left, such as Edward Heath and his supporters. She felt that the EU was too large a **bureaucracy** and too dominated by French and German socialists. She felt it her duty to put the interests of Britain and its citizens (and their wallets) before those of a more abstract 'European' ideal.

Thatcher felt that the federal ideal put forward by the more enthusiastic supporters of the EU would lead inevitably to the end of democracy and the rise of a centralised bureaucracy. The thought of 'foreigners' interfering in UK internal matters appalled her. She felt that further union would lead to the 'Bank of England becoming a local branch of the **Bundesbank**'. Her approach remained typically British – wary, pragmatic and unenthusiastic – but she was content to remain in the EU as it brought so many economic benefits to the UK.

Britain had joined the EU in 1972, when Thatcher had been a member of the Conservative cabinet. The UK had attempted to join under earlier governments, both Labour and Conservative. Opposition to joining in the UK had come usually from both the right of the Conservative party, and the left of the Labour party.

Thatcher's first EU victory – the budget rebate

Like membership of any club, there was a subscription fee to be paid to the EU. Thatcher felt very strongly that the fee charged to the UK by the EU was far too high. She felt, probably correctly, that in his desperation to get in, the despised Edward Heath had accepted terms which were unfair to the UK. She felt that the UK was paying in more than it was getting out, and that UK citizens were subsidising inefficient foreigners out of their taxed income.

Many historians, such as Martin Holmes in *Thatcherism* (1989) or Peter Jenkins in *Mrs Thatcher's Revolution* (1987), and contemporary commentators, such as Hugo Young of the *Guardian* at the time, agree that she was probably right. She was able to negotiate a substantial rebate and reduce the UK contribution to EU funds. This was primarily done by her dominating the discussions with other EU leaders and simply refusing to talk about anything until 'our' money had been sorted out. However, in doing so she showed her contempt for the European 'idea', the Foreign Office, the EU Commission and the leaders of France and Germany.

Her methods of negotiating were not the polite diplomacy of the Foreign Office. Her blunt and simple requests for a return of 'my money'

The media sometimes felt that Thatcher's methods of dealing with her EU partners were a little rough.

were not the normal language of diplomacy. She got her way and the money was refunded – about £1.5 billion over a three-year period. Britain's contribution was now much more fair. The public were delighted and the right-wing press gave great prominence to Britain's 'defeat' of the foreigners. However, the fact that this method of negotiating did considerable harm to the idea of further European unity, and later possible support when it came to the Falklands wars, ought to be considered. Many felt that she could have attained her praiseworthy objectives without making quite so many enemies.

Was Thatcher able to reform the Common Agricultural Policy?

Thatcher herself, in her memoirs *The Downing Street Years* (1993), maintains that her inability to reform the Common Agricultural Policy (CAP), which she intensely disliked, was one of her greatest failures. The way in which she had antagonised her European partners over the rebate meant that her ability to influence change in agriculture was limited.

The CAP was a system where large-scale subsidies (other people's taxes!) were paid to farmers to protect farm prices and farmers' jobs. Often there was no demand for their products, so governments simply stored them. The famous butter 'mountains' and wine 'lakes' became objects of ridicule. Thatcher felt that these subsidies protected the inefficient, and harmed the efficient UK farmer. She felt that this sort of state intervention damaged the free market and prices were kept artificially high. Subsidy and protection were things she loathed. In many respects, the CAP was the exact opposite of Thatcherism.

However, she had limited credibility and influence in Europe, and her own party was split on all matters to do with the EU. Those from the New Right wanted an end to the CAP, but there were many Tory MPs who came from rural/farming constituencies who saw the CAP as vital to their Conservative voters. In the end, political reality dictated hot air but no action.

The decision-making process within the EU

The European Council

Made up of the Chief Executives (such as the French President, the UK Prime Minister) and the relevant Ministers. This is the central decision-making body in the EU. Note that it is the elected leaders of the EU who make the key decisions.

↓

The European Commission

The Executive of the EU. Their main role is to carry out the policies laid down by the Council. The UK has the right to appoint two Commissioners.

↓

The European Parliament

Made up of MEPs elected by the individual members. The UK has the right to send 87 MEPs to the European Parliament. It has a limited role, but serves to check the work of the Commission.

Why did Thatcher negotiate the Single European Act?

To see Thatcher as just anti-European is much too simple, although judging by her public utterances by 1986 that was a reasonable assumption to make. She referred to the EU in her memoirs *The Downing Street Years* (1993) as 'government by bureaucracy for bureaucracy'. Perhaps her most important work, as far as the EU was concerned, was put through at the height of her powers in 1986. This was the **Single European Act** (SEA), which many commentators feel is the most important Act passed by Parliament concerning the EU since the UK actually joined. It led the way to the great Maastricht Treaty in 1991.

The SEA was an important step towards making the EU a single market, with no barriers between any of the member states. It enabled labour, goods and capital to move freely around Europe. A British businessman could sell his goods and services in other EU countries freely. British business could, and did, invest for profit in the EU, and others could invest in plant and equipment in the UK.

The key elements of the SEA were:

- The European Community (EC) became formally known the European Union (EU).

- There would be gradual progress towards much more integration, through the free market and economic policy.

- It was now a common goal that the **Single Market Programme** should be complete by 1992.

- It streamlined the decision-making process at the highest level – the European Council – where the Prime Ministers of the member states met.

- The role of the European Parliament was strengthened.

- There would be greater co-operation over foreign policy within the EU.

As Thatcher was Prime Minister and responsible for passing the Single

The Single European Act: At the Luxembourg Intergovernmental Conference 1985–86 the European Community agreed to move to a single market by 1992. The SEA stated that Europe would 'make concrete progress to closer integration'. However, the actual provisions for deeper integration were not very radical, strengthening the role of the European Parliament and European Court of Justice, and making it harder for nations to veto decisions for themselves.

Single Market Programme: aimed at lifting all barriers to people, capital or goods moving throughout Europe.

Jacques Delors (1925–)
This French civil servant and politician was socialist Minister in France 1976–84. An economics specialist, he became President of the European Commission in 1985 and remained in office for ten years. He was a strong supporter of the drive to give greater powers to the EU.

EMU: European Monetary Union – a European Central Bank and a single European currency.

European Act through the UK Parliament, she cannot be viewed as opposing the EU totally. However, Thatcher felt that the SEA was as far as the UK ought to go when it came to the EU – but trouble arose almost at once when Jacques Delors became the President of the European Commission.

How important was Thatcher's Bruges speech?
No sooner was the ink dry on the UK signature to the SEA, than the seemingly pro-EU stance of Thatcher changed. Jacques Delors became President of the EU Commission (the head of the official EU bureaucracy based in Brussels). Not only was he a strong socialist, but he was also a committed federalist, a combination (to Thatcher) of two particularly obnoxious characteristics. She referred to him as one of a 'new breed of unaccountable politicians', whose philosophy 'justified centralism'. Delors' plans for **EMU** appalled Thatcher.

She had fought against 'centralising bureaucratic socialism' before, and she was not having it imposed again on the UK from the EU. Her views on socialism were well known, and she referred to federalism as 'the ending of democracy by centralisation and bureaucracy'. The idea of Brussels interfering with internal British matters was unthinkable to her.

This came to a head in her Bruges speech in 1988, where she stated her views on the EU very clearly, and started a process which badly split her own party and was to play an important part in her downfall. In this speech, Thatcher argued that:

- the EU was going in the wrong, federalist, direction

- clearly separate national identities had to be maintained within the EU

- there was to be no EU 'super state' controlled by Brussels

- the original ideal behind the EU, which she had supported, had been damaged by 'waste, corruption and the abuse of power'.

What she argued for was a 'willing and active cooperation between independent sovereign nations', and she claimed it would 'be folly to try and fit them into some sort of identikit European personality'. The single market she felt was vital – with a minimum of regulation by anyone. She wanted a 'Europe of enterprise' and she had her eyes firmly fixed on the huge potential markets of the Eastern European countries. She really wanted the UK to share the benefits of a large single market, but also to lead it.

Nigel Lawson (1932–)
A financial journalist by trade, Lawson was a Conservative MP 1974–92 and Minister 1979–83. He was appointed Secretary of State for Energy in 1981 and played an important role in the planning of privatisation. He became Chancellor of the Exchequer in 1983 and remained in the position during the key Thatcherite years until 1989, when he resigned over her dominating style and attitude to the EU.

Exchange Rate Mechanism: Europe-based system of deciding the exchange rate for European currencies, including the pound, with the aim of bringing stable interest rates throughout the EU. It was designed to help investment and also stabilise the value of the currencies of all EU members.

The SEA was possibly a major error by Thatcher. She had agreed to something that went against what she hoped for for the UK. Even when other key figures in the party – such as Nigel Lawson, Kenneth Clarke, Douglas Hurd and John Major – were obviously moving in a very different direction. The SEA was to divide the party and the country. Furthermore, many ordinary party members were hostile to the EU and needed clear guidance. She was in danger of losing popular support. The *Sun* headline of 'Up yours Delors' (1988) when he produced his federalist plan for a European government in 1988 seemed to voice what many people felt. Thatcher had caused major divisions within the Conservative party.

Why did Thatcher join the Exchange Rate Mechanism?

Much against her better judgement, Thatcher was persuaded to join the **Exchange Rate Mechanism** (ERM) in 1990. It was a logical step on from the SEA and was seen by many as leading to the single currency for Europe (the euro) and a controlling central European bank. Key members of the government, such as Chancellor Nigel Lawson, Deputy

Geoffrey Howe (1926–)
A Conservative MP (1964–92) and Minister (1970–4), Howe was appointed Chancellor of the Exchequer in 1979 until 1983. He was a strong supporter of monetarism. He moved to the position of Foreign Secretary in 1983, where he tried to modify Thatcher's strongly anti-EU line, and then in 1989 became Deputy Prime Minister. In 1990 he resigned over her leadership style and played a key role in her downfall.

Black Wednesday: a serious financial crisis in the UK in October 1992, which damaged the pound by lowering its value and forced the UK to leave the Exchange Rate Mechanism. It severely damaged the Conservatives' reputation for financial competence.

Was Thatcher totally anti-European?

1. Read the following extract and answer the question.

'As Prime Minister I was keen to see the former dictatorships of Spain and Portugal join the EU … I was also keen to widen membership to include the former Communist countries of central and Eastern Europe. The extension of the frontiers of a free and prosperous Europe was an integral part of the programme of a Europe of cooperating nation states, which I had put forward in my speech at Bruges in 1988.'

(Margaret Thatcher, *Statecraft*, HarperCollins, 2002)

Using this extract and your own knowledge, discuss whether Thatcher should be seen as a supporter or an opponent of the EU.

2. How justified is the view that Thatcher's EU policy damaged the interests of the UK?

Deserted by her cabinet colleagues, who were deeply divided over Europe, Mrs Thatcher finally resigned in 1990. This image of her tearful departure from Downing Street has proved to be a lasting one.

Prime Minster Geoffrey Howe and Foreign Secretary John Major, argued for entry to the ERM, and were successful. Many economists have since claimed that we joined 'at the wrong rate and at the wrong time'. Whatever the conditions at the time of the UK entry, however, joining was an error. It was to lead to the catastrophe of **Black Wednesday** in 1992 – under Major – which destroyed the reputation the Conservatives had built as being 'good' at managing the economy.

Thatcher's own advisers, Professor Griffiths and Alan Walters, were hostile to the ERM, while her Chancellor, Deputy Prime Minister and the bulk of the cabinet were in favour. The ensuing row led to her losing both her Deputy Prime Minister and her Chancellor – both Geoffrey Howe and Nigel Lawson attacked her with great bitterness in public, and this was to play a major part in her downfall in 1990. The UK had to withdraw humiliated from the ERM in 1992, and the whole process of entry and withdrawal seriously damaged the economy.

There is much to criticise in Thatcher's attitude and policy towards the EU. She failed to realise that the USA was not necessarily a 'better' ally for the UK and that within Europe the UK could play a valid and viable role, which was of real benefit to the UK. She did not understand what the impact of the SEA would be on the UK or her party, and failed to provide effective leadership in this area.

There was too much noisy posturing on Thatcher's part for the benefit of the press and public opinion. She should have worked much more closely with the UK's European partners for the common good. The UK gained much from membership of the EU. Co-operation and not confrontation could have gained much more.

While there was much for the British taxpayer to complain about in the CAP, the problems here remained even when she left office. She had failed to become an 'insider' within the EU and sort it out. The public needed educating in the benefits of UK membership, but all it ever heard was a repeated emphasis on its demerits. Furthermore, the UK was now seen as a hostile and negative influence within the EU.

The debate on Thatcher and the EU
The strongest critics of Thatcher's policies on the EU come from her own party. Ian Gilmour (one of the many 'Old' Tories she sacked) launches a blistering attack on her lack of feeling for the 'right' ideas on the EU in *Dancing with Dogma* (1992), and Nigel Lawson's *The View from No. 11* (1992) is also strongly opposed to her views. The clearest defence of her position and policies can be found in Thatcher's own memoirs, *The Downing Street Years* (1993). Other academics, such as Andrew Gamble in *The Free Economy and the Strong State* (1988) offer some support, but against this there are also those who criticise her savagely, such as Will Hutton in *The State We're in* (1996). There is really no published balanced critique – the subject still arouses huge controversy.

6.8 Did Margaret Thatcher's attitude towards her European partners help or harm Britain's standing in Europe?

Margaret Thatcher was a strong-willed, determined character, sometimes called the 'Iron Lady'. She introduced sweeping changes to Britain's society, economy and politics. Her attitude towards Europe was something of a paradox. In private, she was hostile towards the Europeans. She believed in British strength and national pride. However, in practice, she took Britain further into Europe. By the end of her 11—year rule in 1990, Britain had signed the Single European Act for a single European market, and withdrawal from the EC (as the EEC was later called) was unthinkable.

The British budgetary question

From 1979–84, Community business was dominated by the question of the amount of money Britain contributed to the Community budget. Thatcher believed that Britain paid too much money to the EC and determined to get some of it back. She fought for this for four years to the exclusion of other Community business. At the Fontainebleau Summit in 1984, the Community agreed that Britain should have two-thirds of its money returned each year.

Stephen George in *An Awkward Partner: Britain and the European Community* (1990) argued that Thatcher's negotiations over the budget made Britain 'a skilful and normal actor in the Community game'. Her policy could be described as 'pragmatic involvement'. The budget question also helped British standing in Europe because Thatcher's fighting style was popular with the public. However, her style, characterised by her banging her handbag on the table and demanding 'our money' back, annoyed the Europeans. She failed to develop a good relationship with the new French and German leaders, Francois Mitterand and Helmut Kohl. They stored up hostility against her, which inevitably meant that Britain would not get its own way all the time in the future. In the 1970s the Community had developed along intergovernmental lines with the European Council. The British Budgetary debate gave France and Germany the will to overcome this 'Euro-paralysis' and continue with supranational economic integration.

The Single European Act

In 1985, Margaret Thatcher signed the Single European Act (SEA). This committed Britain to greater institutional integration and to a single market. Thatcher actively contributed to the Single European Act because she was strongly in favour of a single market. A single market was consistent with her ideological belief in free market economics, and therefore she could use Europe to advance 'Thatcherism'. This was the first time since 1973 that a British leader had outlined a positive role for Britain in Europe, and a positive image for the European project in British politics. She circulated her proposals to the EC in 1985, entitled 'Europe: The Future'. She regarded the Single European Act at the time as a success for her single market ideas.

The second main reason for signing the SEA was because she wanted to retain influence in Europe. The French President Mitterand told the European Parliament that Europe could develop in 'two tiers'. Those states that did not want greater federalism could remain outside in the second tier. Thatcher realised that Britain would have no influence in the second tier. She signed the SEA because she realised that Britain had to be at the heart of European decision-making. However, she was not willing to tell the public that this was what she had done. Instead she later claimed that the Europeans had deceived her over the SEA, pretending they wanted a single market when really they intended to move to deeper federalism.

The Social Charter

The SEA promised progress to closer integration. In 1988, the President of the Commission, Jaques Delors, set up a committee to study economic and monetary union. The Delors report, submitted in 1989, recommended three stages to Economic and Monetary Union. Stage one was membership of the Exchange Rate Mechanism. Stage two was currency alignment. Stage three was a single currency and a Central European Bank. Delors also recommended social provisions for minimum conditions of education, employment and social security. Thatcher had ideological objections to the Social Charter. It was at odds with her doctrine of a free market, and of lessening state intervention in social policies. The Labour Party, however, liked the Social Charter because it supported their ideas of social welfare. Under Neil Kinnock Labour moved back in favour of European membership, from its position of total withdrawal in 1983.

Thatcher initially reacted to developments in Europe by continuing with pragmatic involvement in European negotiations. In 1987, she blocked changes in Community funding that would have helped to develop the social policy. But in 1988, the Community again threatened to leave her outside if she did not join with them, and she had to agree to double the amount of money in the Community's social fund. She then made a speech in Bruges which the Europeans saw as hostile. She emphasised the extent to which Britain was a part of Europe, but then attacked Community policies.

The Bruges speech marked a turning point in Thatcher's policy towards Europe. It is possible that she was continuing with the pragmatic involvement of the budget negotiations. In this interpretation, she recognised that Britain must become involved with deeper integration, but wanted to emphasise the British vision of integration, creating the impression that Britain could still 'win' in Europe. Alternatively, Hugo Young described the Bruges speech as the moment when Thatcher could keep her personal hatred of Europeans to herself no longer. She knew Europe would integrate further, and wanted to make British opposition to this clear. In this analysis, the Bruges speech ended Britain's pragmatic involvement with Europe. This analysis seems more likely, because Thatcher initially wanted to deliver a much more hostile speech in Bruges. The Foreign Office, however, forced her to change it.

Economic and Monetary Union

The most important step for the European Community towards greater integration was economic and monetary union (EMU). Britain and Denmark opposed moving towards a union (which would involve supranationality) rather than increased co-operation. The first stage of EMU was membership of the Exchange Rate Mechanism (ERM), established without British participation in 1979. The Chancellor of the Exchequer Norman Lamont, and the Foreign Secretary Geoffrey Howe, both thought that if Britain joined the ERM, it would then be possible to prevent the development of EMU. Outside ERM, however, Britain had no influence. Howe and Lawson forced Margaret Thatcher to tell the European Community at the Madrid summit in 1989 that Britain would join the ERM. Thatcher then sacked Howe from the Foreign Office (although he then became Leader of the House of Commons) and Lawson resigned. Later, Howe also resigned from the government, and his resignation speech in the House of Commons

Source-based questions: Britain and Europe

SOURCE A

Over wide areas a vast quivering mass of tormented, hungry, care-worn and bewildered human beings gape at the ruins of their cities and homes, and scan the dark horizons for the approach of some new peril, tyranny or terror. The remedy … is to recreate the European family, and provide it with a structure under which it can dwell in peace, in safety and in freedom. We must build a United States of Europe. … We all know that the two world wars through which we have passed arose out of the vain passion of a newly united Germany to play the dominating part in the world. … The first step in the recreation of the European family must be a partnership between France and Germany. In this way only can France recover the moral leadership of Europe … France and Germany must take the lead together. Great Britain, the British Commonwealth of nations, mighty America, and I trust Soviet Russia, must be the friends and sponsors of the new Europe and must champion its right to live and shine.

Winston Churchill, speech in Zurich, September 1946.

SOURCE B

Britain applied to join the Common Market after refusing to participate earlier, creating a Free Trade Association, and 'putting some pressure on the Six to prevent a real beginning being made in the application of the Common Market … The nature, the structure, the very situation of England differed profoundly from the countries of the six'. She is insular, maritime, linked to distant countries, essentially industrial and commercial and with slight agricultural interest. The whole question is whether Britain can place herself 'inside a tariff which is genuinely common', renounce all Commonwealth preference, give up agricultural privileges, and 'more than that', regard her EFTA engagements as 'null and void' …. The defence of Europe has become of secondary importance to the United States. Cuba illustrated this … This has led to the French determination to equip themselves with their own atomic force … The Polaris offer is of 'no apparent interest to France.'

Summary of de Gaulle's Press Conference, 14 January 1963.

SOURCE C

Britain does not dream of some cosy isolated existence on the fringes of the European Community. Our destiny is in Europe, as part of the Community. That is not to say that our future lies only in Europe. But nor does that of France or Spain or indeed any other member …. Willing and active co-operation between independent states is the best way to build a successful European Community … We have not rolled back the frontiers of the state in Britain only to have them reimposed at European level, with a European super-state exercising a new dominance from Brussels … The Treaty of Rome was always intended as a Charter for Economic Liberty … And that means action to free markets, action to widen choice, action to reduce government intervention … Europe should not be protectionist … Europe must continue to maintain sure defence through NATO.

Margaret Thatcher's speech in Bruges, 20 September 1988.

1. **Look at Source A.**

a) **What did Winston Churchill mean when he said 'we must build a United States of Europe'?**

b) **What were Churchill's intentions in making this speech?**

2. **Look at Source B.**

a) **How reliable is de Gaulle's account of his motives in vetoing Macmillan's application?**

b) **Was de Gaulle justified in his criticisms of British policy?**

3. **Look at Source C.**

a) **Was Margaret Thatcher right to see the Treaty of Rome as a charter for economic liberty?**

b) **Was Thatcher pro or anti-European?**

c) **What was Thatcher's intention in making the Bruges speech?**

4. **Study Sources A, B and C and use information from this chapter. To what extent were the British 'Reluctant Europeans' after 1945?**

in November 1990 sparked off events leading to the end of Margaret Thatcher's premiership.

Europe and Thatcher's legacy

By the end of Margaret Thatcher's years as Prime Minister, Britain was committed to Europe to a far greater degree. Her fighting talk hid the extent of Britain's involvement with Europe, creating the impression that Britain had to 'win' in Europe. More seriously, in 1989, the Cold War ended and changed the context of British foreign policy completely.

Thatcher attempted to resist the reunification of East and West Germany. She could not, and Britain was left in 1989 facing the prospect of a dominant, wealthy Germany taking Britain's place in the 'special relationship' with America, as well as the prospect of the ex-communist states becoming members of the European Community. British foreign policy was ill-equipped to deal with these new challenges.

1. Was Margaret Thatcher pro or anti European?

2. To what extent was Britain a fully involved member of the European Community in 1990?

3. Did the European leaders deceive Thatcher over the Single European Act?

6.9 Why was the Conservative Party so divided on the question of European integration in the 1990s?

Margaret Thatcher was deposed by pro-Europeans in her Cabinet in November 1990. In the leadership election, the pro-European Michael Heseltine stood against her, but failed to win. The post of Prime Minister instead went to the relatively unknown John Major. Major did not have a large following in the party, and won the election more because he did not have any enemies. A weak character who liked to compromise rather than fight, he came to be seen by the media as grey and uninteresting.

Europe after the Cold War

The end of the Cold War posed three main challenges to European integration. The first was the reunification of Germany, which would make Germany the undisputed dominant partner in the European Community. The British and the French did not want Germany to reunify. However, like the aftermath of the Second World War, the French wanted to control German dominance and wealth through increased integration in EMU. French support for EMU led to the agreements at the Maastricht negotiations in 1991 for a single currency (the Euro). The United States wanted German reunification, because it would help American trade, and because Germany was wealthy enough to pay for European defence. Britain risked losing her 'special relationship' with the United States as the United States preferred to deal with Germany.

The second challenge was enlargement of the Community to incorporate the eastern European countries. Western Europe and America regarded it as important to attract eastern European states to help ensure stability and prosperity, and to prevent the re-emergence of communism. The prospect of enlarging the Community led to a debate at Maastricht about whether the Community should be more supranational, or more intergovernmental. The Dutch proposed supranational decision making for foreign policy and for home affairs. Britain and France both rejected this, preferring intergovernmental decision-making instead.

The third challenge was on defence policy. Economic collapse in the Soviet Union meant that the Soviet Union was no longer likely to invade Europe, or start a nuclear war against the United States. The United States, under President Bill Clinton, therefore wanted to withdraw its troops from Europe, meaning that Europe would have to organise, and pay for, its own defence policy. The European Community realised that the main threat to European stability was regional conflict in the new states of Central and Eastern Europe, for example the ongoing war in the former Yugoslavia. At Maastricht, the Europeans agreed to hold intergovernmental meetings to decide on common foreign and defence policies, although there was little agreement on what those policies should be. Without common defence policies, it was difficult for the European Community to claim to be a major world power.

Conservative policy towards the Maastricht negotiations.

The Maastricht negotiations decided the future of Europe. From the European Community, the European Union (EU) was born, with powers over a larger number of policy areas, such as foreign policy, and home affairs and justice. John Major, keen to put Britain at the heart of Europe, committed Britain further to the EU by agreeing these changes. The victory of intergovernmental decision-making over supranational decision-making meant that it was easier for Britain to accept the European way of making policies. Influential pro-European Conservatives like Michael Heseltine and Kenneth Clarke thought that increased British participation in Europe was inevitable. The end of the Cold War meant that Britain had no other role to play in the world, and furthermore, as Europe expanded, Britain would be unable to survive without European trade.

Anti-Europeans like John Redwood, Michael Portillo (whose father was Spanish) and Michael Howard, however, reacted against British participation in Europe partly because it was inevitable, and because it was becoming more acceptable. They saw it as their last chance to alter Britain's destiny. Anti-European pressure meant that Major opted out of the EU's Social Chapter. He, like Thatcher, tried to create the impression that Britain was winning in Europe, declaring a complete British victory at the Maastricht negotiations.

Economic and Monetary Union (EMU)

The most serious question about which the Conservative Party divided was that of EMU. The first stage of EMU was membership of the ERM, which Britain had joined in 1989. In 1992, however, Britain was forced to pull out of the ERM and devalue the pound. The Bank of England lost £4 billion in one day. The ERM crisis confirmed anti-Europeans' belief that the EMU was not in Britain's economic interests. The ERM crisis was caused by high interest rates in Germany, and anti-Europeans thought that the Germans would use EMU to take over Europe. Pro-Europeans thought that if Britain had entered the ERM earlier, the pound would not have been so weak in the first place, and so could have influenced German interest rates. They also thought that non-participation in EMU would relegate Britain to the 'second tier' of European decision-making.

Domestic party politics
Most of the Conservative anti-Europeans were on the right wing of the Conservative Party. Part of the reason behind their opposition to Europe was that it was one way of attacking John Major, whom they hated for winning the leadership election in 1990. Margaret Thatcher herself became increasingly anti-European, claiming she had been deceived by European federalists when she signed the Single European Act in 1985. Her opposition led other MPs who had supported the SEA, for example Kenneth (now Lord) Baker, to turn against Europe and against Major. In 1995, the right-wing John Redwood tried to take over directly by standing against Major in a leadership election that Major narrowly won.

The famous *Sun* front page, 1st November 1990.

1. Why did the anti-Europeans argue that Britain should be 'in Europe, but not run by Europe'?

2. What changes did the pro-Europeans think that Britain had to make to her foreign policy after the end of the Cold War?

3. Which was the most important in creating Conservative divisions on Europe, hostility to the EU or domestic political considerations?

Anti-Europeans were also encouraged because Major's small parliamentary majority gave them a chance to influence matters. In 1992, anti-Europeans voted against the Maastricht Bill, and nearly managed to stop it coming into law. In Cabinet, anti-Europeans bullied Major. In 1995, they forced the government to change its policy on enlargement of the EU, although Britain had been in favour of enlargement for years.

Anti-Europeans saw opposition to the Euro (the end result of EMU) as the only way to win the 1997 election, and also thought that opposition to the Euro would win support for themselves. In 1994, Major expelled eight 'Euro-rebels' from the party. They gained more publicity than ever before in their political careers. The ERM crisis and the crisis over British beef in 1996 made Europe increasingly unpopular with press and public opinion. The *Sun* led the anti-European tabloids, for example with its famous headline 'Up Yours Delors'. In the 1997 election, the maverick businessman Sir James Goldsmith created a new political party, the Referendum Party, to campaign for a referendum on the Euro. As with the Labour Party in the 1970s, hostility to Europe mixed with domestic and personal political ambitions.

The consequences of the Conservative split over Europe

The Conservative civil war on Europe was a major factor in their landslide defeat in the general election of 1997, and their obsession stopped the most senior and able Conservative politician, Kenneth Clarke, becoming party leader, his pro-European views preventing his election as leader in 1997, 2001, 2003 and 2005.

Between 1997 and 2001, William Hague adopted an anti-Europe stance, but his 'Save the Pound' campaign against the Euro failed to attract the public's imagination. After his resignation, his successors – Iain

Conservative Party leader William Hague on the 'Save the Pound' campaign trail in May, 2001

Duncan Smith and Michael Howard – continued their opposition to further European integration. Following his election as party leader in 2007, David Cameron campaigned hard on a referendum on the Treaty of Lisbon which had been a manifesto commitment by the Labour Party.

6.10 How European were the British by 2007?

Society and culture

The influence of European culture could be seen throughout British society. Every British citizen was a 'citizen of the union'. They carried European Union passports, and could travel and work freely throughout Europe. Many British people took holidays in Spain – Tenerife or Majorca – or Greece. For young people and students, European holidays became commonplace, and initiatives such as InterRail train tickets became possible because of increased co-operation between EU member states. The development of the Channel Tunnel and the Eurostar made travel to the continent even easier: from London, it was quicker to get to Brussels than to Edinburgh.

Food, also was one area in which the British were becoming increasingly 'European'. The fact that Europeans could also travel and work here improved the quality and variety of restaurants enormously. Pizza and pasta from Italy was the most obvious example of European food becoming as common as British 'national' dishes, like fish and chips. Supermarkets were full of food imported from Europe. Products like yoghurt, pizza, salami and wine were hardly available in Britain before membership of the EEC in 1973. In schools, the National Curriculum originally made the teaching of one foreign language obligatory up to the age of 16. The result was that most British pupils left school with at least a rudimentary grasp of French, Spanish or German, and many had travelled to the continent on school exchanges. Improved education made growing links with the continent easier.

How does this photograph explain the increased involvement of Britain in Europe?

A train about to depart from the Eurostar terminal at St Pancras International Station, London

Football was another element of British society where European membership had a large, visible effect. The free movement of workers made it possible for footballers to move to any other club in Europe once their contracts expired. European footballers played in all Premier League teams by 2007. Britain's heroes were Europeans: Eric Cantona, Thierry Henry and Cristiano Ronaldo became household names. By 2007, Arsenal were often fielding teams without any British players and the top teams had European managers. Europe had become a fact of British life.

Trade, business and economics

In 1999, over half of all British trade was conducted with the European Union. This made the EU far too important to markets and business to seriously contemplate withdrawal. Europe was likely to expand into eastern Europe. The Czech Republic, Estonia, Poland, Hungary, Cyprus and Slovenia were involved in enlargement talks in 1999, with suggestions for talks to be extended to Bulgaria, Latvia, Lithuania, Malta, Romania and Slovakia. This would create a market of 500 million people. It would simply be inconceivable for Britain to sustain itself as a trading nation outside this gigantic union.

Membership of the EU meant that business was attracted to Britain in order to take advantage of the huge market. Non-EU countries, like Japan and America, were encouraged to invest in Britain because of the market opportunities. The Japanese car company, Nissan, was one of the largest employers in the north-east, and late in 1999 was part-bought by the French company Renault. Huge continental companies like Siemens and Phillips had bases in Britain, employing British people. British companies like the drugs company SmithKline Beecham could use the opportunities presented by the European market to expand into Europe. London Electricity and SWEB were owned by a French company, which in turn was part owned by the French government. The abolition of customs duties meant that British people could take cheap crossings to France, stock up on alcohol and cigarettes, which were much cheaper in France because of lower taxes, and take them back to Britain without additional charges. European economies were intertwined.

European law

The importance of the EU as a law-making body was still not widely appreciated by the end of the 20th century. In fact, British law could be overridden by EU law. The EU provided half of all national legislation, including 80 per cent of economic and social legislation and 70 per cent of business legislation.

The European Court of Human Rights also had an important bearing on the everyday life of the British. The Court was not part of the EU, but arose from the Council of Europe, and was expected to ensure that the United Nations' Universal Declaration of Human Rights was upheld throughout Europe. The Court was used increasingly by British citizens by the end of the 20th century, as the Convention on Human Rights was incorporated into British law. For example, the Court ruled it illegal for the army to exclude gays and lesbians. The parents of the murdered teenager Stephen Lawrence used the Court to rule that the police could not be exempted from charges of negligence. British citizens also used the European Court of Justice, which upheld European law. Female pensioners over the age of 60 got payments from the government towards their fuel bills, whereas male pensioners were not eligible until they were 65: a 63—year-old postman used the Court of Justice to win the same right for male pensioners.

Politics and Europe

Government civil servants spent up to a third of their time dealing with European affairs. The EU extended into policy-making for home affairs and justice, as agreed at Maastricht. European politics were absolutely central to the everyday running of British politics, yet the political debate about Britain's future in Europe was underdeveloped. The Labour government was still, in 1999, reluctant to come out in favour of a single currency, saying instead that Britain would join the Euro if the conditions were right, and if the people voted 'yes' in a referendum. The Conservative Party became more anti-European, with some right-wingers arguing that Britain must never join the Euro and should withdraw from the EU.

The Labour government declared it wanted to be at the heart of Europe. However, Britain did not participate in the first wave of the Euro in 1999. This meant that Britain was excluded from the Euro-committee of European politicians, who made important decisions about European finance. Labour did make some changes that suggested that eventually the British would go into the Euro, such as allowing companies to sell shares in Euros, and giving the Bank of England control over interest rates. However, Labour has been criticised by the Europeans for failing to educate the public in favour of the Euro.

Tony Blair also adopted the Social Chapter in 1997, and initiated policies on job creation and environmental protection. Blair was the first British Prime Minister to speak French to the Europeans, at the French National Assembly. Labour also made proposals for a more co-ordinated European foreign and defence policy, and agreed to participate in creating the 'Euro-fighter' military plane. However, Britain's support of America's bombing of Iraq in 1997–98 seemed to indicate that Britain still attached much importance to the 'special relationship'. During the Kosovo crisis in 1999, Britain sided with America in calling for NATO to bomb Yugoslavia, although other NATO partners were more reluctant.

Britain's association became even closer to the USA from 2001, with the Global War on Terror after the 9/11 attacks on the USA. Britain participated in the overthrow of the Taliban regime in Afghanistan from 2001 and, more importantly, Britain distanced itself from Germany and France with its involvement in the invasion and occupation of Iraq from 2003.

Press and public opinion

The media in Britain were also on the whole opposed to closer monetary union. The tabloid press believed that Britain should 'save the pound' and did not want to see the Queen's head removed from national currency. They believed this would appeal to their readers, capitalising on nationalism and on a latent dislike of foreigners in the public, in particular stereotyping the Germans.

An opinion poll in 1998 showed that 60 per cent of the public were opposed to joining the single currency. The elections to the European Parliament in 1999 showed also that Europe was not a popular issue. The turn-out of the electorate was very small, averaging around 23 per cent with the smallest ever recorded turnout in Sunderland, at 1.5 per cent. Labour lost seats, and the sceptic Conservatives gained. The 'UK Independence Party', in favour of withdrawal, and with alleged links to the fascist British National Party, gained three seats. 'Saving the pound' seemed to be popular among the public at large. The battle for the hearts and minds of the people over Britain's future relations with Europe was therefore far from won. By 2007 there was a strong campaign in the

THE TREATY OF LISBON, 2007

Signed by the European Union's twenty-seven member states

Originally called the Reform Treaty, the Treaty of Lisbon was drawn up to replace the draft European Constitution, after that was thrown out in 2005 by voters in France and the Netherlands. All twenty-seven EU countries will be expected to ratify the Treaty in 2008, with a view to it coming into force in 2009.

The Treaty brings in the following changes:

- A politician chosen to be president of the European Council for two-and-a-half years, replacing the current system where countries take turns at being president for six months.

- A new post combining the jobs of the existing foreign affairs supremo, (Javier Solana) and the external affairs commissioner (Benita Ferrero-Waldner) to give the EU more clout on the world stage.

- A smaller European Commission, with fewer commissioners than there are member states, from 2014.

- A redistribution of voting weights between the member states, phased in between 2014 and 2017.

- New powers for the European Commission, European Parliament and European Court of Justice – in the field of justice and home affairs, for example.

- Removal of national vetoes in a number of areas.

Ireland and the UK currently have an opt-out from European policies concerning asylum, visas and immigration. Under the new treaty they will have the right to opt in or out of any policies in the entire field of justice and home affairs.

The treaty should come into force in 2009 but different parts will take effect at different times:

- The High Representative on foreign affairs could start work by late 2008, as long as the treaty has been ratified.

- The new-look European Parliament would not appear until after the European elections in June 2009. In fact, that poll will be seen partly as an endorsement of the new arrangements.

- The new president of the European Council could also start work at that point.

Prime Minister Gordon Brown signs the Treaty of Lisbon, December 13th, 2007

- Although a new commission will be chosen in 2009, its size may not be slimmed down until 2014.

- Some extensions of qualified majority voting (QMV) in the European Council are already in place, such as the appointment of the commission president and the High Representative for Common Foreign and Security Policy – but Poland's objections over voting weights mean that the redistribution of votes will not come in until after 2014.

---

1. In what ways had Europe influenced British society by 2007?

2. Did Tony Blair's policies suggest that Britain was really 'at the heart of Europe'?

3. Why was Europe so unpopular in Britain at the end of the 20th century?

British press, led by the *Sun*, in support of a referendum on the Treaty of Lisbon.

British European deputies demonstrate for a referendum during the vote about the Lisbon Treaty at the European Parliament, Strasbourg, February 2008

Further Reading

Britain and European Unity 1945–1992 by John Young (Macmillan, 1993)

Britain and European Co-operation Since 1945 by Sean Greenwood (Blackwell, 1992)

From Reconstruction to Integration, Britain and Europe since 1945 edited by Brian Brivati and Harriet Jones (Leicester University Press, 1993)

An Awkward Partner: Britain in the European Community by Stephen George (Oxford University Press, 1990)

More advanced reading

The European Union and British Politics by Judge Andrew Geddes (Palgrave Macmillan, 2003)

Britain in the European Union Today by Duncan Watts and Colin Pilkington (Manchester University Press, 2005)

7 Social and economic history, 1945–2007

Key Issues

- How far did British society change between 1945 and 2007?

- How far did the British economy experience change between 1945 and 2007?

- What impact did the arrival of migrants from the Commonwealth and from Europe have on Britain?

7.1 Historical interpretation: How successful has the British economy been since 1945?

7.2 In what way did British society change between 1945 and 2007?

7.3 Has Britain become a multi-cultural society since 1945?

7.4 What impact have changes in the mass media had on Britain since 1945?

7.5 The rise and fall of the British trade union movement, 1945–2007

Framework of Events

1947	Nationalisation of the coal industry and railways
	Sterling crisis
1948	Establishment of National Health Service
1949	Economic crisis forces devaluation of pound
1951	Festival of Britain
1953	Coronation of Queen Elizabeth II
1955	Start of commercial television
	Introduction of frozen food to Britain
1956	Rock and roll comes to Britain
1958	Race riots in Notting Hill, London
1960	Trial of Penguin Books for obscenity for publishing *Lady Chatterley's Lover*
1961	First issue of *Private Eye*
1962	Commonwealth Immigration Act introduces first controls on migrants to Britain
1963	The Beatles have three number 1 hits
1964	Start of BBC2
1965	Abolition of the death penalty
1966	England win soccer World Cup
1967	Start of colour television transmissions
	Devaluation of pound as a result of the economic crisis
	Abortion legalised
	Homosexuality 'between consenting adults' legalised
	Pirate radio banned as Radio One is launched.
1968	Commonwealth Immigration Act restricts immigration, particularly Kenyan Asians, to Britain
	Abolition of theatre censorship
1969	White Paper 'In Place of Strife' proposes controls over strikes and trade unions
	Divorce Reform Act liberalises divorce
1970	Equal Pay Act introduces legal enforcement of equal pay for women
1971	Immigration Act effectively ends non-white immigration
	Industrial Relations Act gives government broad powers of intervention in strikes
1972	Miners' strike

1973	Britain joins Common Market (European Economic Community)
	Oil crisis
	Beginning of commercial local radio
1974	Miners' strike
	First commercial flight of Concorde
1975	Referendum confirms Britain's membership of Common Market (EEC)
	Sex Discrimination Act establishes Equal Opportunities Commission
1976	IMF crisis
	Establishment of Commission for Racial Equality
	Introduction of public expenditure cuts
1977	Queen Elizabeth II's Silver Jubilee
	Sex Pistols reach number 2 in the charts with the banned record 'God save the Queen'
1978	Government introduces 5 per cent pay norm for wage increases – rejected by the unions
	Unemployment rises above 1 million for the first time since 1945
1979	'Winter of Discontent': widespread industrial action in the public sector
	Margaret Thatcher elected Prime Minister
1980	Unemployment rises above 2 million for the first time since 1939
1981	Employment Act outlaws secondary picketing in industrial disputes
	Social Democratic Party splits from Labour Party
	Widespread riots in Brixton (London), Toxteth (Liverpool) and Moss Side (Manchester)
1982	Start of Channel 4
1984	Miners' strike
	First major privatisation with sale of British Telecom
1985	Live Aid concert for famine relief
1986	Privatisation of British Gas, the largest of the decade
	Serious riots outside Wapping headquarters of Rupert Murdoch's News International after 5,000 printers dismissed over dispute about introduction of new technology
1989	Introduction of Poll Tax in Scotland
1990	Introduction of Poll Tax in England and Wales: widespread riots
1992	Start of national commercial radio with Classic FM
	'Black Wednesday' departure of Britain from the Exchange Rate Mechanism
1996	Sale of the railways: the last major privatisation scheme
1999	Start of the European Single Currency
	Inflation at lowest level since 1963
2002	Railtrack, a private company, is replaced by government-owned Network Rail after financial difficulties
2006	According to official estimates, British Gross Domestic Product grew by 2.75 per cent in and is expected to grow by 3 per cent in 2007. Growth is expected to slow slightly in 2008 to between 2 per cent and 2.5 per cent
2007	Northern Rock bank fails and is taken over by the government.

Overview

Capitalism: The economic system prevalent in Britain and western society, sometimes called the free market or private enterprise economy. Economic decision-making is highly decentralised with a large number of companies selling goods and services and consumers choosing which services and goods most suits their needs.

Why the extraordinary economic and social changes that have taken place since 1945 happened is by no means clear, especially as to many contemporary observers the economic depression of the 1930s had proven that the **capitalist** system had failed. Even historians as eminent as Eric Hobsbawm remain baffled. In his *Age of Extremes: a history of the world, 1914–1991* (1994) he confesses 'there are no really satisfactory explanations for the sheer scale of the "great leap forward" of the capitalist world economy and consequently for its unprecedented social consequences'.

Professor B. W. E. Alford, however, is more certain. He argues in *British Economic*

Economic growth: The expansion (or decline) of the real output of an economy usually measured by percentage increase or decline annually to the Gross Domestic Product (GDP) the total size of the economy.

Welfare transfer payments: Taxation spent on the welfare state.

General Agreement on Tariffs and Trade: An international organisation established in 1947 to promote the expansion of international trade through the removal of tariffs and other restrictions on cross-frontier trade. Now called the World Trade Organisation.

World Bank: The World Bank, or International Bank for Reconstruction and Development, also set up in 1947 to provide economic aid to member countries – mainly developing countries – to strengthen their economies.

Oil crisis: In the autumn of 1973 the Organisation of Petroleum Exporting Countries (OPEC) forced up the price of oil, a commodity upon which many countries in the west (including Britain) were heavily dependent for fuel, and as the raw material of plastics and other items.

Productivity: Increase in the efficiency of making goods or operating services.

Cartel: A group of producers or companies who agree to maximise profits by artificially raising the price of their goods to consumers.

Inflation: An increase in the general level of prices that is sustained over time. The annual increase may be small or gradual (creeping inflation) or large and accelerating (hyperinflation). Inflation can be caused by an increase in the cost of raw materials which is then passed on to the consumer, or by a shortage of goods the demand for which pushes prices up.

Performance, 1945–1973 (1988) that the 'combination of elements favourable to **economic growth** in the major economies … were post-war reconstruction, a production gap between the USA and the rest which drew American dollars and know-how into Europe and Japan, a sharp upward shift in peacetime levels of public expenditure (caused by defence needs and **welfare transfer payments**) and the absence of general synchronisation in the downswings which took place in the major economies from time to time. Arising out of these conditions, and at the same time reinforcing them, was a widespread and buoyant expectation of economic growth which was powerful enough to ride out random shocks.'

There is no doubt that the leaders of the western world, guided by economic advisers such as John Maynard Keynes, learnt well the lessons of the 1930s. By the end of the Second World War they had set up an international monetary system guided by the International Monetary Fund (IMF), the **General Agreement on Tariffs and Trade** (GATT), and the **World Bank** to prevent such a slump occurring again. Governments also accepted that they had a duty to intervene more heavily in the running of national economies. The White Paper on employment policy, published in 1944, committed the post-war government to a 'high and stable' level of employment. Hugh Dalton, Chancellor of the Exchequer in Clement Attlee's Labour government, set the tone by announcing in 1946, 'twice in our lifetime we have banished unemployment in wartime. Now we must banish it in peace. I will find, with a song in my heart, all the money necessary for sound constructive schemes.' As well as this commitment to full employment, the government was committed to the provision of a welfare state, and close links to both trade unions and industry itself.

The period between 1945 and the onset of **oil crisis** of 1973 was a 'golden age'. Unemployment, which had hit 22 per cent during the depression of the 1930s, stayed well below 500,000. Economic growth rose by 3 per cent per annum, as did **productivity**, and investment grew by around 6 per cent a year from 1950 until the 1960s, when it tailed off to stagnate during the 1970s. The position became more difficult after 1973 when the **cartel** of oil-producing nations quadrupled petroleum prices. In any case the relentless rise of **inflation** was making a mockery of government spending plans as well as the real wages of millions of working people. The Labour governments between 1974 and 1979 were caught between this new economic reality and the expectations of its supporters which led to the 'Winter of Discontent' in early 1979 and the election of the Conservatives under Margaret Thatcher. Her victory was seen by most commentators to spell the end of state spending to achieve full employment, state-subsidised welfare and the power of the trade unions.

The early years of the new economics were hardly encouraging. While other economics grew by 6.3 per cent between 1979 and 1981, Britain's fell by 2.5 per cent. Unemployment rose to 13.3 per cent, the highest in western Europe. However the stern economic policy of Margaret Thatcher and her successors eventually began to work. These policies of rigorously controlling public spending and the encouragement of business were adopted by the 'New Labour' administration of Tony Blair.

The changes dealt with in this chapter have not been without their critics. In particular there have been increasing concerns about:

Acid rain: Pollutants, produced especially by coal and oil power stations, which are found in rainfall and which kill trees.

Global warming: The warming of the earth as a result of greenhouse gases, including carbon dioxide, produced by industry and motor vehicles.

Nuclear family: A household consisting just of mother, father and two children.

Why has crime increased so much since 1945?

Magneto: The ignition switch for the combustion engine.

Place the issues in the mind map in order of importance on how they affected British society and the economy in the period 1945 to 2007. Give reasons for your choice.

● **The environment, pollution and the increasing use of the motor car.** Economists and environmentalists, such as Fritz Schumacher in *Small is Beautiful* (1974), have warned of the consequences of uncontrolled economic growth on the planet. During the 1980s great concern was shown about **acid rain**, and by the 1990s scientists were presenting a convincing case for **global warming**.

● **The supposed breakdown of society**, which many conservative commentators argue has resulted in rising crime, the rise of divorce, and the break down of the **nuclear family** There is no doubt that Britain is a much less law-abiding place: crime has risen more than tenfold since 1945 (see table 1).

TABLE 1 Indictable offences

	Total offences (000s)	Rate per million of population
1945	478	12,705
1955	438	11,235
1965	1,134	28,259
1970	1,556	38,031
1997	4,595	88,410
2007	5,428	100,240

● **The spiritual, rather than the material, impoverishment of society.** George Orwell saw this danger in pre-war society, which he described in his essay *The Lion and the Unicorn* (1941) as being 'a civilisation in which children grow up with an intimate knowledge of the **magneto** and in complete ignorance of the Bible'. Other observers have pointed out the paradox that despite an ever-increasing array of machines to help us manage our lives society seems to be running faster and faster to keep up.

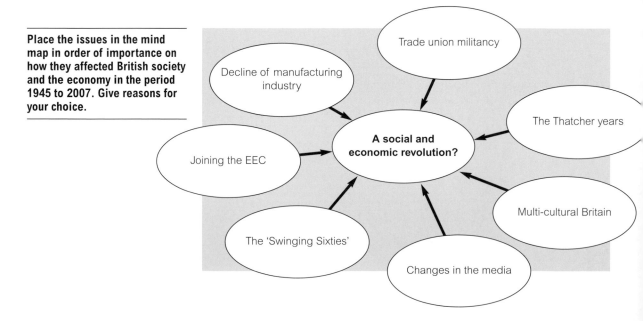

Source-based questions: Statistical analysis

	1956–7	1998–9	2006–7
Average weekly income (women)	£6.16 (equivalent to £80)	£303.70	£394
Average weekly income (men)	£11.89 (equivalent to £155)	£420.30	£498
Average hours worked (women)	41.5	37.6	37.4 (2002)
Average hours worked (men)	48.5	41.7	40.9 (2002)
Unemployment rate	1.3%	4.5%	5.5%
Trade union membership as percentage of workforce	41.5%	29.8%	25.8%
Annual rate of inflation	3.7%	1.1%	2.7%
Percentage of income spent on food	35%	16%	15%
Price of pint of beer	9p	£2.00	£2.52
Percentage of households owning a television	27%	98%	98%

Look at the table above and others in this chapter.

1. Outline the major changes which have taken place since the end of the war to both the British economy and society in general.

2. Make suggestions as to how and why these changes have taken place.

7.1 How successful has the British economy been since 1945?
A CASE STUDY IN HISTORICAL INTERPRETATION

1945–1951

In 1945 Britain had just fought and won the greatest war in its history, at great cost to both the economy and the people themselves. The Labour government under Clement Attlee, which had been swept to power in July 1945, was pledged to rebuild the country. Attlee was determined not to repeat the mistakes that had been made after 1918 that had led to high unemployment and low economic growth for most of the inter-war period. The Labour Party, whose 1945 manifesto stated that the people 'deserve and must be assured of a happier future than so many of them faced after the last war', shared this determination.

In this task both the Labour government, and its Conservative successor under Winston Churchill, were largely successful. The decade after 1945 was one of rapid growth, low inflation, and full employment. The welfare state and the National Health Service guaranteed better living standards and health for everybody, rich and poor. About 20 per cent of British industry was nationalised.

But there were considerable problems along the way. Almost as soon as Attlee came to power, the Americans ended the Lend-Lease system that had supported the British war effort. Officials negotiated a further loan of $3.5bn in December 1945, but the whole incident showed the weakness of Britain's economic position. Further crises in 1947 and 1949 forced the devaluation of the pound, which had the effect of boosting Britain's exports as they were now cheaper to buy, but cast doubts on the handling of the economy by Labour.

In order to repay wartime debts, and to finance the necessary imports for recovery, exports had to be rapidly increased (see table 2). 'Export or die' was the dramatic slogan used by the government. Britain was helped, but perhaps in the long term hindered, by the fact that apart from the

United States her economic competitors were still rebuilding after the war. There was high demand for almost everything that British industry could make. But in concentrating on manufacturing for export, Britain failed to modernise its industry. This hampered its ability to effectively compete in the post-war world.

Why do you think the balance of trade worsened in 1951?

TABLE 2 British trade and payments, 1946–52 (£ million)

	1946	1947	1948	1949	1950	1951	1952
Exports	900	1125	1550	1790	2221	2708	2836
Imports	1100	1574	1768	1970	2374	3497	2927
Balance of trade	−200	−449	−218	−180	−153	−789	−91

American–European Recovery Programme: Universally called Marshall Aid, after the American Secretary of State, George C. Marshall, who introduced it.

During the late 1940s, Britain as well other countries in western Europe was considerably helped by the **American–European Recovery Programme**. Marshall Aid was designed to kick-start war-torn European economies, by supplying financial aid and allowing access to American technology and production methods. It was also thought that this would reduce the likelihood of a Communist takeover. The British received $2.7 billion, the largest amount of any country. West Germany received $1.7 billion. Aid helped to reduce Britain's dollar deficit rather than rebuild its industry.

On the outbreak of the Korean War Britain supported the United Nations by sending troops to South Korea. This was accompanied by a massive rearmament programme introduced by the Chancellor of the Exchequer, Hugh Gaitskell, in April 1951 that would have doubled armaments production within two years. Cuts were made to the welfare state to pay for the programme, and it slowed down economic recovery by directing scarce resources away from the export drive to the armaments industry at a time when industries of Britain's main European rivals, France and Germany, were finally recovering from wartime devastation. This meant that Britain lost important export markets that were difficult to recapture. It also led to a sharp increase in inflation as the price of imports also rose. On coming to power in October 1951, the Conservatives quickly scaled down the rearmament programme. The economist Alec Cairncross concludes that 'rearmament in Britain probably did less harm to the economy in the short run at least than the rise in import prices that resulted from rearmament elsewhere'.

Commentators are divided about Labour's economic record between 1945 and 1952. One of the most critical is Correlli Barnett, who argues in *The Lost Victory* (1995) that Britain was 'in need of being rebuilt from the keel upwards, she had instead only undergone a superficial refit, with items of new technology bolted on to her Victorian structure'. Other historians recognise the achievements and difficulties that Clement Attlee and his ministers had to face. Catherine Schenk, in *Twentieth Century Britain* (1994), concludes 'The transition from wartime production and distribution had been accomplished within a short period of time and the seemingly insurmountable problems posed by the war were overcome'.

1951–1973

Many commentators, such as Larry Elliott and Dan Atkinson in *The Age of Insecurity* (1998), have argued that the period between about 1951 and 1973 was a 'golden age'. There was high economic growth, low unemployment and inflation, and a constantly rising standard of living. Yet the picture was not all golden. In particular Britain's economic growth lagged consistently behind that of its European competitors.

Gross Domestic Product: The total money value of all final goods and services produced in an economy over a one year period.

Between 1951 and 1973 the British economy, in terms of **Gross Domestic Product** (GDP) grew at a rate of 2.8 per cent per annum, a third higher than in the inter-war period and double that of the pre-1914 rate. In the same period, however, the economies of Britain's economic rivals grew rather faster (see table 3). Britain's share of world trade declined from a quarter in 1950 to just over 10 per cent in 1970 (see table 4). This decline caused great anguish. According to Alford in *British Economic Performance, 1945–1975* (1988), 'Britain's poor economic performance has been the dominant theme of political debate and economic discourse since the 1950s'.

1. Why was British economic growth slower than its main economic rivals?

2. Why did Britain's share of world trade decrease?

TABLE 3 Growth rates of real Gross Domestic Product per head, 1913–2007 (%)

	1913–50	1950–73	1973–89	1989–2007
France	1.1	4.0	2.8	1.4
Germany	0.7	4.9	2.1	1.4
Japan	0.9	8.0	3.1	1.2
United Kingdom	0.8	2.5	2.8	2.2
United States	2.6	2.2	2.6	1.7

TABLE 4 UK comparative trade performance 1950–88: Percentage shares of world exports of manufactures

	1950	1960	1970	1988
United Kingdom	25.5	16.5	10.8	8.3
France	9.9	9.6	8.7	9.1
Germany	7.3	19.3	19.8	20.6
Japan	3.4	6.9	12.7	18.1
United States	27.3	22.6	18.5	14.9

Many reasons for this general economic decline have been advanced including government policies towards industry, the strength of the trade unions, inadequate management, and low levels of investment. According to Sean Glynn and Alan Booth in *Modern Britain: An economic and social history* (1996), however, 'no single answer can fully explain the timing and pattern of the British slide'.

An important element was the decline of industries in which the British had traditionally been strong. By the 1980s the shipbuilding industry, for example, had almost totally collapsed. British shipbuilding declined between 1945 and 1975, the time of the most rapid and sustained expansion in the history of world shipbuilding. Britain had a head start after the war: in 1950 it had a 37 per cent share of the market measured in tonnage launched. However, by 1974 Britain's share had slumped to 3.7 per cent. Companies remained small and yards were troubled by **restrictive industrial practices**. Both factors kept productivity low by international comparisons. But companies were very reluctant to consider specialisation or expansionist investment programmes to meet international competition head on. British shipbuilders were therefore unable to take advantage of the new market for tankers and container ships, preferring to build general cargo ships for which there was a declining demand. As a result, according to Glynn and Booth, the industry suffered 'a slow and painful death'.

Restrictive industrial practices: Curbs placed on production by inter-union rivalry or out of date working practices.

The car industry, perhaps the most important modern industry in post-war Britain, also had serious problems. The industry expanded rapidly after 1945, accounting in 1966 for 7.5 per cent of manufacturing output. The effects of the war on European and Japanese car makers allowed British and American firms to dominate the world markets until the mid-1950s. West

Germany overtook British annual output in 1956, and the productivity in British car factories soon fell behind that of Europe and Japan. In 1973 *The Economist* magazine revealed that British factories needed between 67 per cent and 132 per cent more labour than German or Belgian producers to make apparently identical vehicles. In addition, by the late 1960s British cars had an increasing reputation of poor reliability, which helped fuel imports of foreign vehicles and reduced exports. The number of new foreign cars registered increased from 5 per cent in 1964 to 31 per cent by 1973 and 62 per cent by 1979. Nowhere is there a better example of this decline than British Leyland (renamed Rover in 1985). In 1968 it was the largest British car company (and the fifth largest in the world), building approximately 1 million vehicles, accounting for just under 40 per cent of total UK production. In 1991 it had barely 13 per cent of the British market representing an output of 400,000 vehicles.

Industry was naturally heavily affected by economic policies dictated by the government, in which politicians and their advisers tried to juggle competing interests of industry, the consumer in the context of the wider economic position. The 1950s saw the emergence of the 'Stop-Go Cycle'. In the 'Go' phase the domestic economy grew, reducing unemployment, and increasing spending, which increased demand and fuelled inflation. The government used tax increases and credit restrictions to curb demand. As demand fell, economic growth slowed down and unemployment would rise – the 'Stop' phase.

The Stop-Go Cycle was particularly important between 1951 and the devaluation of the pound in 1967. In July 1961 there was a 'Stop' budget increasing taxes, imposing new controls of overseas investments and introducing a pay-freeze for public sector workers. Two years later with an election looming, the Conservatives attempted to boost the economy to reduce unemployment and encourage consumer spending, under policies that became known as 'the dash for growth'.

A production line making Morris Marina cars at the British Leyland factory, 1971

Economists are divided about the effects of the policy on economic growth. Many argue that Stop-Go created an unstable climate that hindered long-term growth of the economy. Its cumulative effect was to harm long-term objectives, such as full employment, growth and structural changes to the economy. Industry was thus often unable to plan ahead and make the necessary investment because it was uncertain whether a change in economic policy would curtail demand for its products. The lack of new investment made it harder to increase productivity through new technology, which in turn meant that British goods were over-priced compared with those produced in other countries. The economic historian Sidney Pollard, for example, argued in *The Development of the British Economy* (1983) that the cycle helped to encourage imports at the cost of exports and thus created a downward spiral that made Britain's continued relative decline inevitable.

Other economists, such as Michael Surrey, are supportive of the policy and point out that the cycle actually provided a stable policy framework which was committed to full employment, a stable exchange rate and economic growth. Indeed the effect of the policies may be exaggerated, for all the changes made seem to have had relatively little impact on underlying growth. Alford concludes, 'comparisons with other economies suggest that stop/go was not the problem – rather it was the weakness of the underlying trend of growth which exaggerated the effect of stop/go phases'.

Other reasons often put forward for Britain's relative economic decline in the 1950s, 1960s and even afterwards, have been poor management and poor labour relations. Glynn and Booth argue that 'British managers have been notably ill-equipped' both in terms of training and in vision. Most British firms did not recruit graduate managers before the 1950s. The engineering industry was especially reluctant to recruit graduate engineers. Even by the late 1980s only 24 per cent of senior British managers were graduates, compared with 85 per cent in the United States and Japan.

During the 1960s the small businessman was often, in the words of Larry Elliott and Dan Atkinson in *The Age of Insecurity* (1998), portrayed as being 'hidebound and reactionary, as much an enemy of economic progress as he was of social progress'. There is certainly an element of truth in this assertion, for managers were often cautious and unwilling to invest in new processes or to take opportunities, making Britain weaker than its major competitors. These problems were identified by the Labour government that came to power in 1964. Its solution was to encourage the merger of smaller companies into larger ones, under a general business ethic that 'big was beautiful'. Through a government agency, the Industrial Reorganisation Corporation (IRC) the government acted as a marriage-broker for mergers between Leyland Trucks and the British Motor Corporation to form British Leyland, English Electric and General Electric, and various smaller companies into International Computers Ltd (ICL).

A particular feature of the 1950s and 1960s was low unemployment, which meant that there was much competition, particularly for skilled labour (see table 5). In the spring of 1956, there were 216,000 registered unemployed and some 400,000 unfilled vacancies. Governments regarded unemployment figures of 500,000 or more as being a major catastrophe. Historically these figures were remarkable considering the high unemployment of the inter-war period, where in the 1930s it had averaged 13 per cent compared to an average of 2 per cent between 1951 and 1973. Such low unemployment had an impact in two ways on people's lives, particularly those of the working classes: it became very easy to switch jobs and it also forced wages up as employers competed for workers.

Why have there been increases and decreases in unemployment?

TABLE 5 United Kingdom Unemployment rates, 1937–2007 (percentage)

1937	1951	1964	1973	1979	1986	1989	1992	1998	2007
10.1	1.3	1.7	2.0	4.7	12.3	7.9	13.3	6.2	5.2

Women also had an increasingly important part to play in the workforce (see table 6). Before the war, middle-class women in most occupations, such as teaching and the civil service, were expected to give up work when they married. Many working-class women, however, continued to work even after marriage as their families needed the extra income. Women were encouraged to enter the labour market during the war and nearly 8 million were in paid work in June 1943. Many however returned to the home once the war had ended and only 6 million were working by June 1947. During the 1950s and 1960s women, particularly among the middle classes, returned to work once they had had their children. Others turned to part-time working as a way of juggling family commitments. The percentage of part-time women workers rose from 12 per cent in 1951 to 34 per cent of the female workforce by 1972.

Why did more women work part-time during the period under consideration?

TABLE 6 Women in the labour force, 1951–81

	1951	1961	1971	1981
As % of total labour force	31	33	37	40
As % of women aged 20–64	36	42	52	61
Part-time as % of total labour force	12	26	35	42
% of all married women aged 15–59 in labour force	36	35	49	62

What did not change was the work that women undertook. Most remained concentrated in lower-status, poorly-paid white collar, service and industrial occupations. While women were increasingly employed in the expanding service sector such as banking or the civil service, it was often as clerks or secretaries. Few women entered the professions: in 1961 women made up only 15 per cent of doctors and just 1,031 (3.5 per cent) of the whole legal profession. However, women increasingly turned away from that mainstay of pre-war employment – domestic service. In 1921 there had been 2.4 million servants: in 1962 there were only 362,000.

What also remained unchanged was the fact that women were paid less than men, often for doing exactly the same work. In January 1945 the average earnings of women in industry was 53 per cent of those of men. The issue was a contentious one. Women and trade unionists in the public sector continued to press the government – their employer. In 1955 the government began to introduce equal pay into the civil service, local government and teaching.

Pressure for equal pay throughout industry mounted during the 1960s. One of the last accomplishments of the 1964–70 Labour governments was to introduce the Equal Pay Act that established equal rates of pay for the same work. The Act, however, did not fully come into effect until 1975. It has helped close the gap between men's and women's pay, with women's full-time earnings rising from approximately two-thirds to nearly three-quarters of the average male rate.

1973–2007

If with hindsight the period between 1955 and 1973 was a period of smooth growth and a gentle progression towards prosperity, then changes in British life between 1973 and 2000 have been more of a roller-coaster ride. Since the early 1970s the British economy, and British industry in particular, has experienced two major depressions and several shorter periods of growth. The 1970s, however, were largely a period of stagnation in the economy. The economy grew roughly at about 2.5 per cent per annum while there was little or no growth in manufacturing itself.

Government economic policies have increasingly played a part in the management of the economy, for better and for worse. Edward Heath came to power in 1970 with a determination to let industry 'stand on its own two feet'. He initially adopted what might be called proto-Thatcherite policies, abolishing price and income controls, refusing to get involved in strikes, and cutting public expenditure. But his administration was soon overwhelmed by events. Some were of the government's own making, particularly the failure to regulate the trade unions, 'U-turns' on incomes and prices policies and providing support for failing industries such as Upper Clyde Shipbuilders and Rolls-Royce Engineering. The early refusal to introduce wage and price curbs led to a rapidly rising rate of inflation. Huge rises in commodity prices during 1973 also help fuel inflation. Non-oil prices rose by 62 per cent during the year, the largest recorded annual increase.

But other events, especially the end of fixed exchange rates in 1972 and the oil crisis of late 1973, were outside the control of the government. The ending of a fixed rate badly hit oil exporting countries because their prices were in dollars, which had effectively been devalued. But they found they could flex their muscles and through the Organisation of Petroleum Exporting Countries (OPEC) raised prices dramatically. During the year oil prices quadrupled from $2.50 to over $12.50 a barrel.

The Labour governments of 1974 to 1979, under Harold Wilson and his successor James Callaghan, had their own economic problems. With the co-operation of the trade unions, wage rises were gradually reduced. Industrial production, however, remained static, and unemployment slowly rose, reaching 1 million in 1978 for the first time since the 1930s.

The real problem facing Labour was the lack of confidence in the government felt by the financial markets. In early 1976 the pound began a seemingly endless slide against the dollar from $2.00 in March to a low of $1.64 in October. The government decided that its only course of action was to buy time, using a loan from the International Monetary Fund (IMF) to create a breathing space secure from outside pressure. The IMF were willing to help, provided cuts were made to public expenditure. Denis Heally, the Chancellor of the Exchequer, negotiated a loan of $3.9 billion worth of credit in exchange for a £2.5 billion cut in government expenditure. In the end little of the credit was actually taken up, but great damage was done to Britain's reputation and led to much speculation about Britain as 'the sick man of Europe'. The *Wall Street Journal* commented 'Goodbye Britain, it was nice knowing you'.

There was, however, modest economic recovery between 1976 and 1978, helped by the arrival of North Sea oil. The balance of payments and the inflation position both improved, while the pound rose to nearly $2.00. The government increasingly abandoned its belief in Keynesian economic policies in favour of more orthodox economic strategies. Writers such as Larry Elliott and Dan Atkinson in *The Age of Insecurity* have argued that 'Callaghan provided the overture for Thatcherism, pioneering many of her themes'.

Margaret Thatcher came to power with a radically different agenda to any previous Prime Minister. Chief among her policies was the adoption of monetarist policies along the lines advocated by the American economist Milton Friedman. Unfortunately, the effect of these new policies spelled disaster for the economy, which in any case was plunging into recession at the time of her election. Output and employment plummeted. The worst effects were felt in manufacturing, with output falling by 17 per cent in 21 months. The loss of jobs in industry was substantial: 2 million manufacturing jobs were lost during the 1980s, of which three-quarters disappeared between 1980 and 1982. High interest rates (rising to nearly 16 per cent in 1980) and the effects of North Sea oil led to a rapid rise in the exchange rate (reaching $2.45 in October 1981). All this devastated British manufacturing industry, driving firm after firm to the wall in sectors like engineering and textiles.

Although many of the monetarist policies were quietly abandoned, the effects of the recession lingered. In 1983, for the first time since the mediaeval period, Britain imported more manufactured goods than it exported. Thereafter the United Kingdom was kept in the black by earnings from the service sector of the economy, especially the financial services in the City of London.

The economy began to recover during 1983 and growth rates rose to about those during the 1950s and 1960s, (about 2.5 per cent per annum). In particularly productivity grew quickly during the whole of the 1980s. In 1977 German manufacturing productivity was 46 per cent above Britain's: by 1989 it was 15 per cent. Yet British manufacturing found it hard to recover from the slump of the early 1980s. Despite the shedding of labour, new factory building and re-equipment by industry during the latter part of the 1980s, British firms still had difficulty competing with foreign rivals. Indeed, as demand for goods rose in the boom of the late 1980s, British industry lacked the capacity to meet it and imports rose to meet the demand.

Manufacturing output only grew by 1 per cent or less per annum. The share of manufacturing in gross domestic product declined from 27 per cent in 1973 to 20 per cent in 1990. Britain's share of world trade continued to decline (see table 7). The long, increasingly inflationary, upswing of 1982 to 1990 eventually collapsed into a deep protracted slump that the economy only pulled out of in 1993 and 1994 (see table 8).

TABLE 7 Average annual growth rate of Gross Domestic Product (percentages)

	1965–80	1980–90	1991	1992	1993	1994	1995	2000	2005	2007
Japan	6.4	4.1	4.3	1.1	0.1	0.6	0.5	2.9	1.9	2.1
US	2.7	3.4	−0.7	2.6	3.0	4.1	2.9	3.7	3.1	2.2
Germany	3.3	2.1	2.0	2.1	−1.2	2.9	2.8	3.2	0.8	2.5
Britain	2.3	3.1	−2.2	−0.6	1.9	3.8	2.7	3.8	1.8	3.0

TABLE 8 Selected indicators of economic performance, 1960–89 (percentages)

	1960–73	1973–79	1979–89
Real earnings increase (average growth per annum)	2.1	0.5	2.8
Inflation (retail price index average annual increase)	4.8	14.7	8.0
Unemployment rate (percentage of workforce unemployed average)	1.9	3.4	9.1

1. Using table 7 and information in this section, has Britain done better than its economic competitors during this period?

2. From figures in table 8 explain whether people were getting better off during the period under consideration. What other factors would you take into consideration to make a reasoned judgement?

As industry faltered, unemployment became a significant problem for the first time since the 1930s. In the first recession of the early 1980s unemployment fell disproportionately on northern England, South Wales and Scotland. The recession of the early 1990s affected the south-east as well: The *Guardian* called it the 'nightmare on Acacia Avenue' because it affected prim suburban streets in Streatham and Shenfield as much as terraced rows in Salford or Sedgley. The government, however, accepted unemployment as a necessary evil in order to control inflation. Despite the costs to the economy, unemployment never became a political issue: political parties preferred to focus their attentions on the employed. The unemployed became a marginalised group, increasingly seen to be themselves responsible for their situation.

Margaret Thatcher also began privatising many of the industries that the Labour government had nationalised in the late 1940s. Initially **privatisation** formed only a small part of Conservative policy, but as the 1980s and 1990s progressed it became increasingly important (see table 9). The first major privatisation was of the medical research group Amersham International in 1982. British Telecom and British Airways followed in 1984 and British Gas in 1986.

Privatisation: The act of transferring an industry from public ownership to the private sector.

TABLE 9 Total revenue from privatisation: financial years 1982/3–1991/2 (£m)

1982/3	1983/4	1984/5	1985/6	1986/7	1987/8	1988/9	1989/90	1990/1	1991/2	1992/3
455	1139	2050	2706	4458	5140	7069	4226	5346	7923	7962

When do you think privatisation became an important source of income for the government?

The government argued that privatisation could enable these industries to benefit from the rigours of the private sector and would be able to manage their affairs without interference from the state. In general however the privatised utilities became private sector monopolies with very little competition. The public was generally in favour, largely because they could make gains by buying shares when they were first issued and then selling them for considerable profits a short time later. By the end of the 1980s the government was making £5 billion a year from privatisations. The money, however, was not invested in long-term capital projects, such as the modernisation of the crumbling transport system, but was largely frittered away on current spending. In effect this income was given back to the electorate as a tax cut.

The Major administration from 1990 was in many ways a continuation of Thatcherite policies. John Major's record for economic competence was mixed. He won the 1992 election during a deep slump, but lost the 1997 contest at a time when the economy was booming. His government will mainly be remembered for the fiasco of the **European Exchange Rate Mechanism** (ERM), which, although offering the prospect of stability, was entered at too high a rate for sterling and the British economy to benefit. Above all there was the extraordinary episode of 'Black Wednesday', 16 September 1992, when Britain left the ERM in considerable confusion. Outside the ERM the government was able to cut interest rates sharply and allow the pound to fall. Recovery began almost immediately. Both unemployment and inflation began to decline. 'Black Wednesday', however, largely destroyed the public's faith in the Conservatives' economic policies and contributed to their humiliation at the polls in May 1997.

European Exchange Rate Mechanism: A system whereby many countries in the European Community agreed fixed exchange rates with each other. It was a forerunner to the Euro.

From this table say whether Britain has done as well as its economic competitors during the 1990s.

TABLE 10 Changes in gross domestic product (1990 = 100)

	1985	1990	1993	1995	1998
USA	87	100	104	111	127
Japan	80	100	105	107	111
France	86	100	101	105	113
Germany	87	100	104	108	115
Britain	85	100	99	109	115

The late 1990s saw a sustained boom, accompanied by slow falls in unemployment towards the 1 million level. Inflation too fell away, so by the middle of 1999 it was as low as it had been in July 1963. According to at least one commentator, the economy had been remarkably stable, with few signs of the 'boom and bust' cycle of the 1970s, 1980s and early 1990s. As

1. What have been the major changes to the British economy since 1945?

2. What do you think are the major factors that have caused these changes?

3. How important do you think government policy has been in British economic development?

4. Why have historians and economists offered different interpretations of Britain's economic performance since 1945?

a result, British economic growth has matched that of its main economic competitors. Yet many structural problems still remain. In particular there remains a lack of the highly-trained, highly-skilled workers that are increasingly needed to run modern industry.

From 1997 to 2007 Tony Blair and his chancellor, Gordon Brown, maintained many of the economic policies inherited from their Conservative predecessors. The United Kingdom economy has grown every quarter since 1992, the greatest sustained period of growth for over 150 years.

In 1997 the Bank of England was made independent from the government in the setting of interest rates to control inflation. During the Blair years Britain experienced steady economic growth, low, stable inflation and low unemployment. The Labour government had been able to get Britain away from the 'boom' and 'bust' policies which had plagued previous governments.

In 2007 the United Kingdom had the fifth largest economy in the world and the second largest economy in the European Union, after Germany. It is also one of the world's most globalised countries, ranking fourth in one recent survey. London is one of the three major financial centres of the world, along with New York City and Tokyo.

7.2 In what way did British society change between 1945 and 2007?

1945–1951

As well as damaging the economy, the Second World War had impoverished people's lives. The British in 1945 may have shared common interests, and endured common problems, but life was drab and heavily regulated. Extensive rationing addressed the shortages in food, in clothing and in consumer goods. The amount of consumer expenditure subject to rationing rose from about 25 per cent in 1946 to 30 per cent in 1948, before dropping away to 12 per cent in 1949. Most foods remained rationed for many years after the war, as did clothing until 1949.

It was clear by 1950 that Britain was slowly emerging into what Tony Benn later called 'a decade of hope'. One sign of this new confidence was the Festival of Britain, held on London's South Bank. The Festival was to be a showcase for all that was best about British industry and innovation. It was also a designed to be in the slogan of the period 'a tonic to the nation': a celebration of the fact that the country was confidently looking towards a better future.

1951–1973

The Conservative administration that came to power in 1951 made few changes to its predecessor's policies. It was to remove the remaining restrictions. This philosophy was summoned up by Churchill in a broadcast in 1952, 'we think that it is a good thing to set the people free, as much as possible in our complicated modern society, from the trammels of state control and bureaucratic management'. The result was the first of many consumer booms. It was encouraged by cuts in taxation. Income tax was reduced by sixpence (2½ p) to nine shillings (45p) in the pound [today the basic rate is 22p] and purchase tax was also cut. As a result there was a dramatic rise in the sale of consumer goods (see table 11). As Catherine Schenk in *Twentieth Century Britain: Economic, Social and Cultural Change* (1994) suggests, 'the British people seemed finally to have been rewarded for their earlier sacrifice as the era of mass consumption arrived'.

TABLE 11 Consumption of selected consumer durables

	1949	1950	1951	1952	1953	1954	1955	1956	1957
New car registrations (000s)	13.8	11.1	11.4	15.7	24.7	33.7	41.9	33.4	35.5
TV sets (000s)	17.4	43.4	57.6	65.3	95.4	104.2	140.5	119.4	151.3

Why did consumption of these items increase?

By 1957 the new Prime Minister, Harold Macmillan, was famously able to assert in a speech at Bedford that 'Most of our people have never had it so good. Go around the country, go to the industrial towns, go to the farms and you will see a state of prosperity such as we have never had in my life-time – nor indeed ever in the history of this country.'

There is no doubt that living standards improved considerably during the period. Consumer goods that once only the rich could afford were increasingly becoming available to the middle and working classes. The Conservative Home Secretary R. A. Butler, in an election broadcast during the 1959 general election suggested, 'we have developed ... an affluent, open and democratic society in which the class escalators are continuing moving and in which the people are divided not so much between the "haves" and the "have-nots" as between "haves" and "have-mores".'

This rise can be seen by the rise in the average weekly earnings: the average male factory worker saw his weekly earnings rise from £7.83p in 1950 to £41.52p in 1973 (see table 12). At the same time the average number of hours he worked fell slightly from 48 to 45 a week. Women's earnings, however, lagged behind men, even so as more women worked, their wages were an increasingly important part of household budgets.

Have wages increased more than prices during this period?

TABLE 12 Average annual wage

	Average annual wage £	Average annual wage index 1935–6 = 100
1935–6	134	100
1955–6	469	350
1960	581	434
1970	1,289	962
1978	3,827	2,856
1991	12,220	9,119
2006	24,000	n/a

Modest increases in inflation reduced some of the effect of the rapid rise in wages (see table 13). Between 1955 and 1960 retail prices rose by 15 per cent, by 1969 they were 63 per cent higher than in 1955. When overtime is taken into account average weekly earnings rose 130 per cent between 1955 and 1969. This almost exactly matched the 127 per cent rise in earnings by middle-class salaried earners during the same period.

TABLE 13 Increases in earnings and retail prices 1981–1997 index

	1981	1995	1997
Average earnings (1990 = 100)	125	336	386
Retail prices (1987=100)	75	149	157

The most obvious sign of this increased affluence was in the ownership of consumer durables. In 1949 only 7 per cent of adults owned a car, but by 1966 over half the adult population had a vehicle of some kind. Many goods, such as television sets and washing machines, cost less year by year and so became more affordable. During the 1950s and particularly during the 1960s an increasing proportion of households had central heating. By 1970, houses were on average 5°C warmer than they had been in 1950. There was an increasing array of household consumer goods, which either entertained, such as televisions and transistor radios, or were labour-saving such as washing machines and frozen food. By 1968 over 90 per cent of households had televisions (see table 14).

How could households afford the increasing array of consumer goods on sale?

TABLE 14 Consumer durables: availability in households (%)

	1955	1975	1995	2006
Vacuum cleaner	51	90	96	n/a
Washing machine	18	70	91	96
Refrigerator	8	85	98	99
Freezer	n/a	15	79	95
Television	35	96	98	99
Telephone	19	52	92	99
Central heating	5	47	85	95
Dishwasher	1	2	12	30
Microwave oven	n/a	n/a	47	91
Video recorder	n/a	n/a	70	82
CD-player	n/a	n/a	63	90
Home computer	n/a	n/a	20	67

(n/a – not available)

By the mid-1960s the children born in the baby-boom of the mid- and late-1940s had become teenagers. There were more young people around than before and they increasingly had more disposable income. By the late 1950s this was 50 per cent higher than it had been pre-war. There were now goods for them to spend it on, clothes, transistor radios, and records. The writer Colin MacInnes suggested in 1958 that 'the great social revolution of the past fifteen years may not be the one which redivided wealth amongst among adults in the Welfare State, but the one that has given teenagers economic power'.

With the slow decline in working hours, teenagers had time to enjoy their new found affluence in milk and coffee bars or, for the well-off, jazz clubs. Above all it was rock and roll which summed up the period. The

To what extent does this differ from a typical kitchen in the 21st century?

A kitchen in the 1950s

music arrived in Britain with the film *Rock around the Clock* (1956). The broadcaster Ray Gosling, then a teenager in Northampton, remembers, 'it was like an electric shock, and we all stood on our chairs and the aisles and howled'. As a result of the film there were riots in Croydon and the Elephant and Castle in London. In Northampton, however, Gosling 'remembered no aggro – it was just the experience of our lives'.

Teenage rebellion seemed more extreme in a society which was dull and conformist. Post-war austerity had been replaced by a natural desire to make up for the privations of a decade and a half. Britain during the 1950s was backward-looking, uncertain of its role in a very different world. Britain in the 1950s and early 1960s was increasingly criticised for its greyness.

For many the first break in this dull conformity was the prosecution and acquittal of Penguin Books in 1960 for obscenity in publishing *Lady Chatterley's Lover* by D. H. Lawrence, a book not available in Britain since the 1920s. It was then possible for books containing explicit material to be published.

What many called the 'permissive society' finally arrived between 1963 and 1966, when as Arthur Marwick noted, 'British society seemed to have broken out of the straitjacket of dullness and conformity'. In practice, however, the sexual and other freedoms excitedly talked about in newspapers and magazines, such as the contraceptive pill, hardly touched most ordinary people. By 1970, for example, only 8 per cent of women used the Pill. London was singled out as 'Swinging London' for a reason. Many of the changes in social mores began in the capital and only slowly filtered out to the provinces.

The middle and late 1960s saw legislation passed by the Labour government that significantly relaxed the old Victorian code. Politicians, however, were reacting to events of the time, rather than taking a lead. Among acts passed during this period were:

● The abolition of hanging for criminal offences in 1965.

● The legalisation of abortion in 1967.

● The legalisation of homosexuality in 1967.

● Local authorities were allowed to set up family planning clinics in 1967, which in effect made these clinics legal for the first time.

● Abolition of theatre censorship in 1968 and a notable relaxation in cinema censorship which took place during the period.

● Divorce was made easier with the passing of the Divorce Reform Act, 1969.

Britain in the early 1970s was very different from 20 years before.

1973–2007

Post-war affluence had given people goods their parents could not have imagined, let alone afforded. Until the mid-1970s, affluence was almost universal, but although for many the rise in prosperity continued at an ever increasing rate, for the first time since 1945 this prosperity was not universal. The gap between rich and poor increased more dramatically than at any time in the 20th century (see table 15). This gap was encouraged by government policy offering tax cuts for the affluent and cuts in benefit for the poorest.

From this table indicate whether or not Britain has become a more equal country in the period 1977 to 1992.

TABLE 15 Share of income by household group, 1977–2006

	Bottom 20%	Bottom 40%	Top 40%	Top 20%
1977	4	14	69	43
1979	2	12	70	43
1985	3	10	74	47
1992	2	8	76	50
2006	3	10	75	51

Individualism: The concept that individuals, and individual rights, are more important than society as a whole.

This has also been accompanied by what Elliott and Atkinson describe as 'a gradual erosion of the collectivist element that held the West together in the era of Beveridge and the Beatles'. Politicians, both of left and right, are increasingly committed to encourage **individualism** and individual achievements. The Conservative Prime Minister Margaret Thatcher summed up this new belief when she once declared in a speech that 'there is no such thing as society', meaning that individuals and their families were more important than society as a whole. 'New Labour' too has largely abandoned the collectivist traditions of the Labour Party.

Yet Britain has not really become an individualistic society, generally remaining resistant to official encouragement to become more entrepreneurial and go-getting. Nowhere is this truer than in attachment to the National Health Service, the greatest collective achievement. Even at the height of her powers, Thatcher time and again had to repeat that the 'National Health Service is safe in our hands'. Although reforms were made, neither Thatcher nor John Major attempted to abandon the principle of free medical care.

Inevitably changes had led to a much more divided society. The groups hardest hit by the changes have been the ethnic minorities, particularly the black and Muslim communities. Men in general were also badly affected. In the 20 years since 1979, men's employment rates fell while women's rose. In 1975 more than 92 per cent of working-age men had a job, but by 1998 this had fallen to 81 per cent, while for women over the same period the figure rose from 59 per cent to 69 per cent.

Women in 2000 were also earning more, thus beginning to close the gap on their male colleagues. By the end of the 20th century one in five women earned more than their working partners, compared with only one in fourteen in the 1970s. In 1998 women earned on average 75 per cent of the average male hourly wage, compared with only 62 per cent in 1974. Women were increasingly being accepted in management and professional circles, despite complaints of a 'glass ceiling' preventing them from progressing beyond a certain point. The share of women in senior positions rose from 7 per cent in 1989 to 14 per cent in 1998.

During the 1970s and 1980s the moral revolution launched in the mid-1960s finally percolated down throughout society. It was increasingly easy for people to adopt a lifestyle that suited them without fear of persecution. Homosexuality, finally legalised in 1967, for example, has become more widely tolerated. Gay scenes developed in many cities, like Canal Street in Manchester. Finally after a long campaign the age of consent for homosexual men was first lowered to 18 and then attempts were made to lower it to 16 as the century ended.

Among the British population as a whole there was increasing sexual freedom. By the late 1990s about 95 per cent of couples had slept together before marriage, whereas in the early 1970s the figure was perhaps 30 per cent. Young people were becoming sexually active at a younger age. In part this was due to the wide availability of contraceptives, especially the pill. As the result of legislation in 1967, many local authorities and hospitals set up family planning clinics making it very much easier for people of all ages to get both advice and contraceptives themselves. The acceptance of the contraceptive pill by women took rather longer than has commonly been supposed, largely because of fears over side-effects. In 1971 only 19 per cent of married women were taking the pill, while two fifths of couples were taking no precautions at all. By the 1990s the pill, closely followed by condoms, was the favourite means of contraception.

Cohabit: To live together as a couple.

The period from the 1970s saw a decline in the institution of marriage. Increasingly couples preferred to live together before marriage, or not get married at all. In 1992 those **cohabiting** without actually getting married amounted to 18 per cent of the total number of unmarried adults. By the end of the decade this figure was almost certainly higher. The number of marriages declined from 396,000 in 1984 to 318,000 in 1996; about a third of these marriages were people marrying for a second or subsequent time. Divorce too became more common, partly because legislation made divorce easier and as social taboos against it relaxed (see table 16). By the late 1990s a third of marriages ended in divorce.

Why have the number of divorces increased?

TABLE 16 Decrees made absolute (000s)

1930	1950	1960	1970	1980	1990	2002	2006
4	33	26	62	159	166	147	133

Opposition to these changes has been surprisingly quiet. Mrs Mary Whitehouse, through her National Viewers and Listeners Association, campaigned with some success during the 1970s and 1980s to reduce the amount of sex and violence shown on television. Legislation was passed in the late 1980s controlling what could be taught about homosexuality in schools. Conservative politicians in particular have tried to reverse the trend, stressing 'family values' and the need to 'return back to basics.'

By and large the political parties were unable and unwilling to halt the social changes which were taking place, indeed they increasingly sought to mould their appeal to the new social groups and their aspirations. Politicians increasingly crafted their appeal to what became known as Middle England – the middle classes and the prosperous working classes. From the late 1970s the Tories owed a lot of their electoral success to their appeal to 'Essex woman' and 'Mondeo man'. It took over a decade for the Labour Party to realise that they had to do the same.

Judicious tax cuts and cheap privatised shares ensured that incomes remained buoyant. A constant stream of new goods appeared on shop shelves to tempt consumers: videos, microwaves, home computers and mobile phones. The rapid pace of technological developments ensured that prices kept falling while the machines themselves were more efficient and effective. The memory and speed of the first home computers in the early 1980s were the tiniest fraction of what was offered by even the most modest computers by 2007.

Another effect of affluence was that people began to travel more. The package holiday had started in the late 1950s, first to Spain and Italy and then to Greece, Cyprus and Turkey. In the early 1970s, 7 million people travelled abroad for their holidays. These figures grew dramatically during the 1980s and 1990s as fares, particularly across the Atlantic and to Australia fell. By 1998 39 million visits a year were being made abroad (see table 17). Young people especially could benefit from cheap flights to go on holidays clubbing in Ibiza or to more exotic locations during 'gap years' between school and university.

Why did more Britons travel abroad?

TABLE 17 Leisure visits abroad (millions)

1951	1961	1971	1978	1986	1997	2003
2	4	7	9	22	39	41

Has material wealth made Britain a happier place? There now seems a sense of unease about the future, in contrast with the optimistic predictions that began the twentieth century. What is clear however is that life at work and at home has become much less secure than it was in the decades after the end of the Second World War. There are predictions that workers will have nine to five jobs in a career where welfare provision and the protection offered by trade unions will be minimal. In *The State We are In* (1995) and other writings, the journalist and economist Will Hutton argues that the net effect of these changes has been to shrink to just 40 per cent of the population those who could be said to be secure in their work and homes. A further 30 per cent were unemployed or economically inactive and a middle 30 per cent were in 'structurally insecure' employment.

1. What have been the main changes in British society since the war?

2. How has the role of women changed?

3. What changes have there been in what people can buy?

During the Blair years, 1997–2007, the average household income continued to rise. As Blair stated in his farewell speech as prime minister, in 2007:

> Go back to 1997 … Think about your own living standards then and now … There is only one government since 1945 that can say all of the following: more jobs, fewer unemployed, better health and education results, lower crime, and economic growth in every quarter – this one.

7.3 Has Britain become a multi-cultural society since 1945?

Before the Second World War there were very few West Indians and even fewer Asians in Britain. Outside the dock areas of London, Liverpool, Cardiff and South Shields (where there was a lively Somali community) it would have been rare to have seen a black face, except for an occasional student. Black people were often objects of curiosity. It was not uncommon for migrants from the West Indies in the 1940s and 1950s to be touched for luck, while some small children were threatened by the warning, 'If you don't behave yourself the black man's going to get you'.

Of what value is this photograph to a historian writing about multi-cultural Britain?

Men from Jamaica arriving at Tilbury on the *Empire Windrush* in 1948.

The Second World War saw the arrival of large number of black troops from the United States. The authorities in Britain were reluctant to accept them, fearing racial problems, although in general they were warmly received. Volunteers also came from the West Indies, Africa and the Indian sub-continent to serve in British forces. Large numbers of people, particularly from Ireland, were recruited to work in factories. They included several parties of men from the West Indies, the first 155 of whom came over in 1942 and worked in power stations in north-west England.

During the 1950s shortage of labour meant that the government, and to a lesser degree private employers, encouraged migration into Britain. Migrant workers were attracted from the Caribbean and the Indian sub-continent in increasing numbers, beginning with the 492, mainly young men, who travelled from Jamaica on the *Empire Windrush* in 1948. One of the 'pioneers', as he described himself was Dan Lawrence who remembers, 'I wanted to see the country that influenced my education very greatly and my values in life. Most of us were young men who just came over on a wave of excitement to try life in a new country. There were a few older men who had worked in England during the war. They went back home to Jamaica and they couldn't settle down there so they came back on the boat with us.' (BBC Radio WM, *The Century Speaks*, 1999).

Immigration from the West Indies and the Indian sub-continent ran at about 14,000 a year during the 1950s, but in 1961 there was a large rise prompted in part by fears that the government planned to introduce restrictions on immigration (see table 18). There were a number of limited schemes recruiting West Indian workers (such as those for London Transport and regional hospital boards) to carry out jobs for which they had difficulty finding British workers. Most migrants, however, came independently, seeking to better themselves and their families. There were also substantial inflows of Irish throughout the whole period, and Poles in the late 1940s and Italians in the 1950s and 1960s.

Do the numbers arriving in Britain show any decline as result of the Commonwealth Immigrants Act, 1962? What figures should be included to show fully the effect of the Act?

TABLE 18 New Commonwealth immigration into Britain, 1956–62

	West Indians	Indians	Pakistanis and Bangladeshis	Total
1956	26,400	5,600	2,100	34,100
1957	22,500	6,000	5,200	33,700
1958	16,500	6,200	4,700	27,400
1959	20,400	2,900	900	24,200
1960	52,700	5,900	2,500	61,100
1961	61,600	23,750	25,100	110,850
1962	35,000	22,100	24,900	82,000

The 'Mother Country' turned out to be far less welcoming than migrants had been led to expect. Mohammed Ayyub remembers arriving in Birmingham from the Punjab in December 1961, 'I tried to find a job, but I couldn't get a job at all. I ultimately applied in the West Midlands Transport for a conductor's job. My degree from Punjab wasn't recognised so it was useless. Being a graduate I didn't want to do that job but I was forced. Most of the people who turned us away from the gate, they said "no jobs". It was a surprise because we had heard stories that the English were very decent.' (*The Century Speaks*).

Official attitudes to migration from the **New Commonwealth** ranged from mild hostility to indifference. Half-hearted attempts were made to dissuade passengers on the *Empire Windrush* from coming to Britain, although once the ship had docked at Tilbury work was quickly found for most people. Administrations, both Labour and Conservative, were

New Commonwealth: Those members of the Commonwealth of Nations who were either still dependencies or had gained independence from Britain after 1947.

keen to avoid alienating Commonwealth governments, but they were also sensitive to mounting calls for immigration controls within Britain itself. In effect during the 1950s they neither controlled migration into the country, nor did they attempt to combat the rising tide of racism. The first attempt to control immigration came with the clearly racist Commonwealth Immigrants Act 1962 that placed restrictions for the first time upon entry of people from the New Commonwealth who were overwhelmingly black, but not on people from the Irish Republic, which had left the Commonwealth when it became a Republic. Further legislation controlling immigration was enacted in 1968 and 1971, which effectively reduced the number of migrants so that by 1973 only 4,000 were arriving each year.

What do you think accounts for the decline of migrants from the New Commonwealth?

TABLE 19 Acceptances for settlement in the United Kingdom, 1963–2002 from the New Commonwealth

1963	1968	1973	1978	1983	1988	1991	2002
56,071	60,620	32,247	30,514	27,550	22,800	27,930	43,635

From which other Commonwealth countries did sizeable numbers of migrants come?

TABLE 20 New Commonwealth immigrants in the United Kingdom (defined as living in households whose head was born in the relevant area according to census returns) (000s)

	West Indian	Indian sub-continent	Total for whole of Commonwealth
1961	173	116	597
1971	302	462	1,294
1981	295	629	1,666
1991	434	1,296	2,635
2001	n/a	n/a	3,371

Tackling racism was more difficult. Although increasingly aware of the problem, the government initially took little action preferring to rely on voluntary measures. Even racist riots in Nottingham and Notting Hill in London during 1958 and overwhelming evidence of discrimination against migrants failed to make the government act. A number of industries operated an unofficial colour bar, refusing to employ black or Asian workers, while other employers took on migrants from the New Commonwealth as long as they were never seen in public.

The new migrants tended to settle in inner-city areas, leading to tension with the established working-class communities. This was particularly the case in the West Midlands and parts of London (such as Indians in Southall and West Indians in Brixton) where a third of all immigrants settled. A lot of these tensions came to the fore in the Black Country constituency of Smethwick during the 1964 election campaign, where the openly racist Conservative candidate, Peter Griffiths, defeated the sitting Labour member Patrick Gordon-Walker. Slogans such as 'If you want a nigger for a neighbour vote Labour' appeared throughout the constituency.

Matters were not helped by a speech made by a senior Conservative politician, Enoch Powell, at Birmingham in April 1968 in which he called for the repatriation of black and other Commonwealth immigrants. Powell was immediately dismissed from the **Shadow Cabinet**, but his views attracted much sympathy among white working-class people in inner city areas. There was for example a march of dockers to the Houses of Parliament in Westminster in his support.

The position of the Labour government elected in 1964 was in practice

Shadow Cabinet: A collective term for the opposition front bench spokespeople.

little different to their Conservative predecessors. Politicians were split between the anti-racism of the political classes, and the concerns of Labour's working-class supporters. The liberal-minded Home Secretary, Roy Jenkins, was determined to stamp out racism and established the Race Relations Board in 1965 and helped prepare the Race Relations Act (1968). On the other hand the government quickly acted to stem the flow of Kenyan Asians forced to leave Kenya in the late 1960s. Legislation was hurriedly passed in early 1968 to restrict the entry of these people, despite their having British passports and a legal right to settle in Britain. The result was misery for many of the 125,000—strong community as well as for the smaller Ugandan Asian community forced to flee neighbouring Uganda by Idi Amin in 1971 and 1972.

During the 1970s the first generation of 'Black Britons' grew up. In 1976, Mark Bonham-Carter, Chairman of the Community Relations Commission, warned that Britain's black community, 40 per cent of whom were now born in the country, would not settle for second-class citizenship. He said that they take 'the phrase "equality of opportunity" for what it means. I have no doubt that we have not kept pace with the expectations of British-born blacks'. The Race Relations Act 1976 tried to tackle these problems by making discrimination unlawful in employment, training and education, and in the provision of goods and services. The Act also made it an offence to stir up racial hatred.

Even so racist attacks and discrimination continued. Occasionally the frustrations of the black communities at the poor conditions in which they lived and their lack of opportunities had vented themselves in outbreaks of rioting during the early 1980s. They began in the St Pauls district of Bristol in 1980, followed by riots in Brixton in London, Toxteth in Liverpool, and Moss Side in Manchester in 1981. These protests were more than race riots, for they were often joined by whites equally frustrated at the conditions they lived in. The **Scarman Report** on the Brixton riots spoke eloquently of the despair of unemployed young blacks and their sense of alienation from the community and especially from the police, whose intolerance and insensitivity were deplored.

The Scarman Report: The result of a committee investigation by Lord Scarman, a senior Law Lord with a liberal reputation.

What reasons can you give to explain why unemployment was higher for ethnic minorities rather than for whites?

TABLE 21 Unemployment rates by ethnic origin (%)				
	1979	1990	1998	2002
White	5	7	6	5
Black	10	13	15	14
Indian	6	10	9	7
Pakistani/Bangladeshi	11	20	20	19
Mixed and others	3	12	13	12

Despite depressingly high levels of racial attacks and accusations of institutional racism in the police force during the 1970s and 1980s the West Indian and Asian ethnic minorities were slowly being integrated into the mainstream of society. The first Labour Asian and black MPs were elected in 1987 and the first Conservative one in 1992. Perhaps the greatest sign of assimilation has been the popularity of Asian food, even if the dishes served at Indian restaurants bear little resemblance to native Indian cuisine. In 1950 there were only six Indian restaurants in Britain. By 1970 there were 2,000 and in 1994 there were 7,500 Indian restaurants nationwide. Chinese food was equally popular. A national catering survey in 1970 found that of those who ate out regularly or occasionally, 31 per cent had eaten at Chinese restaurants, while only 5 per cent had eaten at French restaurants.

There was much to be done however, as the Stephen Lawrence case in

1993 showed, particularly in tackling the 'institutional racism' which the report into the affair found to be prevalent in the police and some other public services. At the end of the 1990s, one in ten London Asian or Afro-Caribbean households had suffered racial harassment in or near the home and one in three felt threatened by the existence of racism. Arthur Marwick however concludes that 'the levels of integration achieved by Britain in the mid-1990s were better than might well have been predicted ten years earlier; at the bottom of the scale black youths were suffering disproportionally, but this (as in America) was becoming more of a class, than a purely racial, issue – in the "enterprise culture" all the poor were getting poorer (while some small businessmen, particularly Asian and Chinese were doing well.)'

Since 2004 Britain has experienced another major wave of migration. In addition to the immigration from outside Europe, Britain experienced considerable migration from the new countries of the European Union, most notably Poland and Lithuania. Official estimates vary, but approximately one million migrant workers from the EU entered Britain after 2004. These migrants – including plumbers, bricklayers and electricians – brought much-needed skills which the growing UK economy required. EU migrant workers also did low paid jobs in agriculture and manufacturing. The strength of the British economy was reflected in the fact that this influx did not lead to unemployment. By 2007, however, it did raise questions of community cohesion, with the influx of such a large number of workers in such a short time.

1. What problems do you think these migrants encountered in Britain?

2. Have these communities become assimilated?

7.4 What impact did changes in the mass media have on Britain between 1945 and 2007?

Since 1945 Britain has seen an explosion in the choice in what we watch and hear. In 1948 less than 10 per cent of the population had a television set, but within 15 years over 90 per cent of households had television. Newspapers are bigger, cheaper and full of colour compared with their counterparts in 1945. At the end of the war the **BBC** operated just two radio stations, whereas by 2007 there were several national radio stations and a network of local radio stations including newer digital stations. Numbers going to the cinema declined dramatically with the introduction of television, but films still remain popular and, indeed, audience numbers have risen steadily since 1985 (see table 22).

BBC: British Broadcasting Corporation founded in 1922 (as the British Broadcasting Company) as the national broadcaster.

Why do you think the number of visits to cinemas increased in the 1990s?

TABLE 22 Cinema attendance 1960–1998

	Screens	Admissions (000s)	Average visits per person
1960	3,034	501	9.6
1970	1,529	193	3.5
1980	1,715	101	1.8
1990	1,715	91	1.6
1998	2,581	136	2.3
2007	3,440	156	2.6

The programmes and other services offered by the media itself have changed, reflecting British society more closely than they did in the 1940s and 1950s. The 1960s in particular saw the media begin to tackle subjects that had previously been taboo, notably sexual relations, and take a much more critical view of politicians. New forms of popular music, particularly rock and roll in the 1950s and 1960s, showed the spending power that teenagers now had and emphasised a dissatisfaction with the place young people had in society.

Until the 1970s the media was, however, generally a unifying force. Choice was limited to two or three TV channels and three or four radio stations. People tended to watch and listen to the same programmes. During the 1980s and particularly the 1990s this changed with a proliferation of channels on **terrestrial**, **satellite** and **cable** television. Video recorders meant that people could record and watch programmes when it suited them. Popular music too split into various types, such as rap, hip-hop, indie/alternative and electronica, whereas previously people had not much choice outside the Top Forty hits.

Terrestrial: Television broadcast through the air and available to everyone with a television aerial.

Satellite: Television broadcast via satellites in space and picked up by special receivers.

Cable: Television broadcast through special cables and picked up with decoders.

The media in 1945

In 1945 the British people got much of their news from newspapers and the radio (then called the wireless). For entertainment they turned to the wireless and cinema. The media had played a major part in the war effort keeping up morale with films like *In Which we Serve* (1942) and *Henry V* (1944), while the radio entertained with programmes such as *Bandwagon* and particularly *ITMA* (*It's That Man Again*) that gently satirised the bureaucracy and shortages of Britain in the 1940s.

Because of the shortage of paper, newspapers generally consisted of four or eight pages. Despite being heavily censored – no weather reports, for example, were carried during the war for fear of giving information to the enemy – they still remained extremely popular. Two newspapers were especially important. The Labour-Party-supporting *Daily Mirror* was the firm favourite of servicemen, who particularly followed the 'Adventures of Jane' a daily strip cartoon featuring a scantily clad heroine. The middle classes generally preferred the conservative *Daily Express*, owned by Lord Beaverbrook, a friend of Winston Churchill and a minister in the wartime government.

The most popular form of entertainment, however, was the cinema. In 1946 about a third of the population went to see a film at least once a week and one in eight twice a week or more. Cinemas were warm and comfortable and the films themselves offered an escape for an hour or two from the dreary existence of wartime and post-war Britain. Newsreels provided by Pathé and Movietone were shown between films and proved an important source of news for audiences.

However the most important source of both news and entertainment was the BBC. At the outbreak of war in September 1939 there were some 9 million wireless sets, about one for every four members of the population. As with British films the BBC reinforced a cosy image of a Britain at peace with itself. The Corporation rigorously censored programmes and even the lyrics of popular songs. The BBC maintained that it had the duty, in the words of its Director-General Sir William Haley, to 'use … broadcasting to develop true citizenship and the leading of a full life'.

The rise of television

The BBC broadcast the first commercial television programmes in the world from Alexandra Palace in North London on 2 November 1936. Transmission ceased on the outbreak of war in September 1939 and resumed on 7 June 1946. Most viewers lived in the south-east. Hours were limited and the new service closed down for a period in the early evening to allow parents to put their children to sleep. There were fears almost from the first programme that television would corrupt the young and bring unhealthy American influences.

What made television really popular was the Coronation of Queen Elizabeth II in 1953, which was watched by half the British population, and also the launch of Independent Television (ITV) on 22 September

1955. The new service was to be funded by advertising and was seen as dangerous by people such as the Archbishop of York. Fears over the quality of programmes shown on the new channel were unfounded. An American commentator observed, 'the British have decided to paint the gaudy thing a sombre grey to blend with the general fog'.

What set ITV apart from the BBC was an innovative news service provided by Independent Television News (ITN) which the BBC was soon forced to emulate. The resulting competition for viewers between the two channels led in general to the development of many more popular television programmes. As a result the numbers of television sets in people's homes soared (see table 23). The television set in the front room was the symbol of the affluent society that Britain had become by the late 1950s. Sets may have been plentiful, but the choice of viewing remained limited and until 1967 was entirely in black and white. The third television channel, BBC 2, was not launched until April 1964.

Why do think there was an increase in TV licences?

TABLE 23 Television licences (thousands)

1947	1950	1955	1960	1965	1975	1985	2007
15	344	4504	10,470	13,253	17,701	18,716	25,000

The 1960s, however, have often been seen as being a golden age of broadcasting with the combination of well-funded broadcasting companies with increasingly liberal and permissive attitudes. There were certainly groundbreaking programmes such as the satirical series *That was the Week that Was* (broadcast in 1963 and 1964) and later *Monty Python's Flying Circus* (broadcast between 1969 and 1972). Controversial television plays such as *The War Game* on the effects of a nuclear warhead dropped on Chatham (which the government banned in 1965) and *Cathy Come Home* (broadcast in 1966), which exposed the plight of single mothers, kept television very much in the public eye. These were combined with popular and long-running series like *Steptoe and Son*, *Dr Who*, and especially *Coronation Street*, which has been running since 1960.

There had long been pressure for a second commercial channel. Channel 4 went on air in November 1982 aiming to provide programmes designed to appeal to minority audiences. In this it has generally been both commercially and artistically successful. Terrestrial television was completed in March 1997 with the appearance of Channel 5.

But the big challenge to broadcasters from the mid-1980s has been satellite and, to a much lesser extent, cable television. In 1999 subscribers could receive 50 or more different channels. In particular Sky TV, which went on air in February 1989, posed a big threat. The major share-owner in the company, News International, controlled by Rupert Murdoch, realised that it could only prosper by buying up the rights, previously owned by terrestrial television, to show sporting fixtures, particularly football. To watch these events people had to subscribe to British Sky Broadcasting (as it is now called). Both ITV and, particularly, the BBC were unable to compete with the money offered by BSkyB to the various sporting federations.

By 2007 cable and satellite television had become firmly established in Britain. BSkyB and Setenta had arranged financial deals with the Football Association for exclusive rights to show Premier League matches. The BBC also announced in 2006 that by 2010 digital television would become the norm.

Digital Terrestrial Television (DTT) was launched in the UK in 1998. After initial commercial failure of a pay-TV proposition, Freeview launched in 2002. Throughout the decade television became more 'on-demand', with viewers able to record their favourite programmes through a 'Digi-box' at the expense of the video recorder.

Radio

At the end of the war the BBC had two radio stations – the Home Service (now Radio 4) and the Forces Programme which was renamed the Light Programme (now Radio 2) in July 1945. It was soon joined by the Third Programme (now Radio 3) in September 1946, intended to serve the intellectual elite. The programmes broadcast were listened to by millions of people from *Dick Barton: Secret Agent* and *Children's Hour* for the young, to *Have a Go* and *Mrs Dale's Diary* for the middle-aged.

Radio listening soon declined in popularity with the growth of its great rival, television. During the mid-1960s the BBC also faced increasing competition from pirate radio stations broadcasting pop music from ships moored outside British territorial waters in the North Sea. Radio Caroline, set up in 1964, was the most popular. Eventually the BBC bowed to pressure and set up its own pop music radio station – Radio 1 – in 1967. At the same time legal action closed down the pirate stations. The BBC effectively had a monopoly of radio broadcasting until 1973 when the first commercial local radio stations were licensed. The first national commercial radio station, Classic FM, started broadcasting in September 1992.

In the 21st century DAB (Digital Audio Broadcasting) provided radio of a higher audio quality and enabled more stations. The BBC expanded its five national analogue stations with a further five digital-only stations. Listeners could now listen via a DAB radio, through their digital televisions or on the internet and download podcasts of their favourite programmes.

Newspapers

Newspapers have changed out of all recognition since 1945. In particular the number of pages have increased in each issue, expanded the coverage of subjects such as sport and travel, and used technological developments to improve the layout of the paper and (especially during the 1990s) colour photography. National newspapers have generally prospered at the cost of provincial and local newspapers. Many provincial daily and evening papers have closed, while local newspapers contain more national and less local news. The numbers of people buying and reading national newspapers have remained very high despite the challenge of television (see table 24).

From the table what do you think have been the main trends in newspaper circulation since the war? Explain your answer.

TABLE 24 Newspaper circulation (000s)

	1939	1951	1960	1970	1980	1990	1999	2007
Daily Express	2,486	4,193	4,130	3,607	2,325	1,585	1,091	737
Daily Herald	2,000	2,071	1,467					
Daily Mail	1,510	2,245	2,084	1,917	1,985	1,708	2,357	2,295
Sun				1,509	3,837	3,855	3,701	3,077
Daily Mirror	1,367	4,567	4,545	4,697	3,651	3,083	2,341	1,500
Daily Sketch	850	777	1,152	806				
Daily Star					1,033	833	613	723
Daily Telegraph	640	976	1,155	1,402	1,456	1,076	1,044	867
Guardian	51	140	190	303	375	424	393	356
Independent (founded 1986)						411	224	252
News Chronicle	1,317	1,586	1,206					
The Times	213	254	255	402	316	420	727	613
Today (1986–1995)						540		
TOTAL circulation	**10,434**	**16,809**	**16,184**	**14,643**	**14,978**	**13,935**	**12,491**	**10,420**

Front page of the *Sun* newspaper in 2007 when Prince Harry was photographed at a fancy dress party.

What does this picture tell us about the *Sun* as a British daily newspaper?

Since 1945 the national newspaper scene has remained remarkably consistent. Three new national daily newspapers have been launched – the *Sun* (1964), *Daily Star* (1978) and the *Independent* (1986), while newspapers that closed include the *Daily Sketch* (1971), the *News Chronicle* (1960), and the *Daily Herald* (1964).

The freedom of the press against the privacy of the individual has remained a constant issue. Newspapers, especially the tabloids, have always included many stories about celebrities, but until the 1970s the lives of the Royal Family and politicians were generally left alone. This changed, however, largely as a result of the massive media interest in the lives of the Royal Family, particularly Princess Diana who was being followed by the paparazzi at the time of her death in 1997. The royals continue to attract a lot of attention. The private lives of politicians also increasingly came under the scrutiny of the press and a succession of minor Conservative ministers resigned from office during the 1990s when their stories hit the front page.

This has increasingly led to calls for regulation of the press to ensure the private lives of people in the public eye and particularly lives of ordinary citizens are respected. Back in 1949 a royal commission on the press recommended the establishment of a press council to act as a forum for the industry. The Press Council was duly set up in 1953 and could hear complaints about invasion of privacy. It was later re-established in 1991, as the Press Complaints Commission. Both the Council and the Commission have proved unable to regulate the press to prevent abuses happening.

There has also been considerable debate about the influence of newspapers in politics. Most newspapers in the 1980s and early 1990s were firmly behind the Conservative government and used their pages to denigrate the Labour Party, its policies and its leaders. The *Sun* after the 1992 election which saw the Conservatives unexpectedly returned to power, proclaimed, 'It was the Sun wot won it'. By 1997, however, most newspapers had switched their allegiance to 'New Labour' reflecting their readers' views that the Conservatives were out of touch with the concerns of the voters.

Film

The common language and, very largely, culture with America has meant that the British film industry has found it difficult to survive. Many of the most talented producers, directors and actors have been lured to Hollywood or, from the 1950s, preferred to work in television. In addition the government has been reluctant to support the film industry in the way that is common on the continent.

Even so a number of notable films have been made and shown to both critical and public acclaim. The late 1940s probably saw the peak of the British film industry, supported by the 'Eady Levy' and heavy import duties on American films. The best films were probably those made by Ealing Studios, such as *The Lavender Hill Mob* (1951) and *Passport to Pimlico* (1949).

Eady Levy: A tax levied on cinema tickets in order to provide grants to the British film industry. Named after Sir William Eady, Chairman of the National Film Production Council.

British films of the period in general tended to avoid controversial issues, preferring to follow the traditional stereotypes in presenting a familiar, reassuring, tolerant, kindly British people to itself. There was no new artistic form as seen on the continent. There was a resurgence of British film-making during the 1960s, beginning with a series of films looking at working-class life of the period, unkindly dubbed 'kitchen sink dramas' by critics. Notable examples were *Saturday Night and Sunday Morning* (1960) on the life of a factory worker in Nottingham and *This Sporting Life* (1963) about a rugby league player. Later in the decade came the first of the James Bond films and *The Italian Job* (1969) which celebrated a newly modernised, confident Britain. The 1960s also saw the heyday of the *Carry On* films, particularly *Carry on Cleo* (1965) and *Carry on up the Khyber* (1967).

The 1980s and 1990s did not see the same number of films being made, but a few highly popular films were still released, including *Gandhi* (1982), *Four Weddings and a Funeral* (1994), *The English Patient* (1996) and *Lock, Stock and Two Smoking Barrels* (1998). From the mid-nineties, with renewed private and public investment, American productions began to return to British studios including the *Star Wars* prequels and the Bond films. The 2000s also witnessed a number of significant films that were British-made with the backing of major American studios. The *Harry Potter* series (2001–2011), *28 Days Later* (2002), *Love Actually* (2003), *The Constant Gardener* (2005) and *Atonement* (2007) and a crop of fresh British acting talent proved that by 2007 the British film industry was in good health.

1. What changes have happened to the mass-media since the end of the Second World War?

2. Why do you think these changes have occurred?

7.5 The rise and fall of the British trade union movement, 1945–2007

The trade union movement has played an important part in shaping post-war Britain. The experience however has not been a happy one for the unions because, particularly after 1979, they have seen most of their power and much of their influence disappear.

1940–1968

The place of trade unions in the war effort was recognised by the appointment of Ernest Bevin, the leader of Britain's biggest union, the Transport and General Workers Union (TGWU), as Minister of Labour in 1940 with responsibility for ensuring war factories got the workers they needed. Bevin fully mobilised the trade union movement in this work. In turn the unions had insisted on the reintroduction of pre war working practices after the war.

The trade unions emerged after 1945 as powerful partners with government and the employers in the management of the economy. Nearly half the working population were members of unions (see table 25). The unions naturally enjoyed warm relations with the Attlee administration. The union leadership in particular did much to contain protests from members about working conditions and ensured that wage rises remained low, thus helping to keep inflation low. In return they ensured that the government took into consideration their concerns, particularly over nationalisation. Clement Attlee also repealed the Trades Disputes Act, 1927 which had done much to shackle union activity during the 1930s.

Why do you think union membership declined in the 1980s and 1990s?

TABLE 25 Membership of trade unions, 1936–2005

	Members of trade unions (000)	% union members as proportion of workforce
1938	5,842	30
1951	9,289	44
1961	9,897	43
1970	11,179	48
1974	11,756	50
1981	12,947	44
1993	7,762	28
2005	6,390	26

The Conservatives elected in 1951 were determined to continue this close relationship. A symbol of this was the appointment of Sir Walter Monckton as Minister of Labour. 'So conciliatory was Monckton,' John Charmley remarks in *A History of Conservative Politics, 1900–1996* (1996) that 'there were many who wondered whether he was the minister *for* labour'. What lay behind this was a recognition that Conservative politics were constrained to operate within the framework of Labour's post-war settlement that had brought significant benefits to working class voters.

Even so there was an increasing belief that poor industrial relations were affecting industrial growth. A stream of press and television stories encouraged this impression, although most strikes were concentrated in one or two industries. A Department of Employment study showed that, between 1971 and 1973, some 98 per cent of manufacturing establishments had no strikes at all (see table 26).

Why have there been dramatic increases and decreases in industrial action as shown by this table?

TABLE 26 Industrial disputes 1931–97

	Working days lost (000s)	1931 = 100	Number of stoppages in year	1931 = 100
1931	6,983	100	420	100
1946	2,158	31	2,205	525
1951	1,694	24	1,719	409
1956	2,083	30	2,648	630
1961	3,046	44	2,686	640
1966	2,398	34	1,937	461
1970	3,906	56	10,980	2,614
1975	2,282	33	6,012	1,413
1980	11,964	171	830	198
1985	6,402	92	903	215
1990	1,903	27	630	150
1995	400	6	211	50
1997	200	3	n/a	n/a
2005	157	n/a	116	n/a
2006	747	n/a	155	n/a

(n/a – not available)

Where they occurred in industry, strikes were often short 'wildcat' strikes over minor job demarcation or manning levels. Over time these had serious long-term effects on output, quality, delivery dates, and labour costs, all of which contributed to the loss of markets at home and abroad. The shipbuilding, car and newspapers industries, which had a large number of competing craft unions, were particularly prone to strikes of this kind.

Strikes increased during the 1960s. There were a number of well-publicised strikes particularly in the docks. The best known of these was probably the seamen's strike during the summer of 1966, which caused immense damage to Britain's export trade and resulted in heavy pressure on sterling. Governments seemed powerless to act, although ministers were well aware of the damage to the economy.

One strategy to curb the unions would have been a change in economic strategy to end the policy of full employment, for the demand for labour and the ease of changing jobs gave unions considerable leverage in arguing for wage increases. But to do so would have struck at the very heart of the consensus that governments, of both left and right, were striving to build. During the 1960s and 1970s many politicians still had vivid memories of the misery that mass unemployment caused between the wars and had no wish to see this happen again. It would take the Conservatives under Margaret Thatcher, and the end of full employment in the late 1970s and early 1980s, to control the unions effectively.

1968–1979

In 1965 the government decided to set up a royal commission, under Lord Donovan, to look at industrial relations. When the commission reported in 1968 it advised against sanctions to curb union power. Barbara Castle, the Secretary of State for Employment, however proposed stiffer measures to regulate industrial disputes in the White Paper *In Place of Strife* (1969). These fairly moderate proposals were overwhelmingly rejected by the trade union movement, as well as by the Labour Party itself, forcing a humiliating retreat by the government. In the end the Trade Union Congress (TUC) and the government agreed a weak compromise.

The Conservative government in 1970 took a rather different approach. It passed the Industrial Relations Act 1971, which introduced unprecedented legal regulation of union activities in an attempt to stop wildcat strikes. This was bitterly resisted by the trade union movement, which refused to register, as the Act directed. This largely rendered the legislation ineffective. In addition the government's approach was also condemned by the **Confederation of British Industry** (CBI). The Act was abolished in 1974 after Labour was returned to power.

Confederation of British Industry: Represents industry in dealings with the government. Formed in 1965.

The Heath government collapsed in early 1974 as the result of a bruising clash with the National Union of Miners. Between 1971 and 1972 the miners had, in the first national strike in the coal mines since 1926, successfully gone on strike for a large pay rise. The strike had caused widespread disruption to industry, including power cuts and compulsory short-term working known as 'the three day week'. The miners, and other trade unions, angered by the falling behind of wages, threatened industrial action. Heath's reaction was to call an election for late February, specifically on the question 'Who governs Britain?' The electorate inconclusively decided that the Conservatives didn't, returning a minority Labour government that resolved the dispute with the miners within days of the election.

Like Heath, James Callaghan would eventually fall foul of the trade unions, though this is more surprising considering Callaghan's background in the trade union movement. Initially relations were warm. Many of the long-standing demands of the unions were met, such as the Health and Safety At Work Act (1974), which improved conditions in factories and offices across Britain. Unions also fully co-operated in attempts to reduce inflation. A voluntary code was introduced in 1976 which lasted for nearly two years; far longer than most observers had predicted.

By the middle of 1978 the pressure on trade union leaders from members after several years of wage restraint was almost irresistible. The government, however, decided to ignore the warning signs when it introduced a 5 per cent pay rise limit in October 1978, without consulting the unions. The figure was rejected first by the Labour Party conference and then opposed by various key groups – firemen, lorry drivers, and Ford workers – who obtained substantial settlements well into double figures. Public sector workers, always poorly paid, tried to follow suit. Months of sporadic industrial action followed which became known as the 'Winter of Discontent'. Eventually the government caved in and awarded a 9 per cent pay rise. The damage, however, had been done. The feeling that the trade unions had got out of control greatly benefited the Conservatives at the general election in 1979.

1979–2007

The new Thatcher government had no qualms in taking on the trade unions. In this the government was helped by the economic slump, which had seen a massive increase in unemployment including many hundreds of thousands of former union members. The government also learnt from the mistakes made by Edward Heath and avoided a full frontal attack, instead preferring a piecemeal approach with a series of acts restricting union activities. Chief among them were requirements for ballots before strike action and restrictions on picketing. Union opposition was muted, partly because it was clear that this legislation was popular among

National Union of Mineworkers leader Arthur Scargill (with loudspeaker) and demonstrators, 1977

members; a majority of whom had indeed voted for the Conservatives in 1979. Days lost due to industrial disputes fell from 6.2 million days in 1981 to 528 in 1982.

The last great act of union resistance was the miners' strike of 1984–85, in which the National Union of Miners under Arthur Scargill was comprehensively defeated by a determined government, who perhaps remembered the bruising contests with the miners in 1972 and 1974. Although the strike attracted considerable public sympathy, it was badly-led by Scargill. As Neil Kinnock told the Labour Party, the miners were 'lions led by donkeys'. However popular the strike might have been it was ultimately doomed to failure, for British industry was no longer as dependent on coal as it had once been. Indeed stocks had been increasing for some months before the strike in anticipation of industrial action.

The defeat of the strike allowed the Conservatives to pass further laws controlling the unions and the power of industrial action. As a result strikes fell to an all-time low.

New Labour had an ambivalent relationship with the unions. Although it was willing to accept trade union money to help fund the party, the leaders were keen to be seen as keeping the unions at arm's length. The Blair administration introduced a number of reforms for which the unions had campaigned, such as a national minimum wage. However, the trade union laws passed by the Thatcher/Major government remained. To Blair 'New Labour' meant his party was no longer in league with the unions. Attempts to find alternative sources of finance led to

1. Why were the unions so powerful after the Second World War?

2. Why was there so much industrial unrest in the 1960s and 1970s?

3. How similar were the Conservative and Labour governments' policies towards the trade unions from 1979 to 2007?

major problems for Blair's third government, after 2005, when it was discovered that the Labour Party had received loans from private donors which had not been paid back.

Further Reading

Texts designed specifically for AS and A2 students

British Society since 1945 by Arthur Marwick (Penguin, 1996)
From Blitz to Blair: A New History of Britain since 1939 edited by Nick Tiratsoo
    (Weidenfeld and Nicolson, 1997)
The People's Peace by Kenneth O. Morgan (Oxford University Press, 1990)
Twentieth Century Britain: Economic, Social and Cultural Change edited by Paul
    Johnson (Longman, 1994)

More advanced reading

The Age of Insecurity by Larry Elliott and Dan Atkinson (Verso, 1998)
British Economic Performance since 1945 by B.W.E. Alford (Macmillan, 1988)
Modern Britain: an Economic and Social History by Sean Glynn and Alan Booth
    (Routledge, 1996)

Websites

A useful site giving basic statistical information about the United Kingdom is the Office for National Statistics http://www.statistics.gov.uk

8 Britain and Ireland, 1914–2007

Key Issues

■ How did British policy change towards Ireland between 1914–2007?

■ Why were Nationalists and Unionists in conflict in Ireland?

■ Why has it been so difficult to find a permanent solution to British-Irish relations?

8.1 Why was Ireland partitioned between 1914 and 1922?

8.2 How did relations between Britain and the Irish Free State/Eire develop between 1922 and 1949?

8.3 Historical Interpretation: Why did civil and political disorder develop in Northern Ireland by 1969?

8.4 How effective was British policy towards Northern Ireland between 1969 and 1985?

8.5 Why was it so difficult to find a political solution in Northern Ireland between 1985 and 2007?

Framework of Events

1914	Home Rule becomes law but its operation is suspended for the duration of the First World War
1916	Easter Rising in Dublin
1917–1918	Irish Convention
1918	General Election: Sinn Fein wins 73 seats
1919	Dail Eireann established in Dublin
1920	Government of Ireland Act
1921	Anglo-Irish Treaty
1922	Irish Free State created
1922–3	Civil War within the Irish Free State
1926	Balfour Declaration on dominion self-government
1931	Statute of Westminster
1932	Fianna Fail win Irish Free State general election
1932–36	Fianna Fail government begins dismantling links between Irish Free State and Britain
1937	New Constitution: Irish Free State becomes Eire
1938	Anglo-Irish agreements: Treaty ports given to Eire
1939	Eire stays neutral in the Second World War
1949	Eire becomes Republic of Ireland and leaves the Commonwealth
1956–1962	IRA Border Campaign
1965	Meetings between Prime Ministers of Northern Ireland and the Republic
1968	Civil Rights Movement develops in Northern Ireland. Civil disturbances begin
1969	British government orders troops into Northern Ireland. Beginning of the 'Troubles'
1971	Northern Ireland government introduces internment
1972	'Bloody Sunday' in Londonderry. Northern Ireland government suspended
1973	Britain and the Republic of Ireland join the EEC
	Sunningdale Agreement on setting up a power sharing executive in Northern Ireland
1974	Ulster Loyalist strike against power sharing. Sunningdale Agreement collapses
1976	'Peace People' movement against violence. The two leaders Mairead Corrigan (Catholic) and Betty Williams (Protestant) win Nobel peace prize
1981	Hunger Strike by Republican prisoners. One of them, Bobby Sands, is elected MP for Fermanagh and South Tyrone. He and nine other hunger strikers die
1982	Prior's 'Rolling Devolution' Proposals

1984	Margaret Thatcher and members of the Cabinet survive Brighton Bombing by Provisional IRA
1985	Anglo-Irish Agreement: Margaret Thatcher and Garret Fitzgerald, Prime Minister of the Republic of Ireland sign agreement on Northern Ireland
1993	Downing Street Declaration
1994	IRA ceasefire
1996	IRA ceasefire collapses after failure to reach agreement on decommissioning paramilitary weapons
1998	'Good Friday Agreement'
1999	Creation of Northern Ireland Executive
	Northern Ireland Executive and Assembly suspended for first time due to Unionist claims that IRA had not decommissioned its weapons
2001	IRA offer to decommission weapons leads to reopening of Northern Ireland Assembly
2002	October: Northern Ireland Secretary, Dr John Reid suspends the Northern Ireland Executive and Assembly because of an IRA spy ring uncovered at Northern Ireland parliament. Assembly remains suspended until May 2007.
2004	Negotiations held in a bid to re-establish Assembly. Comprehensive Agreement replaces Royal Ulster Constabulary with Police Service of Northern Ireland.
2005	Sinn Fein leader Gerry Adams asks IRA to 'lay down its arms'
2006	St Andrew's Agreement leads way to elections for Northern Ireland Assembly
2007	March: Elections lead to dominance of Democratic Unionist Party in Unionist community and Sinn Fein in Nationalist/Republican community
	May: New Northern Ireland Executive formed, with Ian Paisley of DUP as First Minister and Martin McGuinness of Sinn Fein as his Deputy
	July: British army ends Operation Banner, name for its involvement in Northern Ireland which began in 1969. The 'Troubles' officially come to an end.

Overview

BRITAIN'S Irish problem, or Ireland's British problem, has been a dominant theme of United Kingdom politics between 1914–22 and since 1969. In September 1914 a political solution to British-Irish relations seemed to have been made. A Home Rule Act, granting limited self-government, was passed by the Westminster Parliament but was suspended for the duration of the First World War. However, by 1922, Ireland was partitioned between Northern Ireland and the Irish Free State. The latter was a state within the British Empire with internal self-government. These political developments occurred mainly because of the effects of a failed armed rebellion against British rule made by extreme Nationalists in Dublin in 1916.

From the founding of the Irish Free State to the creation of the Republic of Ireland in 1949, some Irish politicians attempted gradually to weaken the links with the British Empire. The most notable was Eamon de Valera. From 1932 to 1937 he severed many of these links. In 1937 he introduced a new constitution which created an independent republic 'in all but name'. In addition, he laid claim to Northern Ireland as part of a united Ireland. In 1949 Ireland became a fully independent state outside the Commonwealth.

Northern Ireland did receive Home Rule. From 1921 to 1972 it was dominated by the Ulster Unionist party. This party was predominantly Protestant. It discriminated against Catholics, who were seen as Nationalists who wanted a united Ireland. By 1968 Catholic civil rights had become a major issue in Northern Ireland politics.

Hillsborough Agreement: Hillsborough Castle is the Secretary of State for Northern Ireland's official residence.

Decommissioning: The handing in for destruction of military equipment including rifles and bomb making equipment.

It sparked off a Protestant unionist reaction which led to major sectarian violence in 1969. The British government first sent troops to Northern Ireland in 1969 in an attempt to maintain law and order. In 1972 the government suspended the Northern Ireland Parliament and ruled the area directly from London.

From 1969 to 1998 Northern Ireland was badly affected by political violence. The Provisional IRA and Loyalist paramilitary groups engaged in guerrilla warfare and sectarian murder. Successive British governments, both Labour and Conservative, had attempted to find a political solution. Attempts to involve both Nationalist and Unionists in government failed. In 1985 a new attempt was made with the Anglo-Irish (**Hillsborough**) **Agreement** which involved co-operation between the British and Irish governments. By the 1990s attempts to solve the conflict in Northern Ireland involved a fusion of previous attempts at a political solution: co-operation in government between political parties within Northern Ireland and co-operation between Britain and Ireland. A major turning-point in British-Irish relations came following the landslide victory of the Labour Party in the 1997 General Election. Under the leadership of Tony Blair, and with the support of US President, Bill Clinton, a landmark agreement was made in 1998. The Good Friday Agreement, between Britain, the Republic of Ireland and political parties in Northern Ireland offered the basis of a permanent agreement. However, there were still problems. The Democratic Unionist Party (DUP) of Ian Paisley did not sign up to the Agreement. Also, an important part of the Agreement was the **decommissioning** of IRA weapons, something the IRA were reluctant to do. However, a new Northern Ireland Executive and Parliament were chosen involving both Nationalists and Unionists. The Good Friday Agreement faced a stern test after 2000 when the UK government was forced to suspend the Northern Ireland Executive and Parliament because of disputes over decommissioning. However, by 2006, the IRA had formally renounced violence and decommissioned its weapons. Also the St Andrew's Agreement of 2006 led to the reestablishment of the Northern Ireland Executive and Parliament, this time with the historic inclusion of the DUP, working together with Sinn Fein.

Political Parties in Northern Ireland

The Ulster Unionist Party
The main party since the creation of the state in 1921. Wants to maintain the union with Britain. Moderate party, which signed the Sunningdale Agreement and the Good Friday Agreement.

The Democratic Unionist Party
Founded in 1971 by Ian Paisley. Wants the return of a Stormont-style government to Northern Ireland. Completely opposed to any involvement of the Irish Republic in Northern Ireland politics. Opposed to Sunningdale Agreement, Anglo-Irish Agreement and Good Friday Agreement all because of links with the Irish Republic.

The Social Democratic and Labour Party
Founded in 1970 by Gerry Fitt. Originated from the Civil Rights movement. Attracts about two-thirds of the Nationalist vote. In favour of a reunification of Ireland by consent. Main aim: to defend the rights of the Nationalist community.

Sinn Fein
Originally Arthur Griffith's party in 1906. Became associated with the demand for an independent Irish republic after 1916. From 1919 it opposed parliamentary representation of Ireland in the British (Westminster) Parliament. From 1922 it opposed representation in the Irish Free State, which was still part of Britain's Dominions. Present party is the political wing of the Republican movement in Northern Ireland. Initially in favour of the 'armed struggle', it moderated its views in the 1980s to support the twin policy of the political violence and democratic politics (the armalite and ballot box strategy). Received about 40% of the Nationalist vote by 1990s. Now supports representation in the Northern Ireland Assembly and Dublin Parliament.

Paramilitary groups in Northern Ireland since 1969

Provisional IRA
Formed in 1970 through split with the Official IRA. Led armed struggle to expel the British from Northern Ireland since that date. In favour of a united Irish republic. Have adopted various policies such as political assassination; bombing in Northern Ireland and Britain; organising demonstrations such, as the 'Dirty Protest' for political status in Northern Ireland's prison in late 1970s, and the Hunger Strike of 1981. Well-armed through support from Libya and money from supporters in the United States.

Irish National Liberation Army
A faction which split from the Provisional IRA in 1975. Military wing of Irish Republican Socialist Party. Engaged in campaign of violence which included the murder of Lord Mountbatten and Airey Neave. Also killed 17 people in Dropping Well pub bombing. Nearly fell apart with faction fighting in 1987.

Real IRA
Another faction which split from the Provisional IRA in November 1997. Responsible for the Omagh bombing of 1998.
UDA (The Ulster Defence Association)
Formed in 1972. Contained 40,000 members and remained legal until 1992. Sees itself as defender of Protestant working-class communities. Active in Ulster Workers' Strike of 1974. Mainly engaged in sectarian murders of Catholics.

UVF (The Ulster Volunteer Force)
Originally formed in 1912 to oppose Home Rule. Mainly engaged in sectarian murders of Catholics. For instance in 1992 11 Catholics were murdered by the UVF.

(Of the 3,600 deaths in the Northern Ireland conflict since 1969 43% have been Catholic [1,548]. Most were killed by Loyalist gunmen.)

Dirty Protest: The name given to the protest by Republican prisoners when they refused to wear clothing and 'dirtied' themselves with their own excreta.

1. What do you regard as the political solution which has had the greatest influence on British–Irish Relations between 1914 and 2007? Give reasons for your answer.

2. What do you regard as the greatest 'missed opportunity' in bringing lasting peace in British–Irish relations in the period 1914 to 2007?

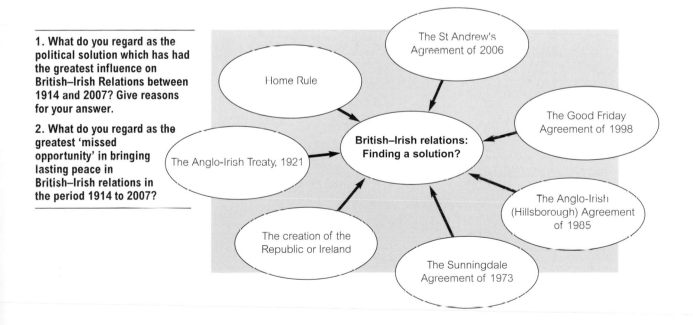

- The St Andrew's Agreement of 2006
- Home Rule
- The Good Friday Agreement of 1998
- British–Irish relations: Finding a solution?
- The Anglo-Irish Treaty, 1921
- The Anglo-Irish (Hillsborough) Agreement of 1985
- The creation of the Republic or Ireland
- The Sunningdale Agreement of 1973

8.1 Why was Ireland partitioned between 1914 and 1922?

The Irish Question: The term given to the problem posed by Ireland to British governments.

In September 1914, it seemed that the British government had found a solution to the **Irish Question**. A Home Rule Act was passed. This granted limited self-government to Ireland within the United Kingdom and seemed to be the end of a political process, which had begun with Gladstone's conversion to Irish Home Rule in 1886.

However, within eight years Ireland was partitioned between Northern Ireland and the Irish Free State. Why did the plan to introduce Irish Home Rule fail?

The problem of Ulster

During the political crisis which led to the passage of the Home Rule Act, a political crisis occurred over Ulster. North-east Ireland contained a Protestant/Unionist majority which was opposed to Home Rule. In 1912 100,000 Ulster Unionists formed the Ulster Volunteer Force (UVF) to oppose Home Rule by force if necessary. When the First World War broke out Ireland seemed to be on the verge of civil war. In addition to the UVF, Nationalists in Ireland formed the Irish Volunteers in 1913 to defend Home Rule. It numbered 200,000 men but was not as well armed as the UVF.

The First World War prevented an armed clash. The UVF and large numbers of the Irish Volunteers volunteered for the British Army. In addition, when the Home Rule Act was passed the Prime Minister, H. H. Asquith, promised to introduce an 'Amending Bill' which would exclude the six north-eastern counties of Ireland from the operation of Home Rule for a period of time.

How did the Easter Rising of 1916 affect British-Irish Relations?

Explain the impact of the Easter Rising, 1916, on British-Irish relations.

During the early years of the war Nationalist opinion in Ireland was upset by a number of developments. At the outbreak of war the UVF were allowed to form their own division of the British Army (the 36th Division). The Irish Volunteers were not allowed the same privilege. In addition, the son of John Redmond, the leader of the Irish Nationalist Party, was denied

Edward Carson (1854–1935)
Carson was educated at Trinity College, Dublin. Irish Solicitor-General from 1892 and MP until 1918 he was a leading Irish Unionist opponent of Home Rule. Carson was a member of British Cabinet 1915–18.

Irish Republican Brotherhood: Originally founded in 1858 the IRB were once known as Fenians. They wanted to create an independent Irish Republic by violent means and engaged in an uprising in 1865–67 and bombing London in the 1880s.

Irish Citizen Army: A small group of socialist trade unionists led by James Connolly who became armed to defend trade unionists during strikes.

Dail: The Parliament of the Republic of Ireland and historically of the Irish Free State and Eire.

Guerrilla war: A plan of campaign fought against a regular army by small bands of armed men and women.

Black and Tans: Volunteers recruited by the British Government after the First World War to supplement the work of the Royal Irish Constabulary and the regular army in countering Irish republican attacks. The Black and Tans became notorious for the violence of their 'reprisals' against the nationalist population. The name is thought to derive from their dark berets and khaki tunics.

a commission to become a British army officer. When a coalition government was formed in May 1915, Sir Edward Carson, leading Irish Unionist and opponent of Home Rule, joined the Cabinet.

Of greater significance was the decision by the **Irish Republican Brotherhood** (IRB) to stage an armed uprising against British rule. Their aim was to create an independent Irish republic. The IRB had infiltrated the organisation of the Irish Volunteers. Around 11,000 men had decided to stay in Ireland and not join the British army. In league with other separatist groups, such as the **Irish Citizen Army**, an uprising involving fewer than 2,000 Volunteers occurred in Dublin at the end of April, 1916. The Rising lasted less than a week and was easily defeated by the British garrison.

Although the Easter Rising was a military failure it did have a profound effect on Irish public opinion. The decision by the British authorities to execute sixteen leaders helped turn the rebels into Nationalist martyrs. However, the Allied powers were hoping the United States would join the war on their side and Britain did not want to alienate Irish-American opinion, so in 1917 several hundred rebel prisoners were released and allowed to return to Ireland. This created a powerful Republican political force. Finally, in 1918 the British government outraged Nationalist opinion by attempting to introduce compulsory military conscription into Ireland. Irish Nationalist MPs and Republicans campaigned jointly against the plan.

British government policy to solve Irish problems came to nothing. Lloyd George, the Prime Minister, called an Irish Convention of all Irish political groups to discuss problems. It met between 1917 and 1918, but was boycotted by Republicans and Unionists opposed any attempt to introduce Home Rule. A turning-point in British-Irish relations came in the December 1918 general election. The Irish Republicans, now known as Sinn Fein, won 73 out of 106 seats in Ireland. In January 1919, instead of going to Westminster, they set up their own parliament in Dublin, **Dail Eireann**. Between 1919 and 1921 Irish Republicans attempted to create an independent state outside the United Kingdom.

Why was the Irish Free State created in 1922?

In Ireland the years 1919–21 are known as the War of Independence. Armed groups of Republicans, known as the Irish Republican Army (IRA) fought a **guerrilla war** against the armed police force, the Royal Irish Constabulary, and the British Army. IRA activity was masterminded by Michael Collins who was Minister of Finance in the Dail Government.

British policy towards this problem was two-fold. Firstly, through the Government of Ireland Act (1920), the government tried to find a political solution. Two Home Rule parliaments and governments would be established in Ireland. One would be for the six counties of the north east (Northern Ireland), the other for the remaining twenty-six counties (termed Southern Ireland). Only part of the act was implemented. In the May, 1921 elections in Ireland, Sinn Fein won an overwhelming vote in the South. They refused to accept the Act.

At the same time, the British government attempted to defeat the IRA by military means. The Royal Irish Constabulary was reinforced by two groups of volunteer forces from Britain, the Auxiliaries and the '**Black and Tans**'. These groups engaged in reprisal raids on the civilian population in retaliation for IRA attacks on British forces. This policy was unpopular in the United States and among Liberals and Labour politicians in Britain.

In the summer of 1921, Lloyd George, the Prime Minister, changed British policy. He called a ceasefire with the IRA and began political negotiations with Sinn Fein.

Michael Collins (1890–1922)

Collins was born in Clonakilty, county Cork. He took part in Easter Rising, later becoming President of the IRB. He was Minister of Finance in the Dail Government of 1919, raised the National Loan 1919–21 and organised the IRA. A member of the Irish delegation for Anglo-Irish Treaty talks, he succeeded Griffith as Prime Minister of the Irish Free State, but was assassinated a few weeks later in August 1922.

Arthur Griffith (1871–1922)

Griffith was born in Dublin, and educated by the Christian Brothers. He was a member of the IRB 1893–1910. In 1906 Griffith founded the Sinn Fein Party. He wanted internal self-government for Ireland similar to Hungary's position in Austria-Hungary, and opposed the Home Rule Bill. He didn't take part in the Easter Rising but became Vice-President of the new Sinn Fein party in 1918. He headed the Irish delegation in the Anglo-Irish Treaty talks 1921 and was elected President of the Dail [Prime Minister] in January 1922, but died seven months later.

In December 1921 an agreement was signed in London. Representatives of Sinn Fein, led by Arthur Griffith and Michael Collins, accepted the creation of a self-governing state, outside the United Kingdom but part of the British Empire. This became the Irish Free State. Initially, the six counties of Northern Ireland were to be excluded. It was agreed that a Boundary Commission would study the border between the Irish Free State and

1. How did British policy towards Ireland change between 1914 and 1922?

2. Who benefited most from the Partition of Ireland and the creation of the Irish Free State?

a) The British government?

b) Irish Unionists?

c) Irish Republicans?

Give reasons to support your answer

3. How far did the political settlement of 1920–22 differ from the Home Rule Act 1914?

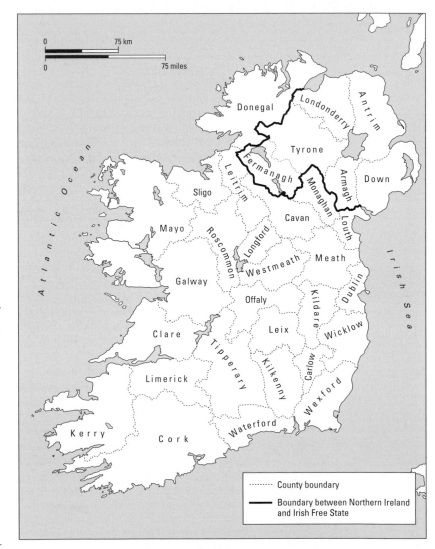

.... County boundary

———— Boundary between Northern Ireland and Irish Free State

The partition of Ireland, 1920–21

Northern Ireland and would recommend changes. Michael Collins believed that the Boundary Commission would give the Irish Free State large parts of Northern Ireland. This would have the effect of forcing Northern Ireland into a united Irish state.

The Anglo-Irish Treaty of 1921 upset extremists on both sides. 'Die hard' Conservatives disliked the breakup of the United Kingdom. Irish republicans, led by Eamon de Valera, were opposed to staying within the British Empire. De Valera's stance seems odd because he had been notified by Lloyd George in secret negotiations in July 1921 that this was the best he could offer. It does explain why de Valera did not lead the Irish negotiating team in London in November and December 1921. The split over the Treaty led to civil war within the Irish Free State. Between June 1922 and 1923, Free State forces defeated Irish Republican forces. The main casualty was Michael Collins, then Prime Minister of the Irish Free State. He was killed in an ambush on 22 August 1922.

8.2 How did relations between Britain and the Irish Free State/Eire develop between 1922 and 1949?

In his defence of the Anglo-Irish Treaty Michael Collins claimed that it gave 'freedom to achieve freedom'. By this he meant that the creation of the Irish Free State would be the beginning of a process which would eventually lead to the creation of a completely independent Irish state. Between 1922 and 1949 the Irish Free State did follow this route. However, the chief architect of this development was Collins' political rival Eamon de Valera.

The creation of Eire

Fortunately for Irish nationalists, political developments within the British Empire assisted this change. At the Imperial Conference of 1926 the 'Balfour Declaration' gave the dominions of the British Empire full internal self-government. The dominions were Canada, Australia, New Zealand, South Africa, Southern Rhodesia, Newfoundland and the Irish Free State. By the Statute of Westminster (1931) the self-governing dominions were declared independent states within the British Commonwealth. These were all held together by common allegiance to the British monarchy.

In 1932, Eamon de Valera became Prime Minister of the Irish Free State. He used the position to sever the political links with Britain. He abolished the Oath of Allegiance to the British Crown which every Irish MP had to take. The position of **Governor-General** to Ireland was reduced to a position of political insignificance. De Valera nominated an obscure Irish politician, D. Buckley, to the post. Instead of living at the Vice-Regal Lodge, the Monarch's residence in Dublin, he was banished to a small house in the Dublin suburbs. Finally de Valera abolished the right of Irish people to send legal cases to the Judicial Committee of the Privy Council.

Governor-General: The Monarch's representative in Commonwealth countries which regard the Monarch as Head of State. Between 1939 and 1949 Britain was represented in Dublin by the UK Representative in Ireland, Sir John Maffey, later Lord Rugby.

Eamon de Valera (1882–1975)		
De Valera was born in New York, USA and raised in County Limerick. He took a leading part in the Easter Rising but escaped execution. Elected President of Ireland in	1919 he opposed the Anglo-Irish treaty of 1921 and sided with anti-Treaty forces in the Irish Civil War 1922–23. He founded the Fianna Fail Party in 1926. De Valera became Prime Minister of the Irish Free State in 1932. Following the	creation of Eire in 1937 he became its Prime Minister 1937–49, 1951–54 and 1957–59 and then President of the Republic of Ireland 1959–73. Throughout his life he worked to achieve a united Irish Republic.

Political Parties in Eire/Republic of Ireland

Fianna Fail
Founded in 1926 by Eamon de Valera when he split from the IRA. Entered the Irish Parliament in 1927 and became the governing party in 1932. Has been the largest party in the Republic of Ireland since 1932. In favour of a 32-county independent Irish Republic to be achieved by democratic means. However, in 1971 two leading members of Fianna Fail, Charles Haughey (future Taoiseach) and Neil Blaney, were accused of gunrunning to the Provisional IRA.

Fine Gael
Founded in 1933. Supported the Anglo-Irish Treaty of 1921. A more pro-British party than Fianna Fail. Has taken a more conciliatory line towards cross-border security and extradition.

Prime Ministers of Irish Free State (1922–1937),
Eire (1937–1948) and the Republic of Ireland (1948 onwards)

1922–32	William T. Cosgrave (Cumann na nGaedhael)
1932–48	Eamon de Valera (Fianna Fail)
1948–51	John Costello (Coalition)
1951–54	Eamon de Valera (Fianna Fail)
1954–57	John Costello (Coalition)
1957–59	Eamon de Valera (Fianna Fail)
1959–66	Sean Lemass (Fianna Fail)
1966–73	Jack Lynch (Fianna Fail)
1973–77	Liam Cosgrave (Fine Gael)
1977–79	Jack Lynch (Fianna Fail)
1979–81	Charles Haughey (Fianna Fail)
1981–82	Garret Fitzgerald (Fine Gael)
1982 (Mar–Dec)	Charles Haughey (Fianna Fail)
1982–87	Garret Fitzgerald (Fine Gael)
1987–92	Charles Haughey (Fianna Fail)
1992–94	Albert Reynolds (Fianna Fail)
1994–7	John Bruton (Fine Gael)
1997–	Bertie Ahern (Fianna Fail)

In 1937 de Valera introduced a new constitution. The Irish Free State became Eire.

The position of Governor-General was abolished. Instead Eire would have an elected President as Head of State. Eire was a 'republic in all but name'. At the Imperial Conference of 1937 it was declared that the creation of Eire did not substantially change Ireland's links with the British Commonwealth. However, the only constitutional link between Eire and Britain was the External Relations Act. This stated that Irish diplomats abroad were seen as representatives of the British Crown.

Eire and the Second World War

A major development in British-Irish relations was the Second World War. Eire was the only part of the British Empire and Commonwealth to stay neutral in the war. Given Eire's strategic position in the Battle of the Atlantic Irish neutrality created serious problems for Britain. This position had been made worse in 1938 when Neville Chamberlain had signed an Anglo-Irish Agreement with de Valera. Under the Agreement a trade war between the two states, which had existed since 1932, came to an end. Of greater significance was the British decision to hand over to Eire the 'Treaty

Ports' of Cork Harbour, Bere Haven and Lough Swilly. These ports could have provided important British naval bases during the War.

On a number of occasions Britain attempted to end Eire neutrality. In June 1940, Malcolm McDonald, former Dominions Secretary and son of Ramsay McDonald, was sent to Dublin on a secret mission. He offered de Valera the reunification of Ireland if Eire entered the War on the Allied side. De Valera refused mainly because the Northern Ireland government had not been consulted. He also believed that the British Prime Minister, Winston Churchill, did not have the political will to honour the agreement.

On two occasions the British considered military intervention to occupy Eire: in June/July 1940, shortly after the fall of France and again in the early summer of 1944, shortly before D-Day. Intervention was ruled out in 1940 because the Cabinet Committee dealing with the issue thought the action would alienate American opinion and lead to guerrilla warfare in Eire. In 1944 intervention was considered because the German and Japanese embassies were still functioning in Dublin. The Allies feared the Germans might find out about the D-Day landings because Northern Ireland was an important staging area for that operation.

By the end of the war Eire's neutrality had greatly distanced it from Britain and the Commonwealth. In his victory speech to the British Empire on V.E. Day, Winston Churchill made specific reference to the problems caused by Irish neutrality in the War. De Valera did not help matters when he signed a book of condolence at the German Embassy in Dublin on the news of Adolf Hitler's death.

The creation of the Republic of Ireland

In 1948, Costello, the Eire Prime Minister, declared, on a trip to Canada, that Eire would become an independent Republic outside the British Commonwealth. This development should have led to a widening of relations between Britain and Ireland. However, under the Ireland Act (1949) Irish citizens still retained considerable rights within the United Kingdom. Unlike any other **aliens** they could stand for the British Parliament and vote in British elections if they were resident in Britain. They could also join the British armed forces and police.

Alien: A person who is not a citizen.

The main reasons behind this British policy concerned other parts of the Commonwealth. Both Australia and New Zealand lobbied the British Government not to change the status of Irish citizens in the United Kingdom: with elections due in 1949 they feared the effects of a change in policy on the large Irish electorates in both these countries. Britain was also concerned about India's relations with the Commonwealth. India had become independent in August 1947, but remained within the Commonwealth. The British government knew that India planned to declare itself a republic. Therefore, in order to keep India, as a republic, within the Commonwealth, relations with Ireland were not changed.

There is another significant aspect of the Ireland Act. The Act stated that no attempt would be made to alter the constitutional position of Northern Ireland without the consent of the people of Northern Ireland. As Unionists had a permanent majority in Northern Ireland (they comprised about 66% of the population) this declaration created the 'Unionist veto'. This had an important impact on British policy in Northern Ireland after 1969.

1. How did the Irish Free State become a completely independent state by 1949?

2. Who or what do you regard as most responsible for this political development? Give reasons for your answer.

3. How significant was the Ireland Act, 1949 to British-Irish relations?

8.3 Why did civil and political disorder develop in Northern Ireland by 1969?
A CASE STUDY IN HISTORICAL INTERPRETATION

The outbreak of widespread civil and political disorder between the Nationalist and Unionist communities in Northern Ireland was a constant feature of British politics from 1969 to 1999. The causes of this disorder, known by some as 'the Troubles', is the subject of much controversy. Both sides in Northern Ireland have widely differing interpretations of these events. Such differing perceptions are a major, if not the major reason why a political solution to Northern Ireland's problems has been so difficult to find.

The background

When Northern Ireland received Home Rule under the Government of Ireland Act, 1920, it was a political solution which Irish Unionists did not seek. They wanted to prevent any form of Home Rule for Ireland. As a result of the Irish political settlements made from 1920 to 1922 only a small number of Irish Unionists (around 100,000) lived in the Irish Free State. The majority of Irish Unionists lived in Northern Ireland.

Between 1921 and 1972 Northern Ireland politics was dominated by the Ulster Unionist Party, which held power continuously over this period. The Ulster Unionists at Westminster (there were 12 in this period) usually voted with the Conservative Party.

Nationalists, who made up around one-third of the Northern Ireland population, made very little impact on Northern Ireland politics. Some of their elected representatives abstained from attending the **Stormont** Parliament. More significantly, the electoral system ensured Unionist dominance.

Nationalists also felt discriminated against in other fields such as housing and employment. By the 1960s resentment felt against the Northern Ireland government by one-third of the population led to the creation of the Northern Ireland Civil Rights Association (NICRA) and a student organisation called People's Democracy. These groups comprised Nationalists, liberal members of the Unionist community and Churchmen. Inspired by the African American Civil Rights movement in the United States the NICRA called for 'one man one vote' and the end to discrimination in housing and employment. People's Democracy had similar aims. Its origins were similar to the student radicalism which affected much of Western Europe and North America from the mid-1960s.

These groups used similar tactics to the African American Civil Rights Movement. Demonstrations and walks were organised. In 1968 a NICRA march took place at Dungannon, County Tyrone. In October, serious rioting accompanied a Civil Rights march in Derry City. The Civil Rights movement was opposed by the Northern Ireland Government and various Unionist organisations. The latter attempted to disrupt marches and demonstrations. Following the **Apprentice Boys' March** in Derry City, in August 1969, rioting by Nationalists became so serious that the police force, the RUC, was finding it difficult to keep control. In addition, armed Unionist groups began attacking Nationalist areas in Belfast and Derry City.

Following a poor showing in the Northern Ireland general election of 1969, the Northern Ireland Prime Minister Captain Terence O'Neill resigned. He was replaced by another Unionist, Major James Chichester-Clark. Faced with ever-mounting sectarian violence, Chichester-Clark

Stormont: The site of the Northern Ireland Parliament, in a Belfast suburb. The name is also used to describe the Northern Ireland government.

Apprentice Boys' March: Celebration by a group of men of the apprentices who defended Derry from the troops of James II during the siege of 1689.

Terence O'Neill (1914–1990)
Born in London, and educated at Eton, O'Neill was a Captain in the Irish Guards 1939–45. He was leader of the Ulster Unionist Party and Prime Minister of Northern Ireland 1963–69.

James Chichester-Clark (1923–)
Eton-educated Chichester-Clark was leader of Ulster Unionist Party and Prime Minister of Northern Ireland, May 1969 to March 1971. He resigned because the Heath government would not send more troops to Ulster.

The Civil Rights March from Coalisland to Dungannon, Country Tyrone, in 1969

How useful is this photograph to a historian writing about the Civil Rights Movement in Northern Ireland in the late 1960s?

requested the support of the British army to maintain peace. On 15 August 1969 British troops were sent to Northern Ireland in a 'peace-keeping role'.

The events of 1968–1969 were a turning point in British-Irish relations. Until 1968 Northern Ireland issues were rarely discussed at Westminster. The Speaker's rules stipulated that Northern Ireland issues be discussed by Northern Ireland ministers at Stormont not in Britain. However, the Civil Rights Movement and the Unionist opposition to it meant that Northern Ireland issues could no longer be ignored by a British government. From 1968 the Northern Ireland problem has been a major issue in British politics.

A Nationalist view of the causes of conflict in Northern Ireland

To most Nationalists, Northern Ireland is an artificial sub-state. It was created in 1920 by Lloyd George as an attempt to solve the Irish problem by providing a political unit within Ireland where there was a built-in Protestant/Unionist majority. The plan was to defend British strategic interests by preventing the unification of Ireland.

This Nationalist view is supported by the failure to create a Council of Ireland. This body was meant to be set up under the Government of Ireland Act. It was to contain representatives from Northern and Southern Ireland. The aim was supposedly to create an All-Ireland political body, which might one day lead to the end of partition. The other failure was that of the Boundary Commission to make any significant changes to the border between the Irish Free State and Northern Ireland. The Commission had been created by the Anglo-Irish Treaty of 1921. When it reported, in 1925, it left large numbers of Catholic/Nationalists within Northern Ireland.

Northern Ireland terminology

The conflict in Northern Ireland has produced a series of inter-connected and sometimes slightly confusing titles for political groups and place names.

Nationalists are those members of the Northern Ireland community who would like to see a united Ireland. They include moderate democratic politicians and extremists.

Republicans are those members of the Nationalist community most closely associated with the idea of creating a united Irish state by force if necessary. Groups such as Sinn Fein, the Provisional IRA and INLA are republican.

Catholics: In Northern Ireland there is a very strong link between Nationalism and Catholicism. The vast majority of Catholics regard themselves as Nationalist, so much so that the terms Catholic and Nationalist are virtually interchangeable.

Unionists are those who want Northern Ireland to remain part of the United Kingdom. They include moderate democratic politicians as well as extremists who engage in sectarian violence.

Loyalists are those members of the Unionist community who engage in political violence to prevent Northern Ireland becoming part of a united Ireland. They include paramilitary groups such as the UDA, the UFF and the UVF. Most recently they have been associated with political parties such as the Ulster Democratic Party and Ulster Progressive Party.

Protestants: The link between Protestantism and Unionism is very strong; again the terms are virtually interchangeable. An important Protestant/Unionist organisation is the Orange Order. This organisation aims to defend religious liberties and the Union with Britain. It is anti-Catholic.

Place names: The most noticeable split between the Nationalist and Unionist communities is over the name of Londonderry/Derry. The former term is used by Unionists, the latter by Nationalists. Since the 1980s the official use has been Derry City for the county town and Londonderry for the county.

Prime Ministers of Northern Ireland

1921–40	Sir James Craig (Lord Craigavon)
1940–43	J. M. Andrews
1943–63	Sir Basil Brooke (Lord Brookeborough)
1963–69	Capt. Terence O'Neill
1969–71	James Chichester-Clark
1971–72	Brian Faulkner

James Craig (1871–1940)
Craig was born in Belfast. A Unionist MP for East Down, 1906, he was a leading Ulster Unionist opponent of Home Rule from 1912. He became the first Prime Minister of Northern Ireland in 1921 and held the post until his death. He was made Lord Craigavon in 1927.

British indifference to Irish Nationalism was confirmed by the failure to stop Unionist dominance of Northern Ireland. Sir James Craig, a leading Ulster Unionist, described Stormont as 'a Protestant Parliament for a Protestant people'. From the moment Northern Ireland was created, Catholics were made to feel like second-class citizens. In 1929 Nationalist fears seemed to be confirmed when the Unionist government changed the electoral system. Proportional representation was abolished. It was replaced by the 'first-past-the-post' system, which ensured Unionist dominance at Stormont.

In local government, votes were given to rate payers rather than all adults. This discriminated against Catholics, because many did not own their own homes. In addition, **gerrymandering** took place. In Derry City, even though Catholics comprised two-thirds of the population, a Unionist city government was in control.

Gerrymandering: The deliberate drawing of electoral boundaries in order to manipulate the election result.

Discrimination against the Catholic minority was also seen in policing. The Royal Ulster Constabulary (RUC) was a predominantly Protestant force. It was supported by a part-time police force known as the 'B' specials – Protestants who harassed the local Catholic community. Both forces possessed considerable law and order powers. These were established under the Civil Authorities (Special Powers) Act, Northern Ireland (1922) and gave the police wide powers to stop, search and detain anyone they believed might be engaged in illegal political activity.

The problem also entered social and employment fields. A government Commission under Lord Cameron was set up to look into the causes of the disturbances of 1968–69. It reported in 1969 that favouritism towards Protestants in the allocation of council housing was rife in Dungannon, Armagh and, most notably, in Belfast and Derry City. In employment Protestants tended only to employ Protestants. As a result, unemployment was over twice as high among Catholics, because Protestants dominated the employer class.

The anti-Catholic/Nationalist nature of the Unionist majority was shown by the reaction to Prime Minister O'Neill's attempts to forge relations with the Republic of Ireland. In 1965, for the first time, a meeting took place between the prime ministers of Northern Ireland and the Republic. This led to opposition to O'Neill within the Unionist community. It created an opportunity for a young Presbyterian cleric, Ian Paisley, to make his political mark by opposing links with Catholics and the Republic.

In February 1969, O'Neill called a general election in Northern Ireland. He narrowly defeated Paisley in the Upper Bann constituency and the election returned a large number of anti-O'Neill Unionists. O'Neill was forced to resign.

To the Nationalists, the causes of the conflict stemmed from Britain, which had a selfish interest in maintaining control over part of Ireland. Successive British governments had allowed a Unionist-dominated government to discriminate against the Catholic minority. When Catholics engaged in legitimate political protest to highlight their grievances they were met by opposition from Unionist thugs, and the RUC and 'B' Specials.

Ian Paisley (1926–)
A founder member of Free Presbyterian Church of Ulster in 1951, Paisley was born in County Armagh, educated at Barry School of Evangelism and Bob Jones University, USA. He was imprisoned for obstructing a Civil Rights March, November 1968. In September 1971 he founded the Democratic Unionist party. He has been an European Parliament MP since 1979 and Westminster MP for North Antrim since 1970 and has opposed the Sunningdale, Anglo-Irish and Good Friday Agreements.

Local government employment in County Fermanagh, March 1969

(County Fermanagh had a Catholic/Nationalist majority)

Jobs	Catholics	Protestants
County Council Administration	0	33
Housing Department	0	10
County Library	1	14
Planning and Tourism	0	5
Public Works Dept	4	60
Education Office	4	120
Health and Welfare Department	21	88
Total	30	330

How useful are these two tables in explaining the degree of discrimination against Catholics in Northern Ireland in the 1960s?

Local representation in Derry City, 1966: The problem of gerrymandering

There were 24 local government councillors for Derry city. Each ward elected eight councillors.

South Ward	14,125	anti-Unionist votes	1,474	Unionist votes
North Ward	3,173	anti-Unionist votes	4,380	Unionist votes
Waterside Ward	2,804	anti-Unionist votes	4,420	Unionist votes

Both of the above inserts are from *Divided Ulster* by Liam de Paor (1971)

A Unionist view on the causes of conflict in Northern Ireland

The majority of the population of Northern Ireland came from English and Scots stock. They had colonised the north east of Ireland from the end of the 16th century. They regard themselves as British rather than Irish. These colonists faced hostility from the Catholic Irish majority: in 1641 an Irish Rebellion led to the massacre of Protestants in Ulster. In 1688–90 the Catholic James II, in league with Louis XIV of France, attempted to force Catholicism on Britain and Ireland. He was defeated by William of Orange at the Battle of the Boyne in 1690. This victory protected the civil and religious liberties of the Protestant population of Ireland and saved Britain from absolutist government.

The link between north-east Ireland and Britain was strengthened in the 19th century by the industrial revolution. Shipbuilding and textiles industries flourished in north-east Ireland as part of an industrial British economy. The area had much more in common with central Scotland and northern England than the rest of Ireland.

As a minority in the whole of Ireland, Protestants feared domination by what they saw as an alien religion and culture. This was reinforced by the Catholic Church's insistence that in a mixed marriage between a Catholic and a Protestant, all the offspring had to be brought up as Catholics. Fear of the Catholic majority was reinforced during the political instability of 1919–22. Irish nationalists attempted to force the Unionist/Protestants of the north east into a united Ireland against their will. When Michael Collins, the Prime Minister of the Irish Free State, was shot on 22 August 1922, he was planning a major IRA campaign to destroy Northern Ireland.

Fifth column: Individuals or groups within a country who support an enemy force.

From the very start of Northern Ireland's existence Catholics were seen as a dangerous **fifth column**. They supported unification with the Republic of Ireland. From 1937, under Articles 2 and 3 of the Eire constitution, the Republic claimed Northern Ireland as part of their national territory. The anti-British position of Irish Nationalists was emphasised by the neutrality of Eire during the Second World War. Between 1956 and 1962 the IRA launched a border campaign of terrorism, attacking border posts and killing RUC officers.

Catholics had also created problems for themselves by opposing Northern Ireland from the start. Many Catholics believed that Northern Ireland wouldn't last long as a sub-state within the United Kingdom. They therefore abstained from participating in government. The Catholic Church refused to co-operate with the creation of a province-wide system of education. It insisted on running its own schools so that from an early age Catholics and Protestants were kept separate, thereby reinforcing the split within Northern Ireland society.

Unlike Nationalists, Unionists do not believe there was any historical justification for a united Ireland. Throughout history, Ulster had a separate

Sean Lemass (1899–1969)
Born in County Dublin in 1899 Lemass was in his teens when he took part in Easter Rising. He was Deputy Prime Minister 1945–49 and Taoiseach 1959–65. He re-established free trade with Britain in 1965 and was the first Irish Prime Minister to visit Belfast. He held talks with Terence O'Neill, Prime Minister of Northern Ireland on improving North South relations in 1965.

1. What were the main grievances of the Catholic/Nationalist minority towards the Northern Ireland government by the mid-1960s?

2. To what extent are the differences between the Nationalist and Unionist views on the causes of conflict based on religion?

identity and the only time Ireland was united as one political entity was under British rule.

The disturbances which occurred in Northern Ireland had their origin in an attempt by Nationalists to push the province into the Republic of Ireland by force. The Official IRA had links with the NICRA and People's Democracy. These were seen as front organisation for this Republican plan. Attempts by the Irish Prime Minister, Sean Lemass, to meet and forge links with Captain Terence O'Neill was seen as part of a broader Nationalist conspiracy to achieve unification.

Protestant fears included the Second Vatican Council of the Catholic Church which began in 1963. Other Christian groups, including Protestants, were invited to attend as observers. This was seen as some as part of a global attempt by Catholicism to dominate Christianity. In *God Save Ulster!* (1989), S. Bruce quoted the Rev. Ian Paisley who stated: 'The aim is a super one-world Church. Rome, of course, already sees herself as that Church'.

There are important social and economic considerations in opposition to an all-Ireland state. Catholic influence in the Republic of Ireland meant that contraception was illegal. The Catholic Church also provided a form of censorship with a list of prohibited books. Northern Ireland, on the other hand, benefited from the National Health Service and the Welfare State, and the standard of living was much higher than in the Republic of Ireland.

8.4 How effective was British policy towards Northern Ireland between 1969 and 1985?

Between 1969 and 1985, British government policy was affected by a number of factors:

- high levels of political violence, which began in Northern Ireland but spread to both Britain and the Republic of Ireland. Political violence involved assassination, car bombs, and the shooting of police and soldiers. It involved paramilitary groups from the Loyalist and Republican communities (see panel on page 272), the RUC and the British army;

- attempts to find a political solution within Northern Ireland between Unionists and Nationalists;

- attempts to find a political solution between Northern Ireland and the rest of the United Kingdom;

- attempts to find a political solution which would involve the Republic of Ireland.

In trying to develop a coherent British policy, developments such as a change in government (from Labour to Conservative) or a change in the Secretary of State for Northern Ireland would have great significance. In addition, the Northern Ireland problem was affected by public opinion in the United States (in particular Irish-American opinion) and in Europe. (After January 1973 both the United Kingdom and the Republic of Ireland were part of the European Community.)

How did the policy followed by the Labour and Conservative governments towards Northern Ireland develop between 1969 and 1973?

After decades of disinterest and neglect the British government was faced with a major domestic political crisis in August 1969. Normally, the responsibility for maintaining law and order within Northern Ireland lay with the Stormont government. However, in *A House Divided* (1970) the Labour Home Secretary, James Callaghan, expressed his belief that military intervention was required by the British army to protect Catholic areas from attacks by Protestant mobs. This was most apparent in west Belfast. During the disturbances of 1968–69 Catholic areas felt that they lacked protection. Walls in these areas were daubed with slogans such as 'IRA, I ran away' condemning the IRA for its failure to defend them.

Direct British involvement under Labour was welcomed by the Catholic/Nationalist community. Their homes were now protected by the British army. A report by the Hunt Advisory Committee to the British government recommended the disarming of the RUC, the disbanding of the 'B' Specials and a transfer of council-house allocation from local authorities to the Stormont government. In April 1970 the 'B' Specials were replaced by a part-time regiment of the British Army, the Ulster Defence Regiment (UDR). Unfortunately, the UDR contained large numbers of former 'B' Specials.

The Republican reaction to the 1968–69 disturbances led to a split within the IRA. An IRA convention in 1969 saw the creation of the Provisional IRA. This group split from the Official IRA mainly because it wanted to engage in armed defence of the Catholic community. The Provisional IRA leader was Sean MacStiofain.

By the time Edward Heath became Conservative Prime Minister in June 1970 the political situation in Northern Ireland had begun to change. The continued existence of a Unionist-dominated Stormont government meant that the Catholic/Nationalist community began to regard the British Army as defenders of Unionism. This development was made worse by the decision of the Provisional IRA to go on the offensive in early 1971. The first British soldier (Gunner Curtis) was shot dead in February 1971 by the Provisional IRA.

With the escalation of political violence the British Government faced a difficult problem. British policy on the ground in Northern Ireland was determined by the senior army officer (General Officer Commanding – GOC – Northern Ireland) working with the Stormont government. A clash had occurred in October 1969 between the Chief Constable of the RUC and the GOC over security, which led to the GOC's role being restricted to co-ordination, and not overall control, of army and police. However, ultimate control lay with Westminster. In April 1971 the Northern Ireland Prime Minister, Chichester-Clark, resigned because the Heath government refused to increase troop levels in the Province.

In August 1971, the Heath government made a major tactical error by agreeing to the introduction of internment without trial, proposed by the new Northern Ireland Prime Minister, Brain Faulkner. With poor police and military intelligence about who was in the Provisional IRA, British troops and the RUC arrested large numbers of Catholic/Nationalists. They were placed mainly in an old military camp near Belfast known as Long Kesh. (It later became the Maze Prison.) The Catholic/Nationalist reaction to internment led to a large increase in support for the Provisional IRA.

The policy of using the army and police to restore law and order in the Catholic/Nationalist community reached crisis point on 30 January 1972. An illegal Civil Rights march in Derry City was stopped by the RUC and

Brian Faulkner (1921–1977)
Faulkner was born in County Down. He was leader of Ulster Unionist Party and Prime Minister of Northern Ireland March 1971 to March 1972. He introduced internment, signed Sunningdale Agreement in December 1973 and became Chief Executive of Power Sharing government January–May 1974. He founded the Unionist Party of Northern Ireland 1974.

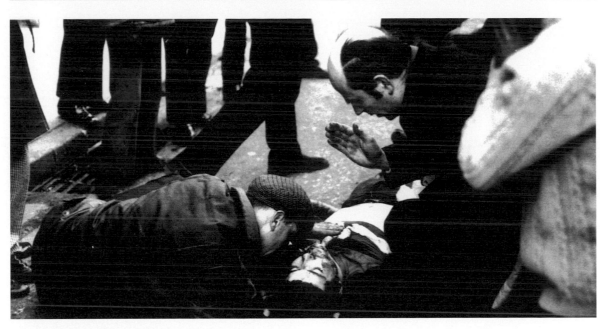

'Bloody Sunday', Derry City, January 1972

Why do you think photographs such as this helped bring about the suspension of the Stormont Government?

SDLP: The Social Democratic and Labour Party – see box on political parties in Northern Ireland, p.271.

The Alliance Party: A non-sectarian political party representing both Catholics and Protestants, and mainly supported by the middle class. It has made very little impact on the Northern Ireland political scene.

Consociational democracy: Democracy achieved by bringing together representative groups into government rather than having a ballot.

the Army. Fourteen marchers were killed by the Army, mainly by members of the Parachute Regiment. To this day the precise circumstances surrounding 'Bloody Sunday' have yet to be revealed. It was, however, a major setback for British policy. It caused uproar in the Republic of Ireland and the British Embassy was burned down. It also led directly to the Heath government's decision to suspend the Stormont government in March 1972, introducing Direct Rule from Westminster. From 1972 Northern Ireland affairs were under the responsibility of a member of the British Cabinet, the Secretary of State for Northern Ireland.

Under the first Secretary of State, William Whitelaw, the Heath government engaged in a major attempt to find a political solution within Northern Ireland. On 19 August 1969, the Labour Prime Minister, Harold Wilson, had made 'The Downing Street Declaration'. In it he declared British commitment to maintaining Northern Ireland's union with Britain as long as the majority of the Northern Ireland community agreed. Whitelaw took the bold step of opening negotiations with all sides of the conflict. In July, 1972 he even met Sean MacStiofain of the Provisional IRA but these talks came to nothing mainly because of the Provisional IRA's insistence on British withdrawal.

By the end of 1973 Whitelaw had been able to get moderate Unionists, led by Brian Faulkner, and moderate Nationalists of the **SDLP** with the **Alliance Party** to agree to the Sunningdale Agreement. The Agreement involved the passage of two acts of parliament: The Northern Ireland Assembly Act, May 1973, and the Northern Ireland Constitution Act, July 1973, and an agreement between the British and Irish governments in December 1973. Direct Rule was to be replaced by 'Power-Sharing'. The government of Northern Ireland was to contain representatives from both the Unionist and Nationalist communities. This was a version of **consociational democracy**. It was introduced because the normal operation of democracy meant that Unionists would always hold power.

Another important feature of the Sunningdale Agreement was the

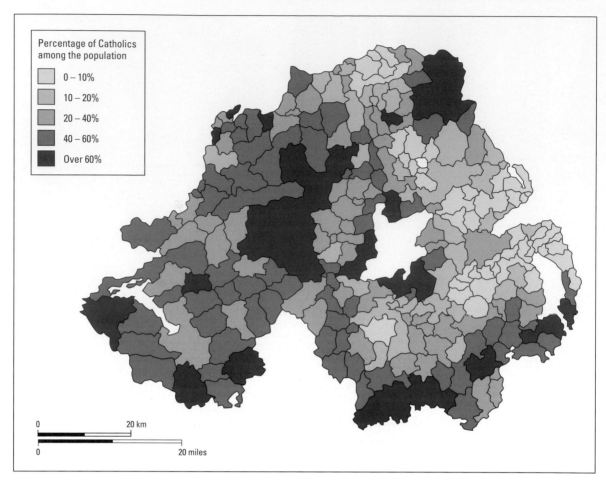

The percentage of Catholics among the population of Northern Ireland in 1971

Percentage of Catholics among the population

- 0 – 10%
- 10 – 20%
- 20 – 40%
- 40 – 60%
- Over 60%

On the evidence of this map, why do you think the partition of Northern Ireland has not been regarded as a serious political solution to the political and civil disorder since 1969?

Taoiseach: The Prime Minister of the Republic of Ireland.

inclusion of an All-Ireland dimension. Since September 1971, the **Taoiseach**, Jack Lynch, had been conducting talks with Edward Heath about Northern Ireland. Both prime ministers wanted an end to political violence. In the course of 1972 the Fianna Fail government in Dublin had introduced harsh measures against the Provisional IRA within the Republic. In December 1973 the Irish dimension of the agreement included the creation of a Council of Ireland. This would be an advisory committee involving political representatives from Northern Ireland and the Republic with limited executive power. It was a similar institution to the one proposed under the Government of Ireland Act, 1920.

The Sunningdale Agreement seemed to offer political stability for Northern Ireland. It was supported by moderate Unionists, moderate Nationalists, and the British and Irish governments. However, it was opposed by paramilitary groups on both sides, the Provisional IRA, the UDA and the UVF. It was also opposed by many Unionists. Most prominent were the Democratic Unionist Party of the Rev. Ian Paisley and the Vanguard Unionist Party of James Craig, a former Northern Ireland Home Secretary.

Secretaries of State for Northern Ireland

1972–73	William Whitelaw (Con)
1973–74	Francis Pym (Con)
1974–76	Merlyn Rees (Lab)
1976–79	Roy Mason (Lab)
1979–81	Humphrey Atkins (Con)
1981–84	James Prior (Con)
1984–85	Douglas Hurd (Con)
1985–89	Tom King (Con)
1989–92	Peter Brooke (Con)
1992–97	Sir Patrick Mayhew (Con)
1997–99	Dr Mo Mowlam (Lab)
11999–2001	Peter Mandelson
2001–2002	John Reid
2002–2005	Paul Murphy
2005–2007	Peter Hain
2007–	Shaun Woodward

Why did the Sunningdale Agreement fail?

The Power Sharing Executive operated for only four months. The collapse of the Sunningdale Agreement was brought about by a general strike organised by the Ulster Workers' Council in May 1974. This group included Unionist politicians, Loyalist paramilitaries and trade unionists. Although it lasted only 14 days, the strike brought Northern Ireland to a standstill.

One reason behind the failure was a change in government. In February 1974 Edward Heath had called a general election over the miners' strike. He was replaced by a minority Labour government under Harold Wilson which lacked the political power to act decisively.

Secondly, there was a lack of decisive leadership by the Labour Secretary of State for Northern Ireland, Merlyn Rees. He allowed the general strike to become established during the second week in May although he could, for instance, have used troops to operate power stations. Instead of supporting the Power Sharing Executive he allowed it to fail and suggested a Constitutional Convention to discuss other ways of finding a political agreement. In elections for the convention, in May 1975, anti-Power Sharing Unionists did well. By November 1975, when the Convention reported, it was split between Unionists who wanted a return of the Stormont government and a minority in favour of Power-Sharing. The Convention was dissolved, a failure, in March 1976.

Did Labour Policy towards Northern Ireland achieve anything between 1974 and 1979?

Diplock Courts: Special courts in Northern Ireland for trying terrorist cases. They were named after Lord Diplock, whose report in 1973 suggested that terrorists should not be tried by jury, because of widespread evidence of intimidation of jurors by paramilitaries.

Birmingham Pub Bombings: On 21 November 1974, the Provisional IRA placed bombs in two city centre pubs – the Tavern in the Town and the Mulberry Bush. Nineteen people were killed and 182 wounded.

Although Rees has been criticised over the failure of Power Sharing he did bring an end to internment. By 1976 the prisons contained convicted criminals, many tried by **Diplock Courts**. The Labour Government also introduced the Prevention of Terrorism Act in November 1974 following the **Birmingham Pub Bombings** by the Provisional IRA. This Act gave the British police powers of arrest and detention for anyone they suspected of terrorist offences. It also allowed the government to prevent people in Northern Ireland travelling to the mainland if they were suspected of being a security threat.

When Rees was succeeded by Roy Mason as Secretary of State in 1976, Mason abandoned attempts to find political agreement. Instead he concentrated on making Direct Rule work by attempting to reduce the level of

Deaths due to political violence and terrorism in Northern Ireland

1969–2005

1969	13	1977	112	1985	54	1993	90	2001	11
1970	25	1978	81	1986	61	1994	68	2002	10
1971	174	1979	113	1987	93	1995	9	2003	8
1972	467	1980	76	1988	93	1996	21	2004	2
1973	250	1981	101	1989	62	1997	23	2005	5
1974	216	1982	97	1990	76	1998	30	2006	3
1975	247	1983	77	1991	94	1999	8		
1976	297	1984	64	1992	84	2000	12		

Deaths due to terrorism associated with Northern Ireland but occurring in the Republic of Ireland, Britain and Europe

1970–1992

1970	3	1977	4	1984	6	1991	3
1971	3	1978	1	1985	4	1992	6
1972	11	1979	9	1986	0		
1973	8	1980	6	1987	6		
1974	2	1981	4	1988	9		
1975	17	1982	13	1989	16		
1976	6	1983	10	1990	6		

political violence. He gave greater responsibility to the RUC for security, and used the SAS for counter-insurgency operations against the Provisional IRA.

Unfortunately, the success of Mason's policy forced the Provisional IRA to reorganise itself into cells, a structure which was impossible for the British Army to break. A secret government report, the Glover Report, in 1968, declared that the Provisional IRA could not be defeated militarily. In his book *Final Term, the Labour Government 1974–1976* (1979) Harold Wilson declared that Labour policy seemed negative and almost defeatist in character. He declared that the political solution to Northern Ireland's problems lay within Northern Ireland. However, after Margaret Thatcher's victory in the 1979 general election British policy took a more dynamic turn.

How far did British policy change under Margaret Thatcher between 1979 and 1985?

Political violence associated with Northern Ireland reached a new intensity in 1979. Airey Neave, the Conservative Shadow spokesman on Northern Ireland, was murdered by the INLA in the House of Commons car park. In the Republic of Ireland INLA murdered Lord Mountbatten, a close relation of the Queen. At Warrenpoint, County Down, close to the border with the Republic 18 members of the Parachute Regiment were blown up by a large bomb detonated by the Provisional IRA.

However, the main problem facing the Thatcher government during its first term was the Hunger Strike by Republican prisoners in 1981. They were demanding the status of political prisoners. This crisis came to a head when a hunger-striker, Bobby Sands, was elected as MP for Fermanagh and South Tyrone. Sands' subsequent death from starvation, and the deaths of nine other hunger strikers, led to a major rise in support for the political wing of the Provisional IRA, Sinn Fein. It also gained considerable international publicity, particularly with the Irish-American community.

Garret Fitzgerald (1926–)
Fitzgerald was born in Dublin and educated at University College, Dublin where he was a lecturer in Political Economy from 1959–73. He was leader of Fine Gael 1977–87, and Taoiseach June 1981 – March 1982 and again December 1982 – March 1987. He signed the Anglo-Irish Agreement of 1985.

Throughout the period 1979 to 1985 the Conservatives tried a number of political initiatives to break the political deadlock. The Secretary of State in 1982, James Prior, tried 'rolling devolution'. This meant political power would be handed back to Northern Ireland gradually if political violence subsided. More significant were the continued links between the British and Irish governments. These discussions, however, were affected by political changes in the Republic of Ireland. When the Fine Gael Taoiseach, Garret Fitzgerald, was in power relations were cordial. When Fianna Fail Taoiseach, Charles Haughey, held power relations were more difficult. These difficulties were made worse during the Falklands Conflict of 1982, when Haughey failed to support Britain. However, by 1985 a new departure in British policy occurred with the Anglo-Irish (Hillsborough) Agreement. It was jointly signed by Margaret Thatcher and Garret Fitzgerald.

To what extent was the Anglo-Irish Agreement of 1985 a turning point in British Irish relations?

The agreement established an Inter-Governmental Conference between the British and Irish governments. This would contain representatives from both governments. It would discuss Northern Ireland and the relations between Northern Ireland and the Republic of Ireland. Matters to be discussed involved cross-border security arrangements and justice. The latter involved the issue of extradition, the returning of terrorist suspects either to Britain or the Republic by the other state to face trial.

Why was the Anglo-Irish Agreement of 1985 significant in the development of British-Irish relations?

This was a major new departure. It formally involved the Republic of Ireland in the affairs of Northern Ireland for the first time. However, the Agreement also recognised that no change in the political status of Northern Ireland would occur without the consent of the majority. This meant that, for the first time, the Republic of Ireland officially recognised the existence of Northern Ireland. This went against Articles 2 and 3 of the Eire Constitution of 1937.

Margaret Thatcher and Garret Fitzgerald, the architects of the Anglo-Irish Agreement of 1985

1. What reasons can you give to explain why British policy changed towards Northern Ireland between 1969 and 1985?

2. What do you regard as the main obstacles to finding a political settlement in Northern Ireland between 1969 and 1985?

3. Who was more effective in dealing with the problems of Northern Ireland between 1969 and 1985: the Labour governments or the Conservative governments? Give reasons for your answer.

From the British point of view this agreement was driven by increasing concerns about the growth in support for Sinn Fein. By 1985 the Republican movement had altered its strategy. It now followed a policy of 'the armalite and the ballot box'. This involved continuing the 'armed struggle' against the British but at the same time seeking election to local government and the Westminster parliament. The Anglo-Irish Agreement, by adding an 'Irish dimension', was a political strategy to stunt the growth of Sinn Fein's political power.

According to Paul Norris in 'Northern Ireland, the Long Road to Peace', published in *Talking Politics* (1998): 'The Anglo-Irish Agreement was a watershed in that it established the Irish government as a legitimate player in the internal affairs of Northern Ireland. The agreement sparked a sustained expression of a sense of absolute betrayal in the unionist community and among its political leaders. The agreement was a political boost for the SDLP who were seen to have top level access to British ministers at a time when Sinn Fein had entered politics and were capturing up to 40% of the nationalist vote.'

8.5 Why was it so difficult to find a political solution in Northern Ireland between 1985 and 2007?

Although the Anglo-Irish Agreement was a major new departure in Northern Ireland affairs, obstacles to peace still remained.

● The continuation of political violence. In 1987 the SAS virtually wiped out the East Tyrone Active Service Unit of the Provisional IRA at Loughgall. In November 1987 the Provisional IRA exploded a bomb at the Remembrance Day service at Enniskillen killing 11 and injuring 63. On 22 September 1989, 11 British servicemen (musicians) were killed by a the Provisional IRA bomb in Kent, England.

● The continued political success of Sinn Fein. The Agreement failed to stem the advance of Sinn Fein. They continued to win about 40% of the nationalist vote. They also ended their boycott of elections in the Republic of Ireland in 1986.

● The Unionists were politically divided. Since the 1960s the once-united Unionist community had split into many factions. The largest group was the Official Unionist Party. However, Ian Paisley's Democratic Unionist Party usually represented three Westminster constituencies. Ian Paisley also topped the poll in the last three European Union elections. Other Unionist groups have appeared over the past 30 years. The UK Unionist Party held the North Down constituency in the 1997 general election. Both the DUP and the UK Unionists have been completely opposed to links with the Republic of Ireland.

● The existence of paramilitary groups on both sides. The commitment of paramilitary groups to violence created a wider gap between two communities. Any attempt by democratic politicians to exclude them from a political agreement meant that it would be difficult to find a lasting peace.

● Limited support for a lasting peace involving both communities. Between 1976 and 1977 there was a brief but popular attempt to try to bring the two communities in Northern Ireland in a bid to create a climate for peace. It followed the deaths of three children after the Provisional IRA bank raid in August 1976. Under the cross-community leadership of Mairead Corrigan and Betty Williams, a women's movement both North and South of the border led a campaign for peace. The 'Peace People' gained international publicity and the two leaders won the Nobel Peace Prize but their movement produced nothing tangible.

What changes were made by the Downing Street Declaration of 1993?

A major move towards peace came on 15 December 1993 with a joint statement by the British and Irish governments. It declared that Britain had no selfish strategic or economic interest in Northern Ireland. It stated that a political settlement should be based on 'the right of the people on both parts of the island to exercise the right of self-determination on the basis of consent north and south to bring about a united Ireland, if that is their will'.

The declaration occurred for a number of reasons.

- Firstly, as in 1976, there was public indignation about political violence in Britain and Ireland. On 20 March 1993 two boys had been killed by a Provisional IRA bomb in Warrington, England. It was followed by bombing in both Britain and Northern Ireland.

- Secondly, the United States government was putting pressure on the British government to find a solution. The Clinton administration was sympathetic to Irish nationalist opinion in the United States. The president appointed a pro-nationalist ambassador to the Republic in 1993, Jean Kennedy-Smith. Congress had already accepted the '**MacBride Principles**' in the mid-1980s concerning trade with Northern Irish companies.

- Thirdly, Albert Reynolds had become Taoiseach in February 1991. His diplomatic skill was important in persuading the Major government to made a political statement.

- Finally, John Hume, leader of the SDLP, had several secret talks with Gerry Adams, leader of Sinn Fein. The aim was to bring Sinn Fein into the peace making process.

Following the Downing Street Declaration, the Provisional IRA declared a ceasefire on 31 August 1994, claiming that 'an opportunity to secure a just and lasting settlement had been created'.

Why did the Downing Street Declaration fail to bring an all-round peace agreement?

In 1995 and 1996 progress towards a peace agreement seemed possible. The Twin Track Initiative by the British and Irish governments on 28 November 1995 attempted a bridge-building exercise between the two communities. It established an International Commission led by ex-US Senator George Mitchell to investigate the issue of decommissioning paramilitary weapons.

The Downing Street Declaration failed to produce an all-round peace agreement in advance of the 1997 general election. The major obstacle to peace was the decommissioning of paramilitary weapons. The Conservative government was heavily dependent on Ulster Unionist support to stay in power and the Ulster Unionists demanded decommissioning before Sinn Fein should be allowed into talks.

This impasse led to the end of the Provisional IRA ceasefire with the Canary Wharf bombing of 9 February 1996. Even though elections took place for a Northern Ireland Forum to discuss peace on 30 May 1996, any genuine attempt at a peace settlement was still-born until after the election.

MacBride Principles: Passed by Congress in 1984. This was an attempt to end religious discrimination in Northern Ireland. US government firms could only agree contracts with Northern Ireland firms if the latter was proved not to discriminate against Catholics.

John Hume (1937–)
Born in Derry City, Hume was educated at Queen's University, Belfast. He was a member of the Civil Rights Association in 1968–69, founder member and Deputy Chairman of SDLP in 1970, MP for Foyle since 1983 and member of European Parliament since 1979. A major influence in the Anglo-Irish Agreement of 1985 and Good Friday Agreement of 1998, Hume received the Noble Peace Prize in 1999.

Gerry Adams (1949–)
Adams has been President of Sinn Fein since 1983. He was interned in 1971 and active in the Provisional IRA in the 1970s. He became MP for West Belfast 1983–92 and again from 1997. Adams had talks with John Hume of SDLP and with Hume and Albert Reynolds he formed a broad nationalist alliance in 1993. He signed up to the Good Friday Agreement of 1998.

Will the 'Good Friday Agreement' of 10 April 1998 bring lasting peace?

Following Blair's landslide victory in the 1997 general election the Provisional IRA announced a new ceasefire on 20 July 1997. Under the guidance of a new Secretary of State, Mo Mowlam, all sides in the Northern Ireland conflict were invited into a peace process. This included Sinn Fein and representatives of the Loyalist paramilitaries. The DUP and the UK Unionists boycotted the talks.

The Good Friday Agreement proposed change in the constitutions of Britain and the Republic of Ireland to include the principle of consent for the place of Northern Ireland within the United Kingdom. It also recognised the identity and aspirations of the Nationalist minority.

The Agreement created a Northern Ireland Assembly, a Power-Sharing Executive and a Council of Ireland between North and South. In many ways it seemed to be similar to the Sunningdale Agreement of 1973. However, this time the agreement included representatives from the paramilitaries. Sinn Fein, the Ulster Democratic Party and the Ulster Progressive Party signed up to the agreement. In return paramilitary prisoners were to be released. The Agreement was also backed by a Referendum in Northern Ireland and the Republic which supported the agreement (see table on page 294). It was also supported by the Clinton administration in the United States. However, a number of obstacles remain:

David Trimble (1944–)
Trimble was the leader of the Official Unionist Party and was First Minister of Northern Ireland 1998–2002. Unionist MP for Upper Bann, he was elected leader in 1995. Trimble is a member of the Orange Order and participant at the Drumcree Marches in 1995 and 1996. Formerly a lecturer in Law at Queen's University, Belfast, he lost out to Mary McAleese (President of the Republic of Ireland) for the post of professor of Law at that university. He received the Nobel Peace Prize with John Hume in 1999.

- There was opposition from within the Unionist community. Both the DUP and the UK Unionist Party opposed the Agreement. Even within the Ulster Unionist Party, David Trimble, the leader, faced criticism mainly from Jeffrey Donaldson MP.

- The Agreement and the Provisional IRA ceasefire resulted in a further split in the IRA. The Real IRA was formed in November 1997. On 15 August 1998, the worst atrocity since 1969 occurred in Omagh, County Tyrone when a car bomb planted by the Real IRA killed 29 people and wounded a further 200. Even though the Real IRA declared a ceasefire on 8 September 1998 there is still the possibility of breakaway groups within the IRA returning to political violence.

- Punishment beatings and murders continued in Republican and Loyalist areas. These were so frequent that in August 1999 Mo Mowlam investigated the possibility that the Provisional IRA had broken its ceasefire.

- One of the last acts of the Major government was to establish a Parades Commission in January 1997. This organisation had to deal with the issue of parades, usually Orange parades. Flashpoints since the Agreement were Drumcree Church, Portadown, the Lower Ormeau Road, Belfast and Derry City. The banning or rerouting of Parades caused considerable resentment in the Unionist community.

- The issue of paramilitary decommission proved to be a major problem. As part of the Mitchell Review of the Good Friday Agreement, in December 1999, the IRA appointed a go-between to Discuss decommissioning with Canadian General de Chastelan.

- Linked with the decommissioning issue was the resentment felt by some members of the Northern Ireland Community about the early release of paramilitary prisoners. Many of them had been convicted of multiple murders.

Referendums on the Good Friday Agreement of 1997

In the Republic of Ireland

The results of the vote to change the Irish Constitution in line with the agreement were:

Votes in favour	1,442,683	(94.4%)
Votes against	85,748	(5.6%)
Electorate	2,753,127	
Turnout	1,545,395	(56%)
Valid votes	1,528,331	
Spoiled votes	17,064	

In Northern Ireland

The results of the vote on the Agreement were:

Votes in favour	676,966	(71.1%)
Votes against	274,879	(28.9%)
Electorate	1,175,403	
Turnout 9	53,583	81%)
Valid votes	951,845	
Spoiled votes	1,738	

By the end of December 1999 the prospect of permanent peace seemed possible. Former US Senator George Mitchell's review of the Good Friday Agreement had led to the creation of the Northern Ireland Executive containing members of Sinn Fein. Deputy Leader of Sinn Fein, Martin McGuinness became Minister of Education in this new Northern Ireland Government. Although two DUP members became ministers, they refused to attend meetings if Sinn Fein ministers were present.

As a result of the referendum on the Good Friday Agreement in the Republic of Ireland, the Irish government agreed to change Articles 2 and 3 of the Irish Constitution which made a claim of sovereignty over Northern Ireland. Also the 'Council of the Isles' – containing representatives of the British and Irish governments and representatives of the devolved governments of Scotland, Wales and Northern Ireland – met for the first time.

The new parliament and executive of Northern Ireland soon ran into difficulties. The key issue was IRA decommissioning. The Unionists, in particular the DUP, wanted the IRA to decommission its weapons in an open way. The Head of the Decommissioning Body, General de Chastelain, made claims that the IRA had decommissioned some of its weapons, but this did not satisfy many Unionists. One of the Ulster Unionist (UUP) MPs, Jeffrey Donaldson, defected to the DUP as a result of lack of progress on this matter. This issue was compounded by continued IRA activity, including punishment beatings in Nationalist areas and the murder of Robert MacCartney, in January 2005. This caused considerable resentment among the Nationalist community against the IRA. Meanwhile, in Colombia (South America) IRA members were arrested and accused of training anti-government guerrilla fighters.

On a number of occasions the Secretary of State for Northern Ireland had to suspend the Executive and Assembly. In 1999, the disagreement over decommissioning was the main dispute. In 2002, an IRA spy ring was uncovered working within the Northern Ireland Assembly building at Stormont. This led to a suspension which lasted until 2007.

However, elections still occurred in Northern Ireland (see tables on page 296). In the elections between 2003 and 2007 there was a drop in support for the two parties most closely associated with the Good Friday Agreement – the Ulster Unionists (UUP) and the SDLP, and the main Unionist opponents of the Good Friday Agreement, the DUP, saw major gains.

From 2004 the British and Irish governments still attempted to find a negotiated settlement based on the Good Friday Agreement. The first part of the negotiations led to the 'Comprehensive Agreement' of 2004. It was hoped that this would form the basis of a future deal between the Northern Ireland parties, including the DUP and Sinn Fein. Part of this agreement replaced the Royal Ulster Constabulary with the Police Service of Northern Ireland, which had been an important demand of Sinn Fein since 1998.

A breakthrough came in April 2005 when Sinn Fein leader, Gerry Adams, made a public appeal for the IRA to lay down their arms. This was followed in July 2005 by an announcement by the IRA that it had decommissioned all its weapons. Instead of doing so publicly, as the DUP demanded, it invited leading Catholic and Protestant clergymen to witness the event. This move was supported by General de Chastelain's Commission which confirmed, in September 2005, that the IRA had indeed completed decommissioning.

Although the IRA's decision to destroy all its weapons seemed significant at the time it paled into insignificance compared to the St Andrew's Agreement of October 2006. This agreement between the British and Irish governments and the political parties of Northern Ireland achieved the re-establishment of the Northern Ireland Executive and Assembly. In doing so, for the first time, the DUP agreed to join an Executive with Sinn Fein. In return, Sinn Fein agreed to support fully the new Police Service of Northern Ireland which it had previously boycotted. This agreement became the Northern Ireland (St Andrew's Agreement) Act of 22 November 2006.

A key part of the agreement was the decision to hold Assembly elections in March 2007, with the subsequent creation of a new Executive by May 2007.

In the March elections the DUP and Sinn Fein confirmed their positions as Northern Ireland's two major parties. As the DUP was the largest party its leader, Ian Paisley, became First Minister. Martin McGuinness of Sinn Fein became Deputy First Minister. To those who witnessed and remembered the violence and division of the 'Troubles' from 1969, the sight of the uncompromising Unionist, Ian Paisley, sitting and joking with former IRA commander Martin McGuinness was remarkable.

The achievement of peace was the work of a wide variety of people. The preliminary moves to peace had occurred under Conservative Prime Minister John Major and Irish Prime Minister Albert Reynolds in the early 1990s. However, the major breakthrough, the Good Friday Agreement, owed much to British Prime Minister, Tony Blair, Irish Prime Minister, Bertie Ahern and David Trimble and John Hume, leaders of the Ulster Unionists (UUP) and SDLP respectively. An important supporter of this process was US President Bill Clinton.

However, permanent peace was unlikely until both the DUP and Sinn Fein were willing to accept the Good Friday Agreement in full. It took a further eight years, until 2006, before all major parties within Northern Ireland were willing to accept all parts of the Good Friday Agreement.

British Prime Minister Gordon Brown (right) meets with Northern Ireland First Minister Ian Paisley, (2nd right), Deputy First Minister Martin McGuiness (2nd left) and Irish Prime Minister Bertie Ahern (left) at Stormont Parliament Buildings, in Belfast, Northern Ireland, July 2007.

Elections in Northern Ireland 2003–2007

2003 Elections to the Northern Ireland Assembly
(The Assembly was suspended at the time, and remained so until 2007)

(%)	% votes	Number of seats	Change since 1998 election
DUP	25.6	30	+7.5
UUP	22.6	27	−1
SDLP	17	18	−6
SF	24	24	+6
Other Unionist	2.5	2	−3
Alliance	3.6	4	0
Others	4.7	1	−2

2004 Elections to the European Parliament (3 MEPs)

	DUP	UUP	Others	SDLP	Sinn Fein
Seats won (2004)	1	1	0	0	1
Vote share (2004)	32.0%	16.6%	9.1%	15.9%	26.3%
Seats won (1999)	1	1	0	1	0
Vote share (1999)	28.4%	17.6%	8.5%	28.1%	17.3%

2005 Elections to the UK Parliament (18 MPs)

	DUP	UUP	Alliance	Others	SDLP	Sinn Fein
Seats won (2005)	9	1	0	0	3	5
Vote share (2005)	33.7%	17.7%	3.9%	5.1%	17.5%	24.3%
Seats won (2001)	5	6	0	0	3	4
Vote share (2001)	22.5%	26.8%	3.6%	5.1%	21.0%	21.7%

2005 Elections to the 26 Northern Ireland District Councils

	DUP	UUP	Alliance	Others	SDLP	Sinn Fein
Seats won (2005)	182	115	30	28	101	126
Vote share (2005)	29.6%	18.0%	5.0% 6.8%	17.4%	23.2%	Seats won
(2001)	131	154	28	44	117	108
Vote share (2001)	21.4%	22.9%	5.1%	10.5%	19.4%	20.7%

2007 Elections to the Northern Ireland Assembly (108 seats)
(Under the St Andrew's Agreement of November 2006)

	DUP	UUP	Alliance	OthersS	DLP	Sinn Fein
Seats won (2007)	36	18	7	3	16	28
Vote share (2007)	30.1%	14.9%	5.2%	8.0%	15.2%	26.2%
Seats won (2003)	30	27	6	3	18	24
Vote share (2003)	25.6%	22.7%	3.7%	7.5%	17.0%	23.5%

1. What have been the major obstacles to finding a permanent peace in Northern Ireland since 1985?

2. To what extent is the Good Friday Agreement of 1998 different from the Sunningdale Agreement of 1973?

3. Answer using information from the whole of this chapter:

'Why has the Irish problem been such a difficult problem for British government to deal with from 1914 to 2007?'

Source-based questions: The Peace Process, 1992

SOURCE A

The problem we have to resolve in relation to Northern Ireland is the notoriously difficult one of two sets of conflicting rights. There is no argument for the self-determination of the unionist community that cannot be applied, with at least equal force, to the nationalist community in Northern Ireland. That community sees itself locked into a political entity it bitterly opposed. Its aspirations to independence were denied. It was cut off from the rest of Ireland and consigned to minority status which repeated itself at every level of politics and society. The symbols of the state, like the working of majority rule, might be neutral in Great Britain. They were, and are, both far from neutral in Northern Ireland.

From the opening statement by the Representative of the Republic of Ireland at the British-Irish Round Table talks, 6 July 1992.

SOURCE B

As to British constitutional arrangements 'Her Majesty's Government reaffirms their position that Northern Ireland's present status as part of the United Kingdom will not change without the consent of a majority of its people'.

Though perhaps not everyone will agree, I believe that the Anglo-Irish Agreement would give effect to any wish that might in future be expressed by a majority of the people of Northern Ireland for any alternative status.

As to Articles 2 and 3 of the Irish constitution, HMG fully accepts the sincerity with which the unionist delegations argue that any successful outcome from the talks process must include the repeal or amendment of those Articles.

From a statement by the Secretary of State for Northern Ireland, Sir Patrick Mayhew, on British-Irish Talks, 18 September 1992.

SOURCE C

British propaganda now claims that while 'preferring' to keep the Six County Statelet within the 'United Kingdom' it has no selfish strategic or economic reason for doing so.

British preference in relation to matters internal to Ireland holds no validity against the preference of the clear majority of the Irish people for national independence as expressed for generations.

Moreover, there are multiple democratic and practical reasons why partition should go:

It defies the wishes of the Irish people as a whole.

It rejects the wishes of the population in Britain as expressed in opinion poll after opinion poll.

It flouts international law.

It is undemocratic.

It is permanently abnormal and can only be maintained by extraordinary means.

It has created a generation of casualties in the Six Counties.

It cannot produce lasting peace.

From 'Towards a Lasting Peace in Ireland' a Sinn Fein publication, 1992.

SOURCE D

Commitment to the Army is total belief in the Army, in its aims and objects, in its style of warfare, in its methods of struggle, and in its political foundation.

Commitment to the Republican Movement is the firm belief that its struggle both military and political is morally justified, that war is morally justified and that the Army is the direct representatives of the 1918 Dail Eireann parliament, and that as such they are the legal and lawful government of the Irish Republic, which has the moral right to pass laws for the whole geographical fragment of Ireland and all its people regardless of creed or loyalty.

From 'The Green Book', the Provisional IRA Training Manual.

---

1. From information contained within this chapter explain the meaning of the following phrases underlined in the sources above.

a) 'Articles 2 and 3 of the Irish Constitution' (Source B)

b) The 'Republican Movement' (Source D)

2. Study Sources C and D and use information in this chapter.

How far do the points raised in these Sources reflect the view of Irish nationalists?

3. Study the Sources above and use information contained in this chapter. 'The failure to produce a lasting settlement to British-Irish relations since 1914 was the creation and maintenance of Northern Ireland within the United Kingdom.'

Assess the validity of this statement.

Further Reading

Texts designed specifically for AS and A2 students

The Irish Question in British Politics 1868–1986 by D.G. Boyce (Macmillan, 1988)
Ireland 1828–1923 by D.G. Boyce (Historical Association Studies, Blackwell, 1992)
Politics UK edited by B. Jones (Prentice Hall, 1998)
The Ulster Question 1603–1973 by T.W. Moody (Mercier, 1974)
Understanding Northern Ireland by D. Quinn (Baseline, 1993)

More advanced reading

Modern Ireland 1600–1972 by R.F. Foster (Allen Lane, 1988)
The Origins of the Present Troubles in Northern Ireland by C. Kennedy-Pipe (Longman, 1997)
The Northern Ireland Question in British Politics edited by P. Catterall and S. McDougall (Macmillan, 1996)
Northern Ireland since 1968 by P. Arthur and K. Jeffrey (Blackwell, 1988).

Index